THE ADAGES OF

Selected by William Barker

Erasmus' *Adages* is a collection of 4151 ancient proverbs, each accompanied by a commentary explaining its history and possible uses. Though most of these commentaries are very short, some just a few lines of scholarly explication, others are lengthy essays on social and political topics. The most famous of these is 'War is sweet to those who have not tried it,' a major anti-war tract. Many of the proverbs have passed into modern usage ('Know thyself,' 'To give someone the finger,' 'Well begun is half done'), some even retaining their Latin form (*Deus ex machina*). And a few, as it turns out, were created by Erasmus himself through occasional misinterpretations of the ancient sources ('Pandora's box,' 'To call a spade a spade'). The massive compendium, characterized by wit, elegance, seriousness, and occasional bursts of satire, was among the most learned and widely circulated of Latin books during the early modern period. This annotated selection of 116 proverbs, which includes all the longer essays, is based on the translation in the Collected Works of Erasmus.

WILLIAM BARKER is Professor of English at Memorial University of Newfoundland in St John's.

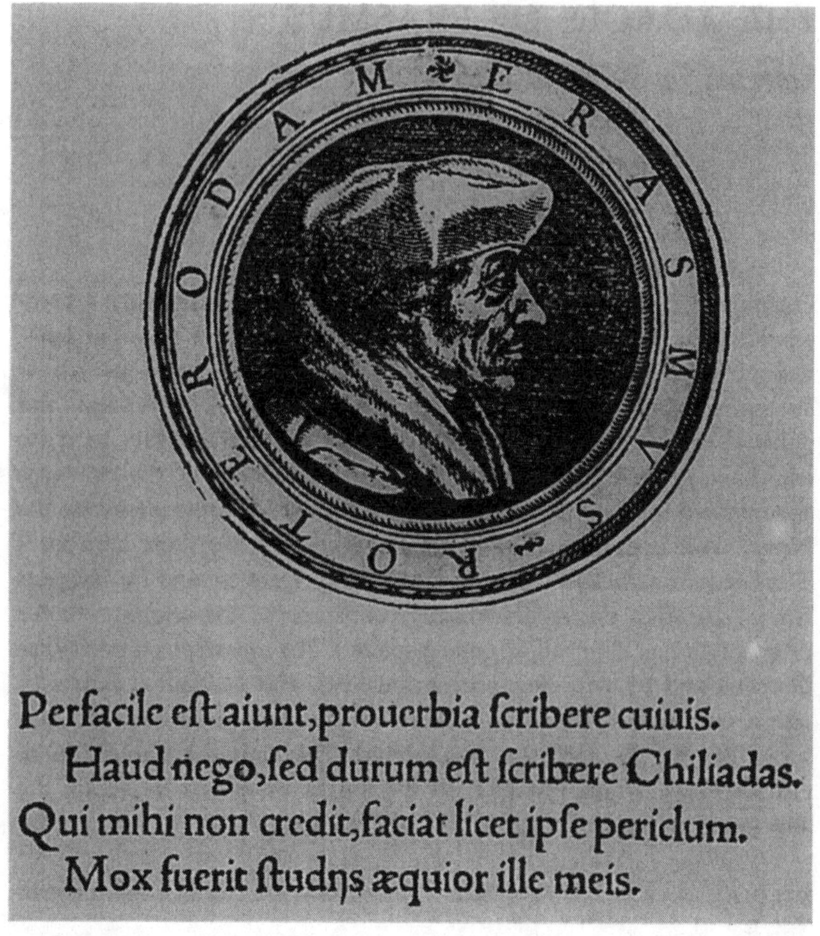
ERASMVS · ROTERODAM ·
Perfacile eſt aiunt, prouerbia ſcribere cuiuis.
Haud nego, ſed durum eſt ſcribere Chiliadas.
Qui mihi non credit, faciat licet ipſe periclum.
Mox fuerit ſtudijs æquior ille meis.

Portrait of Erasmus This roundel by Hans Holbein the Younger appeared in the preliminary pages of *Adages*, in the edition of Basel, Froben 1533. Beneath it is the poem that Erasmus wrote about the composition of this work (for translation and discussion, see introduction, page xx). (Centre for Reformation and Renaissance Studies, Victoria University in the University of Toronto)

THE ADAGES OF ERASMUS

Selected by William Barker

UNIVERSITY OF TORONTO PRESS
Toronto Buffalo London

Toronto Buffalo London
Printed in the U.S.A.

Reprinted 2005, 2010, 2012, 2013

ISBN 8020-4874-9 (cloth)
ISBN 8020-7740-4 (paper)

Printed on acid-free paper

National Library of Canada cataloguing in publication data

Erasmus, Desiderius, d. 1536
The adages of Erasmus

Translations selected from the Collected works of Erasmus, v. 31–34, and 36.
Includes index.
ISBN 8020-4874-9 (bound) ISBN 8020-7740-4 (pbk.)

1. Proverbs, Latin – History and criticism. 2. Proverbs, Greek – History and criticism. I. Barker, William (William Watson), 1946– . II. Title.

PN6140.E84 2001 878'.0402 C00-933116-6

The translations of the *Adages* are selected from the Collected Works of Erasmus: volume 31, translated by Margaret Mann Phillips with notes by R.A.B. Mynors; volumes 32–4, translated and annotated by Mynors; volume 35 (forthcoming) by Denis Drysdall; and volume 36 (forthcoming) by Betty Knott Sharpe and John N. Grant. Most of the endnotes are taken from the work of Mynors, with additional material by Drysdall and Grant. The whole was assembled, and is introduced, by William Barker.

University of Toronto Press acknowledges the financial assistance to its publishing program of the Canada Council for the Arts and the Ontario Arts Council.

University of Toronto Press acknowledges the financial support for its publishing activities of the Government of Canada through the Book Publishing Industry Development Program (BPIDP).

Contents

Illustrations

Editor's Introduction

When I look at that Iliad ... of elegance in Greek and Latin that [Erasmus] calls his *Proverbs*, I seem to see Minerva's own arsenal of language.

Guillaume Budé to Cuthbert Tunstall, May 1517 (Ep 583:221–2)[1]

The *Adages* is an extraordinary work of Renaissance erudition. Into this vast compilation Erasmus gathers Greek and Latin sources for thousands of such proverbs as 'To have one foot in the grave' (II i 52), 'To be in the same boat' (II i 10), or 'To put the cart before the horse' (I vii 28*).[2] He often analyses how these proverbs might be used in a good Latin style. Most entries are quite short. Now and then, though, he expands his commentary beyond the merely philological, and writes lengthy and elaborately crafted essays on morality and religion. These essays, some of them long enough to merit separate publication, began as notes on such proverbs as 'Hasten slowly' (II i 1*), 'The Sileni of Alcibiades' (III iii 1*), or 'War is sweet to those who have not tried it' (IV i 1*).

Though dictionaries and collections of word lore are popular, a massive compilation of Greek and Latin proverbs would not today attract much of an audience outside of specialists or amateurs of the history of language. But in the early sixteenth century, when good Latin style had a social importance and could actually get you a job, the *Adages* became a best-seller and received accolades from many readers. In 1517, for instance, Niccolò Sagundino, a Venetian ambassadorial secretary, wrote to Erasmus: 'I can hardly say what nectar sweet as honey I sip from your most delightful [*Adages*], rich source of nectar as they are, what lovely flowers of every mind I gather thence like a honey-bee, carrying them off to my hive and building them into the fabric of what I write. To their perusal I have devoted two hours a day' (Ep 590:45–9). There are other such compliments written directly to Erasmus (who would have immediately recognized the topos of the honeybee from Seneca's *Moral Epistles* 84). And, even greater testimony, there are still extant many copies of editions published in his own time, well thumbed and annotated by assiduous early readers.

As an expression of the Renaissance love of antiquity and as a work of instruction and reference, the *Adages* is unsurpassed in its sweep. It showed what an individual reader could accomplish in reading almost all extant classical literature. Even with its occasional carelessness (for Erasmus, though obsessed with accuracy, was a quick worker who sometimes was not inclined to verify his references until *after* publication – 'who does not slip up sometimes?' he asks in III i 1*), it was a demonstration of inspired scholarship. The longer essays, full of asides about both the past and the present, demonstrate an eccentricity that works against what we would today recognize as the 'objectivity' of the reference book; yet this same eccentricity gives us the voice of the author, a stylistic signature, hence its interest as a literary work to Erasmus' contemporaries and to us as well. There is a close relationship between the *Adages* and Erasmus' other widely known works, from the *Praise of Folly* to the *Colloquies*, his lively and widely published correspondence, even his writings in religion that lie at the centre of his project as a thinker. A renewed sense of language and its history informs all of Erasmus' writings, and his works are marked not only by challenging ideas, but by a confidence in the power of rhetoric and stylistic invention.

Erasmus and His *Adages*

What was to become so massive first appeared in 1500 as a modest 152-page book called *Adagiorum collectanea*, or *Collection of Adages*. Erasmus was in his early thirties (31 or 34, depending on which year of birth one accepts) and not yet a religious controversialist, still hard at work in his studies and reading through the classics. He had just acquired some proficiency in Greek, and was perfecting his deft style in Latin prose. Though none of his notebooks survives, it seems pretty clear that for part of his training he was following the practice of collecting interesting phrases in a notebook in order to use them later in his rich and highly allusive style.

Like most of his writings, the *Adages* grew out of immediate personal circumstances. Twenty-four years later, in an autobiographical letter, he described the genesis of the book:

> when I considered the important contribution made to elegance and richness of style by brilliant aphorisms, apt metaphors, proverbs, and similar figures of speech, I made up my mind to collect the largest possible supply of such things from approved authors of every sort and arrange them each in its appropriate class, to make them more accessible to those who wish to practise composition with a view to securing a rich and ready diction. (Ep 1341A:576–82)

The book originated, he goes on to say, from a strange event. He had been staying in England, and before he left he had been given a gift of money by his youthful patron, Lord Mountjoy. But on arrival at the port of departure, to his astonishment, most of this money was confiscated by the customs officials, it being illegal to export English currency. When he arrived in Paris he was broke and unwell, and furthermore was worried that his patron, who had misinformed him about his right to export the gift, would think that Erasmus was now angry with him.

> I decided to publish something forthwith. Having nothing ready at hand, I accumulated at random from a few days' reading some sort of a collection of adages, guessing that this book, such as it was, might find a welcome among those who wish to learn, at least for its utility. This I used as evidence that my friendship had not grown cold. (ibid:603–8)

The result was quickly composed (Erasmus says he dictated from his sickbed), with a full and generous dedication to Mountjoy that was intended to maintain the relation of patronage. The book came out in Paris from the workshop of the German printer Johann Philippi as the *Collectanea*, the full title reading *A Collection of Paroemiae or Adages, Old and Most Celebrated, Made by Desyderius Herasmus Roterodamus, a Work Both New and Wonderfully Useful for Conferring Beauty and Distinction on*

All Kinds of Speech and Writing. At the beginning of the book was the letter to the young Lord Mountjoy, and at the end were added a poem on the virtue of the English king Henry VII and a letter to the young prince Henry (thus emphatically situating the work in the context of English patronage).

There were 818 unnumbered proverbs in this first edition of the *Collectanea*. They were gathered from Virgil, Terence, Cicero, the two Plinys, Quintilian, Jerome, Augustine, and others, altogether several dozen authors. Noteworthy were 154 proverbs with Greek citations, based on Erasmus' recent reading of a Greek proverb collection under the name of Diogenianus (it was actually medieval, and had been falsely attributed to a grammarian of the time of the Emperor Hadrian). Erasmus' discussion of each proverb was short, with little supporting analysis or discussion. A typical entry, *Herculei labores*, reads simply

> **The Labours of Hercules**
> Thus those labours are proverbially described, which are useful to others but bring nothing but envy to the doer.[3]

In later editions the notes grew with added citations and with commentary. This tiny note was to become a long essay (III i 1*), a labour of Hercules itself, about Erasmus' own labour in collecting and preparing the *Adages*, and about the ingratitude and envy of certain of Erasmus' readers.

The *Collectanea* was well received. Humanist education as it had been developed in Italy in the fifteenth century placed a great premium on gathering and ordering phrases for literary style. It was not enough to have the lexicon; students also needed a better sense of idiom, of turns of phrase. Proverbs (as we'll see below) were an important source of verbal authority, and so Erasmus had identified a great need. Though he liked to claim to be the first, he was not the originator of the humanist proverb collection. Polydore Vergil (Polidoro Virgilio), an Italian scholar who later moved to England, had published his *Proverbiorum libellus* (Little Book of Proverbs) in 1498. Nevertheless, with the expanded editions and epitomes of the *Adages*, Erasmus became known as the first collector of proverbs. In correspondence with Polydore, whose proverb book he later helped get republished (Ep 1606), he reluctantly acknowledged that the Italian had published before him, yet he still maintained he had come to the *Adages* on his own (a claim that later scholarship supports). Their little conflict shows the importance of priority in the competitive world of humanist scholarship. Ironically, neither disputant ever mentions his prior models in the many medieval florilegia or in the late-classical or medieval Greek collections by Johannes Stobaeus, Diogenianus, Zenobius, and Suidas (a name traditionally but incorrectly given to the anonymous compiler of the *Suda* or *Fortress*, a massive Greek lexicon compiled in the late tenth century), or the large mid-fifteenth-century collection of *sententiae* (or sayings) by Michael Apostolius, even though Erasmus relied heavily on these works, especially when they began to come his way in 1508 and later.[4]

A continuing dissatisfaction with his own work sets Erasmus apart from the run-of-the-mill scholar. Throughout his life he constantly revised, corrected, and expanded in all areas of his writing and research. Five years after its publication, he wrote to John Colet (Ep 181:90–5) that he regretted his 'poor and meagre' *Collectanea*, for in it there were too many printers' errors and he had not by that time read sufficiently in the Greek authors. In the years following the edition of 1500, while he prepared his other works, he gathered citations for a vastly expanded text.

The new *Adages* came to press in 1508, during his first visit to Italy. Immediately on his arrival in Venice, Erasmus attached himself to the household of Aldo Manuzio, already the most famous printer of his age. Aldus, as he is called by his neo-Latin name, had begun printing in the late 1490s. His prestige came from his skill as a printer, exemplified by the beautiful *Hypnerotomachia Poliphili* (Francesco Colonna's *Poliphilus' Strife of Love in a Dream*, published in 1499) and by the (for then) wonderfully compact editions of the classics, produced during the first decade of the 1500s.

In a supportive workplace, surrounded by books and other scholars, Erasmus plunged into the new edition, now to be called the *Adagiorum chiliades*, or *Thousands of Adages*. Erasmus' labours during the months of production in Venice are described in another of the long essays, 'Hasten slowly' (II i 1*). Aldus had already taken as his printer's mark the ancient symbol of the dolphin and anchor, traditionally associated with the proverb that appeared in Greek as Σπεῦδε βραδέως and Latin as *Festina lente*. The proverb was an occasion for Erasmus to write a lengthy tribute, placed quite notably at the beginning of the second thousand of the *Adages*. There he explains the great advantage of working with the famous Aldus:

> When I, a Dutchman, was in Italy, preparing to publish my book of *Proverbs*, all the learned men there had offered me unsought authors not yet published in print ... Aldus had nothing in his treasure-house that he did not share with me ... I was bringing nothing to Venice with me except the confused and unsorted materials for a book that was to be, and that material was confined to published authors. With the greatest temerity on my part, we both set to work together, I to write and Aldus to print. The whole business was finished inside nine months more or less, and all the time I was coping with an attack of the stone, a trouble in which as yet I had no experience. Just consider what advantages I should have lost, had not scholars supplied me with texts in manuscript. Among them were Plato's works in Greek, Plutarch's *Lives* and also his *Moralia* ... the *Doctors at Dinner* of Athenaeus, Aphthonius, Hermogenes with notes ... (II i 1*)

Aldus' example is set as a rebuke to unnamed scholars and printers of northern Europe who, in their ignorance, are unwilling to share. Indeed, Erasmus takes pains to show how the spirit of generosity can enrich the giver: 'Aldus, making haste slowly, has acquired as much gold as he has reputation, and richly deserves both.'

The 1508 *Adagiorum chiliades* is a new work. The earlier *Collectanea* was meant for the practical stylist, a fairly compact book that could fit in a large jacket pocket, and it continued to be revised and reprinted even after this time. The Venice edition is very different, a three-inch-thick folio, richly printed on heavy paper with ample margins. The new edition offered far more than its predecessor: elaborate histories of proverbs, now 3260 of them, sometimes with close philological discussion of sources, comparative analyses of the way a proverb is used in one author then another, interspersed throughout with witty comments on the state of scholarship and literary composition in the Latin culture of the time. It also includes an important new essay at the beginning of the work, analysing the nature of the proverb (Erasmus' introduction*). In this new text there is far more Greek, but now the Greek is consistently translated for the convenience of Latin readers, the translations actually imitating the verse metres of the originals wherever possible. Though Erasmus was later criticized for the translations, they were now a major feature of the *Adages*, and signalled his desire to reach more than the specialist reader. The two indexes are another important feature, the first listing the adages alphabetically, the second giving them under topical headings (*Liberalitas*, *Tenacitas*, *Profusio*, *Rapacitas*, and so on). As the work shows only a minimal internal organization, these indexes must have been very helpful for writers, and remained a standard feature in all the later full-text editions. Curiously, it was only after Erasmus' death that the editions began to include more detailed indexes by keyword and subject – from our modern perspective, essential aspects of a book like this.

Even though 1508 was an expansion, many proverbs – the majority – were still in the short form familiar from the *Collectanea*. For instance,

War is sweet to those who haven't tried it
Γλυκὺς ἀπείρῳ πόλεμος, War is sweet to those who haven't tried it. To care for dangers freely warns those who are inexperienced in things. Aristotle in his *Rhetoric* gives the reason why youth is bolder and old age is more cautious, because to the former inexperience of things gives them confidence. To the latter, the experience of evils gives them fear.[5]

This tiny note is typical of hundreds of entries. Yet unlike many others, this one was to grow enormously in the edition of 1515, long enough to be often republished as a separate pamphlet, one of Erasmus' most famous works (IV i 1*).

Even though many of the adages were fairly short, they were nonetheless longer than they had been in the *Collectanea*. For instance, contrast the following:

Twice cooked cabbage is death (1500)
In Pliny, *crambe* belongs to the genus of the plant *brassica*. Suidas writes that it used to be served at banquets, mainly because it prevents drunkenness, but when recooked it brings on such nausea that it became

proverbial in Greek for aversion, for there was extant among them this proverb, Twice cabbage is death, that is, cabbage twice served is death. Juvenal alludes to this when he tells of the tedium of hearing the same speech time and time again: Cabbage twice cooked kills the wretched teachers.[6]

Twice cooked cabbage is death (1508)
Δὶς κράμβη θάνατος, Twice-served cabbage is death. Pliny, book 20 chapter 9, lists *crambe* third among the species of *brassica*. Dioscorides, book 2, gives three kinds of cabbage. The first of these, apart from the fact that at times it is an effective remedy for many things, also takes away the unpleasantness of drunkenness and hangover. Suidas writes that cabbage used to be served at banquets in antiquity, but when recooked it produced such nausea that it became proverbial in Greek for aversion. Whenever they were describing something disagreeable repeated over and over again, not without disgust, they said 'twice cabbage is death' (that is, recooked). Poliziano thinks that Juvenal was referring to this adage in his seventh Satire: 'You teach rhetoric, O iron-hearted Vettius, / When your troop of many scholars slays the cruel tyrants. / For what each has just learnt in his seat / He stands and declaims, reciting the self-same things / In the self-same verses; served up again and again / The cabbage is the death of the unhappy masters.' He means by 'cabbage served up again' an utterly boring speech which has to be listened to over and over again. This is close to the phrase we quoted in another place 'Corinthus son of Jove,' and it is the opposite of that other one, 'Beauty bears repeating twice and thrice.' Something lovely in itself still pleases, as Horace says, even if repeated ten times. A foolish thing is tolerated at the first taste for the sake of novelty, but when repeated is hardly bearable and causes disgust, for which consider the practice with strawberries.[7]

The citations from the Roman encyclopedist Pliny the Elder, Suidas, Angelo Poliziano (the most celebrated of the late-fifteenth-century humanist scholars), and the Roman poet Horace are typical of the range of the 1508 edition. The new *Adages* was immediately recognized as a remarkable work, evidence of a scholarly mastery but also of an imaginative relationship between Erasmus and the classical past.

Soon after the publication of the 1508 *Adages*, Erasmus moved to England, and it seems certain that he began immediately to work towards another edition. By April of 1511 he was already considering a Paris publisher, and the next year was ready to give the manuscript to Josse Bade, who had published certain other of his works. His major concern was Bade's ability to work with the Greek, but he was reassured and in 1513 sent the manuscript off in the hands of a book dealer named Franz Birckmann. But Birckmann instead took an unusual liberty. He carried the manuscript with him to Switzerland and to Erasmus' surprise gave it to the well-known Basel printer Johann Froben. (About ten years later Erasmus satirized Birckmann in the character named 'The Liar' in one of his *Colloquies*, 'Pseudocheus and Philetymus.')

Johann Froben was already an experienced printer, almost on a par with Aldus in the quality of his work. So the move was not in itself a bad thing. But Froben had just undertaken a page-for-page reprint of the 1508 Venice edition and, to Erasmus' great frustration, decided he now had to wait until this reprint had sold out before undertaking the new edition. More than a year elapsed between Erasmus' revisions and the printing – enough time for Erasmus to have moved from England back to the Continent, and to Basel. He was able to make some last-minute adjustments and additions, working, always in haste, from September until the spring of the next year. The book appeared in 1515, greatly enlarged from the 1508 edition, so much so that Erasmus, during its composition, had claimed to Ulrich Zasius, 'My volume of *Adagia* is being so much enriched that it might be thought a new book' (Ep 307:33–4).

Indeed, the 1515 edition does mark a new direction. Most notably, this text contains the powerful adages attacking political abuses and the warmongering of the European monarchs (I iii 1*, I ix 12*, II v 1*, III vii 1*, IV i 1*). Even in many of the shorter adages comments on social and political life are interwoven. It is as though Erasmus has already done the great part of the philological homework and now wants to bring the proverbs into the present, not for the classroom, but for a larger stage. The ancient world is being set into a modern context in this new edition of the *Adages*. The proverbs are increasingly seen within the living experience of readers. The work shows Erasmus' growing confidence: this is just a year before he turned the world of biblical scholarship upside down with his New Testament edition, accompanied by its remarkable set of annotations.

Margaret Mann Phillips, in her fine 1964 study, calls the 1515 *Adages* the 'Utopian edition.'[8] Certainly the work does share in some places the social criticism also found in the *Utopia* of Erasmus' great friend Thomas More (first published in Louvain in 1516). Yet Phillips' new title for the edition is in some ways misleading, for it exaggerates the place of the political commentary, which though prominent in some of the commentaries is subordinate in the overall collection. Most of the adage essays are still short commentaries on classical sayings. In the end, the edition is much more philology than social criticism. What is surprising, though, is Erasmus' ability to blend the two apparently unrelated fields in some of the essays, to give urgency to the philology and historical depth to the social criticism.

Froben remained Erasmus' publisher for the remaining editions. The 1517–18 text is a correction of 1515, with a small number of new proverbs. The 1520 edition gives 21 new adages, 1523 adds 39, 1526 adds 52, and 1528 adds 123. The entries never get smaller, but they do become fuller and more accurate, as Erasmus combs through the collection for things to improve. Typical is his attention in this letter to Conradus Goclenius in April 1524:

> I should like to give some young man the job of reading through my *Adagia* in the latest edition [January 1523] and comparing it with the last but one. Michael Bentinus [Froben's press-corrector] introduced a lot of mistakes [in the edition of October 1520] by taking so much trouble. *οἴῳ* 'alone' he always turned into *οἵῳ*, and he collated some passages I had cited from Homer in Greek with the Homer printed by Aldus, and the same for the Aldine Cicero, though the Aldine editions are highly corrupt. I should like the passages which the young man marked to be examined by you when you have the time. (Ep 1437:174–81)

The last important edition was that of 1533, now called the *Adagiorum opus* (or *Work of Adages*), with 488 new proverbs. The edition of 1536, prepared in the last months of Erasmus' life, adds only 5 proverbs, for a final total of 4151.

Erasmus composing the Adages. This is one of a series of amusing marginal ink-drawings made in a copy of Erasmus' *Praise of Folly* (Basel: Froben 1515). Hans Holbein the Younger was only about 18 or 19 at the time he did this inspired work. The picture refers back to the text, for Folly has just let loose with a series of proverbs, and concludes by saying, 'But enough of quoting proverbs; I don't want you to imagine that I've been plundering the notebooks of my friend Erasmus.' The manuscript note just above the illustration is by a Basel teacher named Oswald Geisshüssler, known as Myconius, who owned this copy of the book. He says, 'When Erasmus came here and saw himself thus represented, he exclaimed, "Aha, if Erasmus looked like that today, he would find himself a wife at once"' (trans Betty Radice, 'Holbein's Marginal Illustrations to the *Praise of Folly*' in *Erasmus in English* [1975]). (Kupferstichkabinett, Kunstmuseum, Basel)

The process of expansion continued through these editions. For instance, 'Cabbage twice cooked,' quoted above from the *Collectanea* and the 1508 edition, kept on growing (see I v 38* for the final version). In this swelling text on such an obscure topic, Erasmus was able to find additional references to Cato and Aristotle, to the Egyptians and the Sybarites, and to Athenaeus and Theophrastus, two ancient collectors of lore. The final result is a lengthy and fascinating essay on an unexpectedly dangerous vegetable.

Erasmus persisted in the effort of revision right up to his death in 1536. Early on he was amused by this process: in a letter to Zasius (Ep 313:4–5) he comments that the 1516 Basel edition 'is now coming to birth for the third time, and goes one better than Bacchus who was born twice.' Later on, however, the task began to wear on him. In the sixth edition of 1526, he included a letter (Ep 1659) in which he expressed some embarrassment at the proliferation of new editions, explained certain types of errors he had specifically corrected, and promised this to be the last of these revisions. Brave words! In the seventh edition, just two years later, he had to add a new letter 'To His Friendly Readers' (Ep 2022), apologizing for having broken his vow, and explaining that this edition appeared out of necessity for correction and the requirements of the publishers. The 1533 edition begins with a short poem to those who accused him of writing the same book over and over again. Echoing the Latin poet Martial (who wrote against those who claimed that writing satire was easy), Erasmus says

To write out proverbs is easy, they say, and it's true.
But to write them in thousands? – a grind!
If you don't believe me, try it yourself –
Of my efforts you'll soon grow more kind.[9]

Erasmus was driven to add constantly, to move things around. The proliferation of new editions did not please contemporary book buyers, and some, including the famous classical scholar Guillaume Budé, thought it a scam (in much the same way purchasers of textbooks or computer programs regard freshly manufactured editions today; Ep 915). Erasmus was sensitive to these charges, and in his long retrospective letter of 1523 to Johann von Botzheim (known as the *Catalogus lucubrationum*, or Catalogue of Works), he offers a different kind of defence (Ep 1341A:1465–87):

> Now, when you complain that your purse is empty because you have to buy the same book so often, I should like you to look at it like this. Suppose my *Proverbia* had just appeared for the first time, and that the moment the book was published I had died: would you have regretted your expenditure? I doubt it. Now suppose something else, that after several years I came to life again and that at the same time the book revived with me, better and fuller, would you regret further expense, or would you be delighted to see again both your friend and his immortal work? ... As long as we live, we are devoted to self-improvement, and we shall not cease to make our writings more polished and more complete until we cease to breathe. No one is so good a man that he could not be made better; and no book has had so much work put into it that it cannot be made more perfect.

The choice is simple: do you wish me to be dead? – 'or from time to time buy a book that has been enlarged and revised' (lines 1496–7)? One might think this to be an unkind set of alternatives. At the end of his 'Labours of Hercules' (III i 1*) he admits a failing in the haste of his production, but in his correspondence he manages to turn the constant revision into a necessary virtue.

Indeed, in this continuing expansion, we see a tendency of Renaissance literary culture that was by that time a feature of literary production in general.[10] Writers seem helpless in the face of the work. It is as though it gains a momentum of its own, and the author must now follow the work, not lead it. Montaigne's essays – which imitate the *Adages* in other fascinating ways as well – are the best-known example of the text that grows by accretion, but we find the same expansion in the emblems of Alciato, the *Faerie Queene* of Spenser, the *Anatomy of Melancholy* of Robert Burton, and even in Shakespeare and Marlowe, with their different versions of *King Lear* and *Doctor Faustus*. Indeed, in the Renaissance, many works seem never to get finished. Of course, the reference work, which tends to gather more and more within its structure, further resists this idea of completion.

Later Editions

Even after Erasmus' death in 1536, the *Adages* continued to be both abridged and expanded, rather in the way that Webster's dictionary has undergone constant rebirths long after Noah Webster died in the mid-nineteenth century. Of Erasmus' work there were a range of epitomes that appeared throughout the sixteenth and seventeenth centuries, either, like the *Collectanea*, set up in an undifferentiated series (for instance, by one of his contemporaries named Adrianus Barlandus), or arranged by the standard topics – where, for example, the adage 'He that gives quickly gives twice' (I viii 91*) might now appear under the formal heading *Liberalitas* or 'Generosity' (in editions by Johannes Brucherius and Johannes Ludovicus Hauuenreuterus). Many follow a model established early on by Theodoricus Cortehoevius, whose 1530 edition is dedicated to Erasmus. In these shorter versions thousands of adages were dropped and the longer ones were radically cut. *Dulce bellum inexpertis* (IV i 1*) appears under 'Imperitia' in a 1533 pocket-sized *Compendium* in this shortened form:

> **War is sweet to those who do not know it**
> Γλυκὺς ἀπείρῳ πόλεμος. War is sweet to the one who has not tried it. Vegetius, *On Military Affairs* 3.14. There are certain things in mortal affairs, which have so much of crisis and of evil that you will not understand until you have been tested by danger. How sweet, untried, the favour of the great, but he who knows it, fears it [quoting, unidentified, Horace *Epistles* 1.18.86–7].[11]

These concise editions were meant as quick guides to usage, in the way a modern pocket dictionary serves us today. Many of them measured a mere 3 by 5 inches, an inch or so thick. Their existence reminds us that many sixteenth-century readers did not turn to the *Adages* to linger over Erasmus' longer essays, but rather used the book for practical information in the work of reading and writing. That Erasmus approved of these shortened versions is shown in a letter to Adrianus Barlandus, c May 1521, used as a preface by Barlandus in his work:

> My *Chiliades* was too large a volume to be within the reach of those in modest circumstances, or to be read in the grammar schools, or to be carried round with them by those who like strolling players are always on the move. And now your epitome at its very low price can be bought by anyone however ill endowed, and thumbed by schoolboys, and will add little weight to a traveller's baggage. And then those who teach your compendium in schools will be able to use my longer work as a commentary. (Ep 1204:12–19)

By contrast, there were the expanded editions. In the 1570s and later, editors began to add other collections of proverbs to the work of Erasmus. Thus, a folio published by Froben's heirs in Basel 1574 has 852 pages of Erasmus and an astonishing 647 additional pages filled with the work of other commentators and proverb-collectors. This includes the *Animadversiones* or corrections and comments on Erasmus' *Adages* by the French scholar-printer Henri Estienne (1531–98); a collection of 840 adages by Hadrianus Junius (1511–75, Dutch scholar and emblem writer); the *Proverbia,* first published in the late 1520s, of Johannes Alexander Brassicanus (1500–39, a neo-Latin poet); an epitome of adages by Johannes Ulpius (d c 1540); a *Sylloge* or collection of 1396 adages by Gilbertus Cognatus (Gilbert Cousin, 1506–72, who was for a time a secretary to Erasmus); shorter collections excerpted from Caelius Rhodiginus (Lodovico Ricchieri, 1469–1525, author of a famous set of *Lectiones antiquae*), Polydore Vergil (Erasmus' predecessor, now absorbed into the Erasmian opus), Petrus Godefredus (fl 1570), Carolus Bovillus (Charles de Bouelles, 1479–1567, a French humanist who translated French proverbs into Latin, and thus brought them into the classical and Erasmian tradition), Hadrianus Turnebus (1512–65, a French philologist), M. Antonius Muretus (Marc Antoine Muret, 1526–85, French humanist), and Gulielmus Gentius (otherwise unknown); a sequence taken from Hadrianus Junius, Gulielmus Canterus (Willem Canter, 1542–75, a scholar of Greek), and Victor Giselinus (who flourished in the 1560s and published an edition of Ovid); and a small collection by Melchior Bredenanus (otherwise unknown). The whole is indexed by adage, topic, and authorial sources.

It seems remarkable that anything could be added to Erasmus' huge and seemingly inexhaustible storehouse of adages, but the other proverb hunters were working with a broader definition of proverb than that held by Erasmus, and with a wider range of acceptable texts, including the Bible (which Erasmus had purposely not used as a main source). So adage 1104 in Cousin's collection is *Nemo propheta acceptus in patria sua* ('A prophet is not recognized in his own country'), with sources in all four evangelists and parallels in the Roman poet Ennius and the letters of Cicero. Erasmus had provided the basic idea, but other writers, some contemporary with him and others just a bit later, were constantly adding to the pile. Many, such as Sebastian Franck or Heinrich Bebel, were collecting proverbs from the vernacular languages as well, in part alerted to the richness of their own languages by Erasmus' work in Latin. By the end of the sixteenth century, a good part of what was still called 'Erasmus' Adages' the author would not have recognized as his own, and the would-be proverb hunter is well advised to turn to these later editions. Early-seventeenth-century folio volumes of *Adagia* published in Frankfurt go further, and conflate Erasmus' work with the many other collections, reorganizing the whole under synoptic topics (though retaining the name of the individual contributor with each adage).[12]

Finally, there were the versions that Erasmus would certainly have recognized as his, even though his name did not appear on the title page and the pronoun 'I' (often used in the original) now appears as 'we' (Latin often blurs the difference between *ego* and *nos*, yet here the change is significant). These are the censored editions published in the later sixteenth century in Florence, Venice, and Paris, usually under the name of the scholar-printer Paolo Manuzio, great-nephew of Aldus (though the text seems to have been prepared by Eustachio Locatelli, a Dominican and papal confessor). Admirably printed, these editions allowed the free circulation of most of Erasmus' text in Italy after his work had been placed on the Index in the 1550s, though stripped of personality and of much of its social criticism. Manuzio and the censors cleverly dedicated 'their' work to Pope Gregory XIII, thus ensuring its protection during the Counter-Reformation. Generally these editions follow the original Erasmian sequence, though with many adages shortened (the challenging 'War is sweet' is now half a column), a few simply removed, and many religious references modified (for instance, the reference to Christ in 'Between friends all is common' I i 1* and to Paul and Christ in 'Adopt the outlook of the polyp' at I i 93*). Of course, such transformations tended, as has been discussed by Jean Céard,[13] to turn the *Adages* into a work of purely antiquarian interest, and few contemporaries using the censored text would have seen the liveliness or passion of Erasmus' scholarship, the very qualities that made the work stand out from other contemporary works of learning.

Despite its readability, and the fact that some of the essays had a long afterlife (especially 'War is sweet to those who have not tried it' [IV i 1*], an important anti-war tract in the nineteenth century), the history of Erasmus' *Adages* as a central text in the European tradition really ends in the eighteenth century, with the beginning of the decline of classics and rhetoric in the schools. After this, the work became important for scholars of Renaissance humanism and the Reformation, even though the full collection is still of use for anyone interested in the classical proverb. As a synthesis of classical and Renaissance proverb lore the *Adages* has never really been superseded.

Defining the Proverb

The *Adages* grew as one of Erasmus' most important projects, and as a popular and significant book for his contemporaries and successors. Yet from the perspective of our own time, a collection of proverbs seems an unlikely means to attain literary fame. In part, this is because the proverb has fallen out of favour in written discourse. To call someone today a 'dog in the manger' (I x 13*) or to say of a piece of writing that it 'it smells of the lamp' (I vii 71*) implies irony rather than any confidence in the lasting truth of these expressions. When we write out a proverb today, we seem to be all too aware that we are borrowing a stance or a way of describing reality that comes from another time (when dogs had access to mangers and people wrote by lamplight). There is a quaintness or obscurity to many proverbs, and while we may still use them freely in speech, we have become cautious when we use them in writing. It is as though the written context forces us to see the proverb literally, even though in speech the literal meaning is suppressed. If someone writes, 'I left no stone unturned,' readers are struck more by the force of a cliché than by a time-honoured expression of truth (the expression is as old as Euripides, and is found in the *Adages* at I iv 30*, in English as Tilley S 890).[14] When proverbs are used today, it is often with an ironic self-consciousness.

The written proverb, so popular among the educated in the sixteenth century, declined by the eighteenth century. Lord Chesterfield expressed what was becoming the new orthodoxy when he informed his son in a letter that 'a man of fashion never has recourse to proverbs or vulgar aphorisms' (27 September 1749). James Obelkevich explains the transformation in an essay on the social history of the proverb in English:

> Proverbs put the collective before the individual, the recurrent and the stereotyped before the unique, external rules before self-determination, common sense before the individual vision, survival before happiness. And with self-fulfilment goes self-expression: educated people make the further assumption that everyone has (or should have) their own unique, ever-changing experience of life, and that experience should be expressed in freshly chosen words on every occasion. To use proverbs would deny the individuality of both speaker and listener ... Proverbs are seen as part of a restricted code that encapsulates experience and imprisons it: they are conversation stoppers.[15]

Obelkevich may go too far with this claim: our suspicion of proverbial wisdom in writing does not mean we are immune to the proverb in speech: proverbs still make up a significant part of idiomatic spoken language. Though they are no longer taught systematically (as they were in textbooks in many North American schools within living memory), they are part of the repertoire of every speaker and are often used in public discourse as forms of significant cliché. Politicians, television newscasters, and radio announcers rely heavily on such cliché, and proverbs are often played with in these media. They may be used by teachers and linguistics scholars to test native command of language. Surprisingly, considering the way they have become ironized in modern written usage, proverbs are still used by psychiatrists and psychologists in mental-status examinations and in IQ tests.

Though proverbs have been on the decline as a rhetorical device in educated written culture, proverb making is far from over. The past one hundred years have seen many new proverbs enter the language, even if many began as clichés from advertising. Some of these are quite powerful: 'A picture is worth a thousand words' sounds as though it could have had its origin in ancient Babylon, yet it first appeared (unillustrated!) in an advertisement of 1921.[16] Though we pretend a suspicion of final truths, the proverb still persists.

A prevailing view among nineteenth- and twentieth-century proverb experts, who have strong connections to research in folklore, is that the proverb persists because it encapsulates the spoken wisdom of the people: 'A saying current among the folk' is Archer Taylor's tentative definition.[17] Erasmus would agree, but only in part. He acknowledges the mysterious origin, the antiquity, and the broad popularity of the proverb, but obviously does not see it as a function of the 'folk' (that eighteenth- and nineteenth-century invention of the nation-state), but argues in part in his introductory essay that it persists and is popularly circulated because of its form – the way that it compresses thought in metaphorical language.

In his emphasis on form Erasmus seems curiously modern, for much modern scholarly discussion of the proverb has settled on its internal structure, though less on metaphor than on other specific verbal features. There are the features of sound: in English, principally alliteration ('Fight *f*ire with *f*ire'), assonance ('A stitch in t*ime* saves n*ine*'), circumsonance ('L*ast* but not l*east*'), and rhyme ('*Might* makes *right*,' '*Haste* makes *waste*'). There are specific semantic features: repetition ('What will be will be'), identification ('Business is business,' 'Boys will be boys,' 'Enough is enough'), negation ('A watched pot never boils,' 'Dead men tell no tales'), comparison ('Better the devil you know than the devil you don't'), cause-effect relation ('Where there's a will there's a way'), negative cause-effect ('You can lead a horse to water but you can't make him drink'), contrast ('One man's meat is another man's poison'). Proverbs often contradict one another yet such apparent contradiction does not seem to limit their truthfulness ('Look before you leap' but 'He who hesitates is lost'). Proverbs may even be studied as acts of linguistic incompletion (the shorthand expression 'a bird in the hand ...' with '... is worth two in the bush' being understood).[18] Tense and verbal mode are important: proverbs are usually in the present tense, or are imperative.[19] The proverb's persistent binary or quadripartite forms seem especially suited to structuralist analysis: such analysis stresses the proverb's closed and autonomous linguistic features, features directly related to its propositional and apparent truth content.[20] In other words, what sounds like 'truth' in English, Latin, and many other languages is found in statements with tight internal organization, compression, apparent autonomy within the immediate context, and generalization. The proverb fulfils these criteria.

For modern proverb scholars, the context of the proverb is very important – the way the proverb moves about so persistently in a spoken context and the way we use the proverb as a linguistic device in the scenes of everyday life. Erasmus is also interested in context. Yet his sense of context is historical and written. His analysis does not acknowledge the context of informal oral performance, even though the proverb's force is largely in the way it is delivered in speech.[21] Even though Erasmus is purportedly training a 'speaker' or 'orator,' for him the proverb seems most often to be found within the context of the written document. He is interested in the way the written can be given the flow of the oral. Yet he does, though only occasionally, acknowledge contemporary oral usage or the way the proverb moves about from one modern language to another.

Erasmus' great strength as an analyst of proverb discourse is in his recognition of the metaphorical force of the proverb. As he says in his *De copia*, probably following Aristotle, '[M]ost proverbs contain either allegory or some form of metaphor,'[22] and by allegory he means sustained metaphor. Though the relation of the riddle to the proverb has certainly been acknowledged, modern paroemiologists do not seem to have paid as much attention to the way – emphasized by Erasmus and by the ancient rhetoricians – that many proverbs conceal their own meaning.[23] These apparently homely or simple devices are complex; they carry with them elaborate histories, bits of scientific or pseudo-scientific lore, or references to customs and beliefs of older times. In this they seem to pose unanswered (and often, in oral situations, unanswerable) questions, and these pique the interest of the listener at the same time that they seem to settle or give closure to discussion.

In his lengthy introduction, in which he gives his analysis of the nature, origin, and use of proverbs, Erasmus has the following definition: 'A proverb is a saying in popular use, remarkable for some shrewd and novel turn' (section i). He insists on a literal meaning of the Greek term *paroemia* as 'a road that travels everywhere' and of the Latin *adagium* as 'something passed around': in other words, he acknowledges the broad popular appeal of the form. Yet he goes on to stress the rhetorical form – generally metaphor, sometimes highly obscure, but always expressing some kind of 'turn' in language. Julius Caesar Scaliger, in his *Poetices libri septem* of 1570, condemned this approach. How, he asked, can something common and often repeated like the proverb be described as 'novel'? Scaliger didn't grasp Erasmus' concept of metaphor, which even when repeated contains a kind of permanent novelty or surprise within it.[24] Erasmus was sensitive to the metaphorical property of the proverb, and uses this property (not entirely satisfactorily as he admits) to distinguish the proverb from many similar devices: gnome or sentence (a maxim or aphorism, less metaphorical and more abstract, usually moral in content) and its related form the apophthegm (or witty saying, often by a named speaker and recorded by a third party); the parallel or similitude (forceful comparison, often taken from philosophy or natural history, found in English in the flowery sixteenth-century style known as euphuism); the fable (often summarized in a brief statement, as in 'sour grapes' for the tale of the fox and the grapes in Aesop); the paradox; and the *skômma* (*facetia*, anecdote, or witty tale). All these are forms of great interest to him and to his humanist contemporaries, who were fascinated by compression and irony in language, and who prepared many collections of each of these forms. Erasmus himself published collections of *Apophthegms* and of *Similitudes*. The proverb seems to touch on these other forms in its compression, its allusiveness, its exaggeration, its ambiguity, its punning, but differs from them in its reliance on metaphor and the way it moves about in discourse, becomes separated from an author or an initial situation, and is applicable generally to the conditions and events of life.

It is the way a particular metaphor or turn can be applied so generally that especially characterizes the proverb. Francesco Guicciardini, the historian, one of Erasmus' contemporaries, wrote, 'In every nation, we find nearly all the same or similar proverbs, expressed in different words. The reason is that these proverbs are born of experience, or observation of things; and that is the same, or at least similar, everywhere'[25] – a strong echo of section vii of the introduction. In his explanatory essays, Erasmus often shows how what appears to be an obscure proverb actually has a broad application and common usage.

Erasmus believed the origins of the proverb were found in primitive philosophy and ancient religious wisdom. For instance, he reads the Pythagorean adage 'Between friends all is common' (I i 1*) to say that 'the sum of all created things is in God and God is in all things, the universal all is in fact one' – 'an ocean of philosophy, or rather of theology, is opened up to us by this tiny proverb.' So it is grounded in an ancient understanding, but serves the present as a powerful tool of instruction. Proverbs may be used to understand, and they may also be used to teach; indeed, for Erasmus their compression and metaphorical point make them ideal for teaching: 'An idea launched like a javelin in proverbial form strikes with sharper point on the hearer's mind and leaves implanted barbs for meditation' (Erasmus' introduction iv).

For Erasmus, the force of the proverb lies in part in its memorable form and common circulation, in part in its mystery and its anonymity. Through its recognizable form, it calls attention to itself (and to language generally). It seems to come from an indeterminate past, though not from any specific prior scene of composition or enunciation. It is unauthored language – even when the author can be named, the form of the proverb allows it to be absorbed into and moved about in language without author attached. The absence of a specific author allows us to use it as ours, to use it to situate ourselves in language itself, not in language with a particular source. Thus, uttering a proverb may be a way of reminding ourselves of a timeless truth, and, though Erasmus does not go so far, it is also a way to step out of the immediate context of the present, to use language to generalize, to remove ourselves from the historical present. At the moment of proverbial utterance, the event being reflected upon appears to be situated outside of history yet – if this does not seem too paradoxical – to be gathered within traditional language.

Erasmus is occasionally able to locate a possible author for a proverb. This comes as a surprise to the reader. Yet Erasmus is careful to show how the proverb, while used by authors, is not tied specifically to them. It is common property. A proverb, even in Erasmus' *Adages*, with its heavy reliance on the ancient authors, is fundamentally anonymous and can be removed from one context to another, even though it may have many authors and contexts for its use.

Although proverbs lack authors in the usual sense, they often come with implied contexts. And it is in the work of contextualization that Erasmus performs his most remarkable scholarly work. Many proverbs are generalized bits of wisdom that are released from the original context. Thus, 'Know thyself' (I vi 95*) appeared on the entrance to the ancient temple at Delphi, but is now regarded as universally applicable and easily understood in fresh contexts. But others refer to customs or objects of specific times or places and do not part from their original context very well – for instance, 'Gardens of Adonis' (I i 4*), 'The ring of Gyges' (I i 96*), 'As rich as Croesus' (I vi 74), 'Owls to Athens' (I ii 11*), or even 'To hold an eel in a fig-leaf' (I iv 95*). These highly referential proverbs need an explanation. In his lengthy discussion of 'The Sileni of Alcibiades' (III iii 1*), Erasmus describes how the ugly outside of the ancient Silenus-figure is so much at odds with its beautiful inside. As Daniel Kinney[26] and others have noted, the Silenus essay describes Erasmus' own method in the *Adages*, how he 'opens up' the gnarled exterior of the confusing proverb by exposing its clear and meaningful interior. He elucidates these meanings not, like the medieval allegorist, by reference to a structured code of signification but by resituating the classical proverbs in their ancient literary contexts, within what may be called the cultural encyclopedia of antiquity,[27] showing, with many direct citations, how they were used and varied by the great authors of the past. In this way, the proverb becomes once more understandable and, now recharged with meaning, may again be released into discourse. Thus, in a paradoxical use of the historical method, Erasmus renews the proverb by giving it back its ancient context.

The *Adages*: Gathering and Framing

Though the *Adages* sets out to collect proverbs and display ancient usage, a main point of Erasmus' work is that these curious, obscure, and sometimes forgotten expressions may be recovered for the use of the modern stylist. He promotes the proverb on two grounds, both closely related to its function.[28] First, Erasmus recognizes the lightness and deftness – *festivitas* – provided to the writer or speaker by the unusual metaphorical force (the *novitas* or novelty) found in the proverb. He emphasizes delight over instruction. Erasmus is very concerned with this aspect of the proverb, for he is working hard to promote a specific style. The ancients spoke of the deliberative, the forensic, and the epideictic or laudatory modes (arguing for or against a proposed course of action, arguing for or against a case in a court of law, or praising or dispraising an individual). Erasmus strongly promotes a full and fluent style, the familiar style (*genus familiare*), which can serve the three main categories but may also stand alone, in correspondence or other popular communication. Though this last category was developed by medieval writers, it was used to characterize ancient writings – for instance, Plato's dialogues, or the letters of Cicero or the younger Pliny. This style welcomes the proverb, which in turn enlivens discourse. The letter to Mountjoy that prefaces the *Collectanea* enthusiastically promotes the proverb, even in serious discourse: 'Even if you provisionally assume what no sensible person believes, that it is irrelevant to take trouble over how one expresses oneself, yet it is just this metaphorical style of expression that has always been the special distinguishing mark, not of professional stylists, but of philosophers and prophets and divines' (Ep 126:183–7).

The other ground for the utility of the proverb is *auctoritas*: its authority as an encapsulation and embodiment of ancient wisdom. The speaker or writer uses the proverb as the anonymous wisdom of earlier times to strengthen an argument and to convince an audience. This aspect of the proverb was recognized by the ancient rhetoricians. Aristotle, Quintilian, and Cicero, for instance, each treat the proverb as a form of proof in their rhetorical treatises. The proverb as testimony is serious, grounded, and wise. Erasmus is emphatic that the adage does not just decorate one's style in its wit and allusiveness; it gives it strength as well through its compression and truth-value. Thus, he says, Quintilian, the greatest of the Roman teachers,

> not only includes them ... among the figures of oratory, but considers that the proverbial example is one of the most effective methods of proof whether your aim be to convince, or to refute your opponent by means of a witty adage, or to defend your own position. For what statement gains readier approval than one that is on everyone's lips? And could anyone remain unmoved by the consensus among so many generations and races of mankind? (Ep 126:60–7)

That the proverb can be employed as a means of proof as well as decoration was of great importance to Erasmus' contemporaries, who sought to provide forms of logical proof to their rhetorical declamations. The system of logical 'commonplaces,' or places of argument, carefully set forth by Rudolph Agricola in the fifteenth century, had developed into a full-blown method of composition in the sixteenth century.[29] At first this method was a fairly austere modification of ancient and scholastic logic, but it was soon popularized in the schools, so that collections of sayings, quotations, and the like, formerly less systematically gathered in the medieval florilegia (collections of *flores* or flowers culled from other writers), were now organized under 'topics' in notebooks and in printed compendia. Proverbs, because of their autonomous structure, were easily assimilated into the florilegium and into the more logically constructed commonplace book, both encyclopedic systems for the organization of style. The writer would gather materials under the headings, and then use the material to generate new writings in a highly methodical system of composition. As Erasmus says, 'So our student will flit like a busy bee through the entire garden of literature, will light on every blossom, collect a little nectar from each, and carry it to his hive. Since there is such an abundance of material that one cannot gather everything, he will at least take the most striking and fit this into his scheme of work.'[30] Here he is following the ancient analogy of Seneca, who describes bees gathering the nectar and transforming it by 'blending something therewith and by a certain property of their breath.' The writer gathers, 'sifts,' and 'blends' so that 'even though [the final product] betrays its origin, yet it nevertheless is clearly a different thing from that whence it came.' The image of 'digesting' the text is bound up with this activity, which in the end is not just one of receiving the texts, but of producing new ones.[31]

Much of Erasmus' work facilitated such bee-like activity, as has been explained by Paul Oskar Kristeller:

> Ancient quotations were treated as authorities, that is, as a special kind of rhetorical argument, and each humanist kept his own commonplace book as a fruit of his readings for later writing, doubly important at a time when there were no dictionaries or indices to speak of. Finally, Erasmus with his *Adagia* earned the gratitude of posterity by supplying his successors with a systematic collection of anecdotes and sentences ready for use, the real quotation book of the early modern period that everybody used but few cared to mention. Superficial as humanist eclecticism tended to be, much more superficial than its ancient counterpart, it still had the merit of broadening the sources of thought and information that an individual moralist was ready to use.[32]

As we have mentioned, the 1508 edition of the *Adages* came with two indexes, the second of which was topical. The headings (mostly under moral-philosophical topics) now gave the work real value to those looking for commonplace material. And the scores of adapted editions tended to push the work even further in the direction of topical organization. This was a fundamental direction of rhetoric and dialectic for the next hundred or so years.[33]

Despite this tendency towards a more mechanical system of organizing the work and the way it might be used, Erasmus did not seem particularly interested in this approach himself. He tended to be more eclectic, less interested in dialectic, than many of the contemporary theorists of rhetoric. His own use of adages provided the most powerful model for those interested in improving their Latin style. Despite his inclusion of proverbs in the section of *De copia* on proofs, Erasmus himself used adages more as stylistic bricolage, as part of his *festivitas*, less as systematic method. We find the best examples of adage use in his letters, which are very much in the ancient tradition of the familiar style, the kind of writing one finds in Cicero's lively correspondence with Atticus and his other friends and in the younger Pliny's deft and amusing compositions. In Erasmus' letters, adages are dropped in lightly, bringing stylistic point or moral emphasis to a particular passage. The same playfulness is also found in the literary writings, in the *Colloquies* and most remarkably in Folly's famous encomium, which is stuffed with proverbs.[34] Indeed, one of the most interesting examples of Erasmus' adage use is in the *Adages* itself, where he will often wittily make reference to another adage, not in a cross-reference, but in a use of the proverb that exemplifies the practice he seeks to encourage (the best example is found throughout III i 1*). This is the kind of stylistic fluidity that he commends in *De copia*.

Though Erasmus' idea of style comes from ancient rhetoric, which was oriented mainly to public speaking, it is now adapted to writing. Likewise, the proverb, charactericaly oral, he now adapts to the condition of writing. Nevertheless, this is writing that attempts to model itself on speech and orality. Style is something that can be 'heard' – it is a manifestation of a personal voice. The proverb enhances this oral quality, even though the proverb is now a device passed on through the medium of writing.

Writing and instruction in writing tend to routinize language. The emphasis on orality pushes a written style towards an appearance of fluid spontaneity. Though he was the most important individual force for the rise of rhetorical education in the sixteenth century, Erasmus recognized the paradox of instruction in written style: imitation of spontaneity leads the imitator to routine practices, to mechanical systems. He wrote strenuously against the mindless imitators of the ancients in *Ciceronianus*. Yet our post-Romantic notion of stylistic originality would have seemed very odd to him. To an experienced reader of Latin Erasmus does have a distinct personal style (most apparent in his correspondence and polemical writings), yet he emphasized the classical models. The *Adages* shows his devotion to the power of ancient materials to lay the basis for a more vigorous and 'original' style. There is no shame in quoting an ancient author or drawing attention to a witty saying already used or in using a proverb to hammer home a truth. His sense of language is deeply historical. Indeed, rather than using proverbs to erase history, he employs them to foreground it.

The *Adages* and the English Proverb Tradition

With the decline of school instruction in classical languages from the late nineteenth century onwards, only a few Latin phrases are in circulation today – either classical, such as *Tempus fugit* (Time flies), or Horace's *Carpe diem* (Seize the day), or *quid pro quo* (tit for tat), or such tags as the U.S. Marine's *Semper fidelis* or MGM's (invented) *Ars gratia artis*. In the United States, some tags are the result of the Founding Fathers' strong knowledge of Latin: *e pluribus unum* or *novus ordo saeclorum* (on the dollar bill). Such few expressions are the extent of most people's encounter with Latin. Sometimes these phrases are invoked proverbially, as anonymous and authoritative phrases of compressed wisdom. Yet interestingly, none of these catchphrases, not even *Tempus fugit* or *quid pro quo*, appears in the *Adages* (though I i 35, 'To render like for like,' comes close to the old *quid pro quo*).

Nevertheless there is a remarkable amount that we do recognize as our own in Erasmus' work, and it gives us an uncanny realization that what seems to us to be of homely, local, and oral origin is in fact sophisticated, widely travelled, and literary. As well as spatial, the effect is temporal: the proverb, which seems to lie outside of history, is historicized when seen in Erasmus' compilation.[35]

Many ancient proverbs came to the English language in the sixteenth and seventeenth centuries through the great influence of humanist education, exemplified above all by the figure of Erasmus. Yet there is not yet a clear scholarly consensus on how much English readers and writers relied on Latin material. Many readers were fluent in Latin and English, others had lost their grammar-school Latin but still retained familiarity with many stock phrases.

The movement of proverbs, like fairy tales, fables, and other mixed oral-written material, is very hard to trace. Many English proverbs are indigenous productions, but many are translated from other languages, and others are constructed by analogy from other languages. Erasmus had an important influence on English proverbs, and nowhere is this more apparent than in the first English translation of the *Adages*, made by Richard Taverner (first extant edition 1539, with an expanded revision in 1545). Taverner radically cuts the Erasmus text, giving only 235 proverbs in his edition of 1545, and each of the adage essays is just a few lines long. For instance, Taverner takes the fairly short essay at I vii 94*, 'One swallow does not make a summer,' and shortens it further:

> *Una hirundo non facit ver.*
> It is not one swalowe that bringeth in somer. It is not one good qualitie that maketh a man good. Swalowes be a token of the beginning of somer yet one swalow is no sure token. Also ye may use this Proverbe, when ye will signifie that one day or littel time is not ynough for the acheving of a great matter. Which is all one with this in English: Rome was not buylt in one day.[36]

Like many collectors, Taverner tends to answer one proverb with another. The addition of the parallel proverb is, however, an interesting feature of his work and shows that it is more than a translation or adaptation of Erasmus. Indeed, rather than pretend to reproduce Erasmus, once or twice Taverner actually tells the reader to turn to the original. His version of IV i 1*, 'War is sweet to those who have not tried it,' is little more than a translation of the adage:

> *Dulce bellum inexpertis.*
> Batell is a swete thing, to them that never assayed it. He that listeth to know more of this Proverbe, let him go to Erasmus, which handleth in his Chiliades, this Proverbe both right copiously, and also eloquent.[37]

Not all his readers appreciated Taverner's efforts. The Cambridge scholar Gabriel Harvey referred in a manuscript note to Erasmus' *Adages* as having been 'turkissed' (unduly cut and mangled) by his English translators.[38]

Taverner was not the only route by which the adages moved into English. Schoolboys studying Latin and Greek would have been introduced to proverbs as part of their training; editions of the *Adages* were found in many English schools of the time, and in some commonplace books one finds compilations generally taken out of Erasmus. For instance, the Elizabethan schoolmaster John Conybeare made a list of almost 400 such proverbs in Latin, with English translations and applications.[39] The *Adages* were also commonly found in the personal library of scholars (of a hundred Oxford wills examined by Erika Rummel, half listed Erasmus' books, and the most popular of these was the *Adages*).[40] The various Latin-English dictionaries of the time also brought the *Adages* into English: Sir Thomas Elyot's *Dictionary,* revised and greatly enlarged by Bishop Thomas Cooper as the *Thesaurus linguae Romanae et Britannicae* (1565) had 303 of the adages in it; John Baret's *Alvearie or Triple Dictionary, in English, Latin, and French* (1573) had 264.[41] Hence, the *Adages* formed an important source of learning for English readers. It extended the linguistic repertoire, giving a much vaster range of reference in language, mythology, history, culture, and ancient religion. And it encouraged writers to spread themselves stylistically, even in English. Thus, the learned schoolmaster Richard Mulcaster in his *Positions* of 1581 says that 'eventes ... be but foolish maisters,' clearly playing on *Eventus stultorum magister est* ('Experience is the schoolmaster of fools'; I i 31*), or makes a comparison, 'as the rowling stone doth gather mosse,' that wittily reverses *Saxum volutum non obducitur musco,* 'A rolling stone gathers no moss' (III iv 74).[42] There is a subtlety in this game of allusion. Even a popular writer like Shakespeare plays with the learned proverb: 'cakes and ale' in *Twelfth Night* (2.1.123) evokes the familiar *Sine Cerere et Baccho friget Venus* 'Without Ceres and Bacchus Venus grows cold' (see headnote to II iii 97*).[43] When Hamlet says to Polonius, 'For yourself, sir, shall grow old as I am – if like a crab you could go backward' (2.2.203–4), is there not an echo of IV i 98, *Imitabor nepam,* 'I shall imitate the crab'? The self-conscious referentiality of proverb use was part of the stylistic repertoire of every English writer. Some of this writing was tied directly to proverbs: most outstanding was John Heywood's remarkable pastiche *A Dialogue Conteinying the Nomber in Effect of all the Proverbes in the English Tongue* (c 1549). By 1670 and 1678, when John Ray's two editions of *A Collection of English Proverbs* were published, many of the classical proverbs had become thoroughly domesticated in their new language.

Many of the classical proverbs seem to have entered English through the distribution of Erasmus' text in the sixteenth century. What is surprising is how many present-day English readers can recognize – 'many hands make light work' (II ii 95), 'to be afraid of your shadow' (I v 65*), 'blind leading the blind' (I viii 40*), 'dog in a manger' (I x

13*), 'like father like son' (I vi 33), 'to look a gift horse in the mouth' (IV v 24), 'to teach an old dog new tricks' (I ii 61), 'to break the ice' (III v 95*), 'thumbs up' (I viii 46*, for us reversed from the classical form described in the *Adages*), and so on. There are also proverbs found in English as analogies to the Latin ('owls to Athens' becoming 'coals to Newcastle'; see headnote to I ii 11*). This transference by analogy is common in other languages and is a fascinating linguistic phenomenon.

A very small class of proverb appears in English directly out of Erasmus' own, sometimes erroneous, interpretation of ancient texts. 'Pandora's box' and 'To call a spade a spade' are two results of Erasmus' misinterpretation of the ancient sources. 'Pandora's box' was actually 'Pandora's jar' until Erasmus translated *pithos* as *pyxis* (see headnote to I i 31*). The Latin expression for 'To call a spade a spade' was something along the lines of 'To call a skiff a skiff'; Erasmus thought that the Latin *scapha* meant 'spade' not 'small boat' and changed *scapha* to *ligo* (see headnote to II iii 5*). It shows the powerful influence of the *Adages* that two such expressions, essentially invented by Erasmus in a work of Latin scholarship some five hundred years ago, should have lasted until the present day.

Our Use of the *Adages*

What is the significance of the *Adages*? Is it even possible to use the word 'significance' about a reference work, the most quickly dated text in the modern library? Yet Erasmus' *Adages* shows us that the reference book can survive. Of course, this work has historical interest: it shows the way proverbs were collected and discussed in a period of the renewal of Greek and Latin learning in Western culture. It offers a window onto the humanist method of collection as a reflection upon antiquity. But it is more. Erasmus shows us the importance of proverbial language as an organizing force for history. The German critic Walter Benjamin wrote, 'A proverb, one might say, is a ruin which stands on the site of an old story and in which a moral twines about a happening like ivy around a wall.'[44] A proverb contains more than its apparent meaning. As Benjamin so richly states, it implies a narrative and the moral thought of a culture. In the *Adages*, Erasmus brings the linguistic curiosities of the past into a strongly foregrounded present. We usually begin with the details of a proverb, its 'story' if one can be reclaimed, its 'origins' and sources, but we often end up by reflecting on the concealed narrative and its relevance for religion, for education, for politics, for history, and, perhaps most important, for language itself.

Even the way Erasmus wrote the book is remarkable. He plays with material. He offers an imaginative way to write a book of information: he gives us a living, ironic voice, in which the style exemplifies content. And not least, he freely shares his joy in the obscure learning of antiquity and in the art of its quotation, and demonstrates his awe before the moral complexity of his ancient sources.

A Note on This Text

This collection reprints 119 from the total of 4151 adages. Included are all of the long essays, though the majority of Erasmus' discussions are just a few lines in length, and concentrate on citation and direct explication. Thus, short proverb essays like 'to carry wood to the forest' (I vii 57*) or 'thumbs down, thumbs up' (I viii 46*) may give a better sense of the *Adages* than the famous 'War is sweet to those who have not tried it' (IV i 1*). In his work, Erasmus occasionally repeats himself. His attempts to analyse the same proverb twice are interesting, and two of them are included here ('said and done' at II ix 72* and III vi 85* and on washing the Ethiopian, at I iv 50* and III x 88*). This selection concentrates on widely circulated proverbs, with a special interest in expressions that are also found in English. Strangeness and obscurity are to some degree diminished, and the reader is invited to turn to the Collected Works of Erasmus to discover the *Adages* in all their complexity.

The translations of the adages up to III iv 100 are from CWE, volumes 31 to 34. Volume 31 is translated by Margaret Mann Phillips and the notes are by Sir Roger Mynors; volumes 32 to 34 are the sole work of Mynors, who did not complete the work before his death in 1989. Volumes 35–36, with the remaining text, are still to come and are now under the general editorship of John Grant. The translations from III v 1 onwards are by Denis Drysdall and John Grant, who are preparing volumes 35 and 36 respectively, the latter with Betty Knott-Sharpe. Volume 30, an introduction with indexes, is also in preparation. Though the headnotes are the work of the present editor, the endnotes are the work, sometimes modified, of Mynors, Grant, and Drysdall; additional information comes from the editors of the fully annotated volumes in the Amsterdam *Opera omnia* (ASD, II–1, 2, 4, 5, 6, 7, 8), and from Renzo Tosi's *Dizionario delle sentenze latine e greche* (1996). The source notes are not elaborate but are intended only to provide the most immediate help for the reader who wishes to find a passage in its classical context; Erasmus usually identifies the author and work for a quotation, often a book number, but rarely gives more detailed references. Likewise, you will find here no indication of Erasmus' additions and deletions to the text, though the history of these changes is fascinating; they are shown most clearly in the modern *Opera omnia* (ASD). The present selection was to have been made by George Story, *omnium horarum homo* (I iii 86*), and it is in his memory that this work was undertaken.

Notes

1 References to Erasmus' correspondence (Ep for epistle number) are to the English translation in CWE, where these have already been published, or to the Latin edition of Allen (see 'Abbreviations and Works Frequently Cited').

2 An asterisk indicates that the adage is included in this selection.

3 Erasmus *Adagiorum collectanea* (Paris 1500) a2v

4 B. Taylor 'Medieval Proverb Collections: The West European Tradition' *Journal of the Warburg and Courtauld Institutes* 55 (1992) 19–35. The ancient tradition is outlined in two articles by K. Rupprecht, '*Paroimia*' and 'Paroimiographoi,' for Pauly-Wissowa *Real-Encyclopädie* XVIII/2 1701–78. The reception of the tradition by Erasmus and other humanists before and during his time (Niccolò Perotti, Ermolao Barbaro, Angelo Poliziano, Filippo Beroaldo, and Polydore Vergil) is described in Felix Heinimann 'Zu den Anfängen der humanistischen Paroemiologie' in *Catalepton: Festschrift für B. Wyss* (Basel 1985) 158–82. On Erasmus' working methods in incorporating new collections and other materials in the successive editions, see R. Hoven 'Les Éditions successives des Adages: Coup d'oeil

sur les sources et méthodes de travail d'Érasme' *Miscellanea Jean-Pierre Vanden Branden* (Brussels 1995) 257–81.

5 From the Aldine edition of Venice 1508, fol 150r–v (no II iv 4)

6 The adage appears in *Collectanea* on fol a3v in 1500 and many of the early editions. The edition of 1517 adds a Pliny reference ('lib.xx.ca.ix.'), for 'Crambe bis posita mors' reads 'bis Crambe mors,' and adds a Juvenal reference ('Saty. vij.'). In other words, 1517 has been checked and added to against the big edition of 1508. This could have been done as early as 1510, but was not, though in his introduction to 1510 the printer M. Schürer refers to the Aldine text.

7 From the Aldine edition of Venice 1508, fol 56r. Erasmus, following Pliny 15.98–9 at adage I ii 49, explains the strawberry as *unedo* or 'one-bite' because 'only one can be eaten.'

8 Margaret Mann Philipps *The Adages of Erasmus* (Cambridge 1964) 96

9 See CWE 85 no 91 for the Latin text and a prose translation.

10 Lisa Jardine *Erasmus, Man of Letters: The Construction of Charisma in Print* (Princeton 1993) discusses the ways in which Erasmus used the print culture of his age to promote himself, his community, and his ideas.

11 From a later edition of Cortehoevius' *Epitome* (Cologne: J. Prael 1533) 201. This is E153 in *Bibliotheca Belgica* ed Ferdinand van der Haeghen, rev Marie-Thérèse Lenger II (Brussels 1964), which lists all the early editions. From 1542 onwards, the Cortehoevius edition was re-edited by Eberhard Tappius and Conrad Brunssenius (E160). Some of the later Continental editions also offered translations of the Latin into the vernacular; for example, the work of J. Servilius, in editions from 1544 onwards (E163).

12 For other information about later editions, see Margaret Mann Phillips 'Comment s'est on servi des *Adages*?' in *Actes du colloque international Érasme (Tours, 1986)* ed Jacques Chomarat, André Godin, and Jean-Claude Margolin (Geneva 1990) 325–6 and 'Ways with Adages' in *Essays on the Works of Erasmus* ed R.L. DeMolen (New Haven and London 1978) 51–60.

13 Jean Céard 'La Censure tridentine et l'édition florentine des *Adages* d'Érasme' in *Actes du colloque international Érasme* ed Chomarat, Godin, and Margolin (Geneva 1990) 337–50

14 Tilley (*Dictionary of Proverbs*) often lists sources of English proverbs in Erasmus and classical authors, but this is not done consistently. An important English work, with greater attention to classical sources, is

F.P. Wilson's revision of *The Oxford Dictionary of English Proverbs* 3rd ed (Oxford 1970).

15 James Obelkevich 'Proverbs and Social History' in *The Social History of Language* ed Peter Burke and Roy Porter (Cambridge 1987) 43–72, 65; Chesterfield is cited on 57.

16 Wolfgang Mieder *Proverbs Are Never Out of Season: Popular Wisdom in the Modern Age* (New York and Oxford 1993) 137

17 Archer Taylor *The Proverb* (Cambridge, Mass 1931) 3; B.J. Whiting 'The Nature of the Proverb' *Harvard Studies in Philology and Literature* 14 (1932) 273–307 runs through many older definitions.

18 For more on these, with further examples, see the essays in *Wise Words: Essays on the Proverb* ed Wolfgang Mieder (New York and London 1994) and *The Wisdom of Many: Essays on the Proverb* ed Wolfgang Mieder and Alan Dundes (New York and London 1981). Some of the key essays are Roger D. Abrahams and Barbara A. Babcock 'The Literary Uses of Proverbs' *Journal of American Folklore* 90 (1977) 414–29 (repr *Wise Words* 415–37); David Cram 'The Linguistic Status of the Proverb' *Cahiers de lexicologie* 43 (1983) 53–71 (repr *Wise Words* 73–97); Alan Dundes 'On the Structure of the Proverb' *Proverbium* 25 (1975) 961–73 (repr *The Wisdom of Many* 43–64); and Peter Seitel 'Proverbs: A Social Use of Metaphor' *Genre* 2 (1969) 143–61 (repr *The Wisdom of Many* 122–39). Cf also Roger W. Wescott 'From Proverb to Aphorism: The Evolution of a Verbal Art Form' *Forum Linguisticum* 5 (1981) 213–25.

19 A.J. Greimas 'Idiotismes, proverbes, dictons' *Cahiers de lexicologie* 2 (1960) 41–61; part of this is reprinted as 'Les Proverbes et les dictons' in his *Du Sens* (Paris 1970) 309–14.

20 In addition to Greimas, see Matti Kuusi *Towards an International Type-System of Proverbs* (Helsinki 1972) (repr *Proverbium* 19 [1972] 699–736); Henri Meschonnic 'Les Proverbes, actes de discours' *Revue des sciences humaines* 41/163 (July–September 1976) 419–30; G.B. Milner 'De l'armature des locutions proverbiales, essai de taxonomie sémantique' *L'Homme* 9/3 (July–September 1969) 49–70 and 'What Is a Proverb?' *New Society* 32 (1969) 199–202; Pierre Crépeau 'La Définition du proverbe' *Fabula* 16 (1975) 285–304; Grigorii L. Permiakov *From Proverb to Folk-Tale: Notes on the General Theory of Cliché* trans Y.N. Filippov (Moscow 1979; first published Moscow 1970 as *Ot pogovorki do skazki: Zametki po obschei teorii klishe*); the positions are summarized and contextualized

in Peter Gzrybek 'Foundations of Semiotic Proverb Study' *Proverbium* 4 (1987) 39–85 (repr *Wise Words* [n 18 above] 31–71). Some of the schemes, especially that of Permiakov, become increasingly complex as they strive towards a simple formulation. Nevertheless, the linguistic and semantic analysis they provide is lacking in older discussions, such as Richard Chenevix Trench *On the Lessons in Proverbs* (London 1853), a spirited account of the moral truths to be found in proverbs. An essay that explains the rupturing and generative force of the proverb in a medieval literary context is Jacqueline and Bernard Cerquiglini 'L'Écriture proverbiale' *Revue des sciences humaines* 163 (1976) 359–75.

21 Natalie Zemon Davis 'Proverbial Wisdom and Popular Errors' in *Society and Culture in Early Modern France* (Stanford 1975) 227–67, 336–46 gives an excellent account of the interrelationship between printed and oral proverb use in the sixteenth century. More concerned with rhetorical uses in recent time are three articles by Roger D. Abrahams: 'Introductory Remarks to a Rhetorical Theory of Folklore' *Journal of American Folklore* 81 (1963) 143–58, 'Proverbs and Proverbial Expressions' in *Folklore and Folklife: An Introduction* ed R.M. Dorson (Chicago 1972) 117–27, and 'A Rhetoric of Everyday Life: Traditional Conversational Genres' *Southern Folklore Quarterly* 32 (1968) 44–59. Kenneth Burke 'Literature as Equipment for Living' in *The Philosophy of Literary Form: Studies in Symbolic Action* 3rd ed (Berkeley 1973) 293–304 treats oral proverbs as our way to name situations in order better to deal with them, and in this way they give us a clue as to the way literature also helps us to understand social phenomena; this approach seems similar in some regards to that of Erasmus. See also Alan Dundes 'On the Structure of the Proverb' *Proverbium* 25 (1975) 961–73 (repr *The Wisdom of Many* [n 18 above] 43–64).

22 Erasmus in CWE 24 335:122–3; Aristotle *Rhetoric* 1412a17 to 1413a17

23 Dundes 'On the Structure of the Proverb' *Proverbium* 25 (1975) 965

24 On the ancient etymologies see Anna Maria Ieraci Bio 'Le Concepte de *paroimia*: Proverbium dans la haute et la basse Antiquité' in *Richesse du proverbe* ed F. Suard and C. Buridant (Lille 1984) II 83–94; on Scaliger, see Christine B. Beuermann 'Le Renouvellement de l'esprit par l'adage' *Bibliothèque d'Humanisme et Renaissance* 47 (1985) 343–55, 344–5.

25 Francesco Guicciardini *Ricordi* c 12, *Maxims and Reflections* trans Mario Domandi (New York 1965) 43–4

26 Daniel Kinney 'Erasmus' *Adagia*: Midwife to the Rebirth of Learning' *Journal of Medieval and Renaissance Studies* 11 (1981) 169–92

27 The cultural encyclopedia (a useful term from the semiotics of Umberto Eco) may be loosely defined as a collection of referents available in a culture at a particular time, a gathering of what might be known to the educated reader (though not strictly limited to material passed through the institutions of learning). An application of the term to medieval allegorical interpretation is provided by Martin Irvine in *The Making of Textual Culture: 'Grammatica' and Literary Theory, 350–1100* (Cambridge 1994) 246.

28 Claudie Balavoine 'L'Essence de la marjolaine, ou ce que, de l'adage, retint Érasme' *La Licorne* (Poitiers 1980) 159–83. See also her 'Bouquets de fleurs et colliers de perles: Sur les recueils de formes brèves au XVIe siècle' in *Les Formes brèves de la prose et le discours discontinu (XVIe–XVIIe siècles)* ed J. Lafond (Paris 1984) 51–71 and 'Les Principes de la parémiographie érasmienne' in François Suard and Claude Buridant *Richesse du proverbe* (Lille 1984) II 9–23. An important analysis of the *Adages* in relation to Erasmus' agenda in style is given by Jacques Chomarat *Grammaire et rhétorique chez Erasme* (Paris 1981) 761–81.

29 Ann Moss *Printed Commonplace-Books and the Structuring of Renaissance Thought* (Oxford 1996) lays out material essential for an understanding of the reception and use of the *Adages*.

30 *De copia* CWE 24 639:1–15

31 Seneca *Epistulae morales* 84.4–5 (Loeb translation)

32 *Renaissance Thought and Its Sources* ed Michael Mooney (New York 1979) 202

33 In addition to the study of commonplace books by Ann Moss (n 29 above), see also Walter J. Ong 'Commonplace Rhapsody: Ravisus Textor, Zwinger and Shakespeare' in *Classical Influences on European Culture A.D. 1500–1700* ed R.R. Bolgar (Cambridge 1976) 91–126; and Mary Crane *Framing Authority: Sayings, Self and Society in Sixteenth-Century England* (Princeton 1993). Crane sets out principles of gathering and framing by which much composition was taught and undertaken in the sixteenth and seventeenth centuries in England. Rebecca Bushnell describes the activity as 'Harvesting Books' in chapter 4 of her *A Culture of Teaching: Early Modern Humanism in Theory and Practice* (Ithaca 1996).

34 Clarence H. Miller 'The Logic and Rhetoric of Proverbs in Erasmus's *Praise of Folly*' in *Essays on the Works of Erasmus* ed R.L. DeMolen (New Haven

and London 1978) 83–98 finds the 285 proverbs in the text to be most abundant in any of Erasmus' works, and Ari Wesseling 'Dutch Proverbs and Ancient Sources in Erasmus's *Praise of Folly' Renaissance Quarterly* 47 (1994) 351–78 shows that Erasmus did on occasion show detailed awareness of Dutch proverbs, which he imported into his Latin writings, a matter that is also explored in the learned older study by W.H.D. Suringar *Erasmus over nederlandsche spreekwoorden en spreekwoordelijke uitdrukkingen van zijnen tijd* (Utrecht 1873). On Erasmus' style of *varietas*, see Balavoine 'Les Principes de la parémiographie érasmienne' (n 28 above) and, for its influence in France, Terence Cave *The Cornucopian Text: Problems of Writing in the French Renaissance* (Oxford 1979).

35 Thomas M. Greene 'Erasmus' "Festina lente": Vulnerability of the Humanist Text' in *The Vulnerable Text: Essays on Renaissance Literature* (New York 1986) 1–17, 237–8

36 Richard Taverner *Proverbes or Adagies, gathered out of the Chiliades of Erasmus, by Richard Taverner. With New Additions, as Well of Latin Proverbes, as of English* (London 1569); repr ed DeWitt T. Starnes (Delmar NY 1977) 24r

37 Ibid 63r

38 Gabriel Harvey's comment is found as a marginal note in his copy of Erasmus *Parabolae* (Basel 1565) 18r (Folger Shakspeare Library H.a.1).

39 Conybeare's list of adages is found in Folger MS v.a.467, leaves 13–22; there is a transcription in *Letters and Exercises of the Elizabethan Schoolmaster John Conybeare* ed Frederick Cornwallis Conybeare (London 1905).

40 Erika Rummel 'The Reception of Erasmus' Adages in Sixteenth-Century England' *Renaissance and Reformation* 18/2 (1994) 19–30

41 These numbers come from DeWitt T. Starnes's introduction to the reprint of Richard Taverner's translation of Erasmus *Proverbes or Adagies* (n 36 above) vii.

42 Richard Mulcaster *Positions Concerning the Training Up of Children* ed William Barker (Toronto 1994), 150 and 159

43 The possible classical basis of either passage is not mentioned in any of the standard editions, though there is learned discussion of Shakespeare and adages in Kenneth Muir 'Shakespeare among the Commonplaces' *Review of English Studies* 10 (1959) 283–9 and F.P. Wilson 'The Proverbial Wisdom of Shakespeare' in his *Shakespearian and Other Studies* (Oxford 1969) 143–75 (repr *Wisdom of Many* [n 18 above] 174–89). T.W. Baldwin *William Shakspere's Small Latine & Lesse Greeke* (Urbana 1944), with *Adages*

discussed at II 342ff, claims that 'Shakspere h
copy of the *Adagia*, perhaps even owned one' (
disagree, seeing Shakespeare as having given a '
encountered in many different places in his readin
of Shakespeare and his contemporary dramatists h
R.W. Dent *Shakespeare's Proverbial Language: An Inde*
Proverbial Language in English Drama Exclusive of Sha
(Berkeley 1984), which go beyond Tilley's wonderful
focus on drama.

44 Walter Benjamin, 'The Storyteller: Reflections on the Work
Leskov,' in his *Illuminations* ed Hannah Arendt and trans Ha
(New York 1968) 108. Benjamin also has a short note 'On Prov
trans Rodney Livingstone in *Selected Writings* ed Michael Jennings
(Cambridge, MA 1999) II 582. He says: 'Proverbs cannot be applied
situations. Instead, they have a kind of magical character: they transfor
the situation.'

ɔnology

,69	27 Oct: Erasmus' birth (or 1466, as it appears in some authorities)
c 1478–83	Attends school of the Brethren of the Common Life at Deventer
c 1483–86	Attends school at 'sHertogenbosch
1486	Enters the Augustinian monastery at Steyn as a novice
1492	Ordained priest
1492/3	Enters the service of Hendrik van Bergen, bishop of Cambrai
1495–99	First stay in Paris, studying theology
1499	First visit to England; association with More and Colet
1500–2	Second stay in Paris, with visits in Orléans and Holland; in 1500, an early short version of *Adages* (*Collectanea*, with 818 proverbs)
1502–4	First stay in Louvain; refuses offer to teach at university; *Handbook of the Christian Soldier* (1504)
1504–5	Third stay in Paris
1505/6	Second visit to England, staying in the house of More
1506–9	Travels to Italy; in 1507/8 working in Venice with Aldo Manuzio, who publishes the first expanded edition of *Adages* in 1508 with 3260 proverbs
1509–14	Third stay in England; visit to Paris 1511; lecturing in Cambridge 1511–14; *Praise of Folly* (1511); *Copia: On Abundance in Style* (1512)
1514–16	First visit to Basel; begins association with Johann Froben, who prints second edition of *Adages* (1515) and first edition of New Testament (1516); stays in England (1515) and Netherlands (1516); made councillor to Emperor Charles v

1517	In Antwerp, with Pieter Gillis; visit to England; move to Louvain
1517–21	Second stay in Louvain, with various trips, including Basel (1518), to supervise second edition of New Testament; becomes associated with faculty of theology at Louvain; *Julius Excluded from Heaven* (1517/18), an anonymous satire attributed to Erasmus; early version of *Colloquies* (1518); *Adages* appears in third (1517/18) and fourth editions (1520); from this time onwards, Erasmus heavily involved in religious controversies
1521–9	Move to Basel; attempts to mediate between Protestants and Catholics; begins the series of *Paraphrases on the New Testament*; *Ciceronianus* (1528); *Adages* appears in fifth (1523), sixth (1526), and seventh editions (1528)
1529–35	Basel turns Protestant; Erasmus moves to Catholic Freiburg im Breisgau; *Adages* appears in eighth edition (1533), with 488 new proverbs
1535	Return to Basel
1536	12 July: death of Erasmus; collected works published in Basel, volume 2 being final edition of *Adages*, with 4151 proverbs

Abbreviations and Works Frequently Cited

To list every work mentioned even in this short selection of the *Adages* would generate a huge bibliography. The sources given in the notes and headnotes refer to standard editions of the classics, sometimes identified by particular editors (for instance, Aesop 60 Halm refers to the standard numbering of the stories in the nineteenth-century edition of Aesop prepared by Karl Felix von Halm). Most of the texts are available in translation, usually in the Loeb Classical Library. Basic facts on the authors can be found most readily in the third edition of the *Oxford Classical Dictionary*, ed Simon Hornblower and Antony Spawforth (Oxford 1996). The ancient proverb collections have not been translated, but most have been collected in Schneidewin, listed below.

Allen	*Opus epistolarum Des. Erasmi Roterodami* ed P.S. Allen (Oxford 1906–58)
Apostolius	See Schneidewin below
ASD	*Opera omnia Desiderii Erasmi* (Amsterdam 1969–)
Collectanea	Desiderius Erasmus *Adagiorum collectanea* (Paris 1500); numbering follows the revised edition of 1506/7
Contemporaries	P.G. Bietenholz and T.B. Deutscher *Contemporaries of Erasmus: A Biographical Register* (Toronto 1985–7)
CWE	*Collected Works of Erasmus* (Toronto 1974–)
Diogenianus	See Schneidewin below
Ep	Epistle of Erasmus from CWE, when translated, or Allen
Kock	T. Kock ed *Comicorum Atticorum fragmenta* (Leipzig 1880–8)
Nauck	A. Nauck ed *Tragicorum Graecorum fragmenta* (Leipzig 1889)

ODEP	*Oxford Dictionary of English Proverbs* 3rd ed F.P. Wilson (Oxford 1970)
OED	*Oxford English Dictionary* 2nd ed rev J.A. Simpson and E.S.C. Weiner (Oxford 1989)
Otto	A. Otto *Die Sprichwörter ... der Römer* (Leipzig 1890)
PG	J.P. Migne ed *Patrologia graeca* (Paris 1857–86)
PL	J.P. Migne ed *Patrologia latina* (Paris 1844–66)
Schneidewin	F.G. Schneidewin ed *Corpus paroemiographorum Graecorum* (Göttingen 1839)
Stevenson	Burton Stevenson *The Macmillan Book of Proverbs, Maxims and Famous Phrases* (New York 1965)
Suidas	*Suidae lexicon* ed A. Adler (Leipzig 1928–38)
Suringar	W.H.D. Suringar *Erasmus over nederlandsche spreekwoorden en spreekwoordelijke uitdrukkingen van zijnen tijd* (Utrecht 1873)
Taverner	Richard Taverner *Proverbes or Adagies* (London 1539, 1569)
Tilley	Morris Palmer Tilley *A Dictionary of the Proverbs in England in the Sixteenth and Seventeenth Centuries* (Ann Arbor 1950)
Tosi	R. Tosi *Dizionario delle sentenze latine e greche* (Milan 1996)
Walther	Hans Walther *Proverbia sententiaeque latinitatis medii aevi* (Göttingen 1963–86)
Zenobius	See Schneidewin above

THE ADAGES: A SELECTION

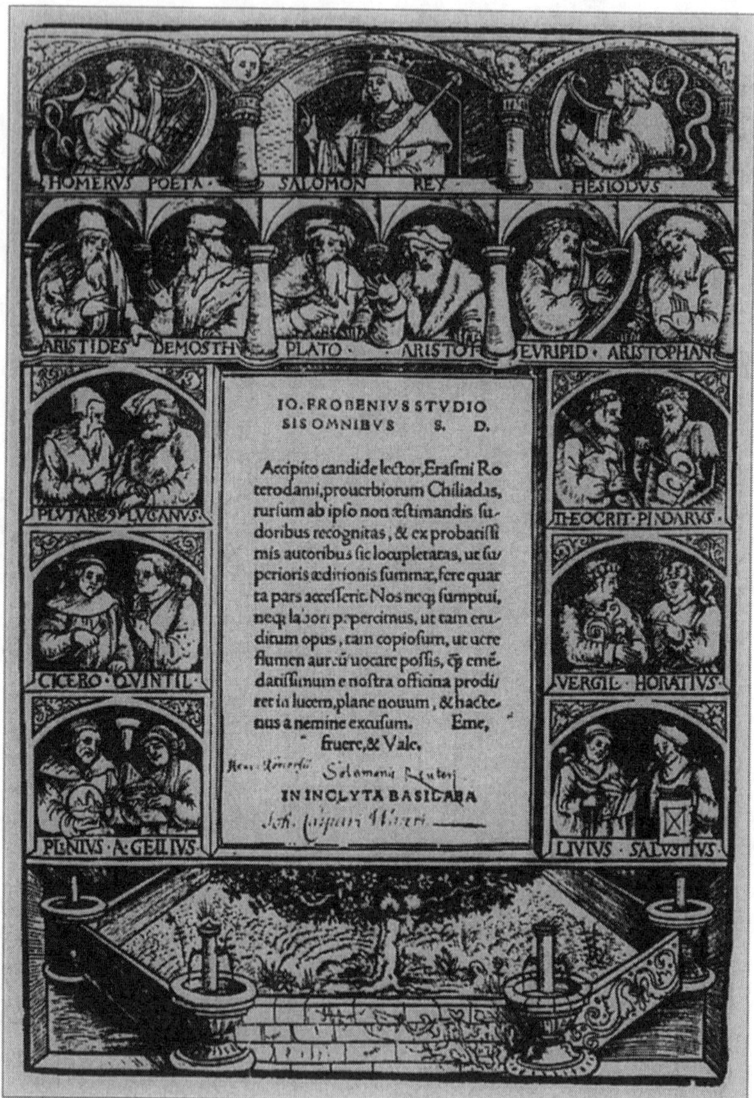

HOMERVS POETA · SALOMON REX · HESIODVS ·

ARISTIDES DEMOSTH PLATO · ARISTOT EVRIPID · ARISTOPHAN

PLVTARCH LVCANVS · THEOCRIT · PINDARVS

CICERO · QVINTIL · VERGIL · HORATIVS

PLINIVS · A · GELLIVS · LIVIVS · SALVSTIVS

IO. FROBENIVS STVDIO
SIS OMNIBVS S. D.

Accipito candide lector, Erasmi Roterodami, prouerbiorum Chiliadas, rursum ab ipso non æstimandis sudoribus recognitas, & ex probatissimis autoribus sic locupletatas, ut superioris æditionis summæ, fere quarta pars accesserit. Nos neq; sumptui, neq; labori pepercimus, ut tam eruditum opus, tam copiosum, ut uere flumen aureum uocare possis, quam emendatissimum e nostra officina prodiret in lucem, plane nouum, & hactenus a nemine excusum. Eme, fruere, & Vale.

IN INCLYTA BASILEA

Erasmus' principal sources portrayed The border for this second edition (Basel: Froben 1515) of the expanded *Adages* shows many of Erasmus' most important classical sources, though the Greek proverb collections have been omitted. As is typical of many title pages of the time (for instance, Aldus' 1508 edition of the *Adages*), there is a message from the printer, here encouraging the reader to buy this recently expanded and corrected edition. (Houghton Library, Harvard University)

Introduction

The introduction by Erasmus first appeared in the enlarged edition of 1508. This remarkably lucid analysis lays special emphasis on the rhetorical uses of the proverb. Erasmus is especially concerned with finding a good working definition of the proverb (not so easy, as he admits in section i, yet obviously necessary for anyone making a collection). He is also concerned with the origins and categories of proverbs. As in his other rhetorical and educational works, he emphasizes the affective as well as the decorative effect of the proverb. Proverbs convince (following Erasmus' argument, in turn derived from Aristotle and Quintilian) because they appeal to authority; 'there is ... in these proverbs some native authentic power of truth. Otherwise how could it happen that we should frequently find the same thought spread abroad among a hundred peoples, transposed into a hundred languages, a thought which has not perished or grown old even with the passing of so many centuries' (section vii). For Erasmus, the greatest effect of the proverb is in its metaphorical 'turn' ('the majority of adages have some kind of metaphorical disguise'; section i). The longest part of the essay, section xiii, dwells specifically on proverbial metaphors, and their numerous types, divided by subject matter. For Erasmus, metaphor works through its compressed and tempting allusiveness, through the way it draws different things together and in a tiny gem-like form forces the reader to make sudden and illuminating connections.

In this essay Erasmus sees the proverb, though spoken and immensely popular, as a specifically literary device, and even when he refers to speech and the 'auditor' or listener, it is speech that is being witnessed through the medium of writing. Later proverb scholarship of the nineteenth and twentieth centuries became more interested in the proverb as a phenomenon of speech (though speech again mediated unselfconsciously through the medium of scholarly writing). The emphasis on writing is very important for Erasmus, because writing allows the proverb to be collected, made an object of study, and incorporated into a literary style.

With its emphasis on metaphor and writing (without entirely overlooking internal formal structures and the spoken or performative features), this essay is a major theoretical statement, one of the most thorough discussions of the proverb up to that time in Western literature, even including those surviving from the ancients, whose writings on proverbs are fragmentary or are included in longer works on rhetoric. Though some of his contemporaries had attempted to write similar pieces (Philippus Beroaldus has an Oratio proverbiorum, *1499), none had the scope of Erasmus, who had, even by 1508, surveyed so many of the sources first hand. He outlines these sources in section v.*

i / What a proverb is

A proverb, according to Donatus,[1] is 'a saying which is fitted to things and times.' Diomedes[2] however defines it as follows: 'A proverb is the taking over of a popular saying, fitted to things and times, when the words say one thing and mean another.' Among Greek authors[3] various definitions are to be found. Some describe it in this way: 'A proverb is a saying useful in the conduct of life, with a certain degree of obscurity but of great value in itself.' Others define it like this: 'A proverb is a manner of speaking which wraps up in obscurity an obvious truth.' I am quite aware that several other definitions of the word proverb exist in both Latin and Greek, but I have not thought it worth while to list them all here, first because I propose as far as possible, in this work especially, to follow the advice of Horace[4] about the brevity required of a teacher; secondly because they all tell the same tale and come back to the same point; but above all because among all these definitions there is not one to be found which covers the character and force of proverbs so as to contain nothing unnecessary and leave nothing diminished in importance.

Setting aside other things for the present, it seems that Donatus and Diomedes regard it as essential for any proverb to have some kind of envelope; in fact they make it into a sort of allegory. They also expect it to contain something *gnomic*, didactic, since they add 'fitted to things and times.' The Greeks too, in all their definitions, introduce either helpfulness in the conduct of life, or the outer covering of metaphor, and sometimes they join the two together. Yet you will find many observations quoted as proverbs by writers of unshakeable authority which are not hidden in metaphor, and not a few which have no bearing at all on instruction in living, and are diametrically (as they say) opposed to the nature of a *sententia* or aphorism. Two examples out of many will suffice. *Ne quid nimis*, Nothing to excess

[I vi 96*], is accepted by everybody as an adage, but it is not in the least disguised. And *Quis aberret a foribus?*, Who could miss the gate? [I vi 36], is given the name of proverb by Aristotle,[5] but I cannot see how it can be useful for the conduct of life. Again, not every proverb is clothed in allegory, as Quintilian[6] makes clear when he says in the fifth book of his *Institutions*: 'Allied to this is that type of proverb which is like a short form of fable.' This indicates clearly that there are other kinds of proverb, which do not come close to allegory. I would not deny however that the majority of adages have some kind of metaphorical disguise. I think the best of them are those which equally give pleasure by their figurative colouring and profit by the value of their ideas.

But it is one thing to praise the proverb and show which kind is best, and quite another to define exactly what it is. I myself think (*pace* the grammarians) that a complete definition and one suitable to our present purpose may be reached by saying: 'A proverb is a saying in popular use, remarkable for some shrewd and novel turn.' The logicians agree that there are three parts to a definition, and here we have them: the word 'saying' indicates the genus, 'in popular use' the *differentia* or species, and 'remarkable for some shrewd and novel turn' the particular characteristic.

ii / What is the special quality of a proverb, and its limits

There are then two things which are peculiar to the character of a proverb, common usage and novelty. This means that it must be well known and in popular currency; for this is the origin of the word *paroimia* in Greek (from *oimos*, a road, as though well polished in use and circulating), that which travels everywhere on the lips of men, and of *adagium* in Latin, as if you should say 'something passed round,' following Varro.[7] And then it must be shrewd, so as to have some mark, as it were, to distinguish it from ordinary talk. But we cannot immediately rank in this category everything which has passed into popular speech, or contains an unusual image; it must be recommended by its antiquity and erudition alike, for that is what I call shrewd. What confers originality on adages I intend to explain soon; at present I shall say a few words about the many ways in which a proverb can achieve a popular circulation.

Proverbs get into popular speech, either from the oracles of the gods, like 'Neither the third nor the fourth' [II i 79], or from the sayings of sages, which indeed circulated in antiquity as if they were oracles, such as 'Good things are difficult' [II i 12]. Or else they come from some very ancient poet, as for instance Homer's 'When a thing is done, a fool can see it' [I i 30], or Pindar's 'To kick against the goad' [I iii 46], or from Sappho 'No bees, no honey' [I vi 62]; for at a time when tongues were as yet uncorrupted, the verses of the poets were also sung at feasts. Or they may come from the stage, that is, from tragedies and comedies, like this from Euripides: 'Upwards flow the streams' [I iii 15*], or this from Aristophanes: 'Off with you to the crows!' [II i 96]. It is comedy especially which by a mutual give-and-take adopts many of the expressions in constant use among the common people, and in turn gives birth to others which are passed on to them for constant use. Some are derived from the subjects of legend, such as the great jar that cannot be filled from the story of the daughters of Danaus [I iv 60], or the helmet of Orcus from the tale of Perseus [II x 74]. Some arise from fables, among which we find 'But we see not what is in the wallet behind' [I vi 90]. Occasionally they are born from an actual occurrence: 'Leucon carries some things, his ass carries others' [II ii 86]. Several are borrowed from history: 'Rome wins by sitting still' [I x 29]. Others come from *apophthegms*, that is from quick witty replies, like that remark 'Who does not own himself would Samos own' [I vii 83]. There are some which are snatched from a word rashly spoken, such as 'Hippocleides doesn't care' [I x 12]. In a word, the behaviour, the natural qualities of any race or individual, or even of an animal, or lastly any power belonging even to a thing, if remarkable and commonly known – all these have given occasion for an adage. Examples of this are 'Syrians against Phoenicians' [I viii 56], *accissare* [II ii 99] which means to refuse coyly what you mean to accept, 'A fox takes no bribes' [I x 18], 'Twice-served cabbage is death' [I v 38*], and 'The Egyptian clematis' [I i 22].

iii / What produces novelty in a proverb

I have already mentioned novelty, and this is by no means a simple matter. For sometimes this is produced by the thing itself, as in 'Crocodile tears' [II iv 60*]; sometimes the metaphor provides it, since the adage may adopt all kinds of figurative variations, which need not be followed up one by one. I will touch only on those which it most frequently assumes. Metaphor is nearly always present, but it embraces many forms. Allegory is no less frequent, though to some people this also is a kind of metaphor. An example of the first is 'Everything is in shallow water' [I i 45], of the second 'The wolf's jaws are gaping' [II iii 58]. Hyperbole is not infrequent, as in 'As bare as a snake's sloughed skin' [I i 26]. Sometimes it goes as far as a riddle which, according to Quintilian,[8] is nothing but a more obscure allegory, as in 'The half is more than the whole' [I ix 95]. Sometimes an allusion gives the proverb its attraction, as in 'Keep it up' [II iv 28]; and 'two heads together' [III i 51]; and 'The good or ill that's wrought in our own halls' [I vi 85]. Occasionally the dialect or idiom itself, the particular significance of a word, gives it a resemblance to a proverb, for instance 'An Ogygian disaster' [II ix 50] for an immense one. It happens sometimes that sheer ambiguity gives grace to a proverb: of this sort are 'An ox on the tongue' [I vii 18*] and 'Like Mys in Pisa' [II iii 67–8]. The point of this is that 'ox' means both an animal and a coin, and in the same way Mys, the Greek for 'mouse,' is the name of an animal and also of an athlete, and Pisa, the name of a town, needs only one letter added to give *pissa*, the Greek for 'pitch.' Sometimes the very novelty of an expression is what makes it into a proverb, like 'Wine speaks the truth' [I vii 17*], for if you say 'Men speak their minds when drunk,' it will not look like a proverb. Similarly, if you say 'Desire fails without food and drink,' this has not the look of an adage; but say 'Without Ceres and Bacchus Venus grows cold' [II iii 97*], and everyone will recognize the adage-form. But of course this kind of novelty, like every other, comes from the metaphor. Age sometimes lends attractions too, as in 'Stand surety, and ruin is at hand' [I vi 97]. Once again, in proverbs you will find humour in all its forms. But to follow out these points in detail might seem to be industry misapplied. However, I shall say rather more later on about proverbial metaphors.

iv / How the proverb differs from those forms that seem to approach it closely

There are however some near neighbours to the proverb, for instance *gnômai*, which are called by us *sententiae* or aphorisms, and *ainoi*, which among us are called fables; with the addition of *apophthegmata*, which may be translated as quick witty sayings, as well as *skômmata* or facetious remarks, and in a word anything which shelters behind a kind of mask of allegory or any other figure of speech associated with proverbs. It is not difficult to distinguish these from the proverb itself, if one knows how to test them against our definition as against a measure or rule; but in order to satisfy the inexperienced as well, I am quite willing to explain more crudely and 'with crass mother-wit' as the saying goes, so as to make it quite clear what my purpose has been in this work. In the first place, the relationship between the aphorism and the proverb is of such a nature that each can be joined to the other or again each can be separated from the other, in the same way as with 'whiteness' and 'man.' Whiteness is not ipso facto man, nor man inevitably whiteness; but there is nothing to prevent what constitutes a man being also white. Thus it not infrequently happens that an aphorism includes a proverb, but a proverb need not automatically become an aphorism or vice versa. For instance 'The miser lacks what he has as well as what he has not' and 'Ill-will feeds on the living but is quiet after death' are aphorisms, but not for that reason adages. On the other hand, 'I navigate in harbour' [I i 46] is a proverb but not an aphorism. Again, 'Put not a sword into the hand of a child' [II v 18] partakes of the nature of both proverb and aphorism, and of allegory as well. There were those, especially among the Greeks, who willingly undertook the task of making *gnomologies*, collections of aphorisms, notably Johannes Stobaeus.[9] I would rather praise their work than imitate it.

Now to consider the rest. Aphthonius[10] in the *Progymnasmata* calls the *ainos* simply *mythos*, a fable. It has, as he says, various secondary names, taken from the inventors: Sybarite, Cilician, Cyprian, Aesopic. Quintilian[11] says that the Greeks call it a *logos mythikos* or apologue, 'and some Latin authors an apologation, a name which has not gained general currency.' He agrees that the fable is close to the proverb, but says that they are to be distinguished by the fact that the *ainos* is a whole story, and the proverb is shorter 'like a fable in miniature.' As an example he gives 'Not my burden: pack-saddle on the ox' [II ix 84]. Hesiod[12] used it in this way: 'Now will I tell the princes a fable, though they know it well: the hawk thus addressed the tuneful nightingale.' Archilochus[13] and Callimachus use it in the same way, although Theocritus in the *Cyniscae* seems to have used 'tale' for a proverb: 'In truth a certain tale is told: the bull went off into the wood' [I i 43].

As for apophthegms, they are differentiated from proverbs in the same way as aphorisms. Just as the phrase 'Who does not own himself would Samos own' [I vii 83] is at the same time both an adage and an apophthegm, so that remark of Simonides[14] to someone who was silent at a banquet 'if you are a fool you are doing a wise thing, but if you are wise a foolish one,' and that well-known saying 'Caesar's wife must not only be innocent, she must be above suspicion' are apophthegms but not also proverbs. Also 'You are used to sitting on two stools' [I vii 2] is both a proverb and an insult. Conversely 'My mother never, my father constantly.'[15] That phrase of Turonius, 'They are at the mills,' is a savage jest, but not also an adage. But there are some of this sort so aptly put that they can easily be ranked as adages, like 'I'm your friend as far as the altar' [III ii 10]. Here we have brevity, aphorism, and metaphor all together. I have emphasized this at somewhat too great length, so that no one may expect to find in this book anything but what falls into the category of proverbs, and to prevent anyone from thinking that an omission is the result of negligence, when I have left it on one side deliberately and on purpose, as not pertaining to the subject.

v / Proverbs are to be respected for their value

Now in case anyone should impatiently thrust aside this aspect of learning as too humble, perfectly easy and almost childish, I will explain in a few words how much respect was earned by these apparent trivialities among the ancients; and then I will show what a sound contribution they can make, if cleverly used in appropriate places, and finally how it is by no means everyone who can make the right use of proverbs. To start with, that an acquaintance with adages was held to be not unimportant by the greatest men is sufficiently proved, I think, by the fact that authors of the first distinction have thought them a worthy subject for a number of volumes diligently compiled.[16] The first of these is Aristotle, so great a philosopher of course that he alone may stand for many others. Laertius tells us that he left one volume of *Paroimiai*. Chrysippus also compiled two volumes on proverbs, addressed to Zenodotus. Cleanthes wrote on the same subject. If the works of these men were still extant, it would not have been necessary for me to fish up some things with such labour out of these insignificant writers, who were both careless and textually most corrupt. Some collections of proverbs are to be found under the name of Plutarch, but they are few in number and almost bare of comment. Often cited among compilers of proverbs, by Athenaeus in his *Deipnologia* among others, are Clearchus of Soli, a pupil of Aristotle, and Aristides, and after them Zenodotus, who reduced to a compendium the proverbs of Didymus and Tarrhaeus. In the brief scholia on Demosthenes proverbs of Theophrastus are also quoted. This makes it clear that these writers too left collections on this subject. I am aware that this work is in circulation under the name of Zenobius. But as I find that in the scholiast on Aristophanes there are some things attributed to that very Zenodotus who summarized Didymus and Tarrhaeus which are to be found word for word in this man's collections, I hope I shall not be blamed if in this work I adduce him, whatever his name was (for what does it matter?), under the name of Zenodotus. This writer refers among others to a certain Milo as a collector of proverbs. One Daemon is also quoted, by many others and particularly by the person who explained a number of words and phrases in the speeches of Demosthenes; he appears to have composed many books of proverbs, since book 40 is quoted. There are also extant the collections of Diogenianus. Hesychius states in his preface that he has given a fuller explanation of the proverbs which had been briefly enumerated by Diogenianus; but the work itself seems to conflict with the prologue, since the earlier writer claims to give a list of the authors and the subjects of the proverbs, while the later is so brief that nothing shorter could be imagined. From this I conjecture that this work was produced in a fuller form by the author, and contracted into a summary by another hand. Suidas, who must himself be placed in this category, mentions a certain Theaetetus as having written a work on proverbs. But why should I be talking of these people, when the Hebrew sages themselves did not hesitate to bring out more than one book with this title, and to enclose the venerable mysteries of the unsearchable deity in proverbs which the intellects of so many and such great theologians have struggled to elucidate, as they are struggling to this day?

It is no light argument too that among good authors it was the most learned and eloquent who sprinkled their books most freely with adages. To begin with the Greeks, who is a greater master of proverbs, so to call it, than the great, not to say the divine, Plato? Aristotle, otherwise a grave philosopher, is always ready to interweave frequent proverbs, like jewels, into his discussions. As in other things, so in this, Theophrastus imitates him. As for Plutarch, a serious, religious-minded writer, not to say austere, how he scatters proverbs plentifully everywhere! Nor was he averse to bringing forward and discussing certain proverbs among his 'Problems,' and in this he was following the example of Aristotle. To turn to Latin, setting aside grammarians and poets in both kinds (unless it is thought that among these we should count Varro, who gave proverbial titles to his *Menippean Satires*, so that there is general agreement that he borrowed the subjects of his fables from no other source than proverbs), the rulers of Rome did not think it was demeaning the imperial majesty to reply in proverbs when they were consulted on great topics, as can be found even now in the *Digest*:[17] 'Not everything, nor everywhere, nor from everybody' [II iv 16].

Then who would dare to despise this mode of speech, when he saw that some of the oracles of the holy prophets are made of proverbs? One example of this is 'The fathers have eaten sour grapes, and the children's teeth are set on edge.'[18] Who would not revere them as an almost holy thing, fit to express the mysteries of religion, since Christ Himself, whom we ought to imitate in all things, seems to have taken a particular delight in this way of speaking? An adage is current in Greek: 'I judge the tree by its fruit' [I ix 39]. In Luke[19] we read the same thing: 'A good tree bringeth not forth corrupt fruit, neither doth a corrupt tree bring forth good fruit.' In Greek, Pittacus[20] the philosopher sent an enquirer to watch boys playing with tops, so as to learn proverbial wisdom from them about taking a wife, and heard: 'Stick to your own' [I viii 1]. Christ[21] cites a proverb from children playing in the market-place: 'We have piped to you and you have not danced; we have mourned to you, and you have not wept.' This is very like that saying in Theognis,[22] if one may compare sacred with profane: 'For Jove himself may not content us all, / Whether he holds rain back or lets it fall' [II vii 55].

If a motive is to be found in reverence for antiquity, there appears to be no form of teaching which is older than the proverb. In these symbols, as it were, almost all the philosophy of the ancients was contained. What were the oracles of those wise old Sages but proverbs? They were so deeply respected in old time, that they seemed to have fallen from heaven rather than to have come from men. 'And *Know thyself* descended from the sky' [I vi 95*] says Juvenal.[23] And so they were written on the doors of temples, as worthy of the gods; they were everywhere to be seen carved on columns and marble tablets as worthy of immortal memory. If the adage seems a tiny thing, we must remember that it has to be estimated not by its size but by its value. What man of sane mind would not prefer gems, however small, to immense rocks? And, as Pliny[24] says, the miracle of nature is greater in the most minute creatures, in the spider or the gnat, than in the elephant, if only one looks closely; and so, in the domain of literature, it is sometimes the smallest things which have the greatest intellectual value.

vi / The many uses of a knowledge of proverbs

It remains for me to show briefly how proverbs have an intrinsic usefulness no less than the respect in which they were formerly held. A knowledge of proverbs contributes to a number of things, but to four especially: philosophy, persuasiveness, grace and charm in speaking, and the understanding of the best authors.

To begin with, it may seem surprising that I should have said that proverbs belong to the science of philosophy; but Aristotle,[25] according to Synesius, thinks that proverbs were simply the vestiges of that earliest philosophy which was destroyed by the calamities of human history. They were preserved, he thinks, partly because of their brevity and conciseness, partly owing to their good humour and gaiety; and for that reason are to be looked into, not in sluggish or careless fashion, but closely and deeply: for underlying them there are what one might call sparks of that ancient philosophy, which was much clearer-sighted in its investigation of truth than were the philosophers who came after. Plutarch[26] too in the essay which he called 'On How to Study Poetry' thinks the adages of the ancients very similar to the rites of religion, in which things which are most important and even divine are often expressed in ceremonies of a trivial and seemingly almost ridiculous nature. He suggests that these sayings, brief as they are, give a hint in their concealed way of those very things which were propounded in so many volumes by the princes of philosophy. For instance, that proverb in Hesiod 'The half is more than the whole' [I ix 95] is exactly what Plato in the *Gorgias* and in his books *On the State* tries to expound by so many arguments: it is preferable to receive an injury than to inflict one. What doctrine was ever produced by the philosophers more salutary as a principle of life or closer to the Christian religion? But here is a principle clearly of the greatest importance enclosed in a minute proverb, 'The half is more than the whole.' For to take away the whole is to defraud the man to whom nothing is left; on the other hand, to accept the half only is to be in a sense defrauded oneself. But it is preferable to be defrauded than to defraud. Again, anyone who deeply and diligently considers that remark of Pythagoras 'Between friends all is common' [I i 1*] will certainly find the whole of human happiness included in this brief saying. What other purpose has Plato in so many volumes except to urge a community of living, and the factor which creates it, namely friendship? If only he could persuade mortals of these things, war, envy, and fraud would at once vanish from our midst; in short a whole regiment of woes would depart from life once and for all. What other purpose had Christ, the prince of our religion? One precept and one alone He gave to the world, and that was love; on that alone, He taught,[27] hang all the law and the prophets. Or what else does love teach us, except that all things should be common to all? In fact that united in friendship with Christ, glued to Him by the same binding force that holds Him fast to the Father, imitating so far as we may that complete communion by which He and the Father are one, we should also be one with Him, and, as Paul[28] says, should become one spirit and one flesh with God, so that by the laws of friendship all that is His is shared with us and all that is ours is shared with Him; and then that, linked one to another in the same bonds of friendship, as members of one Head and like one and the same body we may be filled with the same spirit, and weep and rejoice at the same things together. This is signified to us by the mystic bread, brought together out of many grains into one flour, and the draught of wine fused into one liquid from many clusters of grapes. Finally, love teaches how, as the sum of all created things is in God and God is in all things, the universal all is in fact one. You see what an ocean of philosophy, or rather of theology, is opened up to us by this tiny proverb.

vii / Proverbs as a means to persuasion

If it is not enough to understand something oneself, but one wishes to persuade others, to be furnished with proverbs is by no means unhelpful, as Aristotle[29] himself makes sufficiently clear by classifying proverbs as evidence more than once in his principles of rhetoric: 'for instance,' he says, 'if one wishes to persuade someone not to make close friends with an old man, he will use as evidence the proverb that one should never do an old man a kindness' [I x 52], and again, if one were to argue that he who has killed the father should slay the children also, he will find this proverb useful: 'He's a fool who kills the father and leaves the children' [I x 53]. How much weight is added to the power of persuasion by supporting evidence is common knowledge. Aphorisms too are of no small use; but under evidence Aristotle also classes proverbs. Quintilian[30] too in his *Institutions* also mentions proverbs in several places as conducive to good speaking in more ways than one. For in book 5 he joins proverbs with examples and allots them equal force; and he rates the force of examples very high. Again in the same book he classes proverbs under the type of argument called in Greek *kriseis*, authoritative assertions, which are very frequently used and of no mean power to persuade and move. It may be better to quote Quintilian's actual words: 'Popular sayings which command general assent will also be found not without value as supporting material. In a way they carry even more weight because they have not been adapted to particular cases but have been said and done by minds exempt from hatred or partiality for no reason except their evident connection with honour or truth.' And a little further on: 'Those things too which command general assent seem to be, as it were, common property from the very fact that they have no certain author. Examples are "Where there are friends, there is wealth" [I iii 24] and "Conscience is a thousand witnesses" [I x 91] and in Cicero "Like readily comes together with like as the old proverb has it" [I ii 20]; for these would not have lived for ever if they did not seem true to everyone.' Thus far I have retailed the words of Quintilian. The same author, a little later, makes the oracles of the gods follow proverbs as though they were closely related. And what of Cicero?[31] Does he not use a proverb in the *Pro Flacco* to destroy the credibility of witnesses? The proverb in question is 'Risk it on a Carian' [I vi 14]. Does he not in the same speech explode the integrity in the witness-box of the whole race of Greeks with this one proverb: 'Lend me your evidence' [I vii 95]? Need I mention the fact that even philosophers in person are always supporting their arguments with proverbs? No wonder then if historians often seek to support the truth of their narrative by means of some adage. So true is it that what vanishes from written sources, what could not be preserved by inscriptions, colossal statues, and marble tablets, is preserved intact in a proverb, if I may note by the way this fresh reason to praise adages.

And then St Jerome shows no reluctance in confirming a Gospel maxim with the help of a common proverb: 'A rich man is either wicked himself or the heir of a wicked man' [I ix 47]. Even Paul himself does not scorn to use proverbs as evidence in some passages, and not without cause. For if *τὸ πιθανόν*, the power to carry conviction, holds the first place in the achievement of persuasion, what could be more convincing, I ask you, than what is said by everyone? What is more likely to be true than what has been approved by the consensus, the unanimous vote as it were, of so many epochs and so many peoples? There is, and I say it again, in these proverbs some native authentic power of truth. Otherwise how could it happen that we should frequently find the same thought spread abroad among a hundred peoples, transposed into a hundred languages, a thought which has not perished or grown old even with the passing of so many centuries, which pyramids themselves have not withstood? So that we see the justice of that saying, 'Nothing is solider than truth.' Besides, it happens (how, I cannot tell) that an idea launched like a javelin in proverbial form strikes with sharper point on the hearer's mind and leaves implanted barbs for meditation. It will make far less impression on the mind if you say 'Fleeting and brief is the life of man' than if you quote the proverb 'Man is but a bubble' [II iii 48*]. Lastly, what Quintilian[32] writes about laughter, when he says that the greatest difficulties in pleading a case, which cannot be solved by any arguments, can be evaded by a jest, is particularly applicable to the proverb.

viii / Decorative value of the proverb

It hardly needs explaining at length, I think, how much authority or beauty is added to style by the timely use of proverbs. In the first place who does not see what dignity they confer on style by their antiquity alone? And then, if there is any figure of speech that can confer breadth and sublimity on language, any again that contributes to grace of expression, if finally there is any reason for humour, a proverb, being able normally to adapt itself to all kinds of rhetorical figures and all aspects of humour and wit, will of course contribute whatever they are wont to contribute and on top of that will add its own intrinsic and peculiar charm. And so to interweave adages deftly and appropriately is to make the language as a whole glitter with sparkles from antiquity, please us with the colours of the art of rhetoric, gleam with jewel-like words of wisdom, and charm us with titbits of wit and humour. In a word, it will wake interest by its novelty, bring delight by its concision, convince by its decisive power.

ix / The proverb as an aid to understanding literature

Even if there were no other use for proverbs, at the very least they are not only helpful but necessary for the understanding of the best authors, that is, the oldest. Most of these are textually corrupt, and in this respect they are particularly so, especially as proverbs have a touch of the enigmatic, so that they are not understood even by readers of some learning; and then they are often inserted disconnectedly, sometimes even in a mutilated state, like 'Upwards flow the streams' [I iii 15*]. Occasionally they are alluded to in one word, as in Cicero[33] in his *Letters to Atticus*: 'Help me, I beg you; "prevention," you know,' where he refers to the proverb 'Prevention is better than cure' [I ii 40]. Thus a great darkness is cast by these if they are not known, and again they throw a great deal of light, once they are understood. This is the cause of those monstrous mistakes in both Greek and Latin texts; hence the abominable errors of translators from Greek into Latin; hence the absurd delusions of some writers, even learned ones, in their interpretation of authors, mere ravings in fact. Indeed, I would mention some of these here and now, if I did not think it more peaceable and more suited to my purpose to leave everyone to draw his own conclusions, after reading my notes, as to the extent to which writers of great reputation have sometimes fallen into wild error. And then it sometimes happens that an author makes a concealed allusion to a proverb; and if it escapes us, even though the meaning will seem clear, yet ignorance of the proverb will take away a great part of our pleasure. That remark in Horace is of this type: 'A horse to carry me, a king to feed me' [I vii 20]. And in Virgil: 'And Camarina shows up far away, / Ne'er to be moved; so have the fates decreed' [I i 64]. In one of these is the proverb 'A horse carries me, a king feeds me,' in the other 'Move not Camarina.'

x / The difficulty of proverbs calls for respect

If according to the proverb 'Good things are difficult' [II i 12], and the things which seem easy are scorned and held cheap by the popular mind, let no one imagine it is so simple a task either to understand proverbs or to interweave them into discourse, not to mention myself and how much sweat this work has cost me. Just as it requires no mean skill to set a jewel deftly in a ring or weave gold thread into the purple cloth, so (believe me) it is not everyone who can aptly and fittingly insert a proverb into what he has to say. You might say of the proverb with justice what Quintilian[34] said of laughter, that it is a very risky thing to aim for. For in this kind of thing, as in music, unless you put on a consummate performance, you would be ridiculous, and you must either win the highest praise or be a laughingstock.

xi / How far the use of adages is advisable

In the light of all this I will point out to what extent and in which ways adages should be used. In the first place, it is worth remembering that we should observe the same rule in making use of our adages as Aristotle[35] elegantly recommended in his work on rhetoric with regard to the choice of epithets: that is to say, we should treat them not as food but as condiments, not to sufficiency but for delight. Then we must not insert them just where we like; there are some places where it would be ridiculous to put jewels, and it is equally absurd to apply an adage in the wrong place. Indeed, what Quintilian[36] teaches in the eighth book of his *Institutions* about the use of aphorisms can be applied in almost exactly the same terms to proverbs. First, as has been said, we must not use them too often. Overcrowding prevents them from letting their light shine, just as no picture catches the eye in which nothing is clear in profile, and so artists too, when they bring several figures together in one picture, space them out so that the shadow of one body does not fall on another. For every proverb stands by itself, and for that reason must anyway be followed by a new beginning. This often causes the writing to be disconnected, and because it is put together from bits and pieces, not articulated, it lacks structure. And then it is like a purple stripe, which gives an effect of brilliance in the right place; but a garment with many stripes in the weave would suit nobody. There is also another disadvantage, that the man who sets out to use proverbs frequently is bound to bring in some that are stale or forced; choice is not possible when the aim is numbers. Finally, when anything is exaggerated or out of place, charm is lost. In letters to one's friends, however, it will be permissible to amuse oneself in this way a little more freely; in serious writing they should be used both more sparingly and with more thought.

xii / The varied use of proverbs

Here I think it is not beside the point to indicate shortly the ways in which the use of proverbs can vary, so that you can put forward the same adage now in one shape and now in another. To begin with, there is no reason why you should not occasionally fit the same wording with different meanings, as for instance 'A great jar with holes' [I x 33] can be applied to forgetfulness, extravagance, miserliness, futility, or ingratitude: whatever you have told to a forgetful person slips from the mind, with the spendthrift nothing lasts, a miser's greed is insatiable, a silly chatterer can keep nothing to himself, a gift to an ungrateful man is lost. Sometimes a saying can be turned ironically to mean the opposite: if you are speaking of an arrant liar, you can say Listen to the oracle 'straight from the tripod' [I vii 90]. Occasionally it happens that the change of one small word may make the proverb fit several meanings: for instance 'Gifts of enemies are no gifts' [I iii 35] can be shifted to fit gifts from the poor, from flatterers, from poets; for presents from an enemy are believed to bring ruin, and when poor people, sycophants or poets give anything away, they are fortune-hunting rather than giving. In a word, you may freely arrange this comparison in any way which it will fit. This method applies to almost every instance where a transference is made from a person to a thing or vice versa. Here is an example, applied to a person. 'The proverb says Not even Hercules can take on two [I v 39]; but I am Thersites rather than Hercules; how can I answer both?' It can be twisted to refer to a thing in this way: 'Not even Hercules can take on two; how can I stand up to both illness and poverty?' Or the proverb can be turned the other way, as in 'It is said Not even Hercules can take on two; and do you dare to stand up against two Herculeses?' Or in this way: 'It is the opposite of the familiar Greek proverb [I ix 30]: I expected coals and I have found treasure.' And: 'I have exchanged, not gold for bronze but, quite simply, bronze for gold' [I ii 1]. Sometimes the adage is explained and held up for comparison, sometimes it is an allegory pure and simple which is related. Occasionally even a truncated form is offered, as when you might say to a person whose answer was quite off the point 'Sickles I asked for' [II ii 49], and in Cicero 'Make the best of it' [IV ii 43]. At times it is enough to make an allusion with a single word, as when Aristotle says that 'all such men are potters to one another' [I ii 25]. There are other methods of varying the use of proverbs; but if anyone wishes to follow them out more closely, he may get what he wants from my compilation *De duplici copia*.

xiii / On proverbial metaphors

It remains to set to work on the task of making a catalogue of proverbs, but after first pointing out some proverbial metaphors. For there are some sayings which do not much resemble proverbs at first sight, and some take a proverbial shape, so that they can easily be added to the category of proverbs. Generally speaking, every aphorism approaches the genus proverb, and in addition metaphor and in particular allegory, and among these especially such as are taken from important fields which are generally familiar, such as seafaring and war. Examples of these are: to sail with a following wind, to be shipwrecked, to turn one's sails about, to hold the tiller, to bale out the bilge-water, to spread one's sails to the wind and to take in sail. And these: to give the signal to attack, to fight at the sword's point, to sound the retreat, to fight at long range or hand to hand, to set to, to join battle, and hundreds of others of the same kind, which only need to be drawn out a little to assume the form of a proverb. In the same way there are those which are taken from well-known things and exceedingly familiar in everyday experience, as for instance whenever there is a transference from the physical to the mental, as to turn the thumb down (to show support) [I viii 46*], to wrinkle one's brow (to take offence) [I viii 48], to snarl (to be displeased), to clear one's brow (to grow cheerful). And there are those which come from the bodily senses: to smell out (to get to know), to taste (to investigate). They normally have the look of a proverb about them, whenever expressions peculiar to the arts are used in another sense, as 'the double diapason' from music [I ii 63], 'diametrically' [I x 45] from geometry (another instance is 'words half a yard long'), 'to put it back on the anvil' [I v 92] from blacksmiths, 'by rule' from stonemasons, 'I haven't done a stroke' from painters, 'to add a last act' from the stage. Sometimes without metaphor a tacit allusion contributes something of a proverbial nature. Such an allusion will be most successful when it concerns an author or fact very famous and known to everybody, Homer for instance in Greek and Virgil in Latin. An example of this is that phrase in Plutarch:[37] 'Since many good men and true are here to support Plato.' The allusion is to a liturgical custom: at a sacrifice the priest would say 'Who's here?' and the assembled company would reply 'Many good men and true.' Then there is that phrase in Cicero's *Letters to Atticus*:[38] 'Two heads together' and in Lucian[39] 'the sons of physic' used for physicians.

There is also a resemblance to proverbs in those expressions often met with in pastoral poetry, the impossible, the inevitable, the absurd, likenesses and contraries. The impossible is like this:[40] 'But it were equal labour to measure the waves on the seashore' [I iv 45*] and in Virgil:[41] 'Ere this the light-foot stag shall feed in air, / And naked fish be beach-strewn by the sea.' The inevitable like this: 'While boars love mountain-crests and fish the streams,' and in Seneca:[42] 'While turn the lucid stars of this old world.' An example of the absurd:[43] 'Let him yoke foxes too and milk he-goats.' An instance of contraries: 'E'en the green lizards shelter in the brakes; / But I – I burn with love,' and so in Theocritus:[44] 'The waves are silent, silent are the gales, / But in my breast nothing will silence care.' Of likeness:[45] 'Wolf chases goat, and in his turn is chased / By the fierce lioness,' and in Theocritus:[46] 'The goat pursues the clover, and the wolf pursues the goat.'

There are two other formulae very close to the proverb type, formed either by repetition of the same or a similar word, or by the putting together of opposite words. Examples of this are: To bring a bad man to a bad end, An ill crow lays an ill egg, and A wise child has a wise father. This is almost normal in Greek drama, both comedy and tragedy. Further, The deserving get their deserts; Friend to friend; Evil to the evil, good to the good; Each dear to each; To every queen her king is fair. Also: Hand rubs hand; Jackdaw sits by jackdaw. The type of opposites goes like this: Just and unjust; Rightly or wrongly, in Aristophanes; Will he nill he, in Plato; and again, Neither word nor deed. So too in our own poets:[47] 'With right and wrong confounded' and 'She truth and falsehood spread.' (This figure was used by Valerius Maximus[48] without keeping to its true sense, merely as a means of emphasis: 'protesting' he says 'that against all right and wrong, when he held high command, he was butchered by you, a Roman knight.' For how can it make sense to say that a nefarious outrage was committed 'against all wrong'?) With what justice and what injustice; To do and suffer anything; Worthy and unworthy; What did he say or not say?; At home and at the war; Publicly and privately; What you know, you don't know; Openly and in secret; In jest and in earnest; With hands and feet; Night and day; What you put first or last; Neither great nor small; Young and old; To the applause of gods and men.

To this type belong all those phrases found everywhere in the poets: A maid and no maid, A bride and no bride, A wedding and no wedding, A city and no city, Paris ill-Paris, Happiness unhappy, Gifts that are no gifts, Fear unfearsome, War that is no war, Adorned when unadorned, Thankless thanks, Wealth that is no wealth. This opposition sometimes happens in compound words, like *morosophos*, foolishly wise, and *glukupikros*, bittersweet. So lovers, as Plutarch[49] assures us, call their passion, which is a mixture of pleasure and pain, such that they willingly pine. To this belongs that riddling type of contradiction, for example: I carry and carry not, I have and have not; 'A man no man that sees and sees not / With stone that's no stone hits and hits not / A bird no bird that on a sapling / That is no sapling sits and sits not.' This riddle[50] is recorded both by Athenaeus, citing Clearchus, and by Tryphon, and is also mentioned by Plato. Others of this type are: tongue-tied chatterer, vulnerable invulnerable, hairy smooth, son that was no son. Many things of the kind are put forward and expounded by Athenaeus in his tenth book. The nature of adages does not rule out a riddling obscurity, which is otherwise not recommended; on the contrary, the obscurity is welcome, as though there was some family relationship. An example of this would be to tell a man who was talking nonsense 'to set sail for Anticyra' or 'to sacrifice a pig' or 'to pluck squills from the tombs'; the first of these is in Horace, the second in Plautus, and the third in Theocritus.[51] So too many oracular responses have been naturalized as proverbs, and the precepts of Pythagoras[52] clearly belong naturally among the proverbs.

One thing specially appropriate to adages as a class is hyperbole, as in 'With his arms affrights the sky' and 'Cracks rocks with his clamour' and 'I dissolve in laughter,' especially if there is an admixture of any kind of metaphor. This can be done in various ways, either by using a proper name or with a comparison or with an epithet. Examples are: A second Aristarchus [I v 57], This Phalaris of ours [I x 86], As noisy as Stentor [II ii 37], Like a lioness on a sword-hilt [II x 82], A Stentorian voice [II iii 37], Eloquence like Nestor's [I ii 56]. And I am quite prepared to point out some of the springs, so to say, from which this kind of figure can be drawn.

1 / *From the thing itself*. The figure is sometimes taken from the thing itself, whenever we call a very wicked person wickedness personified, or an infamous person infamy, a pernicious one a pest, a glutton a sink, a swindler shady, a morally vile man a blot, a dirty fellow filth, a despicable man trash, an unclean one a dung-heap, a monstrous one a monster, a trouble-maker an ulcer, a man who ought to be in prison a jail-bird. Every one of these almost can be also expressed by a comparison: for instance, Golden as gold itself, Wicked as wickedness, Blind as blindness, Garrulous as garrulity, Ugly as ugliness, Thirsty as thirst itself, Poor as poverty, As unlucky as ill-luck personified, As infantile as infancy. To this category belong phrases like Father of all famines and Fount of all eloquence and More than entirely speechless and Worse than abandoned.

2 / *From similar things*. Nearest to these are phrases derived from similar things, such as: Sweet as honey, Black as pitch, White as snow, Smooth as oil [I vii 35], Soft as the ear-lobe [I vii 36], Pure as gold [IV i 58], Dull as lead, Stupid as a stump, Unresponsive as the sea-shore [I iv 84], Stormy as the Adriatic [iv vi 89], Deaf as the Ocean, Bibulous as a sponge, Thirsty as the sands, Parched as pumice-stone [I iv 75], Noisy as the bronze of Dodona [I i 7], Fragile as glass, Unstable as a ball, Accommodating as a buskin [I i 94], Thin as Egyptian clematis [I i 22], Tall as an alder, Hard as a whetstone [I i 20], Bright as the sun, Fair as a star, Pale as boxwood, Bitter as Sardonic herbs [III v 1], Despised as seaweed, Seething as Etna, Tasteless as beetroot [II iv 72], As just as a pair of scales [II v 82], As crooked as a thorn, As empty as

a bladder, Light as a feather, Changeable as the wind, Hateful as death, Capacious as the abyss [III vii 41], Twisted as the labyrinth [II x 51*], Worthless as blue pimpernel [I vii 21], Light as cork [II iv 7], Leaky as a great jar full of holes [I x 33], Transparent as a lantern, Dripping like a water-clock, Pure as a crystal spring, Inconstant as the Euripus [I ix 62], Dear as a man's own eyes, Beloved as the light, Precious as life itself, Inflexible as a dry bramble [II i 100], Revolting as warmed-up cabbage [I v 38*], Bright as a purple stripe, Licentious as the carnival of Flora.

3 / *From living creatures.* Similarly from living creatures: Talkative as a woman [IV i 97*], Salacious as a sparrow, Lecherous as a billy-goat, Longlived as a stag, Ancient as an old crow [I vi 64], Noisy as a jackdaw [I vii 22], Melodious as a nightingale, Poisonous as a cobra, Venomous as a viper, Sly as a fox [I ii 28], Prickly as a hedgehog [II iv 81], Tender as an Acarnanian sucking-pig [II iii 59], Slippery as an eel [I iv 95*], Timid as a hare [II i 80], Slow as a snail, Sound as a fish [IV iv 93], Dumb as a fish [I v 29], Playful as a dolphin, Rare as a phoenix [II vii 10], Prolific as a white sow, Rare as a black swan [II i 21*], Changeable as a hydra [I i 95], Rare as a white crow [IV vii 35], Greedy as a vulture [I vii 14], Grim as scorpions, Slow as a tortoise [I viii 84], Sleepy as a dormouse, Ignorant as a pig, Stupid as an ass, Cruel as watersnakes, Fearful as a hind, Thirsty as a leech, Quarrelsome as a dog, Shaggy as a bear, Light as a water-beetle. Lucian[53] too collects some things of the kind: 'While they are as irritable as puppies, as timid as hares, as fawning as monkeys, as lustful as donkeys, as thievish as cats, as quarrelsome as fighting-cocks.' Plutarch[54] in his essay 'On Running into Debt' has 'As untrustworthy as a jackdaw, as silent as a partridge, as lowborn and servile as a dog.'

4 / *From the characters of the gods.* These arise from the characters of the gods: Chaste as Diana, Elegant as the very Graces, Lecherous as Priapus, Lovely as Venus, Eloquent as Mercury, Mordant as Momus [I v 74], Inconstant as Vertumnus [II ii 74], Mutable as Proteus [II ii 74*], Changeable as Empusa [II ii 74*].

5 / *From characters of legend.* From legendary characters: Thirsty as Tantalus [II vi 14], Cruel as Atreus [II vii 92], Savage as a Cyclops [I iv 5], Mad as Orestes, Crafty as Ulysses [II viii 79], Eloquent as Nestor [I ii 56], Foolish as Glaucus [I ii 1], Destitute as Irus [I vi 76], Chaste as Penelope [I iv 42], Handsome as Nireus, Long-lived as Tithonus

[I vi 65], Hungry as Erysichthon, Prolific as Niobe [III iii 33], Loud as Stentor [II ii 37], Blind as Teiresias [I iii 57], Ill-famed as Busiris, Enigmatic as the Sphinx [II iii 9], Intricate as the Labyrinth [II x 51*], Inventive as Daedalus [II iii 62, III i 65], Daring as Icarus, Overweening as the Giants [III x 93], Stupid as Gryllus, Sharp-eyed as Lynceus [II i 54*], Unremitting as the Hydra [I x 9].

6 / From characters in comedy. From characters in comedy come: Boastful as Thraso in Terence,[55] Quarrelsome as Demea, Good-natured as Micio, Fawning as Gnatho, Confident as Phormio, Wily as Davus, Charming as Thais, Miserly as Euclio.

7 / From characters in history. From historical characters come: Envious as Zoilus [II v 8], Strict as Cato [I vii 89], Inhuman as Timon, Cruel as Phalaris [I x 86], Lucky as Timotheus [I v 82], Despicable as Sardanapalus [III vii 27], Religous as Numa, Just as Phocion, Incorruptible as Aristides, Rich as Croesus [I vi 74], Wealthy as Crassus [I vi 74], Poor as Codrus [I vi 76], Debauched as Aesop,[56] Ambitious as Herostratus, Cautious as Fabius [I x 29], Patient as Socrates, Muscular as Milo [I ii 57], Acute as Chrysippus, With as fine a voice as Trachalus, Forgetful as Curio, The Aristarchus of our time [I v 57], The Christian Epicurus, A Cato out of season [I viii 89].

8 / From names of peoples. From peoples: Treacherous as a Carthaginian [I viii 28], Rough as a Scythian [II iii 35], Inhospitable as the Scythotaurians, Mendacious as a Cretan [I ii 29], Fugitive as the Parthians [I i 5], Vain as the Greeks, Drunken as Thracians [II iii 17], Untrustworthy as a Thessalian [I iii 10], Contemptible as a Carian [I vi 14], Haughty as a Sybarite [II ii 65], Effeminate as the Milesians [I iv 8], Wealthy as the Arabs [I vi 74], Short as a Pygmy [IV i 90], Stupid as an Arcadian [III iii 27].

9 / From occupations. From occupations come: Perjured as a brothel-keeper, Soft as a catamite, Boastful as a soldier, Severe as an Areopagite [I ix 41], Violent as a tyrant, Brutal as a hangman.

xiv / Of the need for careful introduction of a proverb

This may seem a tiny and negligible thing, but since I have taken on the role of a teacher, I shall not hesitate to issue a warning for the inexperienced. In making use of adages we must remember what Quintilian[57] recommends in the use of newly-coined phrases or daring metaphors: that one should, as Greek most eloquently expresses it, *προεπιπλήττειν τῇ ὑπερβολῇ*, make an advance correction of what seems excessive. Similarly we should 'make an advance correction' of our proverb and, as it were, go halfway to meet it, if it is likely to prove obscure, or to jar in some other way. For this class of phrase, as I have pointed out just now, admits metaphors of any degree of boldness, and unlimited innovation in the use of words and unashamed hyperbole and allegory pushed to enigmatic lengths. Greek makes this 'advance correction' in ways like these: As the proverb runs, As they say (in several forms), As the old saying goes, To put it in a proverb, As they say in jest, It has been well said. And almost exactly the same methods are in use in Latin: As they say, As the old proverb runs, As is commonly said, To use an old phrase, As the adage has it, As they truly say.

1 *Ars grammatica* 3.6 (*Grammatici latini* ed Keil 4.402)
2 *Ars grammatica* 2 (ibid 1.462)
3 The next two definitions are similar to, but not the same as, those in *Etymologicum magnum* 654.15 (ed Venice 1499) and Suidas Π 733
4 *Art of Poetry* 335–6
5 *Metaphysics* 1A.1 (993b5)
6 *Institutes of Oratory* 5.11.21
7 *On the Latin Language* 7.31
8 8.6.52
9 Compiler about 500 AD of a valuable florilegium, which Erasmus knew only from manuscripts in circulation
10 *Progymnasmata* 1 (21), written by Aphthonius in Greek around the early fifth century AD, in Latin translation a very important textbook in the Renaissance
11 5.11.20
12 *Works and Days* 202–3
13 Archilochus frag 174 ed West; Callimachus frag 194.6–8 ed Pfeiffer; Theocritus 14.43
14 Simonides of Ceos was a lyric poet c 500 BC; this comment comes from Plutarch *Moralia* 644F.
15 Two retorts to the Emperor Augustus, from Macrobius *Saturnalia* 2.4.20 and 28: a young man, said to look like Augustus, was asked by the emperor if his mother had ever been in Rome, and this was his answer; Turonius owned a band of slaves whose musical performance delighted Augustus and who rewarded them with grain for bread but when asked for a repeat

performance was told by Turonius that the slaves were now busy grinding the grain.

16 Here begins a list of Erasmus' main sources, outside of his own vast reading: Aristotle was said to have made a list of proverbs by Diogenes Laertius 5.26; Chrysippus of Soli (third century BC), the Stoic philosopher, has left only a few fragments of his collection *On Proverbs*; Cleanthes was another Stoic; Plutarch was believed to be the author of a small proverb collection; Athenaeus' *Deipnosophistae* is a major source for the *Adages* and Erasmus' marked up copy of an Aldine edition of 1514 is in the Bodleian Library; Zenodotus is more commonly known under the name of Zenobius, author of a major Greek proverb collection; Diogenianus is the author of another major Greek collection, perhaps the first of these consulted by Erasmus; Hesychius of Alexandria (fifth century AD) made a lexicon of a rare words; Suidas is the name given to the author of a tenth-century collection more properly known as the *Suda*.

17 Compilation of opinions of the Roman jurists, published by order of the Emperor Justinian AD 533

18 Jeremiah 31:29, Ezekiel 18:2

19 6:43

20 Pittacus, one of the Seven Sages

21 Luke 7:32

22 Theognis 25–6

23 *Satires* 11.27

24 *Natural History* 11.2–4

25 Aristotle frag 13 ed Rose, cited by Synesius *Praise of Baldness* 22 (*PG* 66.1204B)

26 *Moralia* 35F–36A, from memory

27 Matthew 22:40

28 Ephesians 4:4

29 *Rhetoric* 1.15 (1376a1)

30 5.11.37 and 41

31 Cicero, *Pro Flacco* 27.65 and 4.9 (ie, lend me your evidence, and I shall in turn give you evidence when required, true or false)

32 6.3.8–9

33 *Letters to Atticus* 10.10.3

34 Perhaps a reminiscence of 6.3.6–7

35 *Rhetoric* 3.3.3 (1406a19)

36 8.5.7

37 *Moralia* 698F

38 *Letters to Atticus* 9.6.6

39 *How History Ought to Be Written* 7

40 Theocritus 16.60

41 *Eclogues* 1.59–60, followed by 5.76

42 *Oedipus* 503

43 Virgil *Eclogues* 3.91, followed by 2.9 and 68 run together

44 2.38–9

45 Virgil *Eclogues* 2.63

46 10.30

47 Virgil *Georgics* 1.505 and *Aeneid* 4.190

48 *Facta et dicta memorabilia* 6.2.8 (a manual of 'memorable deeds and sayings' for speakers compiled in the first century AD)

49 *Moralia* 681B

50 A famous riddle, said to be by Panarces, about whom nothing

else is known; it is mentioned in Plato *Republic* 5.479C and in various other ancient texts, including Athenaeus 10.452C, Suidas AI 230, and a rhetorical treatise ascribed to Tryphon (*Rhetores graeci* ed Spengel, 3.194.16); the answer is 'A one-eyed eunuch throws a lump of pumice-stone at a bat hanging on a tall reed, and misses it.'

51 Horace *Satires* 2.3.166; Plautus *Menaechmi* 290ff, 312ff; Theocritus 5.121

52 The precepts of Pythagoras were very well known in the Renaissance, in part through Erasmus' collection of thirty-six of them, with discussion and explication, in *Adages* I i 2; they are cautionary exhortations, taken from a number of ancient sources, some of them fairly obvious ('Exceed not the balance,'), others obscure ('Taste not of anything with a black tail,' 'Do not sit on the grain-measure,' 'Abstain from beans,' 'Do not put food in a chamber-pot,' 'Do not make water facing towards the sun,' 'You shall not have swallows under the same roof,' and so on).

53 *Piscator* 34

54 *Moralia* 830C

55 All characters from the comedies of Plautus and Terence

56 Aesop is here not the fabulist, but a notorious spendthrift of the first century BC (see Horace *Satires* 2.3.239)

57 8.3.37

I i 1
Amicorum communia omnia / Between friends all is common

This proverb always remained first in the numbered sequence in the editions from 1508 onwards (it was no 94 in the Collectanea*). It sums up a position on generosity and social responsibility repeated by Erasmus in his writings throughout his life. As his commentary shows, the proverb appears often in writers in antiquity (see also* Otto 827, Tosi 1305*). But in an uncharacteristic aside, Erasmus also sets the proverb into the Christian tradition – 'nothing was ever said by a pagan philosopher which comes closer to the mind of Christ.' Hence its priority in the overall sequence. In his preceding introductory essay (section vi), Erasmus had already shown how 'an ocean of philosophy, or rather of theology, is opened up to us by this tiny proverb.'*

Despite Erasmus' remarkable range of scholarship, it is interesting to see that the first and last references in the essay are, by modern scholarly stan-

dards, incorrect. The first of these seems to be Erasmus' own slip, the second shows his reliance on a text with faulty readings. Considering the vast amount of material he covers in the Adages, *and the astonishing pace he maintained as a scholar, it is surprising there are not more such errors. Erasmus often worked without the texts immediately before him, and seems to have forgotten more than most scholars have ever learned. The proverb worked its way into English in the form it is given here (Tilley* F 729*).*

Τὰ τῶν φίλων κοινά, Between friends all is common. Since there is nothing more wholesome or more generally accepted than this proverb, it seemed good to place it as a favourable omen at the head of this collection of adages. If only it were so fixed in men's minds as it is frequent on everybody's lips, most of the evils of our lives would promptly be removed. From this proverb Socrates[1] deduced that all things belong to all good men, just as they do to the gods. For to the gods, said he, belong all things; good men are friends of the gods; and among friends all possessions are in common. Therefore good men own everything. It is quoted by Euripides[2] in his *Orestes*: 'Shared in common are the possessions of friends,' and again in the *Phoenissae*: 'All grief of friends is shared.' Again in the *Andromache*: 'True friends have nothing of their own, but with them all is common.' Terence[3] says in the *Adelphoe* 'For there is an old proverb, that between friends all is common.' It is said that this was also in Menander,[4] in a play of the same name. Cicero[5] in the first book of the *De officiis* says 'As the Greek proverb has it, all things are in common between friends,' and it is quoted by Aristotle[6] in the eighth book of his *Ethics* and by Plato[7] in the *Laws*, book 5. Plato is trying to show that the happiest condition of a society consists in the community of all possessions: 'So the first kind of city and polity and the best laws are found where the old saying is maintained as much as possible throughout the whole city; and the saying is that friends really have all things in common.' Plato also says that a state would be happy and blessed in which these words 'mine' and 'not mine' were never to be heard. But it is extraordinary how Christians dislike this common ownership of Plato's, how in fact they cast stones at it, although nothing was ever said by a pagan philosopher which comes closer to the mind of Christ. Aristotle[8] in book 2 of the *Politics* moderates the opinion of Plato by saying that possession and legal ownership should be vested in certain definite persons, but otherwise all should be in common according to the proverb, for the sake of convenience, virtuous living, and social harmony. Martial[9] in book 2 pokes fun at a certain Candidus, who was always quoting this adage, but otherwise gave nothing to his friends: 'O Candidus, what's mine is yours, you say; / Grandly you chant this maxim night and day,' and the epigram ends thus: '"What's mine is yours," yet naught you give away.' An elegant remark of Theophrastus[10] is quoted in Plutarch, in the little essay entitled 'On Brotherly Love': 'If friends' possessions are in common, then friends' friends still more should be in common too.' Cicero[11] in the first book of the *De legibus* seems to attribute this adage to Pythagoras, when he says: 'Hence that word of Pythagoras "Between friends things are in common, and friendship is equality."' In Diogenes Laertius[12] also Timaeus reports that this saying first began with Pythagoras. Aulus Gellius[13] in his *Attic Nights*, book 1 chapter 9, bears witness that not only was Pythagoras the author of this saying, but he also instituted a kind of sharing of life and property in this way, the very thing Christ wants to happen among Christians. For all those who were admitted by Pythagoras into that well-known band who followed his instruction would give to the common fund whatever money and family property they possessed. This is called in Latin, in a word which expresses the facts, *coenobium*, clearly from community of life and fortunes.

1 Apparently a slip of the memory; in Diogenes Laertius 6.37 a similar comment is ascribed to Diogenes the Cynic.
2 *Orestes* 735, *Phoenissae* 243, *Andromache* 376–7
3 *Adelphoe* 803–4
4 Menander frag 10, cited by Suidas K 2549
5 *On Duties* 1.16.51
6 *Nichomachean Ethics* 8.9.1 (1159b31)
7 *Laws* 5.739b–c
8 *Politics* 2.1 (1261a2)
9 2.43.1–2 and 16
10 Theophrastus frag 75, cited by Plutarch *Moralia* 490E
11 *On the Laws* 1.12.34
12 8.10
13 1.9.12 (the word *coenobium*, which attracted Erasmus with its suggestion of a cenobitic or communal life, is a mistaken correction, found in early printed texts, of an old legal formula *ercto non cito*)

I i 4
Adonidis horti / Gardens of Adonis

A 'garden of Adonis' was a pot containing a small plant and was associated with the spring festival for Adonis, the beautiful divine hero and lover of Venus. In the ritual of the burial of Adonis, the plant was thrown away. Erasmus refers to these in Praise of Folly *(*CWE 27 89*). The proverb first appeared in* Collectanea *no 700, from Diogenianus 1.14.*

Ἀδώνιδος κῆποι, Gardens of Adonis, used to be applied to trivial things, which served no useful purpose and were suitable only for giving a brief passing pleasure. Pausanias[1] tells how people used to be very fond of 'Adonis-gardens, well stocked particularly with lettuce and fennel; they would plant seeds in them just as one does in pots. Thus the thing became a proverb directed against worthless, trifling men,' born for silly pleasures – people like singers, sophists, bawdy poets, confectioners, and so on. These gardens were sacred to Venus, on account of her darling Adonis, who was snatched away in his first bloom and turned into a flower. Plato[2] makes mention of this in the *Phaedrus*: 'Would a sensible husbandman who has seeds which he cares for and wants to come to fruition sometime, plant them in gardens of Adonis in the summer and be pleased to see them become beautiful in eight days, or would he do these things for the sake of sport and amusement, if he does them at all?' Thus also Plutarch,[3] in the treatise entitled 'On the Delays of the Divine Vengeance': 'Nay, God is so particular and concerned with trifles that although we have nothing divine in us, nothing which in any way resembles him, nothing consistent and stable, but rather in the manner of leaves, as Homer says, we begin to wither away and shortly die, yet he has such a care for us (just like the women who cherish and care for gardens of Adonis that bloom for a few days in earthenware pots), that he cherishes our short-lived souls sprouting in tender flesh that is incapable of any strong root of life, who are soon, for any chance cause, to perish.' Theocritus[4] recalls this in idyll 15: 'Frail gardens, in bright silver baskets kept.' The proverb is also known in the form: 'more fruitless than gardens of Adonis.'[5]

In a metaphor not unlike this, Isaeus, according to Philostratus,[6] calls youthful pleasures 'gardens of Tantalus' because they are just like shadows and dreams, and do not satisfy the soul of a man, but rather irritate it. Similarly Pollux[7] called the style of Athenodorus the sophist 'gardens of Tantalus' because it was smooth and youthful and gave the appearance of having something in it, where there was nothing at all.

1 Pausanias frag 1.27, cited from Suidas A 517
2 *Phaedrus* 276b
3 *Moralia* 560B–C
4 15.113–14
5 Zenobius 1.49
6 *Lives of the Sophists* 513 and 594–5 (Isaeus was a first-century AD sophist); Tantalus and his punishment are treated at *Adages* II vi 14 (also II i 46).
7 Julius Pollux (second century AD) *Onomasticon* under *Polydeukês* compliments the style not of Athenodorus the sophist but Athenodorus Polydeukes (see ASD II-1, 117).

I i 31
Malo accepto stultus sapit / Trouble experienced makes a fool wise

Repeatedly in his educational writings Erasmus reminds the reader that fools learn only from experience, whereas a wise man with his foresight does not need experience to recognize an evil. This proverb appears in a short sequence on this theme ('The Phrygians learn wisdom too late' [I i 28], 'Once stung, the fisherman will be wiser' [I i 30]). There is an English proverb, 'Experience is the mistress of fools' (Tilley E 220), which may suggest either that fools learn only from experience or that fools remain foolish because experience commands them. The adage here is related to Erasmus' celebrated anti-war essay IV i 1, 'War is sweet to those who have not tried it.'*

Erasmus finds an origin for the proverb (Otto 61) in the ancient story of Pandora, which in turn became the basis of the English proverb 'Pandora's box' (Tilley P 40). But the idea of Pandora's box is Erasmus' own creation, for he translates Hesiod's Greek pithos, *a large jar or Latin* dolium, *as* pyxis, *or 'box.' He also has Epimetheus (Afterthought) open the box instead of Prometheus (Foresight). Erasmus' interpretation and the impact it has had on*

European versions of the Pandora story are told by Dora and Erwin Panofsky in Pandora's Box: The Changing Aspects of a Mythical Symbol *(New York 1962), chapter 2. They argue that Erasmus seems to have conflated 'the crucial episode in the life of Hesiod's Pandora with its near duplicate in Roman literature, the last and equally crucial episode in the life of Apuleius' Psyche' (18). In the story in Apuleius'* Golden Ass, *Psyche carries a* pyxis *down to the underworld, where it is filled with a* modicum *of Persephone's beauty. On her return, Psyche opens the box, is overcome by the vapours and is then rescued by Cupid, who reseals the pyxis. The expression 'Pandora's box' is now found in all the European languages. Ben Jonson may have been closer to the original story when he wrote mockingly of 'Pandora's tub' (in* The Alchemist *2.1.92). Interestingly, when Richard Taverner, the sixteenth-century English adapter of Erasmus, wrote up this adage, he kept it as 'The foole, when he hath taken hurte, wareth wise,' and made no mention of Pandora.*

Hesiod[1] expressed the same thought, though a little differently, when he said in his book entitled *Works and Days*: 'His punishment the wicked man receives / At last, but only pain instructs the fool.' Homer[2] too seems to allude to the same saying in the *Iliad*, book 23: '… so that paying up, you'll know the truth.' Plato[3] in the *Symposium*: 'I am saying this to you also, Agathon, so that you may not be deceived by this, but take warning from the knowledge of what happened to us; and that you should not, like the fool in the proverb, learn wisdom through the experience of evil.' Plautus'[4] phrase in the *Mercator* is to be classed with this: 'Happy is he who learns wisdom at another's cost.' Similarly in the *Elegies* of Tibullus,[5] book 3: 'How happy is he, whosoe'er he be / Who from another's woe learns woe to flee.' This is what those speeches of the tardily-wise mean:[6] 'Now I know what love is.' 'Now I understand that she is wicked and that I am wretched.' 'Ah, fool that I am, I have just tumbled to it at last.'

The adage seems to spring from that very old story about the two brethren, Prometheus and Epimetheus, which is told in Hesiod,[7] more or less in this way. Jupiter was angry with Prometheus because he had stolen fire from heaven and given it to men; and wishing to play a similar trick on him, gave Vulcan the job of making the figure of a girl out of clay, with the greatest possible skill. When this was done, he required each of the gods and goddesses to endow this image with his or her gifts. This is clearly why the name Pandora[8] was invented for the maiden. Then, when the image had been showered with all the endowments of beauty, accomplishment, brains and speech, Jupiter sent her to Prometheus with a box, beautiful indeed, but concealing inside it every kind of misfortune. Prometheus refused the present, and warned his brother that if any kind of gift was brought in his absence, it must not be accepted. Back comes Pandora and, having persuaded Epimetheus, she gives him the box. As soon as he had opened it, and understood, as the diseases flew out, that Jove's 'gifts were no gifts,'[9] he began to be wise, but too late. Hesiod[10] clearly refers to the adage when he says, 'He took it, and touched by woe understood at last.' He says the same in the *Theogony*: she gave birth to Prometheus, 'the cunning one' (so he calls him) 'of many wiles / And Epimetheus, whom mistakes made wise.' Hence Pindar[11] in the *Pythians* calls him 'late-wise.' Their very names indicate this. For Prometheus means in Greek a man who takes counsel before acting, and Epimetheus one who acts first, and only then does common sense enter his head. To act like Prometheus, *prometheuesthai*,[12] is to meet misfortunes when they threaten by taking thought. Lucian[13] in one of his dialogues quotes from some comedy-writer or other the following line, attacking Cleon on the ground that he was only wise too late when the business was all over: 'Cleon is a Prometheus after the fact.' Again, at the end of the same dialogue: 'To take counsel after the event is like Epimetheus, not Prometheus.'

The proverb is also found[14] in the form Παρὰ τὰ δεινὰ φρονιμώτερος, More prudent after hard experience, and again in this form: Ἐξ ὧν ἔπαθες, ἔμαθες, From what you suffer, you learn, or (giving the sense rather than the words) What hurts is what teaches, *Quae nocent docent*. But it is much more circumspect to learn prudence from the ills of others, according to the Greek saying:[15] 'I learnt my lesson watching others' ills.' There is a word going around among my own people: 'It is through shame and loss that mortals grow wiser.'

1 *Works and Days* 217–18
2 *Iliad* 23.487
3 *Symposium* 222b
4 *Mercator* 4.7.40, from a scene falsely attributed to Plautus
5 3.6.43–4
6 Virgil *Eclogues* 8.43, Terence *Eunuchus* 70–1 and his *Andria* 470

7 *Works and Days* 47–105
8 *Pan* meaning 'all' and *dora* 'gifts,' in Hesiod
9 Sophocles *Ajax* 665
10 *Works and Days* 89, *Theogony* 510–11
11 *Pythians* 5.28
12 A very obscure verb-form, found only in the preface to the *Problemata* of Alexander of Aphrodisias
13 *Prometheus es in verbis* 2 and 7
14 This is found at *Adages* IV iii 59 and I iii 99.
15 Menander *Sententiae* 121

I i 68
Deus ex improviso apparens / Unexpected appearance of a god

Ironically, this adage is better known in the English tradition in a Latin form: Deus ex machina *('the God from the machine'). Erasmus gives a variant for the title of this essay, but soon establishes that* Deus ex machina *is indeed the proverb under consideration. As he points out, though the phrase was well known in antiquity, it proved tricky to translate for the early commentators in the Renaissance, who didn't know about the stagecraft being referred to. Marsilio Ficino, the leading Florentine Platonist, cited here, also had the same problem in his version of the pseudo-Platonic* Clitophon *407a (Tosi 1691). Erasmus used this proverb in his* Collectanea *of 1500, though in the Greek form, which he could have found in Diogenianus (2.84). The unexpected descent of a god from a device in the ceiling was found in a number of Renaissance plays, especially in masques.*

Θεὸς ἀπὸ μηχανῆς ἐπιφανείς, A god appearing suddenly from the machine. This is applied to people who find, in the midst of their perplexities, some unhoped-for person who comes to their rescue and solves the problem for them. It is taken from a habitual practice in tragedies, in many of which some god was revealed by means of certain machines, not on the stage itself, but coming down from above so that he could finish off the play by a sudden change in the plot. Cicero[1] witnesses to this in book 1 of the *On the Nature of the Gods*, as when he says this: 'You on the contrary cannot see how nature can achieve all this without the aid of some intelligence, and so, like the tragic poets, being unable to bring the plot of your drama to a dénouement, you have recourse to a god; whose intervention you assuredly would not require if you would but contemplate the measureless and boundless extent of space that stretches in every direction.' There is no doubt that Cicero here is imitating a passage from the *Cratylus* of Plato:[2] 'Unless, just as the writers of tragedy do when they are at a loss, they take refuge in machines, hoisting up gods.' This passage of Plato has been translated quite wrongly, or at least obscurely, by the Latin translator, because he did not know the proverb. For he puts it like this: 'Unless like the tragic poets, whenever they are undecided, they take refuge with the gods by means of some imaginary machines.' The same stumbling-block seems to have got in the way of the writer who translated the life of Lysander from Plutarch.[3] When Lysander decided to make changes in the state and reflected that the proposition was too difficult to tackle by ordinary methods, he did what the poets do in tragedy, he planned how to achieve what he wished by means of false oracles and reverence for the gods. The Greek is as follows: 'Just as in a tragedy, bringing a machine before the public, he composed and concocted oracular replies purporting to come from the Pythian Apollo.' The same is indicated rather vaguely, but with true elegance, by Aristotle[4] in his *Metaphysics*, book 1, in words which one may translate as follows: 'For Anaxagoras uses mind, like some god of tragedy suddenly shown forth as a device for the making of the world. And when he is at a loss in explaining the cause of what necessarily is, then he brings in mind. But in all other matters he ascribes the cause to anything rather than to mind.'

Hence there is the frequent phrase in Greek tragedy,[5] 'Many are the forms of the gods, etc.' They work out the plot by the introduction of a god; as in Euripides' *Orestes*, where Apollo appears in the midst of the uproar and at once settles the disturbed situation. An example of this seems to be taken from Homer,[6] when in the *Iliad*, book 1, he introduces Pallas to placate the enraged Achilles; and he brings forward some divinity in various other places. But Horace,[7] in the *Art of Poetry*, says that this should not be done in comedy, unless the situation is so difficult that it cannot be unravelled by human effort: 'Nor let a God in person be displayed / Unless the labouring plot deserve his aid.' In agreement with this, Plautus[8] introduced Jove into the *Amphitryo* and for that reason called it a tragicomedy. Lucian[9] in *Philopseudes*: 'And I thought that this one was chosen for me by fate as a god from the machine, as the saying goes.' Again in *On Salaried Posts*: 'For these specially pertain to tragedies of this sort; or some other god from the machine, sitting on the mast-head.' Euripides[10] thought of this in the *Iphigenia in Aulis*. 'Truly I appeared to you as a great god.' Lucian[11] in *The Sects*, 'There you stood, like that adage beloved of tragedy-writers, a god appearing from a machine.' In Athenaeus,[12] book 6, some poet or other makes a certain gluttonous fellow complain that the sellers of fish just show their goods and then immediately snatch them away: 'And they quickly remove the goods from sight, / And sell them like gods from the machine.' Just so, whenever salvation comes from some unexpected quarter, it is usually ascribed to a god. Thus Pliny[13] writes in book 25: 'Even in what has been discovered chance has sometimes been the finder; at other times, to speak the truth, the finder was a god.' Again, in book 27: 'Therefore this is chance, this is that god who discovered most things in life.'

1 *On the Nature of the Gods* 1.10.53–4
2 *Cratylus* 425d
3 *Lysander* 25.1
4 *Metaphysics* 1.4 (985a18–21)
5 Euripides *Alcestis* 1159
6 *Iliad* 1.206ff
7 *Art of Poetry* 191–2
8 *Amphitryo* 59
9 *Philopseudes* 29, *On Salaried Posts* 1
10 *Iphigenia in Aulis* 973–4
11 *The Sects* (or *Hermotimus*) 86
12 6.226c
13 *Natural History* 25.17 and 27.8

I i 69
Homo homini deus / Man is a god to man

This proverb, connected as Erasmus notes with the preceding, appears often in sixteenth-century writings in many European languages with its opposite, 'Man is a wolf to man' (the proverb that immediately follows). At the end of this essay, Erasmus stresses the Greek origins of the proverb, as its use by a Christian might seem blasphemous. For modern scholars the earliest citation is a fragment from the comic poet Cecilius (264R; see Tosi 1299). Erasmus found this from his usual Greek sources (Zenobius 1.91; Diogenianus 1.80; Apostolius 3.10; Suidas A 2536) and, as he shows, it appeared in many Latin writers too. It worked its way into English (Tilley M 241), but it is no longer commonly used. It was first cited by Erasmus in Collectanea *no 91.*

Not far from this is the phrase Ἄνθρωπος ἀνθρώπου δαιμόνιον, Man is a god to man, usually said about one who has conferred sudden and unlooked-for salvation, or who has brought help by some great benefaction. To be a god, thought the ancients, was simply and solely to be of value to mortal men; thus the ancient world made gods out of the originators of grain, wine, laws, anyone who had contributed something to the betterment of life. To such an extent was this true, that they worshipped certain animals, as the Egyptians worshipped the stork, because it was believed to seek out, drive away, and kill the snakes which came up at a certain time of year from the marshlands of Arabia. The Romans also held the goose sacred, because its noise woke the guards and so saved the stronghold of the Capitol from the invading Gauls. This is what Cicero[1] means when he writes in the first book of his *On the Nature of the Gods*: 'I will make my point thus: these animals are deified by the barbarians for the benefits which they confer.'

According to Prodicus[2] of Ceos, some inanimate bodies have been held to be gods, such as the sun, the moon, water, earth, because they seemed conducive to life, and mortals particularly rejoiced in their benefits. The Scythians, as Lucian[3] tells us in *Toxaris*, swear by wind and sword as if they were gods, because the one gives breath, the other death. But since, as Cicero[4] says, the advantages and misfortunes of men are for the most part derived from mankind, and the special quality of God is to preserve or do good, thus it comes about that whoever brings rescue in dire peril, or is the means of conferring some immense benefit, performs as it were the office of God, and is said to have stood as a god to the beneficiary. Agreeing with this we have that customary expression used by Homer[5] and by Hesiod,[6] 'the gods, the givers of all good things,' and what Strabo[7] says in his tenth book, 'It is rightly said, that it is when mortals are beneficent that they most closely imitate the gods.' The same writer says, in book 17, that for some Egyptians God was twofold: immortal, the creator of all things, and mortal, of an unknown name; and thus they gave almost divine honours to those who conferred benefits upon them. In common parlance, too, people who are preserved in desperate and involved situations, or in deadly peril, say that some god had preserved them. Horace:[8] 'Thus Apollo saved me.' Again in the *Odes*, he says he was saved in war by Mercury, and once more by Faunus from the fall of a tree. Juvenal[9] makes the same allusion when he says,

Would any god, or godlike man below
Four hundred sesterces on you bestow,
Kinder than fate ...

And Virgil[10] in *Tityrus,*

O Meliboeus, a god gave us this respite;
To me that man for ever shall be God,
And on his altar fume a tender lamb
From our own flocks ...

Then he gives the reason why he will consider Caesar among the divinities, adding the benefit conferred:

He, he it was who gave my cattle leave
To stray thus freely, and myself allowed
The play I wished for with my rustic pipe.

Pliny[11] in the *Natural History,* book 2, is more clearly referring to the Greek proverb, but speaks as irreverently about the gods as he does a little later about the immortality of souls and foolishly about the resurrection of bodies. For after gibing at the multiplicity of gods, and utterly refusing to attribute the care of mortals to the one supreme divinity which he takes to be either the world or some kind of Nature, he says: 'To be a god is to bring aid to a mortal, though mortal oneself. And this is the way to eternal glory. By this went the great men of Rome, by this now advances with divine step, with his children, Vespasianus Augustus, the greatest ruler of all time, bringing help in disaster. This is the oldest way of giving thanks to those who deserved well, to number them with the gods. For even the names of all the other gods, and those I have recorded above of the stars, have sprung from the merits of men.' Thus far Pliny. Ovid[12] says: ''Tis a fitting pleasure for man to save man; / There is no better way of seeking favour.' Plutarch[13] in the essay 'To An Uneducated Ruler' says that the gods are not blessed because they live for ever, but because they are the lords and authors of virtue. Paul,[14] though, places the height of virtue in charity; but charity which consists in doing the greatest good to the greatest number. Gregory of Nazianzus[15] thought of this in his oration *On the Care of the Poor*: 'By imitating the mercy of God you will become God to the sufferer, for man has nothing so divine as kindness.'

Among Christians the name of God ought not to be given to any mortal man even in jest, and such extraordinary and disgusting flattery must be altogether unacceptable to our moral code; yet it can happen that this adage finds a use, and not an immoral or unfitting one. For instance, one might say, 'At a time when I was labouring under such great misfortunes that no mortal man either wished to help me or could do so, you alone came to my aid – it was more than I had hoped for – and not only rescued me by your kindness (otherwise I should have perished) but made me better fitted for life than I had been before. Between us two, if ever, that old Greek proverb can apply, man is a god to man.' Or one might speak thus: 'I owe everything to letters, even my life; but I owe letters to you, who by your liberality procure me leisure and support me in it. What is this, if not what the Greeks mean when they say, "man is a god to man?"' Or in this way: 'To do a small kindness certainly proves a man is a friend; but to spend skill and wonderful care and attention so as to retain a life which is ebbing away, and restore it, as a doctor does, what is that but what the Greeks say, man is a god to man?' Again, 'Matters had come to such a point that not Salvation itself could bring aid.[16] Then you came upon me like the presence of a god, and dispersed my troubles with marvellous speed, and set me back where I was before, not expecting nor hoping for such a thing – so that I might understand that it was no idle word of the Greeks, "man is a god to man."' Or again, 'In other things, indeed, you have always been the greatest friend to me, but in this juncture you were not only my greatest friend, but I might almost say, as the Greeks do, "a man who is a god to man."'

1 *On the Nature of the Gods* 1.36.101
2 Prodicus of Ceos frag 84B5 ed Diels-Kranz
3 *Toxaris* 38
4 Not traced in CWE or ASD
5 *Odyssey* 8.325
6 *Theogony* 46
7 *Geography* 10.3.9, 17.2.3

8 *Satires* 1.9.78, *Odes* 2.17.28–9
9 5.132–3
10 *Eclogues* 1.6–10
11 *Natural History* 2.18
12 *Ex Ponto* 2.9.39–40
13 *Moralia* 781A
14 1 Corinthians 13
15 *Oratio* 14, 26–7 (*PG* 35.892D)
16 Terence *Adelphoe* 761–2

I i 70
Homo homini lupus / Man is a wolf to man

This proverb is more sinister than its opposite, the preceding 'Man is a god to man.' Like the preceding, it first appeared in Collectanea *(no 63). It is found in English (Tilley* M *245). Interestingly, Erasmus makes much less of it than 'Man is a god to man,' even though this proverb may have been more often cited in both antiquity and the Renaissance (Tosi 1181). That one proverb might utterly contradict another is a common phenomenon in wisdom literature and does not seem to bother Erasmus here. After all, as he shows, though they disagree with one another, both proverbs are true.*

Ἄνθρωπος ἀνθρώπου λύκος, Man is a wolf to man. Almost the opposite of the foregoing, and in a way derived from it apparently, is the phrase of Plautus[1] in the *Asinaria*, 'Man is a wolf to man.' Here we are warned not to trust ourselves to an unknown person, but to beware of him as of a wolf. 'A man is a wolf and not a man,' he says, 'to the one who knows nothing of his character.'

1 *Asinaria* 495

I i 93
Polypi mentem obtine / Adopt the outlook of the polyp

This is a proverb on changeability, disguise, trickery, and concealment. The themes are returned to in a number of fascinating proverb essays in the Adages: *'As variable as the hydra' (*I *i 95), 'The ring of Gyges' (*I *i 96*), 'As many shapes as Proteus' (*II *ii 74*), 'The Sileni of Alcibiades' (*III *iii 1*), and*

'More changeable than the chameleon' (III iv 1), the chameleon also being alluded to at the end of this essay. Erasmus also mentioned this adage at II iii 91 'Polyps' ('There will be nothing to prevent us from applying the name "polyps" to those who turn themselves into any and every shape in the wish to stand well with everyone'). Changeableness fascinated Erasmus, and he addresses the theme in many places outside of the* Adages, *for instance,* De copia *(CWE 24 642–3), where he lists in abbreviated form a range of sources for this topic, including the figure of Fortune (I vii 70*) and Nemesis (II vi 38*). He first discussed the proverb in* Collectanea *no 255.*

There is in Greek an adage one can put in this class: Πολύποδος νόον ἴσχε, Adopt the outlook of the polyp. This recommends us to take up for the time being this or that kind of behaviour, this or that kind of face. Homer[1] seems to praise this in Ulysses, and calls him 'a man of many turnings,' changeful in his ways. The adage originates from the nature of this fish, of which Pliny[2] speaks, book 9 chapter 29. Lucian[3] too, in the conversation of Menelaus and Proteus; they write that it changes colour especially in fear. When fishermen are out after it, it attaches itself to rocks, and its body takes the colour of whatever rock it sticks to, obviously to escape being caught. In fact St Basil[4] reports that fish are sometimes taken in by its deceptive appearance, and swim up, offering themselves to be caught. The proverb is taken from Theognis,[5] whose couplet about the polyp exists today. He is also quoted by Plutarch in his essay 'On Having Many Friends': 'Adopt the attitude of the many-coloured polyp; / Moving towards a rock, it straightway takes its hue.' Clearchus[6] quotes this couplet among proverbs according to Athenaeus (the author's name is not given): 'O hero, son Amphilochus, take on the polyp's way, / Whatever nation you shall meet, let you become as they.' Plutarch[7] cites the same poem out of Pindar. Thus there is a well-known proverbial line:[8] ''Tis best in season to be this, or that.'

This advises us to suit ourselves to every contingency in life, acting the part of Proteus,[9] and changing ourselves into any form as the situation demands. In the same way Plutarch[10] said, 'I turn to a different opinion.' Aristophanes[11] makes the same observation in the *Plutus*, telling us to live in the style of the region, in local style. The saying[12] Νόμος καὶ χώρα, Custom of the country, points in the same direction. This means that in every region there are certain established things, which as guests we should not condemn, but do our best to copy and act on them. Let no man think that by this adage we are taught a disgusting type of flattery, which assents to everything in everybody, or an improper changeability in behaviour, of the sort which Horace[13] elegantly castigates in the *Satires*, and which historians remark in Catiline and in the emperor Anedius Cassius,[14] and Holy Scriptures[15] in any bad man when it says, 'the fool is as inconstant as the moon': the wise man is like the sun, always himself.

In Alcibiades[16] one may wonder whether this changeableness is to be taken as a vice or a virtue; he certainly had a happy and enviable dexterity of mind and character, which made him act the polyp, so that 'in Athens he amused himself with jokes and sallies, bred horses, and lived in pleasant elegant style, while among the Spartans he was close-shaved, wore a cloak, and took cold baths. Among the Thracians he was warlike and took to drinking. But when he came to the Tisaphernes, he followed the custom of the people and enjoyed pleasures, soft living, and ostentation.' There is however a kind of downrightness, edgy and harsh and unsmiling, among inexperienced people; they require everyone to live solely in his own way, and whatever pleases others they condemn. On the contrary there is a sensible attitude which makes good men comply on occasion with a different mode of conduct, to avoid either being disliked or being unable to be of use, or else for the sake of rescuing themselves or their households from great dangers. Ulysses[17] acted like this with Polyphemus, making a great many pretences, and with the suitors, when he acted the part of beggar. Brutus[18] too feigned stupidity, David[19] even pretended to be mad. And St Paul[20] too congratulates himself, with a kind of saintly boasting, on having used a pious pretence, and become all things to all men, that he might win all for Christ.

There is also nothing to prevent us from using the adage in a wider sense, when we are observing people's faults, against the conduct of men endowed with versatile minds who take on the character of those with whom they have to do, whoever they are. Plautus[21] aptly describes this kind of person in the *Bacchides*: 'Not a soul can be worth anything, unless he knows how to be good and bad both. He must be a rascal among rascals, rob robbers, steal what he can. A chap that's worth anything, a chap with a fine intellect, has to be able to change his skin. He must be good with the good and bad with the bad; whatever the situation calls for, that he's got to be.' Eupolis[22] in Athenaeus: 'A city man, a polyp in his manners.' Plutarch[23] in his 'On Natural Causes' quotes these lines from Pindar: 'Adapting the mind to the colour of the sea-creature, / He mingles with all cities.' And in the same place he gives the reason why this happens to the fish.

Aristotle[24] draws a similar metaphor from the chameleon, in his *Ethics*, book 1. He says that anyone who is dependent on fortune, with its sudden changes, will be like a chameleon, continually altering, now happy, now cast down; every time chance puts on a different face, this man changes his face and mentality. Pliny[25] mentions the chameleon, book 28 chapter 8, where he writes that this creature is about equal in size to the crocodile, but differs from it by its sharply-curved spine and breadth of tail. No creature, he says, is thought to be more easily frightened, and hence these changes of colour. Plutarch,[26] in his essay 'On Flattery,' writes that the chameleon imitates every colour except white. He also tries, in the 'Table-talk,' to explain why the polyp does not only change colour, which happens to men when they are afraid, but also matches itself to the rock, whatever colour that may be. There are some birds too which change both colour and song according to the season of the year; Pliny,[27] book 10 chapter 29, is the authority, and Aristotle[28] in book 9 on the *Nature of Animals*. This change of song is most notable in the nightingale. This is why Hecuba, in Euripides,[29] orders Polyxena to imitate the nightingale and try all kinds of speech, so as to persuade Ulysses that she should not be killed.

1 *Odyssey* 1.1
2 *Natural History* 9.87
3 *Dialogi marini* 4.3
4 *Homilies on Hexaemeron* 7.3
5 Theognis 215–16, cited by Plutarch *Moralia* 96F
6 Clearchus of Soli frag 75 ed Wehrli, cited by Athenaeus 7.317A
7 *Moralia* 916C and 978E (actually quoting Theognis; just a bit further on in the passage Plutarch does quote Pindar)
8 Zenobius 1.24 and Diogenianus 1.23
9 Proteus in *Adages* II ii 74*
10 *Brutus* 40.8
11 *Plutus* 47
12 'Custom of the country' is *Adages* III vi 55.
13 *Satires* 2.7.6–20

14 Anedius, from Vulcacius Gallicanus *Avidius Cassius* 3.4 (from *Historia Augusta*)
15 Ecclesiasticus 27:12
16 Plutarch *Moralia* 52E
17 Ulysses with Polyphemus and, later, the suitors, from *Odyssey* 9 and 17
18 The story of Lucius Junius Brutus, the first consul, is told in Livy 1.56.8 and Ovid *Fasti* 2.717.
19 1 Samuel 16:23
20 1 Corinthians 9:19–22
21 *Bacchides* 654–62 (trans Nixon)
22 Eupolis frag 101 Kock, cited by Athenaeus 7.316C
23 *Moralia* 916C, citing Pindar frag 43
24 *Nicomachean Ethics* 1.10 (1100b6), and, on the chameleon, also *Adages* III iv 1*, IV viii 35
25 *Natural History* 28.112–13
26 'On Flattery' in *Moralia* 53D; 'Table Talk' is actually 'On Natural Causes' in *Moralia* 916B.
27 *Natural History* 10.80
28 *History of Animals* 9.49 (632b14)
29 Euripides *Hecuba* 336–8

I i 96
Gygis anulus / The ring of Gyges

Like the the preceding proverb on the polyp, this proverb and Erasmus' essay emphasize the significance of disguise and concealment. Though the story is well known from the versions in Herodotus and Plato, the expression never became proverbial in English. Collectanea *no 341, from Diogenianus 4.72.*

Γύγου δακτύλιος, Gyges' ring. This suits either men of fickle character, or the lucky ones who get everything they want by just wishing for it, as by the wave of a magic wand. Lucian[1] recalls this proverb in *Wishes*, where someone wishes he had several rings like that of Gyges, one so that he could get rich, one to make him attractive and lovable, another to help him to fly wherever the fancy took him. In early times superstition credited rings with great efficacy, and indeed they used to be sold as possessing various powers through enchantment, some against the bite of wild beasts, some against slander, some for other purposes, either to repel bad luck or attract good luck for those who wore them. Hence in Aristophanes,[2] in the *Plutus*, Dicaeus says to the sycophant threatening judgment, 'I take no heed of you, because I wear this ring Eudamus sold me for a drachma.' And again in the same play, 'But it has none against the sycophant's blow' (remedy, understood).

He is speaking of a ring, and the allusion is to the bite of wild beasts. The proverb is derived from a story of this sort, which Plato[3] does not disdain to tell in his *Republic*, book 2. I likewise will not find it irksome to go over it here. A certain Gyges, the father of Lydus, was a herdsman in the service of the king who at that time ruled over the Lydians. One day a furious storm arose, torrents of rain fell, finally there was lightning and even an earthquake, so that in the region where Gyges happened to be grazing his flocks the earth split open, leaving a great chasm. When he saw this (he alone, because all the other shepherds had fled in terror) he went down into the chasm, and there, among other sights marvellous to relate, he saw a huge bronze horse, hollow inside. There was an aperture in the horse's flank, and looking through this he saw in its belly the corpse of a man, of more than human size. No clothing was on it nor any accoutrements, only a gold ring on one finger. This Gyges took, and turned back out of the cavern. A few days later he returned to the assembly of shepherds in which the business was to elect an envoy to take the king, month by month, the proceeds of his flocks. When Gyges had taken his place among the rest, he noticed that if he happened to turn inwards the jewel set in the ring, it came about at once that no one could see him, and they all talked about him just as if he had not been present. Amazed at this, he turned the bezel of the ring outwards again and began at once to be visible to the herdsmen. When he had tested this carefully and often, and had ascertained that the ring had this power to make him invisible when the jewel faced himself and visible when it faced towards others, he contrived to get himself sent by the shepherds as their envoy to the king. He went off, seduced the king's wife, and plotted with her to murder the king. After disposing of him, and marrying the queen, he rapidly became king from being a shepherd – and all because of the ring of destiny. Plato[4] mentions the same in the *Republic*, book 10. Cicero[5] also refers to this in the *De officiis*, book 3. Herodotus,[6] in his first book, tells the story very differently, without making any mention of a ring.

Very similar to this is the cap of Orcus, which I shall mention in another place.[7]

1 *Wishes* (or *Navigium*) 42

2 *Plutus* 883–5

3 *Republic* 2.359d

4 *Republic* 10.612b

5 *On Duties* 3.9.38
6 1.8–15 (reference to the famous tale in Herodotus interestingly added rather late, in 1528)
7 *Adages* II x 74

I ii 4
Clavum clavo pellere / To drive out one nail by another

This comes from the Greek and has survived in most European languages. Because it has a relation to the doctrine of similars or homeopathy, by which one treats a disease with the disease or an aspect of it, variations are also found in medical writings (eg, Galen De sanitate tuenda *3.2; Tosi 1629). It is a common older proverb in English (Tilley* N *17). First appeared in* Collectanea *no 50, with only the 'peg' not the 'nail' version.*

Ἥλῳ τὸν ἧλον ἐκκρούειν, To drive out one nail by another, and Πάτταλον πάτταλῳ ἐξέκρουσας, You drove out one peg with another peg, that is, you expelled one evil by another. Lucian[1] in *Philopseudes*: 'And as they say, you are driving out one nail with another.' Again in the *Apologia*: 'I am afraid that in addition to the accusation brought against me I might further find myself accused of flattery, knocking out one nail with another, as they say, a smaller with a greater.' Aristotle[2] writes in the last chapter but one of book 5 of his *Politics*, that wicked men and flatterers are friends to tyrants, for they are the ones who can be useful to them, bad people for bad ends, 'one nail with another, as the proverb says.' Synesius[3] to Olympius: 'Wicked foreigners are attacking the church; attack them. For pegs drive out pegs.' St Jerome[4] to Rusticus the monk: 'The philosophers of the world,' he says, 'are accustomed to drive out an old love by a new love, as one nail with another.' Cicero[5] in book 4 of the *Tusculan Questions*: 'A cure may often be effected by change of scene, as is done with sick people who are slow in making recovery. Some think too, that the old love can be driven out by a new, as one nail may be driven out by another.' Julius Pollux,[6] book 9, writes that the adage is derived from a certain game, which is called *kindalismos*; in this a peg stuck into clayey soil is driven out by another peg being struck against it. He quotes the proverbial line: 'one nail with another, peg with peg.'

There is then a place for this adage, not only when we check one fault with another, an evil by another evil, guile with guile, force with force, boldness with boldness, or slander with slander; but also when we overcome some troublesome thing by another sort of trouble, as when we subdue the incitements of desire by hard work, or master the anxiety of love by other greater cares. Eusebius[7] against Hierocles: 'He drives out demons, one demon by another as they say,' surely referring to this proverb. And that moral maxim of Publius[8] is not unlike these allusions: 'Never is danger conquered without danger.'

1 *Philopseudes* 9 and *Apologia* 9
2 *Politics* 5.11 (1314a4)
3 *Epistulae* 45.186a (*PG* 66.1373D)
4 *Letters* 125.14.1
5 *Tusculan Disputations* 4.35.75
6 *Onomasticon* 9.120
7 *Contra Hieroclem* 34 (30) (*PG* 22.837B)
8 Publilius Syrus N 7 (author of a well-known collection of aphorisms, called his *Mimes*, taught in schools and edited by Erasmus) cited by Aulus Gellius *Attic Nights* 17.14

I ii 11
Ululas Athenas / Owls to Athens

To perform a redundant task. The Greek proverb is translated analogously into the modern European languages (eg, our 'Carry coals to Newcastle' [Tilley C 466], the German 'Bring beer to Munich,' the Italian 'Carry beanpoles [i frasconi*] to Vallombrosa' [Tosi 477]). But 'Owls to Athens' was also used for a long time, especially in the sixteenth century (Tilley O 97), for instance, by Ariosto in his* Orlando Furioso *40.1: Were I to tell you, says the narrator, of all that fought in that battle 'I should be thought, / To beare potts ... to Samos Ile ... / Or Owles to Athens, Crocodills to Nile ...' (translation by Sir John Harington). This proverb first appeared in* Collectanea *no 131. For an analogy noted elsewhere by Erasmus, see I vii 57*.*

Γλαῦκας εἰς Ἀθήνας, Owls to Athens ('you carry' or 'send' understood). This will fit stupid traders who transport their wares to a place where they are more abundant anyway, as if a man were to take grain to Egypt or saffron to Cilicia. It will be more attractive if the metaphor is transferred to the things of the mind: so-and-so teaches a man wiser than himself, he sends poems to a poet, he gives advice to a man wise in counsel. Cicero[1] to Torquatus: 'But again in writing thus to you I am only sending owls to Athens.' And to his brother: 'I will send you the verses for which you ask – owls to Athens.' Aristophanes[2] in the *Birds*: 'What do you say? Who, pray, brought an owl to Athens?' Lucian[3] uses and explains this in his epistle to Nigrinus. The proverb derives from the fact that there is a species of owl peculiar to Attica, and abundant there. It is said that they live in a place called Laureum in Attica, where there are gold-mines,[4] and hence they are also called Laureotic owls. In old times, this bird was specially beloved by the Athenians, and held to be sacred to Minerva, owing to the grey eyes with which it sees even in the dark, and sees what ordinary birds do not see. Hence it is believed to be a good augury in counsel, and this is what is meant by the proverb 'The owl flies.'[5] It is also said of Minerva[6] that she turned the rash plans of the Athenians to a favourable outcome. However Daemon, quoted by the annotator of Aristophanes, thinks that the phrase 'owls to Athens' does not only come from the fact that there are plenty of owls there, but that the owl used to be stamped on the gold and silver coins of Athens together with the head of Minerva. This coin is called a *tetradrachm*, four drachmas; earlier on they used to have two-drachma pieces, the distinguishing mark of which was an ox, whence the proverb comes 'An ox on the tongue.'[7] Some relate that there was also a *triobolus*, which they also call a half-drachma, for the drachma is worth six obols. The coin called the triobol had on one side the effigy of Jove, on the other the owl. Hence it seemed absurd to take an owl to Athens, since the whole place was full of owls. Plutarch[8] refers to the Athenian coinage in his life of Lysander, where he tells the story of the slave who made an enigmatic allusion to a theft of his master's, when he said there were 'many owls sleeping under the tiles,' giving away the fact that there was money hidden there, stamped with the owl.

1 *Ad familiares* 6.3.3 and *Ad Quintum fratrem* 2.16(15).4

2 *Birds* 301

3 *Nigrinus*, prefatory epistle

4 The 'gold-mines' of Laureion were actually silver-mines (see *Adages* II viii 31).

5 *Adages* I i 76

6 *Adages* I viii 44
7 *Adages* I vii 18*
8 *Lysander* 16.2

I ii 21
Simile gaudet simili / Like rejoices in like

Our most commonly used analogue in English is 'Birds of a feather flock together' (Tilley B 393*) though 'Like will to like' (Tilley* L 286*) was also widely known in the sixteenth century. This proverb was often cited in relation to the doctrine of similars (or homeopathy) in medicine. It is interesting to compare this with* I ii 4* *'To drive out one nail by the other'; though the proverbs are related, their meanings are in a way opposed. The adage appeared in* Collectanea *(no 177), in relation to* I ii 20 *'Everyone loves his own age' (see also Otto 1335).*

῞Ομοιον ὁμοίῳ φίλον, Like rejoices in like. Aristotle[1] in the *Ethics*, book 8: 'Like seeks like,' and in book 9: 'Like is a friend to like.' Hence that other phrase: 'Similarity is the mother of affection.' So where there is absolute similarity there is the most violent love, and this is the meaning of the fable of Narcissus.[2] Agathon in the *Symposium* of Plato:[3] 'For the old saying is right, that like always cleaves to like.' Plutarch[4] in the essay called 'How to Tell a Friend from a Flatterer,' quotes the following iambic lines:

The speech of age is pleasant to the old,
Boy suits with boy, woman with woman too,
A sick man with the sick, and one in grief
With one who suffers in dear accord.

Diogenes Laertius,[5] showing that Plato imitated some things from the writings of Epicharmus, quotes his saying that 'a bitch seems most beautiful to a dog, a cow to a bull, a she-ass to an ass, a sow to a boar.' I have said elsewhere[6] 'To every queen her king is fair.' Plato[7] in the eighth book of the *Laws*: 'We say that like is a friend to like as far as virtue is concerned, and equal to equal.' But the adage can rightly be transferred also to those who are linked by a likeness in vice. Directed against those is the line of Catullus[8] 'Well agreed are the abominable profligates,' and Martial's[9] 'Worst of wives and worst of husbands, I am surprised that you do not agree,' and Juvenal's[10] 'Great is the concord among catamites.'

1 *Nicomachean Ethics* 8.1.2 (1155b7) and 9.3.3 (1165b17)
2 A well-known version of the Narcissus story is Ovid *Metamorphoses* 3.339–510.
3 *Symposium* 195b
4 'How to Tell a Friend from a Flatterer' in *Moralia* 51E, an unidentified fragment from a comedy or tragedy
5 3.16
6 *Adages* I ii 15
7 *Laws* 8.837a
8 57.1
9 8.35.2–3
10 2.47

I ii 39
Principium dimidium totius / Well begun is half done

The proverb was especially popular in antiquity (Otto 557; also Diogenianus 2.97 and Suidas A *4097); it was known in the Middle Ages largely through Horace's* Epistles, *which Erasmus quotes below (Tosi 802). The proverb in its rhyming form is still found in English (Tilley* B *254), though often with variations (eg, the schoolteacher's still cited 'Homework begun is homework half done'). Taverner gives it as 'The beginninge is halfe the hole.' Erasmus listed this first in* Collectanea *no 208.*

'Αρχὴ ἥμισυ παντός, Well begun is half done. This adage signifies that it is in the tackling of a task that the greatest difficulty lies. It is a half-line from Hesiod,[1] quoted by Lucian in *Hermotimus.* Aristotle[2] also refers to it in the *Politics,* book 5, and Plato[3] in the *Laws,* book 6: 'For in proverbs it is said that the beginning is half of a whole action, and everyone always praises a good beginning. But, as it seems to me, it is more than half, and no one has ever praised sufficiently a beginning well made.' Suidas[4] quotes from a certain Marinus: 'That was the beginning for us, and not only the beginning, nor as the proverb has it half of the whole, but the complete thing itself.' Aristotle[5] in the *Ethics,* book 1: 'The beginning is said to be more than half of the whole.' Horace[6] in the *Epistles*: 'Who sets about hath half performed his deed; / Dare to be wise.' Ausonius:[7] 'Begin, for half the deed is in beginning; / Begin the other half, and you will finish.' Plutarch,[8] in his essay 'On How to Study Poetry,' quotes these verses from Sophocles: 'For someone who begins well every deed, / 'Tis likely that's the way the end will be.'

1 *Works and Days* 40, cited by Lucian *Hermotimus* 3
2 *Politics* 5.4 (1303b29)
3 *Laws* 6.753e
4 Suidas A 4091
5 *Nicomachean Ethics* 1.7 (1098b7)
6 *Epistles* 1.2.40
7 *Epigrammata* 15 (81)
8 *Moralia* 16A, citing Sophocles frag 747 Nauck

I iii 1
Aut regem aut fatuum nasci oportere / One ought to be born a king or a fool

Like many of the longer essays, this is at the beginning of a new century of proverbs. Though most of the surrounding proverb essays were written in 1508, this was added in 1515, for the proverb itself came from Erasmus' recently published edition of Ludus de morte Claudii *(a 'skit on the death of Claudius,' referred to at the beginning of the adage essay, also called* Apocolocyntosis*), by the Roman writer Seneca. The proverb lays the basis for a lengthy reflection on the qualities and training of the good ruler, a theme given great emphasis elsewhere in Erasmus, most notably in his* Education of a Christian Prince *published just a year later, in 1516, but also in the other anti-war proverb essays (for these, see introduction to* IV i 1* *'War is sweet to those who have not tried it'). Erasmus moves from the proverb very quickly into his remarkable essay of observations and criticisms of sloppy governance and the foolishness of the uneducated ruler, and though he has many examples from the ancient world, these are not, as Erasmus admits at the end, examples of the proverb itself, which was nevertheless quite well known in various forms in antiquity (Otto 1535, Tosi 982).*

Annaeus Seneca was a man, as Tacitus[1] said, of a very pleasant wit; this is clear from that amusing skit which he wrote against Claudius Caesar, and which has recently come to light in Germany. In this short work he mentions an adage, One ought to be born a king or a fool. It is best to give his very words: 'As for me,' he says, 'I know I have gained my freedom from the fact that the end has come for that man who proved the truth of the proverb, One ought to be born a king or a fool.' And again in the same book, 'He killed in one and the same house Crassus, Magnus, Scribonia, Bassionia, the Assarii, although they were noble, while Crassus was such a fool that he might have reigned.' In another place, though the allusion is less clear, he refers to the same thing in his line 'He snapped the royal thread of a stupid life.' If Hesiod[2] is right in the view that a popular saying is never meaningless, perhaps it would not be beside the point to inquire what can have given rise to this proverb, uniting as it does two such dissimilar things – a king and a fool – with the obvious intention of drawing a parallel between the two. Especially as it is the particular distinction of kings (and the only true royal one) to surpass all others in wisdom, prudence, and watchfulness.

Well, everyone agrees that those famous kings of old time were for the most part well endowed with stark stupidity; one can see this in the fables of the poets on the one hand, in the writings of the historians on the other. Homer, for instance (and the writers of tragedy after him), makes his Agamemnon ambitious rather than wise. What could be more stupid than to purchase the title of commander-in-chief by the cruel slaughtering of an only daughter? What could be more idiotic than to be up in arms so childishly for the sake of a chit from a barbarous land, and then when he couldn't keep his sweetheart, to snatch the girl belonging to Achilles, and put the whole army in danger? And then there is Achilles himself – how foolishly he rages when bereft of his lady-love and how childishly he goes crying to his mother! And yet he is the one whom the poet sets before us as the perfect example of an excellent prince. Look at Ajax, and his unwise anger; look at Priam, and his senile maunderings when he embraces Helen – that shameless creature – and calls her his daughter, and declares he has no regrets for that war which brought him such disasters, bereaved him of so many children, plunged him into such mourning so often – and all so that Paris should not fail to possess his girl. Why say more? The whole of the *Iliad*, long as it is, has nothing in it, as Horace[3] says in an elegant line, but 'the passions of foolish kings and foolish peoples.'

The *Odyssey* also has its dense and stupid suitors and characters like Alcinous. Even Hercules himself is described as sturdy and spirited, but heavy and doltish in mind. Indeed Hesiod[4] (whom some think older than Homer) calls princes 'gift-greedy' and 'childish' – I suppose on account of their small wisdom in government, and the way they strained after the accumulation of riches by fair means and foul, rather than after the public good. So they imagine old Midas, wearing his asses' ears as a mark of stupidity.[5] And I think perhaps this is the place to mention how the earliest theologians – that is, the poets – attribute wisdom to Apollo and to Minerva, but to Jove, the ruler of gods and men, they leave nothing but the threeforked lightning, and that nod and that eyebrow which makes all Olympus tremble. Moreover, what profligate, what buffoon ever fooled so foolishly, or was more vilely vile, than this character whom they make ruler of the world? He deceives his wife with tricks, turning himself into a swan, a bull, a shower of gold; he rigs up traps for women, suborns his Ganymedes, fills heaven with bastards. In the same way Neptune and Pluto are painted as fierce and ruthless, but they are not credited with wisdom.

But suppose we dismiss the legends and turn to more recent times, to history: how much sense do you think Croesus King of Lydia had, if he was truly such as Herodotus[6] paints him, so relying on his treasure of jewels and gold that he was angry with Solon for refusing him the name of 'fortunate'? Or what could be imagined more idiotic than Xerxes, when he sent messengers to Mount Athos, to terrify it with most scornful and threatening letters, or ordered so many lashes to be given to the Hellespont? Alexander the Great showed a no less kingly stupidity when he renounced his father and took pleasure in being greeted as the son of Jove, when he competed in drinking to excess, when he allowed himself to be worshipped as god by the flatterers in his banquets, when he complained that this world was too small for his victories, and took to the ocean to find other worlds to conquer. I leave aside all the others, the Dionysiuses, the Ptolemies, the Juliuses, the Neros, the Tiberiuses, the Caligulas, the Heliogabaluses, the Commoduses, and the Domitians – among whom one arrogated to himself the name of god when he was unworthy of the name of man, another exposed himself to be laughed to scorn by his very flatterers, another urged by ambition shook the whole world with meaningless wars.

But I look rather silly myself when I embark on this catalogue, and as they say, seek water in the sea.[7] You merely have to turn over the chronicles of both the ancients and the moderns, and you will find that in several centuries there have been barely one or two princes who did not by sheer stupidity bring disaster to human affairs. A prince, indeed, is either a fool to the immense detriment of the whole world, or a wise man to the immense benefit of all; although it is easier to do badly than well, and the harm he does spreads or rather pervades everything more quickly than the good. But nowadays we see some princes who aspire to anything except the one thing which would make them deserve the name of prince; and stupid subjects, who admire everything in their kings except the one thing needful. 'He is young'; that would recommend him as a bridegroom to a bride, not as a prince to the state. 'He is good-looking'; that is the right praise for a woman. 'He is broad-shouldered, broad-flanked'; if you were praising an athlete, that would be the way to do it. 'He is strong and can stand hard toil'; that is a testimonial for a batman or a houseboy. 'He has a large store of gold'; you are describing an active moneylender. 'He is eloquent'; that's what dazzles me in a sophist. 'He sings well, he dances well'; that is the way to praise flute-players and actors, not kings. 'He has no equal in drinking' – for former princes actually delighted in this commendation! It would be fitter praise for a sponge. 'He is tall, and stands head and shoulders above the rest'; that's splendid, if one wants to reach something down from a high place. As for saying 'He's a skilled dice player, he's good at chess,' that is praise shared with the lowest idlers, and a prince should be ashamed of it. You may heap up everything – public refinement, gold and jewels, ancestral images, a pedigree drawn from Hercules (or from Codrus or Cecrops[8] if you prefer), but unless you tell me of a mind far removed from vulgar foolishness, free from sordid desires for worthless things, and from the prejudices of the herd, I have not heard any praise worthy of a king.

For it was not ill-advisedly that the divine Plato[9] wrote that the only way for a state to attain happiness was for the supreme command to be given to philosophers, or else, inversely, that those who govern should themselves follow philosophy. And to follow philosophy is not just to wear a mantle[10] and to carry a bag round, or let your beard grow. What is it then? It is to despise those things which the common herd goggles at, and to think quite differently from the opinions of the majority. And I don't see how it is possible for a man who thinks he is free to do just what he likes, who marvels at riches as if they were important, who thinks even a sworn oath may be set aside for the sake of power, who is captivated by empty glory, who is a slave to shameful lust, who is terrified of death – I just can't see how such a man can play the part of a beneficent king.

The first requisite is to judge rightly about each matter, because opinions are like springs from which all the actions of life flow, and when they are contaminated everything must needs be mismanaged. The next essential is to recoil from evil and to be led towards good. For true wisdom consists not only in the knowledge of truth, but in the love and eager striving for what is good. You may well find among rulers one who can see that it is not possible to go to war without grave disaster to human affairs, and that an old obsolete claim to sovereignty is not very important – and yet he will plunge everything into war merely out of ambition. There may be one who can see that the greatest curse of a state comes from appointing as magistrates, not those who can be of the most use to the public weal by their prudence, experience, and integrity, but those who can bid the highest sums – and yet he will be impelled by avarice to look after the treasury and let the abuse go on. And there is another who understands that the duty of a prince, who takes taxes from all, is to look after everyone's interest, to preside over trials, to stamp out crime, to watch the magistrature, to amend useless laws. And yet he is called away from this business by pleasures, which do not give him the time to attend to matters worthy of a ruler. Another is conscious that he has it in his power to confer a great benefit on the human race, but at the risk of his life; and anyone who thinks it is the most terrible thing to die, will fail in duty to the state at this point. And so first of all the mind of the prince must be freed from all false ideas, so that he can see what is truly good, truly glorious, truly splendid. The next thing is to instil the hatred of what is base, the love of what is good, so that he can see clearly what is becoming to a prince, and wish for nothing but what is worthy of a good and beneficent ruler. Let him recognize the good where it may be found, and always measure everything by it, never varying from this aim. This is what is meant by wisdom, and it is in this that the prince must so far excel other mortals, as he excels them in dignity, in wealth, in splendour, and in power.

If only all Christian princes would copy that wisest of all kings,[11] who when he was given a free choice of a boon from Him to whom nothing is impossible, wished for wisdom alone, and that wisdom by which he might rightly govern his people! And pray what did he teach his own son, but the love and following of wisdom? It is for this reason that the Egyptians make a symbolic representation of a prince by drawing an eye and a sceptre.[12] Indeed what the eye is to the body, so is a true prince to the people; the sun is the eye of the world, the prince the eye of the multitude. As the mind is to the body, so is the prince to the state; the mind knows, the body obeys. And if the mind commands the body, it is for the body's good; it does not rule for itself like a tyrant, but for that which is in its charge. Above all, the good ruler is the living portrayal of God, who rules the universe. And the closer the prince conforms to the lines of the original, the more magnificent he is. God is all-seeing, all-feeling, and swayed by no passions. He is greatest in power, but at the same time greatest in goodness. He does good to all, even the unworthy. He deals no punishments, except rarely and when he must. He governs this world for us and not for himself. All the reward he asks is to do good. But the evil prince, on the contrary, seems to be the copy of the devil, and to act in his stead. Either he knows nothing, or what he knows is how to bring about public disaster. What power he has, he uses to harm the state. And though it is in his power to do a great deal of harm to everybody, he would like to do even more than he can.

Nothing is nobler than a good king, nothing better, nothing nearer God; equally, nothing is worse than a bad prince, nothing viler, nothing more like the devil. There is something divine about a beneficent prince, but no wild beast is more destructive than a tyrant. And a tyrant is whoever wields power for himself, whatever name his paintings and statues give him. It is not for us to pass judgment, as it were, upon the great ones of the earth, but yet we are obliged – not without sorrow – to feel the lack in Christian princes of that high wisdom of which we have spoken. All these revolutions, treaties made and broken, frequent risings, battle and slaughter, all these threats and quarrels, what do they arise from but stupidity? And I rather think that some part of this is due to our own fault. We do not hand over the rudder of the ship to anyone but a skilled steersman, when nothing is at stake but four passengers or a small cargo; but we hand over the state, in which so many thousands of people are in peril, to the first comer. If anyone is to be a coachman, he learns the art, spends care and practice; but for anyone to be a king, we think it is enough for him to be born. And yet to rule a kingdom well, as it is the finest of all functions, is also the most difficult by far. You choose the man who is to have charge of a ship; but you do not choose the man to whom you are entrusting so many cities, so many human lives? But there it is, the thing is so established that it is impossible to root it out. Kings are born, and whoever may have been picked out by chance, whether he be good or bad, stupid or wise, sane or clouded in mind, as long as he looks like a human being, he is to be entrusted with supreme power in the state. By his will the world is to be thrown into an uproar with wars and slaughter, all things sacred and profane are to be turned upside down.

But if this is a thing which we cannot change, the next best plan would be to improve matters by careful education; and if we may not choose a suitable person to be our ruler, we must strive to try to make that person suitable whom fate has given us. We see with what care and solicitude and watchfulness a father brings up his son, who is the future master of one estate. How much more care, then, should be spent on the education of one who, if good, will be so to the immense benefit of all, and if bad, will bring about the ruin of all – one on whose nod hangs the safety or the destruction of the world? With what rules and precepts of philosophy must that mind be fortified, not only against such great calamities as may arise in a state, but against the favour of fortune, so often accompanied by pride and stupidity; against pleasures, which can corrupt the best natures; still more against the dangerous fawning of flatterers, and that poisonous 'Bravo!' which they chant – particularly when the prince is acting most like a madman. It seems to me that he should have attached to him, while still an infant, some skilful educator; for no one can truly be fashioned into a prince, except long before he knows that he is what he is. In the early days, I say, a preceptor should be appointed, and we should take all the more care in choosing him because we are not free to choose our prince – but we are free to educate him. Let him instil into this childish mind, as yet blank and malleable, opinions worthy of a prince; arm it with the best principles of conduct, show it the difference between a true prince and a tyrant, and lay before its very eyes what a god-like thing is a beneficent ruler, what a loathsome hateful brute is a tyrant. He will explain that a ruler who wields power for himself and not for the state is no prince, but a robber; that there is no difference between pirates and pirate-minded princes, except that the latter are more powerful and can bring so much more disaster on human affairs. He will impress on his pupil that he can be of use to so many thousands of people – nay, to the whole world, by simply behaving as one good and wise man. He will teach that among Christians supreme rule means administration of the state, and not dominion. It may bear the name of supreme rule, but he must remember that he is ruling over free men, and over Christians, that is, people who are twice free. In addition, for a person to be a prince it is not enough to be born, to have ancestral statues, the sceptre, and the crown. What makes a prince is a mind distinguished for its wisdom, a mind always occupied with the safety of the state, and looking to nothing but the common good. He will warn his pupil not to judge himself by the plaudits of the stupid populace or the praise of flatterers, not to do anything on the impulsion of hatred, love, or anger, or at the urge of any passion. When he appoints magistrates, creates laws, or in his other duties, he must work for one end only, for good, and for the people's benefit. It is not enough if he himself does harm to no one – the prince is also the guarantor of the uprightness of his officials. The glory of a prince does not lie in extending his sway, in removing his neighbours by force of arms; but if he happens to acquire the sovereignty of a region, he must make it flourish by justice, by wise economy, and the other arts of peace. The teacher will recommend him to be particularly inclined to serve the cause of good men, to be ready to pardon, and with the attitude towards punishment of a friendly doctor, who amputates or cauterizes the limb which he despairs of healing; to be careful to avoid everything from which he can foresee the danger of evil to the state. Above all, he is to shun war in every way; other things give rise to this or that calamity, but war lets loose at one go a whole army of wrongs. These principles and others like them should be impressed on the child's mind, with the help of the maxims of the wise and the examples of esteemed princes.

What actually happens is that no kind of man is more corruptly or carelessly brought up than those whose education is of such importance to so many people. The baby who is to rule the world is handed over to the stupidest of womenkind who are so far from instilling anything in his mind worthy of a prince, that they discourage whatever the tutor rightly advises, or whatever inclination to gentleness the child may have in himself – and they teach him to act like a prince, that is like a tyrant. Then no one fails to fawn and flatter. The courtiers applaud, the servants obey his every whim, even the tutor is obsequious; and he is not doing this to make the prince more beneficial to his country, but to ensure a splendid future for himself. The cleric who is popularly called his confessor, is obsequious too – he has some bishopric in mind. There is flattery from the judges, flattery from playmates and companions; so that Carneades[13] was right when he said that the only art kings could learn properly was the art of riding, because only a horse makes no distinction between prince and peasant and is unable to flatter. He just tosses off the rider who is not skilful enough to stay on his back, no matter who it may be.

One of the earliest lessons is pomp and pride; he is taught that whatever he wants, he can have. He hears that the property of everyone belongs to the prince, that he is above the law; that the whole paraphernalia of government, laws, and policies exist stored in the prince's mind. He hears the terms *sacred majesty, serene highness, divinity, god on earth,* and other such superb titles. In short, while he is yet a boy, all he learns to play at is being a tyrant. Then he is caught up among the girls; they all allure and admire and defer to him. The effeminate crew of young friends is there, and they have no other topic for jokes or conversation but girls. Next there are other diversions – gaming, dancing, feasting, lute-playing, gadding about;

the best years of his life are used up like this. If he takes a fancy to beguile his leisure by reading, he reads old wives' tales, or what is worse, historical romances. His mind is not in the least equipped with any antidote, and he imbibes from them an enthusiasm – what the Greeks call *zeal* – for some pernicious hero, say Julius Caesar or Xerxes or Alexander the Great. And what suits him best in them is the worst. They furnish the worst example, they foster the craziest urges. Now imagine, if you please, an intelligence not selected from among many, as should be the case, but a very ordinary mind, and an education so corrupt that it would corrupt the mentality of an Aristides;[14] then imagine the poison of flattery, frolic and pleasure (which don't agree very well with wisdom), luxurious living, wealth and magnificence, the sense of power; all this at an age of ruthlessness and inclined naturally to bad courses. Add finally the tainting of the mind by false ideas. And can you wonder if, coming from this early environment to the administration of a kingdom, he doesn't do it very wisely?

'But never mind,' they say, 'he's young, he'll learn by experience.' But the prince must never be young, even if he is young in years. Any prudence which is won from experience is of a sorry kind, and sorriest of all in a prince. The prince's prudence will be too dearly bought by the country, if he only learns by waging war that war is the thing he must avoid at all costs; or if he fails to understand that public offices must be given to upright men, until he sees the state tottering through the audacity of evildoers. Don't tell me that those who wish to learn to sing to the lute will spoil several lutes in the process, before they learn the art, as Xenophon[15] said; that would mean that the prince would only learn to administer his state by the ruin of the state.

It is not therefore much to be wondered at, if we see things going absolutely contrary to the way they should; when instead of the passions which arise from the body being controlled by the mind the disturbances in the mind spread out into the body, when the eyes see less than the rest of the body sees, when the person who is most pernicious and harmful to the public is the very person who should be beneficial to all, acting in place of God. Do we not see fine cities, created by the people, overthrown by the princes? Or a state enriched by the toil of its citizens, and looted by the princes' greed? Plebeian lawyers make good laws, princes violate them; the people seek for peace, the princes stir up war.

I think these are the things which give rise to this adage, from which somehow or other we have digressed a long way; but now we return to it. So it is said, One ought to be born a king or a fool, because the primitive kings were of that sort, as the ancients tell – and may the princes of our day be altogether different! For everything is permitted to fools, because of the weakness of their minds. And everything is praised in kings, because of their power. There is perhaps another way of understanding the saying, in reference to the equal happiness of kings and fools; because whatever a king wants is provided by fortune, and fools are no less fortunate because of their self-satisfaction, it allows them to think they have no lack of good gifts. And in fact the proverb seems to have originated among the Romans, who hated the name of king as barbaric and tyrannous, and contrary to political freedom, of which they at that time were the most enthusiastic supporters.

1 *Annals* 13.3
2 *Works and Days* 763–4
3 *Epistles* 1.2.8; it may be that Alcinous, generous king of the Phaeacians, is a slip here for Antinous, one of the suitors in the *Odyssey*.
4 *Works and Days* 39–40
5 Discussed in the adage 'Midas has ass's ears' I iii 67 (Midas judged Pan to be a superior flute-player to Apollo, who then punished him by giving him the ears of an ass)
6 1.30–3, 7.35
7 Cf Adages I vii 57*, I ix 75 'You seek water in the sea.'
8 Codrus was the last king of Athens, Cecrops the first; both suggest remote antiquity.
9 *Republic* 5.473C–D
10 The mantle or Latin *pallium*, the wallet to contain scraps of food obtained by begging, and the beard were signs in Rome of the typical Greek.
11 Solomon; see 1 Kings 3:9.
12 Plutarch *Moralia* 354F, also mentioned in *Adages* II i 1* and III vii 1*
13 Carneades was a leading philosopher in the Middle Academy; the remark comes from Plutarch *Moralia* 58F.
14 Aristides was the Athenian politician of the fifth century BC, known as 'the just.'
15 *Oeconomicus* 2.13

I iii 7
Quot homines, tot sententiae / So many men, so many opinions

The English version is sometimes found as 'So many men, so many minds' (Tilley M 583), rather than 'opinions.' As with a few others of these classical proverbs, the Latin is sometimes preferred by English writers. Erasmus is correct about the immense popularity of this saying in the Renaissance, usually given as it is found in Terence's Phormio 454, *but sometimes as as he says from Horace or, not mentioned, Ovid* Art of Love 1.759 *(Otto 826; Tosi 537). The jab at contentious theologians is typical: though not afraid of controversy himself, Erasmus deplored it.*

Nothing is more widely known even today than this saying of Terence[1] 'So many men, so many opinions,' and in the same author there is a similar phrase, 'every man has his own way.' Persius[2] also: 'Men are of a thousand kinds, and diverse the colour of their lives; / Each has his own desires; no two offer the same prayer.' In the same class is that remark in an epigram[3] that one may find people who are willing to yield in the matter of family acres, but not one who will give way on a matter of opinion. Horace[4] adds an elegant metaphor: 'Three guests I have, of wishes quite contrary; / As their tastes differ, so their orders vary.' It was Horace, too, who devoted the first ode of all to the subject of this proverb, ie that different people are led by different interests, that some have one thing at heart and some another. Terence,[5] in the *Phormio*, plays upon this in jest when he says of three advisers, 'the first says yes, the second says no, and the third says "Let's think about it."' St Paul[6] the Apostle seems to have made a reference to this when he says that for the putting aside of strife, we should allow every man to have his own convictions. If the general run of theologians had listened to this advice, there would not now be such fierce contention about little questions of no moment at all; for there certainly are some things of which one may remain in ignorance without any lack of piety. The same thought is expressed at greater length by Euripides[7] in the *Phoenissae*:

If what were fair and wise were so to all
Disputing strife would not exist for men,

But now for mortals naught is 'like' nor 'same,'
Only the words may happen to agree,
In deed and fact no likeness can be found.

Again in the *Hippolytus Crowned*: 'This man, this God, is after their own heart / To some, not so to others.' Homer[8] thought of this in the *Odyssey*, book 14: 'For one man takes delight in certain things, / Another in others.'

1 *Phormio* 454; Mynors notes that Erasmus seems to have forgotten that the 'similar phrase' he goes on to quote is actually the second half of the same line in Terence.
2 *Satires* 5.52–5
3 Martial 8.18.9–10
4 *Epistles* 2.2.61–2 and *Odes* 1.1.3–28
5 *Phormio* 449–57
6 Romans 14:5
7 *Phoenissae* 499–502 and *Hippolytus* 104
8 *Odyssey* 14.228

I iii 15
Sursum versus sacrorum fluminum feruntur fontes / The springs of the sacred rivers flow backwards

This peculiar adage is about a reversal, the idea of a river that flows up towards its source. The motif is still found in modern literature: the protagonist of Herbert Read's curious masterpiece The Green Child *(1945) follows a backwards-flowing river, and in Conrad's* Heart of Darkness *(1902), the narrator travels 'down' to the mysterious head of the river. It sometimes happens with paradoxical proverbs that the original sense becomes confused in translation: though this proverb was well known in antiquity (Otto 678; Tosi 440) and appeared correctly in other European languages, in English it took the form 'Streams back to their springs do never run' (Tilley S 931), even though the point of the classical proverb is a contradiction of this. Erasmus' unnamed Greek sources were Zenobius 2.56, Diogenianus 1.27, and Suidas A 2596.*

A proverbial allegory, which we use to signify that something is upside down, that the proper arrangement of things is reversed, as for instance if a boy should admonish an old man, or a pupil try to teach his teacher, or a servant give orders to his master. The adage comes from Euripides,[1] *Medea*:

Upwards flow the streams of sacred rivers,
Overturned are justice and tradition,
The plans of men are treacherous
And trust in the gods no longer fixed.

In these words the chorus is pointing out that the original order of things is reversed: men are using women's wiles and not abiding by their promises, while women are daring to do manly deeds. Lucian[2] in *Terpsion* makes use of this proverb when the deceived legacy-hunter reproaches Pluto because he himself has been carried off by death as a mere youth, while the old man whose money he had desired to inherit is still alive, against all the natural order of things. 'This is a case of Upwards flow the streams,' he says. Again in his *Apology* for the essay *On Salaried Posts in Great Houses*: 'At any rate there is a big difference between your present life and your writing; this would be, as they say, Upwards flow the streams and all things overturned, and a recantation towards what is worse.' Diogenes Laertius[3] uses this in his life of Diogenes the Cynic: he tells how Diogenes sent a message to his master, as if he were the lord and not the servant, that he should do what he had been ordered to do, and the master replied with the proverb, 'Upwards flow the streams of the sacred rivers'; 'but if you were ill,' Diogenes said, 'and had hired the doctor with your own money, would you follow his prescription or reply in that way, "Upwards flow the streams?"' Aristotle[4] makes use of it in his *Meteorologica*. Virgil[5] has an allusion to it in the *Aeneid*, when he says: 'Back flows Aufidus river from Adriatic waves.' Servius remarks here that a proverb is lying concealed, suggesting unlikelihood or inconsistency. Horace[6] expresses it thus in the *Odes*:

Who shall deny that streams ascend
And Tiber's currents backward bend,
While you have all our hopes betrayed;
You, that far other promise made,
When all your volumes, learned store!

The treasure of Socratic lore,
Once bought at mighty price in vain,
Are sent to purchase arms in Spain?

Porphyrion noted that this was a proverb. Ovid,[7] too, in his *Heroides*:

If Paris' breath shall fail not, once Oenone he doth spurn,
The waters of the Xanthus to their fount shall backward turn.
O Xanthus, backward haste; waters, to your springs again,
Oenone has been deserted, and Paris feels no pain.

Propertius[8] again, 'Rivers begin to recall their waters to their fount.'

1 *Medea* 410–13
2 *Dialogues of the Dead* 16.2 (Terpsion is one of the characters) and *Apologia* 1
3 6.36
4 *Meteorologica* 2.1 (353b27)
5 *Aeneid* 11.405 (Servius is the ancient commentator on Virgil)
6 *Odes* 1.29.10–16 (trans Sir Philip Francis); Porphyrion is the ancient commentator on Horace.
7 *Heroides* 5.29–32
8 Propertius 2.15.33

I iii 41
Fumos vendere / To sell smoke

For this proverb, Erasmus provides a very thorough discussion (Otto 730, the modern authority for Latin proverbs, has little to add). The proverb was circulated in the Middle Ages as 'He who sold smoke is punished' (Tosi 286), ie, the aspect of punishment was retained. Our modern 'smoke and mirrors' may have some kind of relation to this proverb about illusion and illegal selling practices. The Elizabethan courtier-poet Sir John Harington gives the witty English translation 'Let fume him choake, that selleth smoke' (from Tilley s *576, who gives other English versions of 'To sell smoke'). This was first listed by Erasmus in* Collectanea *no 659.*

In Martial[1] there is a particularly neat adage, 'to sell smoke,' which means to sell the favour of the great, pretending that one can do a man the service of recommending him because one has a certain proximity to them. Smoke, in fact, begins by seeming something sizeable, but it vanishes in no time. Martial's lines run: 'To sell about the palace no empty smoke, nor applaud Canus, nor applaud Glaphyrus.' So it comes about that we talk of 'smoke and clouds' when we mean a display which is all deceit, and the vain hope of great things. St Jerome[2] against Rufinus: 'From such a forest of books you cannot produce one sprig, one bush. These are mere puffs of smoke, mere clouds.' Rufinus had reproached Jerome with having brought the works of the poets like smoke to the notice of nuns who were not likely to understand them. But Jerome takes the proverb like a clumsily hurled weapon and thrusts it back more skilfully, indicating that the word 'smoke' does not mean obscurity, but vain, false ostentation. Plutarch,[3] 'On the Divine Sign of Socrates': 'But he sent off nonsense to the sophists, as a kind of smoke of philosophy.'

This kind of man, the greatest plague of kingly courts, is neatly and excellently described by Aelius Lampridius[4] in his life of the emperor Heliogabalus. I should like to quote his very words: 'Zoticus,' he says, 'was of such importance under him, that he was regarded by all the highest officials of the court as if he had been the mate of their master. It was this same Zoticus, as well, who making bad use of his familiarity used to sell for bribes all the actions and words of Heliogabalus, hoping for enormous riches from this "smoke," as he made promises to one and another and deceived them all. Leaving the presence of Heliogabalus he interviewed them one by one, saying "I said this about you," "I heard this about you," "This is what is going to happen to you." There are men of this kind, who if they are admitted to too great familiarity with princes, sell the reputation not only of the bad princes but of the good ones; and who live on the proceeds of their infamous scandal-mongering, through the stupidity or innocence of the rulers who do not perceive what is going on.' Thus far Aelius. But the adage is given greater point by the punishment of Thurinus Verconius,[5] which the same Aelius recounts in his life of Alexander Severus in this manner: 'When alone, in the afternoon or in the early morning, he never saw certain people because he knew that they told lies about him, especially Verconius Thurinus, who had been his close companion. This man had put up everything for sale by his deceptions, with the result of dishonouring the rule of Alexander, as if he were a stupid man whom Thurinus had in his power and whom he could persuade to everything. Indeed he convinced everybody that he could do anything by a nod. In the end Alexander caught him by a stratagem. He sent someone to him who was asking publicly for a favour, and approaching Thurinus for it in private, as if asking for his support in interesting Alexander in him in secret. This was done, and Thurinus promised to use his influence, and said that he had spoken to the emperor when he had not spoken at all, but left it to be thought that the request might yet be granted, selling the outcome for money. Alexander ordered him to be spoken to again, and Thurinus, as if thinking of something else, assented by a nod, but still did not say anything. The request was granted, and Thurinus the "seller of smoke" exacted a huge reward from the man who had won his case. Alexander ordered him to be accused, and when everything had been proved by witnesses, those who were present when he had been paid and those who had heard his promises, the emperor ordered him to be tied to a stake in the Passage Market[6] and a fire to be made from burning straw and damp wood, which killed him. Meanwhile the herald proclaimed, "By smoke he is punished, who sold smoke." But as he did not wish to seem cruel in even one case, he made diligent enquiries before pronouncing sentence, and found that Thurinus had accepted bribes from both parties in lawsuits, putting up the result for sale; and from all who had received lucrative posts or provinces.' And a little further on: 'He gave no one of these "sellers of smoke" the chance to speak ill of him, or of others to him, particularly after the death of Thurinus, who had often betrayed him as if he were stupid and senseless.' The phrase he uses, Passage Market or 'open market,' he seems to explain himself in another part of the same Life, when he says: 'The man who "sold smoke" about him, and had accepted a hundred gold pieces from a certain soldier, he ordered to be crucified, beside the road frequently used by his slaves on their way to the imperial estates.' 'The Emperor Avidius Cassius,' we read,[7] 'thought out this kind of punishment, by making a tall wooden stake a hundred and eighty feet high, and tying the criminals on it from the top to the bottom, setting fire to the lowest, so that some were burnt and others killed by the torment of the smoke and even by fear.' Thus far the historian.

A horrible punishment, yet fitting for such heinous crimes. But I could wish it were not true today that the Courts, not only of princes but of bishops were full of this detestable kind of people, and had not only a lot of men like Thurinus but much worse than he; who not only sell an office falsely promised, but even sell silence itself, as it were copying Demosthenes;[8] or indeed, what is still worse, they use the poison of the tongue to thwart those whose bribes they have accepted for their good offices. If only our princes would take care to imitate Alexander Severus. He was a pagan moreover, and a Syrian by race, and a mere youth, and yet he was so violently opposed to flatterers, informers, dishonest judges, sellers of smoke, and all such pests of Courts, that he was implacable towards them, though otherwise a man of the mildest character.

There is a proverbial saying bandied about in our own time regarding the splendid promises of courtiers. For they talk of 'court incense,' thinking of that incense-vapour which is wafted in our sacred rites from a swinging censer. That is not very different from our proverb. They speak too of the 'holy water' of courtiers, thinking of the water which is placed at the door of churches, for those to sprinkle themselves with who go in or come out.

1 4.5.7–8
2 *Against Rufinus* 3.39 (*PL* 23.484C)
3 *Moralia* 580B
4 *Heliogabalus* 10.2–4
5 *Severus Alexander* 35.5–36.3, 67.2, 23.8
6 The Forum Transitorium, a landmark in the heart of ancient Rome, was so called because it connected the Forum of Augustus with that of Vespasian; Erasmus' explanation of the name seem to be imaginary.
7 Vulcacius Gallicanus *Avidius Cassius* 4.3
8 Demosthenes was said to have taken bribes not to speak; mentioned in *Adages* I vii 19, citing Aulus Gellius 11.9.1.

I iii 68
Hinc illae lachrymae / Hence those tears

In English writing up to the eighteenth century one is more apt to find this proverb in Latin (Otto 904) than in English. Thus, in Henry Fielding's Tom

Jones (1749), VIII, *iv, a conversation between Tom and the learned barber Benjamin: '"I conjecture," says Jones, "that thou art a very comical fellow." "You mistake me widely, sir," said the barber, "I am too much addicted to the study of philosophy,* hinc illae lachrymae, *sir, that's my misfortune. Too much learning hath been my ruin."' There was also an English version of the proverb in circulation (Tilley* T *82).*

In the *Andria* of Terence[1] there is a phrase which seems a proverbial allusion borrowed by Horace,[2] 'hence those tears.' Cicero[3] made use of it in his speech in defence of Marcus Caelius: 'Hence those tears, indeed, and this is the cause of all those offences and criminal charges.' It may be said, when the reason for something has remained long concealed and at last the truth is discovered. For instance, suppose someone said that the barbarians despise Greek learning for fear, of course, they themselves should appear uneducated; he could usefully add 'hence those tears' that is, because it makes them uncomfortable. This sort of allusion often appears in good authors; and it takes on a proverbial function even if there is no proverbial metaphor present. Of this kind is the often-repeated Homeric phrase[4] in Cicero's *Letters to Atticus*: 'I fear the Trojans.'

1 *Andria* 126
2 *Epistles* 1.19.41
3 *Pro M. Caelio* 25.61
4 *Iliad* 6.442, cited in Cicero *Letters to Atticus* 2.5.1 and elsewhere

I iii 86
Omnium horarum homo / A man for all hours

A standard English version, 'A man for all seasons,' appears in Robert Whittinton's Vulgaria *(1520). The phrase became attached to Thomas More by Erasmus himself in the preface to the* Praise of Folly, *published three years after this little essay first appeared in the* Adages *of 1508. Robert Bolt's play (published 1961) and film (1966) on Thomas More has kept the English phrase famous. As Erasmus shows, the adage was used by many writers in antiquity (see also Otto 830). He first listed it in* Collectanea *no 760.*

The man who suits himself to seriousness and jesting alike, and whose company is always delightful – that is the man the ancients called 'a man for all hours.' Quintilian[1] tells us that Asinius Pollio was called so. In Suetonius,[2] Tiberius used to call two of his boon companions the merriest of men, and friends for all hours, even in his imperial orders. A friend of this kind is depicted, with vividness and grace, by Ennius,[3] in the person of Geminus Servilius. Although the poem is preserved in the *Attic Nights* of Aulus Gellius, book 12 chapter 4, I have pleasure in transcribing it here:

When he had spoken thus, he called the man
Who shared with him his table and his talk,
And all he had; with whom at close of day,
Wearied with counsel and affairs of state,
He might with jesting tell things great and small
And pour out all he thought and know it safe;
A mind to which he turned with full delight
In public and private, never swayed
By others' views to doing wrong, but light
Of heart, and without malice; learned and loyal;
A man of pleasant ways and power of speech,
Happy, contented with his own, and shrewd,
Speaking a word in season, ready with help,
Sparing with talk, retentive; prizing high
The value of the buried years of old,
Keeping old ways but not despising new,
Wise in the ancient laws of gods and men,
Able to speak but also hold his peace.

Such a one among philosophers is said to have been Aristippus,[4] who did not refuse to obey the command of Dionysius and dance with the rest in the purple worn by women, though Plato objected, adding that even in Bacchanalia one should behave with modesty. Hence Horace[5] says: 'Every colour became Aristippus.' Those on the other hand who have their own code of behaviour and do not find it easy to live with anyone else, are said to be 'men of few men,' as Terence[6] says. In Horace:[7] 'He lacks, we say, the common feelings of a man.'

1 6.3.110, on Asinius Pollio, one of the leading political and literary figures of the first century BC
2 *Tiberius* 42
3 *Annals* 234–50, cited by Aulus Gellius 12.4.4
4 The Cyrenaic philosopher (fifth/fourth century BC); anecdote from Diogenes Laertius 2.78
5 *Epistles* 1.17.23
6 *Eunuchus* 409
7 *Satires* 1.3.66

I iv 30
Omnem movere lapidem / To leave no stone unturned

This proverb is for us a widely circulated cliché (Tilley S 890). The Latin literally means 'to move every stone.' Erasmus' learning here is exemplary (though Tosi 912 lists even more sources). First listed in Collectanea *no 449.*

Πάντα λίθον κίνει, Leave no stone unturned: that is, try everything, leave nothing unattempted. Many writers[1] say that this adage arose in the following way. When Xerxes made war on the Greeks, and was vanquished at Salamis, he himself moved away from there but left Mardonius behind to carry on the war in his name. When the latter had also been worsted in the fight at Plataeae, and had taken flight, a rumour got about that Mardonius had left an immense treasure buried in the ground near his tent. Incited by this prospect, Polycrates, a Theban, bought that piece of ground. However, when he had looked for the treasure long and thoroughly, and had made no progress, he consulted the oracle of Delphi, as to how he could find that money. Apollo replied in these words 'Leave no stone unturned.' As soon as he had done this, he found, they say, a great hoard of gold. Others think the metaphor comes from those who hunt for crabs along the seashore; for the crabs usually lie hidden under rocks which the people looking for them move.

The adage is also found[2] with the word rock *petra* instead of stone *lapis*, Πάντα κινήσω πέτρον, meaning 'I'll risk everything.' Euripides[3] in the *Heraclidae*, where the phrase means 'to leave nothing undone.' Pliny the Younger[4] in one of his letters: 'I make straight for the throat and concentrate on that. He certainly concentrates on his chosen target, but he often makes a bad choice. I pointed out that it might be the knee or shin or ankle when he thought he had the throat. I can't see the throat, I said, so my method is to feel my way and try everything – in fact I leave no stone unturned.' St Basil[5] to his nephews: 'For the preparations for our journey, we must, as they say, leave no stone unturned.'

Perhaps Theocritus[6] is alluding to this in his *Boucoliastae*: 'And from the line she moves the stone.' He is speaking of Galatea wantonly trying everything to make Polyphemus angry with her; I have mentioned this elsewhere.[7] The commentator[8] points out that this is a proverb and means the same as 'to shake out every rope.' He adds that the metaphor comes from some sort of game in which a player who cannot vanquish his opponent by any other means moves from the back line a piece called the 'king.' However, what he says about the stone statue which Galatea could move by her beauty is more far-fetched, in my opinion.

1 Zenobius 5.63 (who provides the anecdote), Suidas Π 223; also Diogenianus 5.41
2 Diogenianus 7.42
3 *Heraclidae* 1002
4 *Letters* 1.20.14–15 (trans Betty Radice); Pliny uses the proverb in Greek, which never was absorbed into Latin.
5 *Ad adulescentes* 10 (*PG* 31.588C)
6 6.18
7 *Adages* I i 25, I ix 97
8 Ancient commentator on the passage in Theocritus' eclogues; 'to shake out every rope' is the next proverb discussed in the *Adages*, I iv 31.

I iv 35
Asinus ad lyram / An ass to the lyre

This proverb was well known in the Renaissance. It first appeared in Collectanea *no 125 but was expanded in the later editions. Erasmus could have used the Greek proverb collections (Zenobius 5.42, Diogenianus 7.33, and Suidas* O *391), but there is no evidence here that he did (there are Latin variations; Otto 183–4). This appears in the* Adages *in a sequence with similar proverbs (36 'The pig heard the trumpet,' 37 'A jackdaw has no business with a lute,' 38 'A pig has nothing to do with marjoram,' and 39*, 'What has a dog to do with a bath?' which follows). A parallel for us* *is the biblical 'Pearls before swine' (Matthew 7:6), not included by Erasmus. The English version is 'To see an ass play on a harp' (Tilley A 366), which follows more from the second part of Erasmus' essay.*

Ὄνος λύρας, An ass [we must supply, listening] to the lyre. This is a hit at people who lack judgment through their ignorance, people who have dull ears. Varro[1] gave this proverbial title to one of his *Satires.* In Gellius are to be found these words of his, extracted from the satire entitled *The Will*: 'If an only son, or more than one, is born to me in ten months, and if they turn out to be asses at the lyre, they shall be disinherited'; meaning by this phrase unteachable, as far as good learning is concerned, and unmanageable. St Jerome[2] to Marcella: 'Although I could justifiably set these people aside, since it is useless for the lyre to play to the ass, yet lest they accuse us of pride, as they usually do ...' and again, against Vigilantius: 'Although it is a stupid thing that I am doing, to seek masters for the master of all, and to place a restraint on him, who does not know how to speak and cannot keep silent. There is a true proverb in Greek, An ass to the lyre.' Lucian[3] *On Salaried Posts*: 'For what communication can there be, as they say, between the ass and the lyre?' And *Against an Ignoramus*: 'But you are an ass listening to the lyre and wagging your ears.' Hence the adage is used in this form, 'the ass twitching its ears,' or again, 'Someone told a story to an ass, and it twitched its ears.' This is turned against those people who understand nothing, and yet make play with nods and smiles to those who are talking, as if there were nothing they did not understand. It is natural to the donkey to twitch its ears as if to convey that it has understood, when it has not even heard.

Sometimes applied to the ass not listening to the lyre, but trying to play itself. Lucian: 'Especially when he plays, he wants to appear merry and charming, an ass, as they say, himself playing on the lyre.' Again in *Pseudologista*: 'As they popular saying goes, an ass seeing the lyre and trying to play.' This line is also quoted: 'The donkey listened to the lyre, the porker to the trumpet.' This can be applied to people who make an unseemly attempt to follow a craft of which they have no experience, having rather a natural unfitness for it. Stratonicus turns it round amusingly in Athenaeus,[4] *Doctors at Dinner*, book 8: There was a certain Cleon, nicknamed the Bull, who sang well, but had not an equal knowledge of the lyre. When Stratonicus heard him play, he said, 'There was an old saying about an ass at the lyre, but now it's the bull at the lyre.'

1 Varro, *Menippean Satires* 543, cited in Gellius, *Attic Nights*, 3.16.13
2 *Letters* 27.1.2 and 61.4.1
3 *On Salaried Posts* 25, *Against an Ignoramus* 4, *Dialogues of Courtesans* 14.4, *False Speaking* 7
4 8.349c–d

I iv 39
Quid cani et balneo? / What has a dog to do with a bath?

The proverb may come from Suidas T *584, but it seems merely to be an excuse for this long, enthusiastic, yet digressive essay. It appears in the* Adages *in a series of other contradictions (see preceding headnote). There seems to be no English equivalent.*

Though Erasmus now and then mentions contemporaries, this lengthy tribute to a single individual is unique in the whole of the Adages *(a shorter version appeared in* Collectanea *no 25). Rudolphus Agricola (1444–85), an early northern humanist, was an important figure in the reform of learning in the late fifteenth century. Immensely learned, as Erasmus describes, his principal work was his* De inventione dialectica libri tres *(Three Books on Discovery in Dialectic), published posthumously in 1521. In the late Middle Ages, dialectic was a logical system of proof taught to scholars in the university. Agricola, however, was drawn to classical rhetoric, the non-logical art of persuasion, which began with 'invention' or 'discovery' (the structuring of arguments using 'common places' which through their aptness and attractive power have the power to convince the listener of a particular position). His treatise is an complex attempt to synthesize logic and rhetoric. It had a great impact on Renaissance education, which quickly shifted about this time from the medieval emphasis on logic to a more literary approach. Erasmus, of course, was one of the prime movers of this shift, and the* Adages *itself is a rich source of commonplace material. Erasmus studied at Deventer with Alexander Hegius, the former pupil of Agricola, and here sees himself as a direct descendant of the two. For more on Agricola, whom Erasmus so greatly admired, see* Contemporaries of Erasmus *I 15–17.*

Τί κοινὸν κυνὶ καὶ βαλανείῳ; What has a dog to do with a bath? I quote this adage with all the more pleasure because it refreshes and renews my memory, and my affection, for Rodolphus Agricola of Friesland, whom I name as the man in all Germany and Italy most worthy of the highest public honour: in Germany, because she gave him birth, in Italy, because she made him a great scholar. No one was ever born this side of the Alps more completely endowed with all literary gifts; let this be said without prejudice.

There was no branch of fine learning in which that great man could not vie with the most eminent masters. Among the Greeks he was the best Greek of them all, among the Latins the best Latin. As a poet you would have said he was a second Virgil; as a writer of prose he had the charm of a Poliziano, but more dignity. His style, even extempore, had such purity, such naturalness, that you would maintain it was not a Frisian who spoke, but a native of ancient Rome herself. Such perfect eloquence was paired with the same degree of learning. He had delved into all the mysteries of philosophy. There was no part of music in which he was not accurately versed. At the very end of his life he had bent his whole mind on the study of Hebrew and the Holy Scripture. In the midst of these efforts he was snatched from this world by the envy of the fates, not yet forty years old, as I am told. There are a few literary remains of his work, some letters, poems of various kinds; the *Axiochus* of Plato translated into Latin, and a version of Isocrates' *To Demonicus*. Then there are a couple of lectures given in public session in the University of Ferrara, for it was there he both learnt and gave open lectures. There were lying hidden in some people's possession his treatises on dialectic, and they have recently appeared,[1] but in a mutilated state. He had also translated some of Lucian's dialogues. But since he himself cared little for glory, and most mortals are, to say the least of it, careless in looking after the work of others, none of these have yet seen the light. But the works which are extant, even if not published by himself, give plain proof of something divine about the man.

Let it not be thought that I as a German am blinded by patriotic feeling; to avoid this I will transcribe the epitaph written for him by Ermolao Barbaro[2] of Venice. It is superb, and one might find it difficult to decide whether it was more worthy of the man who wrote it or the man it was written about. Here it is:

Under this stone, the jealous Fates decreed
The Frisian hope, his country's light, should come,
Rudolph Agricola; in life, indeed,
He brought such praise to Germany his home
As ever Greece could have, or ever Rome.

What ampler or more magnificent tribute could be paid to our dear Rodolphus than this splendid testimony, so complete, and offered not to a living man but to one already dead – so there is no question of its proceeding from affection rather than from judgment? and to a German, so there is no possibility that love for a country they both shared should diminish the weight of the testimony? And it came from that man who had brought glory not only to his native Italy, but to this whole age of ours; whose authority is such among all learned men that it would be most impertinent to disagree with him; whose work in restoring literature is so outstandingly valuable that anyone would have to be utterly impervious to culture, or at least utterly ungrateful, who did not hold the memory of Ermolao as sacrosanct.

Such full and ungrudging praise of this man has, I confess, a singular charm for me, because I happened while yet a boy to have his disciple Alexander Hegius as my teacher. He was headmaster of the once famous school of the town of Deventer, where I learned the rudiments of both languages when I was almost a child. To put it in a few words, he was a man just like his master: as upright in his life as he was serious in his teaching. Momus[3] himself could have found no fault in him except one, that he cared less for fame than he need have done, and took no heed of posterity. If he wrote anything, he wrote as if he were playing a game rather than doing something serious. And yet these writings, so written, are of the sort which the learned world votes worthy of immortality.

So it was not without thought that I plunged into this digression; not to boast of the glory of Germany, but to perform the duty of a grateful pupil, and acquit myself of the debt I owe to the memory of both these men, because I owe to one the loving respect of a son, and to the other the affection of a grandson.

Now to turn to the adage, which I remember having learnt from a certain very learned letter of my beloved Rodolphus, at a time when I was a mere child and as yet ignorant of Greek. In this letter he is trying to persuade the town council of Antwerp, with conviction and eloquence, that they should appoint as master of their school someone proficient in liberal studies, and not (as they usually do) entrust this office to an inarticulate theologian or naturalist, the sort of man who is sure he has something to say about everything but has no notion of what it is to speak. 'What good would he be in a school? As much good, to use the Greek repartee, as a dog in a bath.'

Lucian[4] *Against an Ignoramus*: 'And each one of the onlookers immediately voices that very handy proverb: what do a dog and a bath have in common?' Again in the *Parasite*: 'But to my way of thinking, a philosopher at a drinking-party is just like a dog in a bath.' So this is to be applied to those who are totally useless for certain purposes, just as there is no use for dogs in a bath.

1 In the early editions of the *Adages*, Erasmus had written 'are lying hidden' but the *De inventione dialectica* was finally published in 1521 in Strasbourg, so in 1526 Erasmus changed the wording.

2 Well-known Italian humanist (1454–95)

3 Momus was the Greek god of ridicule.

4 *Against an Ignoramus* 5 and *Parasite* 51

I iv 45
Undas numeras / You are counting the waves

This proverb, apparently taken directly from Theocritus, continues the series of proverbs devoted to impossible tasks (a kind of metaphor called adynaton, *used by many ancient poets, and discussed by Erasmus in his introduction, section xiii). The immediately preceding proverb (referred to here) is 'You are measuring the sands.'*

Κύματα μετρεῖς, You are counting the waves. This had the same meaning as the previous one, and both are elegantly touched on by Virgil[1] in the second book of his *Georgics*:

If you wish to know their number, go and tot up the grains
Of sand that are whirled around by a sand-storm in the Sahara,
Or count the waves that break along Adriatic coasts
When an easterly gale comes down in gusts upon the shipping.

Theocritus[2] in *The Graces*: But is like the toil of measuring the waves on the beach / As many as the wind drives shoreward from the sea.' This seems to have come from an Aesopic fable recounted by Lucian[3] in his *Sects*. Once a man sat by the seashore, trying to count the waves one by one; but he was defeated by the waves following close on other waves, and distressed in his mind because he could not number them. Then a crafty fox encouraged him with a timely piece of advice. 'Why are you distressed,' it said, 'about the waves which pass? You should begin counting from here, and consider the rest as finished with.'

1 *Georgics* 2.105–8 (trans C. Day Lewis)
2 16.60–1
3 *Hermotimus* 84; cf Aesop 60 Halm.

I iv 50
Aethiopem lavas: Aethiopem dealbas / You wash the Ethiopian

Still continuing the series of overwhelmingly difficult or impossible tasks, this one having become a common Renaissance proverb in many languages, including English (Tilley E *186; it is used by the playwrights Dekker and Webster). The story is in Aesop, Pliny, Lucian, and others, the proverb reported in Suidas* AI *125, Zenobius 1.46, and Apostolius 1.68 (see also Otto 32). As sometimes happens in the massive* Adages, *Erasmus repeats a proverb: so, at* III *x 88* we find* Aethiops non albescit, *'The Ethiopian does not become white,' again using the Aesop fable, but in a later edition (1533) adding lines*

You wash the Ethiopian The main figure is black in this picture from Andrea Alciato's *Book of Emblems* (emblem 59, here in the edition of Paris 1540, p 89). He was coloured white in the first (unauthorized) edition of 1531. The epigram, derived from Lucian, the same source used by Erasmus, translates 'Why do you wash, in vain, the Ethiopian? Oh forebear: no one can brighten the darkness of black night.' Erasmus treats this proverb twice, at I iv 50* and III x 88*. (Thomas Fisher Rare Book Library, University of Toronto)

by the Greek writer Lucian, from Greek Anthology *11.428. The proverb gained wide circulation through the* Emblems *of Andrea Alciato (no 59), who translated Lucian's poem from the* Greek Anthology *into Latin under the title 'Impossible' (see accompanying figure). For many sixteenth-century Europeans, the blackness of the Ethiopian would have been a cause for curiosity and suspicion, not yet the sign of cultural inferiority that it was to become by the eighteenth century and the rise of African slavery. Even so, Erasmus' explanation of the proverb ('doubtful morality decorated by a gloss of words') is moving in the direction of intolerance.*

These expressions have the same meaning: Αἰθίοπα σμήχεις, You are washing an Ethiopian, and Αἰθίοπα λευκαίνεις, You are whitening an Ethiopian. Lucian,[1] *Against an Ignoramus*: 'And according to the proverb I am trying to wash an Ethiopian.' That inborn blackness of the Ethiopian, which Pliny[2] thinks to be a result of heat from the nearness of the sun, cannot be washed away with water nor whitened by any means whatsoever. This will be particularly apposite when a matter of doubtful morality is decorated by a gloss of words, or when praise is given to one who does not deserve praise, or an unteachable person is being taught. The adage, it seems, comes from a fable of Aesop.[3] A man bought an Ethiopian, and thinking his colour was not natural, but the result of a former master's negligence, he tried everything which is used to whiten clothes, and so tormented the poor creature with perpetual washing that he made the man ill – but he still stayed the colour he had always been.

1 *Against an Ignoramus* 28
2 *Natural History* 2.189, 6.70
3 13 Halm

I iv 56
In aqua scribis / You write in water

The idea of writing in water is a common metaphor in English poetry for futility; for the proverb see Tilley W *114 (and also Tosi 1417). The proverb was in* Collectanea *(610). The quotation from Catullus, a well-known passage, is interestingly a fairly late addition (1520).*

Καθ' ὕδατος γράφεις, or εἰς ὕδωρ γράφεις, You write in water, that is, you are wasting your time. Lucian[1] in *The Tyrant*: 'Are you joking, Charon, or are you, as they say, writing in water, if you expect anything in the way of an obol from Micyllus?' Plato[2] in the *Phaedrus*: 'Will he not then write these things carefully in black water, sowing with his pen?' There is a line of verse to this effect among the Greek maxims:[3] 'The oaths of wicked men are writ in water.' Xenarchus misquotes this in his *Pentathlon*, cited by Athenaeus[4] in his tenth book: 'To me, a woman's oath is writ in wine.' And then Catullus:[5] 'What a woman says to her ardent lover should be written in wind and in running water.'

1 *Tyrant* (or *Cataplus*) 21
2 *Phaedrus* 276c
3 Menander *Sententiae* 26
4 Xenarchus was a writer of Greek New Comedy, and this is a fragment from his work (6 ed Kock), here cited by Athenaeus 10.441E.
5 70.3–4

I iv 57
In arena aedificas / You are building on the sand

This is one of the very few proverbs taken by Erasmus directly from the Bible, in this case Matthew 7:26 (in Luke 6:49 the image is of a house built upon 'earth'). It is a common poetic motif (Spenser's House of Pride is built upon 'a sandie hill'; see also Tilley S 88). The sequence of hopeless tasks continues.

Εἰς ψάμμον οἰκοδομεῖς, You are building on the sand. The parable in the Gospel seems to allude to this. What one has built on the sand does not remain firm. This can be appropriately applied when someone has undertaken a piece of work which is bound to be useless, because the foundations have not been properly laid.

I iv 95
Folio ficulno tenes anguillam / You are holding an eel in a fig-leaf

Though 'slippery as an eel' (which appears in a list in his De copia *[CWE 24 394]) is still with us, without Erasmus' explanation this proverb (from Dio-*

genianus 8.55) is quite mysterious. The allusiveness and mystery are played on in Alciato's well-known emblem poem 'On One Having Been Caught,' no 21 in his Book of Emblems*: 'For a long time wherever you fled, I pursued you: but now you are finally trapped in my snare. No longer will you be able to elude my power. I've caught the eel in a fig-leaf.' See also III vi 79* 'To hunt eels.' This proverb (Tilley E 62) is near the end of the sequence of futile tasks (eg, I iv 87 'You are singing, or telling a story to the deaf,' I iv 89 'You are speaking to a stone,' I iv 97 'You teach a dolphin to swim,' etc).*

Τῷ θρίῳ τὴν ἔγχελυν, (we must supply, You are holding) the eel in the fig-leaf. This is a little different:[1] used when an otherwise evasive, slippery person is held by a grip too tight for him to escape. A fig-leaf has a rough surface, so much so that Plutarch[2] wrote that its name was synonymous with harshness; and for that reason perfectly adapted for keeping hold of a slippery eel.

1 'A little different' that is from the two preceding, I iv 93 'You are tying a dolphin by a tail' and I iv 94 'You are holding an eel by the tail.'

2 Plutarch *Moralia* 684B (Mynors: it is not clear why the Greek word *thrion* for fig-leaf should suggest roughness)

I V 4
Evitata Charybdi in Scyllam incidi / Having escaped Charybdis I fell into Scylla

Erasmus greatly expands his discussion from Collectanea *(378) to give a very full explanation of what is still a common proverb in many European languages, in English appearing somewhat differently as 'Between Scylla and Charybdis' (Tilley S 169; see also Tosi 1557 and Otto 382). In the* De copia *(CWE 24 639) Erasmus sees Charybdis as a figure of 'insatiable gluttony or woman's inexhaustible lust.' The more modern 'Between a rock and a hard place,' not in Tilley or* ODEP*, but listed in* OED *('Rock' I.2.g) as an American slang expression suggests a similar situation between two dreadful alternatives. Another analogue is 'to fall out of the frying pan into the fire'; this is close to the next proverb, I v 5 'Fleeing from the smoke, I fell into the fire.'*

Τὴν Χάρυβδιν ἐκφυγὼν τῇ Σκύλλῃ περιέπεσον, I escaped Charybdis but fell into Scylla. These are iambic dimeters, *akephaloi*[1] whether produced by chance or created by art is uncertain. The meaning is this: 'While I was avoiding a more serious evil I fell into a different one'. The adage comes from the story in Homer,[2] which tells how Ulysses sailed too close to Scylla for fear of Charybdis, and lost six of his crew. Some say that Scylla was the daughter of Nisus king of the Megarians, who for stealing her father's golden lock of hair was changed into this sea-monster, as Pausanias[3] tells in his book on Corinth. Virgil[4] seems to agree with this in the *Bucolics*, when he says

Or what shall I say of Scylla, Nisus' child,
Whom story pictures as a lovely woman
Ringed round with howling monsters to her waist,
Her sea-dogs' fangs tearing the trembling sailors?

Servius states that Scylla was the daughter of Phorcus and the nymph Crateis. When Glaucus fell in love with her, Circe, who had a passion for him, saw that he was fonder of Scylla than of herself, and mixed magic poison in the spring where the nymph was accustomed to bathe. When she stepped down into it, she was changed from the waist downwards into a variety of shapes. For this was the special quality of Circe, to change human beings into the shape of beasts. Hating her deformity she flung herself into the sea, and became the subject of the legend.

Where the truth lies, opinion differs among writers. Sallust[5] thinks there was a rock jutting out into the sea, which looked like the shape of a woman to anyone who saw it from a distance, and the waves dashing against it seemed to imitate the sound of wolves howling and dogs barking, so it was imagined that she was girdled from the waist down with such wild animals. In the Greek collections[6] I find that there was a trireme, a particularly fleet one, called *Scylla*, from *skyleuein*, to despoil, because the pirates who lurked in her infested the Tyrrhenian and Sicilian seas and whenever they overtook other ships, despoiled them: hence the story arose. As to Charybdis, the fables of the poets tell that she was a ravenous woman who stole the oxen of Hercules and was struck by Jove's thunderbolt, and flung into the sea, there to become a monster which retains its previous nature to this day. For it swallows up everything, and what it has swallowed is driven towards the shore round Taormina, according to Sallust. Thus Horace[7] gives the proverbial name Charybdis to a greedy courtesan of insatiable covetousness:

Wretched youth,
In what a great Charybdis art thou caught,
Lad worthy of a better flame.

Servius says Scylla is in Italy, Charybdis in Sicily. In the *Aeneid* Book 3, Virgil[8] has a beautiful description of the narrow strait between the two perils:

Once on a time, they say, these two lands were a single
Country; then there came a convulsion of nature which tore them
Hugely asunder – the ages can bring such immense geological
Change – and the sea rushed violently in between them, dividing
Italy from Sicily, severing their coasts and washing
Cities and fields on either side with a narrow strait.
Scylla guards the right shore, insatiable Charybdis
The left.

and the same elsewhere: '– not to attempt the passage, there being on either side / So narrow a margin of safety.' In the *Odyssey* Book 12, Homer[9] describes the double danger at great length, and makes Circe warn Ulysses to keep his course nearer to Scylla than to Charybdis, because it would be better to lose six of his crew than have them all perish; she assures him that Charybdis is more hazardous than Scylla:

Heaven keep you from being there when she sucks the waves in her jaws,
For not even Neptune could save you from such disaster.
No; you must hug Scylla's rock and speedily drive your ship by;
It is better you should have to mourn the loss of six
Of your company, than that of your whole crew.

The adage can be used in three ways. First, when we give a warning that if a point is reached where we are in such straits that there is no escape without cost, we must choose the lesser of the two evils, following the example of Ulysses, and tend to the side where the loss is slighter. For instance, if someone is in danger of losing his money or his safety, he chooses to have his money in danger rather than his life, because the loss of possessions can be repaired in one way or another, but life once lost can never be restored. Secondly, we may use it to point out that a transaction is double-sided and dangerous, and that it needs the utmost prudence to keep from erring on either side. In this case there will be no question of deciding which is the greater risk; but this at least is clear, that on each side there is great danger. An example of the first would be, 'Remember it is far better to incur expense through Scylla than to lose health in Charybdis.' It is preferable to have a financial loss, to run into Scylla as it were, than to fall into the Charybdis of dishonour. Of the second: 'Take care to please the people in such a way that you do not offend the ruler. Do your business with caution and circumspection, remembering that you are steering a course between Scylla and Charybdis.' Thirdly, you could turn it the other way, like this: 'By being afraid to seem not very learned, you have brought on yourself the reputation of arrogance; that is exactly what is meant by avoiding Scylla and falling into Charybdis.' In Latin this line is famous, whoever was the author[10] (at present it does not come to mind): 'Into Scylla he fell, in hopes of avoiding Charybdis.'

1 'headless,' referring to a metrical line in which the first syllable is omitted
2 *Odyssey* 12.235–46
3 2.34.7
4 *Eclogues* 6.74–5 and 77, with the commentary by Servius
5 Sallust frag 4.27 of his lost *Histories* (first century BC), cited by Servius on *Aeneid* 3.414
6 Apostolius 16.49
7 *Odes* 1.27.18–20
8 *Aeneid* 3.414–21, 685–6 (trans C. Day Lewis)
9 *Odyssey* 12.106–10
10 A familiar proverbial line, identified by von Leutsch as the twelfth-century Gauthier de Châtillon *Alexandreis* 5.301

I V 18
Multa novit vulpes, verum echinus unum magnum / The fox knows many things, but the hedgehog one big thing

The English form of this proverb is probably best known today from the title of one book: Isaiah Berlin's The Hedgehog and the Fox: An Essay on Tolstoy's View of History *(1953). Yet the proverb circulated in English in the sixteenth century (Tilley* F *636). Erasmus could have found this in Suidas* Π *1931 as well as the Zenobius cited below. The Latin* echinus *meant both hedgehog and sea-urchin and 'urchin' in English used to have the same double sense; hence the apparent digression below. Animals and animal lore from the fable writers and from the writers on natural history (such as Pliny) provided many opportunities for moralizing proverbs such as this one.*

Πόλλ' οἶδ' ἀλώπηξ ἀλλ' ἐχῖνος ἓν μέγα, Many-sided the skill of the fox: the hedgehog has one great gift. Zenodotus[1] quotes this line from Archilochus. It is said about cunning people who are involved in various plots, or rather when we want to show how some people manage to do more with one piece of astuteness than others with their different schemes. The fox protects itself against the hunters by many and various wiles, and yet is often caught. The *echinus*, by which I take it he means the hedgehog (for in this place he is talking of the land-animal, not the sea-urchin[2]) by its one skill alone is safe from the bites of dogs; it rolls itself up with its spines into a ball, and cannot be snapped up with a bite from any side. In the same Zenodotus these lines are quoted from Ion of Chios, a tragic poet; and Athenaeus[3] quotes the same from the same in his *Table-talk*, from a tragedy entitled *Phoenicia:*

> But on land a lion's way I praise,
> But even more the hedgehog's wretched arts:
> When he perceives another creature's smell
> Rolling his spiny self into a ball
> He lies impregnable to touch and bite.

Plutarch[4] refers to the proverb and to the poem in his essay entitled 'Whether Land or Sea Animals are Cleverer.' I will give his words:

'The defending and guarding of their own safety by hedgehogs has provided the proverb: "The fox knows many things, but the hedgehog one big thing." For when the fox approaches, they say, "Rolling his spiny self into a ball, / He lies impregnable to touch and bite."' Plutarch, or whoever was the author of this work, mingled with the lines some words of his own; I say this so that no one will suspect me of the error. But it is Pliny[5] who described most fully the intelligence and astuteness of this animal (book 8 chapter 37): 'Hedgehogs also,' he says, 'prepare their food, and by rolling over the apples lying on the ground spike them on their spines; they take just one in their mouths and carry them into hollow trees. By retreating into their holes they foretell the change of wind from north to south. But when they know of the presence of a hunter, they contract snout, feet, and the whole of their underpart, which is covered with sparse and harmless hair, and they roll up into the shape of a ball, so that nothing can be taken hold of that is not spikes. When driven to desperation they void urine which corrodes their hinder parts and damages their spines.' Anyone who wishes to learn more about this must consult the reference I have given. This is the part which touches most closely on the sense of the proverb.

The sea-urchin also is famous for intelligence; forseeing the raging of the sea, it collects stones and weighs itself down with them, so that the weight will keep it from being easily shifted, and its spines will not be worn out with too much rolling. When sailors see this, they make fast their boats with several anchors. This is what Pliny says in book 9 chapter 31.

The fox is crafty, and knows a great many tricks, as many fables relate, especially this one, which is told by Plutarch[6] in his *Moralia*. Once, when the leopard was making a scornful comparison between himself and the fox, claiming that he had a coat of varying and many-coloured spots, the fox replied that while the leopard's ornamentation was on his skin, his own was in the mind. And truly it was much better to be endowed with cunning brains than with a party-coloured skin. The Greeks[7] call a clever and guileful person *poikilophrôn* and *poikilomêtis*; the Latin words are *vafer* and *versipellis*.

Another story[8] is told, not unlike this proverb: once the fox was talking to the cat, and boasting that he had so many skills at his disposal that one might say he had a bag of tricks; the cat replied that she had only one, to which she trusted in danger. While they were discussing this there was suddenly a noise of approaching hounds. The cat leapt up into a high tree, while the fox was encircled and caught by the pack of hounds. The moral of this story is that it is sometimes worth more to have one plan, if it is realistic and efficacious, than several wiles and trivial schemes. For instance, a poor man might court a girl with manifold devices, but a rich man would have one only, the one described by Ovid:[9] 'Say, "take what you like," you will say well.' The fox knows many things, but the hedgehog one big thing.

1 Zenobius 5.68
2 Erasmus explains the various words for hedgehog (Latin *ericius* or *herinaceus*, then *echinus* from the Greek *echinos*).
3 3.91d–e citing Ion of Chios frag 38 Nauck
4 *Moralia* 971E–F
5 *Natural History* 8.133–4; 9.100
6 *Moralia* 155B and 500C, referring to Aesop 42 Halm
7 In Greek, Mynors notes, words that mean mental agility are compounds of the word for 'many-coloured' *poikilos*; in Latin, a clever man can be described as one who changes his skin. The analogy between versatility of mind and variegation of colour has been built into the language.
8 Not a classical tale (Babrius and Phaedrus, ed Perry, no 605); it is found in La Fontaine's *Fables* 9.14.
9 *Art of Love* 2.161–3

I V 25
Auribus lupum teneo / I hold the wolf by the ears

In English today, we 'hold a tiger by the tail' but the meaning is very close, and the form 'He holds a wolf by the ears' is attested in sixteenth-century English (Tilley W 603). Erasmus first gave the proverb in Collectanea *no 164; it was well known in antiquity (Otto 987) and moved into other European languages (Tosi 1554). The parallel that Erasmus concludes with, 'Neither with thee can I live, nor yet without thee,' is another famous proverb found in Ovid, Martial, and Catullus (Tosi 1401).*

This is in the *Phormio* of Terence:[1] a young man, Antiphon, had a wife at home whom he could not throw out, either because he did not wish to, being desperately in love with her, or because it would

I hold the wolf by the ears An illustrated proverb from an early-sixteenth-century manuscript of moral instruction made for Francis I of France. The Latin, based on *Adages* I v 25*, translates as 'A person is holding a wolf, or some fierce animal that bites, by the ears when he becomes involved in the type of business that is not safe to abandon, and yet cannot be endured for long. For it is regarded as impossible to hold on to something forever, and the biting beast is hardly to be let out of one's hands without great danger' (Jean Michel Massing *Erasmian Wit and Proverbial Wisdom: An Illustrated Moral Compendium for François I* [London 1995] 80). (Courtesy of the Warburg Institute, University of London)

not have been upright to do so, since she had been adjudged to him by the pronouncement of the magistrates; but neither could he keep her, because of the violent resentment of his father. And when his cousin called him happy, because he possessed in his house what he loved, he answered 'It's all very well, I am holding the wolf by the ears, as they say. For I cannot see how I can send her away, nor do I know how to keep her.' Later the pander asserts (as if referring to the proverb) that he has the same experience with Phaedria, whom he can neither keep on, because he pays nothing, nor reject, because he is terribly charming and promises mountains of gold. Donatus[2] adds the Greek proverb in Greek words: 'I hold the wolf by the ears, and can neither keep him nor let him go.' Suetonius[3] in his life of Tiberius: 'The reason for delay was fear of the risks threatening on all sides, so that often he said he was holding the wolf by the ears.' Plutarch[4] in 'Precepts of Statecraft': 'A wolf, they say, cannot be held by the ears,' while men are particularly led by this part, that is by persuasion.

This is said about people who become involved in some affair which it would not be honest to abandon, and yet cannot be borne. It seems to have been derived from some event, like many other proverbs; or at any rate it springs from the fact that while the hare has very long ears and can easily be held by them, the wolf has ears which are short for its size, and there is no holding it in that way, but on the other hand it is most dangerous to let it escape from one's hands, since the beast has such a bite. Caecilius in Aulus Gellius,[5] book 15 chapter 9, has the same idea, but without the metaphor: 'For these are the worst friends, cheerful of face, / Dismal at heart, whom you can neither clasp nor let go.' Theognis[6] alludes to it, even more distantly: 'My heart's so strangely moved by love for you / That I can neither love nor can I hate.' An imitation of this, it seems, is the line[7] 'Not with thee can I live nor yet without thee.' Varro[8] also gives as an example of an adage: I hold the wolf by the ears.

1 *Phormio* 506–7
2 Donatus the commentator on *Phormio* 506
3 *Tiberius* 25.1 in *Lives*
4 'Precepts of Statecraft' in *Moralia* 802D
5 *Attic Nights* 15.9.1
6 Theognis 1091–2

7 Martial 12.46.2 (see also Ovid *Amores* 3.11.39 and Catullus 72.5–8, 75.3–4, 85.1–2, and in a different context, Strabo 14.2.24)
8 *On the Latin Language* 7.31

I V 38
Crambe bis posita mors / Twice-served cabbage is death

A very odd but well-known proverb in both Greek and Latin (Otto 454) that requires the kind of background explanation given here. Erasmus worked on this proverb essay for many years through many editions, beginning with Collectanea *no 20, adding material here and there (see editor's introduction, pp xv–xvi, xx). The proverb moved into English as the obscure 'Coleworts (or cabbage) twice sodden' (Tilley* C 511; ODEP, *97). There are also versions in Italian (Tosi 384). Elsewhere, in the* De copia, *Erasmus sees rewarmed cabbage as 'revolting' but not deadly (*CWE *24 387).*

Δὶς κράμβη θάνατος, Twice-served cabbage is death. Pliny,[1] book 20 chapter 9, lists *crambe* third among the species of *brassica*. Dioscorides,[2] book 2, gives three kinds of *crambe*. The first of these, besides being efficacious otherwise in a number of remedies, even takes away the troublesome results of drunkenness and intoxication, if you eat it raw with vinegar before the meal, as Marcus Cato[3] indicated. Aristotle[4] thinks that the reason for this is that being cold, and having a juice which is mild and dispersive, it draws the vinous liquor into the bowels and the thinner liquor slides into the bladder; the cabbage itself remains in the stomach and cools the body. Thus the humours are drawn off in both ways and the cooled body allows the tipsiness to wear off. There is however a special quality in cabbage, which resists wine, and if it is planted in a vineyard the wine is weaker. Thus it was an accepted custom with the Egyptians and Sybarites to eat cooked cabbage before everything else; the custom of some men was to take cabbage-seed from an amethystine goblet before drinking, so as to be able to indulge in wine without fear of intoxication.

Athenaeus,[5] book 1, says something like this, adding that in early times the cabbage and the radish were held to be the same thing. Theophrastus asserts that the grape-vine, even when growing, shuns the smell of radishes. But to return to the proverb.

Suidas[6] writes that cabbage used to be served at banquets in antiquity, but when recooked it produced such nausea that it became proverbial in Greek for aversion. Whenever they were describing something disagreeable repeated over and over again, not without disgust, they said 'twice cabbage is death' (that is, recooked). Poliziano[7] thinks that Juvenal was referring to this adage in his seventh Satire:

You teach rhetoric, O iron-hearted Vettius,
When your troop of many scholars slays the cruel tyrants.
For what each has just learnt in his seat
He stands and declaims, reciting the self-same things
In the self-same verses; served up again and again
The cabbage is the death of the unhappy masters.

He means by 'cabbage served up again' an utterly boring speech which has to be listened to over and over again. This is close to the phrase we quoted in another place[8] 'Corinthus son of Jove,' and it is the opposite of that other one, 'Beauty bears repeating twice and thrice.' Something lovely in itself still pleases, as Horace[9] says, even if repeated ten times. A foolish thing is tolerated at the first taste for the sake of novelty, but when repeated is hardly bearable and causes disgust.

Yet this plant was highly celebrated in early times, so much so that it was not without veneration, and for this reason was called *mantis*, a prophet. It was the custom to swear by it, especially among the Ionians, 'so help me, cabbage!' and this also might be seen as an origin for the proverb in the sense of aversion, as Athenaeus[10] says in *Doctors at Dinner*, book 9.

1 Pliny *Natural History* 20.79
2 Dioscorides *De materia medica* 2.120–2
3 Cato *De agri cultura* 156.1
4 Aristotle *Problemata* 3.17 (873a37)
5 1.34c–e, citing Theophrastus *History of Plants* 4.16.6
6 K 2318
7 *Miscellanea* c 33, citing Juvenal 7.150–4
8 *Adages* II i 50, I ii 49
9 *Art of Poetry* 365
10 9.370b (Mynors comments that cabbage is a 'prophet' because if your cabbage crop does well, your other vegetables will also prosper, or so Nicander, Athenaeus' source, seems to imply)

I v 65
Umbram suam metuere / To be afraid of one's own shadow

Erasmus used this twice in his early collection, the Collectanea *(nos 262, 400). It is a common English proverb (Tilley S 261) and besides Latin (Otto 1817) is also found in many other languages (Tosi 1602).*

Τὴν αὐτοῦ σκιὰν φοβεῖσθαι, To be afraid of one's own shadow. This is said of people who tremble like children when there is no danger at all. It comes either from those who catch sight of their own shadow and are suddenly frightened, or from the melancholics of whom Aristotle[1] speaks, who on account of weak spirits in the eye see something like an image of themselves in the surrounding air, and then they think they see their own ghosts. Socrates says in the *Phaedo* of Plato,[2] 'But you, afraid of your shadow, as they say,' that is, mistrusting yourself. Quintus to Cicero[3] on seeking the consulship: 'The other indeed, in heaven's name, of what distinction is he? First, of the same aristocracy as Catiline. Of greater? No, but in his valour. For this reason, Manius, the man who feared his own shadow, you will indeed despise.' This passage, however, was corrupted in the manuscripts in more ways than one. Plutarch,[4] decade 7 of the 'Table-talk,' 'The one who refuses and resents the name of "shadow" seems truly to be afraid of a shadow.' He is speaking of 'shadows' so called because they themselves were not invited by the host but followed an invited guest to the feast.

1 The passage in Aristotle not located (not by ASD either)
2 *Phaedo* 101d
3 Quintus Cicero *Commentariolum petitionis* 9
4 *Moralia* 709C; for shadows as uninvited guests, see *Adages* I i 9.

I vi 16
Ne sutor ultra crepidam / Let the cobbler stick to his last

A proverb on respecting one's limits. Literally, 'Let not the cobbler [judge] beyond his sole (or sandal)' (see Otto 462 and Tosi 543) but here translated to fit with the familiar English form ('Let not the cobbler go beyond his last' [Tilley C 480]). This proverb appears in sequence immediately after 'To learn the potter's art on a big jar,' that is, to learn a difficult task by practising on suitable material. This first appeared in Collectanea *no 153.*

Close to this is *Ne sutor ultra crepidam,* Let the cobbler stick to his last – let no one, that is, attempt to judge of matters which are far removed from his own skill and calling. This adage took its rise from Apelles, the famous painter, of whom Pliny,[1] book 35 chapter 10, tells the following story: 'When his work was finished, he would expose it in the porch to the view of passers-by, hiding behind the picture to listen to their comments on its faults, because he thought the public a more strict critic than himself; and they say that he was criticized by a cobbler for painting one loop too few on the inner side of a pair of sandals. Next day, finding his criticism had been attended to, the man went proudly on to criticize the drawing of a leg; and Apelles looked out indignantly and told him when passing judgment to stick to his last. These words became proverbial.' So much for Pliny. There is a similar story in Athenaeus:[2] Stratonicus the lyre-player said to a smith who was arguing with him about music 'Can't you see that you're not sticking to your hammer?' His nephew's remark[3] in his *Letters* points the same way, that no one can judge a work of art properly unless he too is an artist. And Aristotle's saying[4] in the first book of the *Ethics* that everyone is a proper judge of the things he knows about. Also what he wrote in the second book of the *Physics* of a blind man disputing about colours – words which have become proverbial among academics of our own day for disputing on subjects of which a man knows nothing. To the same opinion we may refer what Fabius Pictor[5] says in Quintilian, that the arts would be fortunate if none but artists were their critics.

1 Pliny *Natural History* 35.85

2 Athenaeus 8.351a

3 The 'nephew' refers to Pliny the Younger *Letters* 1.10.4.

4 *Nicomachean Ethics* 1.3 (1094b27) and *Physics* 2.1 (192a7) (compare Tilley M 80 'A blind man should judge no colours')

5 Fabius Pictor (the early annalist) is a mistake for Fabius Quintilianus, the rhetorical writer (for which see the *Institutes of Oratory* 12.10.50, the possible source), the mistake coming from Erasmus' misreading of Jerome *Letters* 66.9.2.

I vi 17
Dii facientes adiuvant / The gods help those who help themselves

Also in English as 'God helps those ...' (though the earlier form often runs somewhat differently as 'Help thyself and God will help thee' [Tilley G 236*]). Erasmus leaves the proverb in a classical form (Otto* 522*), and doesn't try to draw a Christian lesson from it.*

Varro[1] in his *Agriculture*, book I: 'And since, as they say, the gods help those who help themselves, I will invoke the gods first.' He indicates that divine help is commonly available, not to the idle, but to industrious men who try as hard as they can. To this I think we should refer those lines in Homer[2] which have already become proverbial: 'Some things, Telemachus, will you devise / In your own heart; some too will heaven suggest.' Cicero[3] used this in book 9 of his *Letters to Atticus*: 'You have to do everything unprepared, But nevertheless "some you'll devise, some too will heaven suggest."'

1 *Res rusticae* 1.1.4
2 *Odyssey* 3.26–7 (also *Adages* III ix 55)
3 *Letters to Atticus* 9.15.4

I vi 95
Nosce teipsum / Know thyself

The three sayings referred to at the beginning of this essay, and which follow in sequence in the collection, are 'Know thyself,' 'Nothing to excess,' and 'Stand surety, and ruin is at hand' (that is, 'he who gives a guarantee ... makes a promise regarding something which it is not in his power to guarantee'). As Erasmus notes, they were found written over the doors of the temple at Delphi. Of the three, which appeared together in Collectanea *no* 108*, the first is certainly the best known, and has passed easily into English (Tilley* K 175*). It is surprising that Erasmus does not do more with this; there is a massive history of philosophical commentary on the proverb (Otto* 1236*, Tosi* 347*). This and the next proverb are important commonplaces in Renaissance philosophy, especially in the various revisionist forms of Stoicism.*

To the same line of thought[1] belong those three sayings which are easily the most famous of all the utterances of wise men, so much so that, as Plato[2] bears witness in the *Charmides*, they could be seen inscribed by the Amphictyons in front of the doors of the temple at Delphi as maxims worthy of the god. The first of these is Γνῶθι σεαυτόν, Know thyself, which recommends moderation and the middle state, and bids us not to pursue objects either too great for us or beneath us. For here we have a source of all life's troubles: every man flatters himself, and blinded by self-love[3] takes to himself without deserving it all the merit that he wrongly denies to others. Cicero[4] in the third book of letters to his brother Quintus: 'As for that famous *Know thyself*, you must not think it was uttered merely to reduce our self-conceit; we should also recognize our own blessings.' There is also a line preserved among the proverbial maxims:[5] 'That *Know thyself* is useful everywhere.' Nonius Marcellus quotes a satire by Varro,[6] the title of which was *Know Thyself*. Ovid[7] in his *Art of Love*: 'Those world-famous words, / That every man should to himself be known.' Juvenal:[8] 'And *Know Thyself* descended from the sky.' Ovid gives Pythagoras as the author of this rule; Socrates in Plato thinks it started with Apollo. Plato[9] in the *Phaedrus*: 'I cannot yet achieve the self-knowledge of the Delphian inscription.' Some think[10] that this too was taken from that ocean we call Homer;[11] for Hector in Homer, while attacking everyone else, fought shy of Ajax whom he knew to be stronger than himself. As the poet says, 'he shunned an encounter with Ajax son of Telamon.' Diogenes[12] ascribes it to Thales, but cites Antisthenes as giving it to Phemonoe, though he says that Chilon appropriated it. Thales when asked 'What is difficult?' replied 'To know oneself.' Asked 'What is easy?' he said 'To give another man good advice.' Macrobius[13] in the first book of his *Commentary on the Dream of Scipio* records that when someone asked the Delphic Oracle by what road he could arrive at happiness, the answer was: 'If you have learnt to know yourself.' The same reply was given by the oracle to Croesus, as we learn from Xenophon[14] in his *Cyropaedia*. The Greek proverb-collections cite this line from Antiphanes:[15] 'Friend, if you're mortal, think as mortals should.' The same principle is expressed by Pindar[16] in the words 'Mortal desires are fit for mortal men.' Demonax,[17] asked when he had begun to be a philosopher, replied 'As soon as I began to know myself.' Socrates,[18] when judged by the oracle of Apollo to be the only philosopher in Greece, though Greece was full of them, explained this by saying that the others professed to know what they knew not, and that he defeated them because he knew that he knew nothing, and that was the only thing he professed to know. But Socrates was outdone in modesty on this point by Anaxarchus,[19] who used to maintain that he did not even know that he knew nothing. Menander[20] the writer of comedies has one of his characters correct this universally accepted dictum: 'This *Know thyself* in many ways is wrong; / Far better were it, other men to know.'

1 The previous adage is 'Spit in your own bosom,' an action taken to ensure good luck.
2 *Charmides* 164d
3 As in *Adages* I iii 92
4 Cicero *Ad Quintem fratrem* 3.5.7
5 'proverbial maxims' as in Menander *Sententiae* 762
6 Varro, one of his *Menippean Satires*, referred to in the lexicon of Nonius
7 *Art of Love* 2.499–500
8 Juvenal 11.27
9 *Phaedrus* 229e
10 'some think,' possibly from Plutarch *Moralia* 164B–C
11 *Iliad* 11.542
12 Diogenes Laertius 1.40 and 1.36
13 Macrobius *Commentary on the Dream of Scipio* 1.9.2
14 *Cyropaedia* 7.2.20
15 Antiphanes frag 289 Kock from the collection of Stobaeus
16 Pindar *Isthmian Odes* 5.16
17 Demonax, the Cynic philosopher of the second century AD, not in Lucian
18 Socrates in Diogenes Laertius 2.32
19 Anaxarchus in Diogenes Laertius 9.58
20 Menander, a fragment (203) in Stobaeus' collection

I vi 96
Ne quid nimis / Nothing to excess

The second of the three proverbs over the doors of Delphi. This is almost as famous as the one preceding and subject to almost as much ancient commentary and reflection (Otto 1229, Tosi 1761). The proverb came into English in different forms as 'The mean is best' and 'Too much of one thing is good for nothing' (Tilley M *793,* T *158).*

The second embodies almost the same principle in different words: Μηδὲν ἄγαν, Nothing to excess. Terence[1] in the *Andria* puts it in the mouth of one of his characters, Sosia the freedman, as though it were widely known. Diogenes Laertius[2] ascribes it to Pythagoras. Aristotle[3] in book 3 of the *Rhetoric* gives Bias as the source, where he is treating of the ungoverned passions of the young who, he says, go wrong in every field through enthusiasm; for they love to excess and hate to excess too, while the aged are different, for (to borrow Aristotle's own words) 'they follow the advice of Bias, loving as though they might one day hate and hating as though they might one day love.' Some attribute it to Thales, some to Solon, according to Laertius.[4] Plato[5] cites it in one place from Euripides. And there is no lack of people who trace it back to Homer[6] as the fountain-head, who has the following lines in *Odyssey* 15: 'That host I like not who beyond the mean / Both loves and hates; reason is always best.' Again in *Iliad* book 10: 'O son of Tydeus, praise me not too much / Nor too much blame me.' Personally I should prefer to trace it back to Hesiod,[7] who has in his *Works and Days* the line 'Observe the mean; due time is best in all.' So Euripides[8] in several places and especially in the *Hippolytus*: 'So what there is too much of I like less / Than the old rule of nothing to excess.' Pindar,[9] cited by Plutarch: 'The wise have ever praised exceedingly this saying Nothing to excess.' Sophocles[10] in the *Electra*: 'Be not over-angry with those whom you hate, but let not your enemies slip out of mind.' Plautus[11] in the *Poenulus*: 'Moderation, sister, in all things is best.' Here too belongs that Homeric[12] tag, in book 13 of the *Iliad*: 'But in all things there comes satiety, / In sleep and love, sweet song and gracious dance.' Pindar[13] seems to have imitated this in the *Nemeans*: 'In honey lies satiety, and in the delightful flowers of love.' Pliny[14] in his eleventh book: 'Most destructive, even in every walk of life, is that which is carried to excess.' Horace:[15] 'All things are ruled by reason, have fixed bounds, / Within which only can the right hold firm.' And again: 'Virtue's a mean 'twixt vices either side.' Phocylides:[16] 'Measure's the best of all things.' And Alpheus[17] in an epigram: 'This *Nothing to excess* I like excessively.' Quintilian[18] writes that moderation is sovereign in delivery, as in everything else. Finally Plutarch[19] in his life of Camillus tells us that piety is halfway between contempt of the gods and superstition, and that 'piety and the principle of nothing to excess are best.' And there is nothing in the whole world in which one cannot go wrong by excess, except the love of God, as Aristotle[20] too admits in different words, putting wisdom in the place of God. Here belongs a quotation from some poet, given by Athenaeus[21] in his first book, on the virtues of wine: 'All human cares it drives from out the heart / With reason drunk, but to excess, 'tis worse.'

1 Terence *Andria* 61
2 Diogenes Laertius 8.9
3 Aristotle *Rhetoric* 2.13 (1389b24)
4 Diogenes Laertius 1.63
5 *Philebus* 45d–e
6 *Odyssey* 15.69–71 and *Iliad* 10.249, from Plutarch *Moralia* 164C
7 *Works and Days* 674
8 *Hippolytus* 264–5
9 Pindar fragment 216, cited by Plutarch *Moralia* 116D
10 *Electra* 177–8
11 *Poenulus* 258
12 *Iliad* 13.636–7
13 *Nemean Odes* 7.52–3
14 *Natural History* 11.284
15 *Satires* 1.1.106–7 and *Epistles* 1.18.9
16 Phocylides *Sententiae* 36 (the maxims are falsely attributed to him in the Theocritus printed by Aldus in 1495)
17 Alpheus of Mitylene, in *Palatine Anthology* 9.110
18 Quintilian, perhaps 12.6.20
19 *Camillus* 6.4 in *Lives*
20 Aristotle *Eudemian Ethics* 8 (1249b16) or *Nicomachean Ethics* 10 (1177a12) (ASD)
21 Athenaeus 2.37b (not book 1), citing Panyasis fragment 14 Kinkel

I vii 17
In vino veritas / Wine speaks the truth

A proverb known in many languages (Otto 1900, Tosi 732), though English writers often quote the Latin form instead of the English variants ('In wine there is truth,' Tilley W 465, *and 'Wine is the glass of the mind,'* W 481*). As he occasionally does elsewhere, Erasmus adds a second related adage at the end of the essay. This one, 'A slip of the tongue is wont to tell the truth'*

(Tilley S *538), is suggestive of what became known as the Freudian slip (the 'parapraxis' described in Freud's* The Psychopathology of Everyday Life*). The theme addressed here comes close to that of the outside and inside analysed in 'The Sileni of Acibiades' (*II *iii 1*). The Greek sources are Zenobius 4.5, Diogenianus 4.81, and Suidas* OI *134.*

Ἐν οἴνῳ ἀλήθεια, Wine speaks the truth. An adage found in many classical authors, meaning that strong drink strips the mind of its pretences and brings out into the open what is hidden in a man's heart. That is why Scripture[1] forbids wine to be given to kings, because where strong drink reigns there are no secrets. Pliny,[2] book 14 chapter 22, writes that wine 'betrays the secrets of the mind so effectively that men in their cups will say what will cost them their lives and cannot even repress remarks that will recoil and cut their own throats. It is a common saying' he adds 'that there is truth in wine.' There is a well-known saying, attributed to an eminent Persian,[3] that torture is unnecessary to get at the truth; wine is much more effective. Horace[4] confirms this in the *Odes*:

Tough wits to your mild torture yield
Their treasures; you unlock the soul
Of wisdom and its stores conceal'd,
Arm'd with Lyaeus' kind control.

Again in the *Art of Poetry*:

So kings are said to ply with cups galore
(Strong drink their thumbscrew) him they would explore:
Is he the stuff of which a friend is made?

And again elsewhere: 'Drink's the one key that opens every door.' The proverb is also expressed in the second book of Athenaeus[5] in this way: 'Wine and truth,' because those who have drunk too much not only blurt out their own secrets but make rash statements about other people too. In Plutarch's[6] life of Artaxerxes, when Mithridates has said something insolent in his cups, Sparamixas says 'No offence taken, Mithridates, but when the Greeks speak of "wine and truth"' and what follows. Greek has another common proverbial saying:[7] 'What is in the heart of the sober man is in the mouth of the drunkard.' Theognis:[8] 'Silver and gold by fire the craftsman tries; / 'Tis wine displays the mind before our eyes.' Athenaeus[9] cites this line from Euripides: 'Bronze the face mirrors, and strong drink the mind.' He also quotes Ephippus: 'Liquor in plenty forces one to speak, / And tipsy men, they say, will tell the truth.' But he also preserves in book 10 a saying of Anacharsis that men as they get drunk are filled with false ideas, and then tells a story not without its point. One of the guests had said to Anacharsis 'You have married a very ugly wife.' 'Yes' said he, 'I quite agree. Hey, waiter, bring me a good strong drink, and I'll make her look handsome.' So it's not only the lover, but the drinker too, who 'thinks what's foul is fair,' as Theocritus[10] puts it. And yet how can a man speak the truth whose judgment is unsteady? Truth however is not always opposed to falsehood; sometimes its opposite is pretence. A man can speak sincerely and what he says may be false; and what he says can be true though he does not speak the truth.

Last but not least, the proverb aims, not at the madness of intoxication, to which things that are fixed appear to be going round and round and single things appear double or treble, but at the more moderate stage which clears away false shame and disguises. Alcibiades in the *Symposium* of Plato:[11] 'What follows you would never have heard me say, unless first I had recalled the proverb that Wine without children or with children speaks the truth.' From these words it is clear that the same proverbial expression was current about childhood as about wine. A similar proverb is still in common use today, to the effect that you never hear the truth from anyone, save only from three kinds of person: children, drunkards, and madmen.

To this I think one should add another proverbial line:[12] 'A slip of the tongue is wont to tell the truth.' For what a man lets fall unawares is commonly thought to be true, because only then is it free from any suspicion of falsehood. Such slips of the tongue are picked up on as indications that can be trusted: 'For "Neoptolemus" I thoughtless cry / "Orestes" – sign that better days are nigh.'[13] Cicero[14] finally in his *Topica* lists among those whose remarks carry conviction children, sleepers, persons caught off their guard, and drunkards.

1 Proverbs 31:4
2 *Natural History* 14.141 (see also *Adages* I vi 70)
3 Diogenianus 7.28 and Apostolius 12.49
4 Horace *Odes* 3.21.13–16 (trans Conington), *Art of Poetry* 434–6, and *Epistles* 1.5.16. In the first passage, Lyaeus is another name for Bacchus.
5 Athenaeus 2.37e, quoting Alcaeus frag 366 Lobel-Page
6 *Artaxerxes* 15.3 in *Lives*
7 The 'proverbial saying' is from Diogenianus 7.28 (*Adages* II i 55).
8 Theognis 499–500
9 Athenaeus 10.427f citing Aeschylus frag 393 Nauck, not Euripides; ibid 2.38b, citing Ephippus frag 25 Kock; ibid 10.445f, citing Anacharsis
10 Theocritus 6.19
11 *Symposium* 217e
12 Menander *Sententiae* 294
13 In the quotation Hermione cries out for Orestes though she is officially engaged to Neoptolemus, in Ovid *Heroides* 8.115–16.
14 Cicero *Topics* 20.75

I vii 18
Bos in lingua / An ox on the tongue

Erasmus took this well-known classical proverb from the Greek collections: Zenobius 2.70; Diogenianus 3.48; Suidas B *460. In English we have the analogous though different 'cat's got his/her tongue' (this expression has only been collected for the twentieth century; see* OED *'tongue' II 4 d).*

Βοῦς ἐπὶ γλώττης, An ox on the tongue. Used of those who do not dare say freely what they think. A metaphor either from the great mass of the animal, as though it crushed the tongue and did not let it speak, or from the fact that in Athens there was once a coin with the figure of an ox. In Rome too king Servius first struck bronze coins with sheep and oxen on them, according to Pliny,[1] book 18 chapter 3. Plutarch[2] in his 'Antiquarian Problems' tells the same story, the reason being that in early times almost all wealth took the form of flocks and herds, whence some suppose[3] that *pecunia*, the Latin for money, is derived from *pecora*, cattle. And so those who kept their mouths shut for fear of a pecuniary penalty, or had not the face to speak because they had taken bribes, were said to have 'an ox on the tongue.' Julius Pollux,[4] in the ninth book of his *Vocabulary* where he explains this proverb, more or less agrees with this, adding that the coin itself was commonly called an ox. Further, that in the festival in Delos, if someone was due to receive an award, the herald announced by custom 'Such-and-such a man shall receive so many oxen.' An ox in this sense, he says, was worth two Attic drachmas, whence some people supposed it was a Delian and not an Attic coin. He adds that in the laws of Draco[5] there was a mention of a ten-ox payment, which would mean ten coins; and that there were those who thought that Homer too had spoken of the coin, not of the animal, when he tells of exchanging 'gold arms for bronze, arms worth a hundred oxen / For arms worth nine.' But this view is refuted by Julius Pollux in another passage, where he shows that exchange of goods already existed without coins. The author of the scholia[6] on Homer, in the second book, records that the ox was honoured among the ancients for many reasons, but particularly because it is sacred to Apollo; and so on one side of the coin they stamped an ox and on the other a king's head. But he gives the adage in the form Βοῦς ἐπὶ γλώσσῃ βέβηκεν, An ox treads on my tongue, pointing out that this is used when a man kept silent for money. Theognis:[7] 'An ox is on my tongue.' Philostratus[8] in his *Life of Apollonius*: 'He was the first of men to restrain his tongue, inventing "An ox sits upon it" as a principle of silence.' He speaks of Pythagoras, the apostle of silence. Again, in his life of the sophist Scopelianus:[9] 'Nor should we be surprised if some people, who are tongue-tied themselves and have set upon their tongues the ox of silence.' It occurs also in the *Agammemnon* of Aeschylus;[10] 'The rest for me is silence; on my tongue / A great ox treads.'

1 *Natural History* 18.12
2 Plutarch *Moralia* 274F
3 Festus p 291 Lindsay
4 Julius Pollux *Onomasticon* 9.61 (epitome of a Greek word list compiled c 166–76 AD, published by Aldus in 1502)
5 Draco was the Athenian legislator, proverbially known for his severe (or Draconian) laws.
6 Perhaps Eustathius on *Iliad* 2.449 (queries ASD)
7 Theognis 815
8 *Life of Apollonius* 6.11
9 Scopelianus, from Philostratus *Lives of the Sophists* 1.21.1
10 *Agamemnon* 36–7

I vii 28
Plaustrum bovem trahit / The cart before the horse

Erasmus took this from a single source in the satirical writer Lucian, one of his favourite authors (from Terpsion, *in* Dialogues of the Dead *16.2). It also appears in the Greek collections by Diogenianus (3.30) and Suidas (A 1486). See also Tosi 435. There is an analogy in* Adages *V i 30 'To place before.' This proverb is similar to our 'To set the cart before the horse' (Tilley C 103) in the way it shows the inversion of a normal situation, and that is how Sir Roger Mynors translated the title. Yet the meaning of the ancient proverb goes further, because the wagon actually drags the ox.*

Ἡ ἅμαξα τὸν βοῦν ἐλαύνει, literally The wagon drags the ox. Of something that happens the wrong way round: for instance, of a wife laying down rules for her husband, of a pupil correcting his master, of a people giving orders to their prince, of reason subservient to the emotions. Lucian in his *Terpsion*: 'But now, in the words of the proverb, the wagon often runs away with the ox.' The image derives from carts rolling backwards down a slope and dragging their oxen after them.

I vii 57
In silvam ligna ferre / To carry wood to the forest

As Erasmus himself notes, this proverb should be compared with 'Owls to Athens' (I ii 11). It has interesting variants in other languages (Tosi 474), such as the English 'To cast water into the sea' (Tilley W 106). In this essay Erasmus uncharacteristically quotes himself.*

To carry wood to the forest is to wish to supply someone with things of which he already has a large supply. Horace[1] in his *Satires*:

When I, born overseas, would write in Greek,
In after-midnight hour, when dreams speak plain,
I saw Quirinus, and he said 'Refrain:
Wood to the forest would be no more mad
Than to the serried ranks of Greeks to add.'

On the same lines we speak of carrying water to the sea. I have used both images together in one of my epigrams:[2] 'To send my Pietro verses sure would be / Wood to the forest, water to the sea.' They both agree with one I have recorded elsewhere, Owls to Athens.

1 Horace *Satires* 1.10.31–5
2 Poem to Pietro Carmeliano, written about 1506 (given in *The Poems of Erasmus*, CWE 85–6 no 35)

I vii 70
Nosce tempus / Consider the due time

This proverb essay includes the famous proverb 'Take Time by the forelock, for she is bald behind' (Tilley T 311), explained by a long poem from the Greek Anthology, *which Erasmus here quotes in full. The poem was also translated by Andrea Alciato in his* Book of Emblems *(no 122; see accompanying figure) and one image of Time in Renaissance painting was largely derived from this widely distributed verbal and pictorial image (see also Otto 1755, Tosi 575).*

Γνῶθι καιρὸν, Consider the due time. Prominent among the familiar sayings of the Seven Sages;[1] ascribed, like most of them, to several authors and used by almost everyone. Hesiod:[2] 'Observe the mean: due time is best in all.' Theocritus[3] alludes to it in the eleventh idyll: 'Some blooms in summer, some in winter blow.' Isocrates[4] too in the *Ad Demonicum* remarks that in all things there is less satisfaction if they are done out of due season. So important is it in all business to observe the due and proper time. The same message is to be found in the Greek maxims[5] 'Small things are great when in due season given' and in another 'It always pays to know when time is ripe.' Besides there is Pindar[6] in the *Pythians*: 'The proper time likewise is of all things the chief.' And Horace's familiar tag[7] 'Sweet is folly in its proper place.' Such is the force of *Opportunitas*, of Timeliness, that it can turn what is honourable into dishonour, loss into gain, happiness into misery, kindness into unkindness, and the reverse; it can, in short, change the nature of everything. In the beginning and ending of any

In occaſionem.

Lyſippi hoc opus eſt, Sycion cui patria: tu quis?
  Cuncta domans capti temporis articulus.
Cur pinnis ſtas? uſque rotor: talaria plantis
  Cur retines? paßim me leuis aura rapit.
In dextra eſt tenuis dic unde nouacula? acutum
  Omni acie hoc ſignum me magis eſſe docet.
Cur in fronte coma? occurrens ut prendar: at he
  Dic cur pars calua eſt poſterior capitis?
Me ſemel alipidem ſi quis permittat abire,
  Ne poßim apprenſo poſtmodò crine capi.
Tali opifex nos arte, tui cauſa, ædidit hoſpes,
  Vtq; omnes moneam, pergula aperta tenet.

Consider due time The figure of Due Time (or Occasion) in Andrea Alciato's *Book of Emblems* follows the traditional imagery associated with Fortune (emblem 122), from the Paris edition of 1540, p 20. Alciato's accompanying poem is a translation of the same poem quoted by Erasmus in I vii 70*. (Thomas Fisher Rare Book Library, University of Toronto) business it has especial influence, so that the ancients, we may well think, had good reason to endow it with divinity, though in Greek this god is masculine, and his name is *Kairos*, Due Time.

Her image was represented in the old days as follows. She had wings on her feet and stood on a freely-turning wheel, and she spun very rapidly round and round. The forepart of her head was thickly set with hair, the back of it bald, so that her forehead could easily be grasped and the back of it not at all. Hence the phrase 'to seize the opportunity.' Thus both a learned allusion and an elegant image were produced by the unknown author of the line 'Long in the forelock, Time is bald behind.' Besides which, it is a pleasure to add the epigram by Posidippus[8] on this subject, which was unaccountably omitted by Poliziano,[9] and runs as follows: '"Where did the sculptor come from?" Sicyon. "And his name?" Lysippus. "And who are you, the subject?" Due Time, master of all things. "Why go on tiptoe?" I am always running. "Why have a pair of winged sandals on your feet?" I fly with the wind. "Why carry a razor in your right hand?" To show that I am keener than a razor's edge. "And your hair, why so long over your face?" That he who is beforehand with me may seize it. "The back part why so bald?" Because once I have run past a man on my winged feet, never for all his longing shall he seize[10] me from behind. Such, stranger, did the artist make me, and set me in the forecourt to be a warning to you and your fellow men.' My version of these verses is not meant to compete with the Greek original; it is, as usual, uninspired and quite extempore, as the poem itself will have made clear even if I said nothing, my sole purpose being to make it intelligible to those who know no Greek. Nor will it be off the point to add an epigram by Ausonius,[11] which, as Poliziano points out, is evidently derived from the Greek, although it differs in certain respects, and in particular by the addition of Remorse as Opportunity's companion. The poem runs like this: '"The artist's name?" Phidias. "What, the man who made the great statue of Athena?" Yes, and the Jupiter, and I am the third of his masterpieces. I am the goddess Opportunity, so seldom seen, recognized by so few. "Why stand on a wheel?" I cannot stay still in one place. "And why those winged sandals?" I am always in flight, and the good fortune of which Mercury is patron I provide when I please. "Do you hide your face with hair?" I have no wish to be recognized. "But why bald behind?" That I may not be seized as I run past. "And who is your companion?" Let her tell you herself. "Tell me, pray, who are you?" I am the goddess who was not named even by Cicero himself, she who punishes what is done and not done in such a way that there are regrets afterwards; and so I am called Remorse. "Now I turn to you again: you must tell me what business she has with you." When I take wing, she stays behind; if I pass any man by, she remains with him. You yourself, while you ask these questions and waste your time in idle curiosity, will find that you have let me slip.'

1 The Seven Sages were ancient statesmen and philosophers, listed in Plato's *Protagoras* 343a: Chilon, Pittacus, Bias, Cleobolus, Periander, Thales, and Solon.
2 *Works and Days* 694
3 Theocritus 11.58
4 *To Demonicus* 31
5 Menander *Sententiae* 872 and 381
6 *Pythian Odes* 9.78–9
7 *Odes* 4.12.28
8 Posidippus was a poet of the third century BC whose poem cited here is in *Greek Anthology* 16.275.
9 Angelo Poliziano (1454–94) was one of the leading Italian humanists. His *Miscellanea* was an analysis of textual problems in classical literature and one of its essays (c 49) was a full discussion of this poem.
10 To 'seize the opportunity' comes from Cato's *Distichs* 2.26.2 a collection of Latin verses and popular morality widely studied in schools.
11 Ausonius *Epigrams* 33

I vii 71
Olet lucernam / It smells of the lamp

There are two English variations: Tilley C 43 *'It smells of the candle' and* L 44 *'It smells more of the lamp than of wine.' Erasmus takes this from Plutarch's* Moralia *802E and 848C. Demosthenes, the greatest of the Greek orators, was known to work enormously hard at his speeches (see, for instance, in Plutarch's life, 8 and 11).*

Τὸν λύχνον ὄζει, It smells of the lamp, of something which has been the object of thought and much work has gone into the polishing of it. Derived from the practice among keen students of working late by lamplight to finish some elaborate piece, if they want to produce a special effect. It used to be a common criticism of Demosthenes that his arguments smelt of the lamp, because his speeches were all written and thought out in advance before he left home. Hence too the well-known tribute to him, that he used more oil than wine. For he was temperate and drank only water, and even when a very old man could still be found toiling away by the light of his humble and yet famous lamp.

I vii 76
Oppedere, et Oppedere contra tonitrua / To fart in someone's face, or To fart against the thunder

Not conventionally listed in the ancient proverb collections, though there are similar proverbs about which Erasmus comments (eg, I iv 46 *'To fart in front of a deaf man,' rather like our 'to preach to the deaf';* II iii 31 *'The dead man lies there farting'; and* III iv 2* *'Everyone thinks his own fart smells sweet'; and so on). Erasmus got the references in this essay from his own reading. These proverbs do not seem to have an English equivalents in the early modern period, though perhaps they were not collected. Despite its apparent crudeness, Erasmus uses this proverb at the end of his essay on 'The Sileni of Alcibiades' (*III iii 1* *n 65).*

To fart in someone's face I find in use as a proverbial expression for the display of dislike and contempt. Horace[1] in the *Satires*: 'Do you really mean / To fart in the face of a pack of curtal Jews?' Aristophanes[2] in the *Plutus*: 'And fart in the face of penury,' and again elsewhere in the same play: 'And break wind in the face of penury.' This was a way for those who had now become rich to show their contempt for poverty. The same author in the *Clouds*: 'And fain would I out-fart your thunder-claps.' The speaker is Strepsiades, who is making a humble address to the Clouds and showing contempt for Jove's thunderbolts. The scholiast adds that this is derived from a device used on the ancient stage, by which small stones were poured from a great jar into a bronze vessel so that they made a sound like thunder, and this was a way of making a noise in answer to the thunder. I think myself that there is an allusion to the ancient custom of *poppysmos*, smacking the lips; for in the old days when they saw lightning it was the custom to make an answering noise by smacking the lips, which they supposed to be a protection against being struck by lightning. Aristophanes in the *Wasps*: 'And if I send a lightningflash, they smack their lips'; at which some people by way of a joke would break wind, as though this were a clumsy way of imitating the smacking noises made by other men. The Cyclops, in Euripides'[3] tragedy of that name, to show his contempt for Jove's thunder, speaks as follows: 'Then I drink a great bucket of milk, and raise my skirts and rumble fit to match Jove's thunderbolts.'

1 *Satires* 1.9.69–70
2 The first Aristophanes reference is a confused recollection of *Plutus* 618 and *Clouds* 293–4; the second is *Plutus* 618; the third is *Clouds* 293–4; then *Wasps* 626; Mynors also sees a contribution here from Pliny's *Natural History* 28.25.
3 *Cyclops* 327–8

I vii 94
Una hirundo non facit ver / One swallow does not make a summer

A well-known proverb in English (Tilley S *1025) and in other languages (Tosi 1589). It comes from the Greek collections (Zenobius 5.12; Suidas* M *1030). It is interesting to see that Erasmus' interpretation does not accord with the way we would take the proverb (ie, a fleeting sign of arrival does not necessarily mean the thing has come), even though the English proverb certainly came from the Latin, quite possibly through Erasmus. For its presentation in Richard Taverner's English adaptation of the* Adages, *see editor's introduction, p xxxvii.*

Μία χελιδὼν ἔαρ οὐ ποιεῖ, A single swallow does not make a summer, meaning that one day is not time enough to acquire virtue or education. Or that one thing well done or well said is not sufficient to earn you the reputation of a good man or a good speaker, for many good qualities go to make this up. Or that to obtain certainty on some question, one single theory is not enough. If a great many approaches lead to the same result, then and then only will your theory be acceptable. It can so easily happen that one swallow should appear early by mere chance. This is derived from the natural habits of the swallow, which is the herald of early summer, for it flies away when winter comes. Whence Horace's phrase[1] 'When Zephyrs blow and swallows first appear,' which refers to the early summer. Aristotle[2] in the first book of the *Ethics*: 'One swallow makes no summer, nor does one day'; and in the same way it takes more than one day or one short space of time to make a happy man. Aristophanes[3] in the *Birds*: 'He seems to me to need full many swallows,' where the scholiast sees a reference to the proverb I have just recorded, One swallow does not make a summer. There is something akin to this in Sophocles' *Antigone*:[4] 'What one man owns can never make a city.' For just as one swallow does not make a summer, so one man does not make a commonwealth nor one coin a rich man.

1 *Epistles* 1.7.13
2 *Nicomachean Ethics* 1.7 (1098a18)
3 *Birds* 1417
4 *Antigone* 737

I viii 40
Caecus caeco dux / The blind leading the blind

Again a common proverb in English (Tilley B 452*) and in other European languages, from the Middle Ages onwards, often in the biblical form ('If the blind lead the blind, both shall fall into the ditch' from Matthew 15:14; see also Otto 277 and Tosi 1000). The image was painted by Bruegel. Erasmus tends not to give proverbs from the Bible, but here is an important exception, and he mentions the Gospel source right at the start of his essay before he goes on to locate the classical sources at greater length. There is also Apostolius 11.50 (Don't take a blind man as your guide, or a stupid man as your counsellor).*

Τυφλὸς τυφλῷ ὁδηγός, The blind leading the blind. An adage to which the Gospel[1] text has given a wider circulation, and it is therefore a special pleasure to record it. It may be used whenever one ignorant man attempts to instruct another, or an unwise man tries to give advice to an imprudent one. Cicero[2] alluded to the proverb in the last book of the *De finibus*: 'History relates that Gaius Drusus' house was often beset by those who came to him for a legal opinion; the people concerned could not see their own way clear, and chose a blind man to be their guide.' Such are Cicero's words; Drusus was a highly expert jurist, and for the benefit of others looked forward with his mental vision though with his bodily eyes he could see nothing. Close to this is Horace's phrase about a blind man showing the way. Horace,[3] writing to Scaeva: 'Though he were blind who shows you where to go, / Yet listen none the less.' Porphyrion opines that the expression is equivalent to 'A sow teaching Minerva'; for it is to stand the thing on its head if a blind person tries to show the way to a sighted one. In the *Plutus* of Aristophanes[4] the slave Carion is indignant at the way his master, who can see, followed the god of wealth, Plutus, who is blind:

> He does the opposite of what he should
> Who follows a blind man. 'Tis we who see
> Who guide the blind; yet he must follow them,
> And make me do the like.

1 'Gospel' is both Matthew 15:14 and Luke 6:39.
2 Actually *Tusculan Disputations* 5.38.112
3 *Epistles* 1.17.3–4 (Porphyrion is a later commentator on Horace; the reference is to *Adages* I i 40)
4 *Plutus* 13–16 (Plato also uses this image when he describes Wealth as played by a blind actor in *Republic* 9.554b)

I viii 46
Premere pollicem. Convertere pollicem / Thumbs down. Thumbs up

The catchphrase has easily survived into modern usage, though, surprisingly, in reverse of the classical meaning (Otto 1445). For the ancients, 'thumbs down' was the command to the gladiator to lower the weapon, and 'thumbs up' the sign that the victim was to be killed. It is not clear when the meanings became reversed, though in this essay Erasmus seems to suggest that the classical meaning still held. 'Thumbs up' was a popular English gesture of confidence by troops in the First World War (OED). For other gestures, see also II iv 68 'To show the middle finger' and III iv 14* 'To lift a finger.'*

In ancient times the thumb was used as an indicator of interest and support. The supporter used to turn his thumb down; the man who did not support turned his thumb up. These gestures passed into a proverb, so that now to turn the thumb down is used of support in any context, and to turn it up of hostility – Pliny,[1] book 27 chapter 2: 'Our thumbs should be turned down when we support someone, and there is actually a proverb which prescribes this.' Juvenal:[2] 'And if the mob have given their Thumbs up, / They kill whome'er they like to please the crowd.' Horace[3] uses 'both thumbs' to express whole-hearted support: 'And if he thinks that you his taste approve, / With both his thumbs he'll sponsor what you love.' Porphyrion expounds as follows: 'With both his thumbs means With both hands, the part being put for the whole by the figure of speech called synecdoche. Perhaps because a speaker who delivers an encomium closes his hands, joining the thumb to its next neighbour.' Acron in this fashion: 'With both his thumbs means by the figure of speech *synecdoche* With both hands, raised equally and moved to and fro; for this is the gesture of those who deliver a panegyric.' It is pretty clear, as we can infer from their words, that both of them have missed the origin of the proverb.

1 *Natural History* 28.25
2 3.36–7
3 *Epistles* 1.18.65–6 (Porphyrion and Acron are names traditionally given to two of the ancient commentators on Horace's poetry)

I viii 78
Ut sementem feceris, ita et metes / As you have sown, so also shall you reap

This proverb is best known from the Bible, but here Erasmus frames the biblical texts with classical citations (see also Otto 1104). There are also many medieval variations (Tosi 809). The English version 'As they sow, so let them reap' is Tilley S 687.

Cicero[1] used a most elegant metaphor, As you have sown, so also shall you reap, in the sense that you will receive the reward appropriate to what you have done. Plautus[2] in the *Epidicus*: 'A bitter pill indeed, for work well done / To reap a harvest of calamity,' meaning ill-treatment in return for kindness. And in Plato:[3] 'What harvest will this man reap? A wretched one, I am sure.' The image is shared with Scriptures[4] too: 'They that sow in tears shall reap in joy,' and St Paul: 'He that soweth to his flesh shall of his flesh reap corruption; but he that soweth to the Spirit, shall of the Spirit reap life everlasting,' and 'If we have sown unto you spiritual things, is it a great thing if we shall reap your carnal things?' Euripides[5] has it in mind in that line in the *Hecuba*: 'And you may reap what your designs deserve.' In fact, there is almost a regular phrase in Greek poetry of the form 'bad things badly.' Aristophanes[6] in the *Knights*: 'No culture have I but to read and write / A few poor rudiments and very poorly.' And one often finds the threat to bring an evil man to an evil end. The scholiast points out that this is a proverbial turn of speech, on which something has been said in the introduction to this work.[7] Euripides[8] again in the *Hecuba*: 'Bad men to have bad fortune, good men good,' and further on in the same play 'For since you dared to do what is not right, / What is not welcome you shall suffer now.' Laertius[9] tells an amusing anecdote about Diogenes. At dinner some of them were throwing him bones as one would to a dog, because he was a Cynic. His method of avenging this insult was to go up close to them, and as he stood by them to lift a leg, treating them as a dog might in return. But even nearer is a story he tells in his life of Zeno. Zeno one day was beating a slave who had been caught thieving. The slave cried out all the time that it was his fate to steal; to which Zeno replied: 'Yes; and your fate to be beaten.' The slave had heard his master arguing for the inevitability of fate, and made this his excuse for his offence; but the philosopher prettily reversed the argument.

1 Cicero *On the Orator* 2.65.261

2 *Epidicus* 718

3 *Phaedrus* 260d

4 Psalms 125.6, Galatians 6.8, and 1 Corinthians 9.11

5 Hecuba 331

6 *Knights* 188–9 and *Plutus* 65

7 That is, section xiii of Erasmus' introduction to the *Adages*

8 Euripides *Hecuba* 903–4 and 1250–1

9 Diogenes Laertius 6.46 and also in his life of Zeno 7.23 (the term Cynic is derived from the Greek for 'dog')

I viii 91
Bis dat qui cito dat / He that gives quickly gives twice

Erasmus probably knew this as a recollection of a maxim taken from the so-called 'mimes,' or dramatic performances, of Publilius Syrus; this ancient collection of sayings was widely read in schools in the Renaissance and often published with Cato's Distichs. *Publilius was also printed with maxims of Seneca and that may account for Erasmus' hesitant ascription at the beginning of the essay. This was a very common expression in Latin (Otto 248, Tosi 1354) and though a proverb in English (Tilley* G *125) is often found quoted in Latin in English texts.*

I remember reading somewhere, in Seneca if I am not mistaken, that 'He who gives quickly gives twice.' Seneca[1] too in the second book of the *De beneficiis* has 'A gift is less welcome that has long stuck to the giver's fingers.' The lesson of this maxim is that we should not be dilatory or reluctant in helping our friends when they need it, but should do what we can for them on our own initiative without waiting to be asked. Among the Greek epigrams[2] there is a couplet that bears the name of Lucian: 'Swift gifts are sweetest, and the good / That tarries earns no gratitude.' The lines cannot be turned adequately into Latin, because the charm and wit of the epigram lies in the word *charis*, which in Greek sometimes means a kindness, sometimes the grace that makes a thing acceptable, sometimes an actual goddess, one of the Graces. Ausonius[3] cites a similar maxim in Greek: 'Favour slow-footed is favour without favour.' It is the beginning of a hexameter line, taken from some epigram. His rendering is: 'Favour that tarries loses its savour; / Favour done promptly wins answering favour.' And he offers an alternative: 'A good deed should be done with speed; / What is tardy, though kind, no thanks will find.' So it is that Hector in Euripides,[4] in the *Rhesus*, condemns delay in helping friends: 'In helping friends I like not to be late.' There is also an elegant moral maxim[5] to the same effect: 'Twice welcome what we need, when offered free,' and another like it: 'He helps the needy twice whose help is swift.'

1 Seneca *On Benefits* 2.1.2
2 Epigram in *Greek Anthology* 10.30
3 Ausonius *Epigrams* 16 and 17, adapting the preceding
4 *Rhesus* 333
5 The 'moral maxim' is Publilius Syrus B 1 and I 6.

I viii 96
Virum improbum vel mus mordeat / Even a mouse will fasten its teeth in a rascal

The 'heroic hexameter' from which the adage is derived is an epigram by Palladas in the Greek Anthology *9.379. This proverb is obscure, though a variation is found in Diogenianus 5.87 (with 'goat' in place of 'mouse'). The unlucky physician in this strange and unusually personal anecdote may be a Dutchman named Bont, if P.S. Allen is correct (Bont is mentioned in Erasmus' Epistles 225 and 275); the haughty Englishman has not been identified.*

Κἂν μῦς δάκοι ἄνδρα πονηρόν, Even a mouse will fasten its teeth in a rascal. Part of a heroic hexameter, indicating that somehow or other the wicked do not escape punishment but pay the proper penalty in some way. It applies also to those who start a quarrel on some frivolous pretext and complain that they have suffered loss, pretending that they have received an injury in order to avoid paying what they owe. This happened lately in England to a man I know, a physician with whom I am closely linked both by our common country and by the ties of friendship. I should like to tell the story in passing. There was a citizen of London, an extremely rich man and supposed to be highly respectable, whom my friend by his skill and care, and not without some personal risk, had restored to freedom; for he was the victim of a most pestilent fever. As happens in the moment of danger, he had promised the physician mountains of gold if he would attend him without stint in such a desperate situation, appealing also to the friendship there was between them. To cut the story short, my friend agreed. He was young, and a German. He attended him, he did as he could, and the man recovered. When the physician shyly raised the question of payment, the worthless fellow wriggled out of it. He must not worry about his fee; 'but as a matter of fact my wife keeps the keys of the chest where I keep my money, and you know what women are. I should not like her to notice that I had parted with such a large sum.' A few days later he happened to meet the man, who was now in very good shape and showed not a trace of his recent illness; so he appealed to him, reminding him that the fee had not yet been paid. In reply the fellow stoutly asserted that the money had been paid over by his wife in cash on his instructions. The physician said this was not so. Now see what a handle this worthy man seized! The physician happened to address him in Latin in the second person singular; whereat he flared up as though grossly insulted. 'How dare you,' he cried, 'a German like you, use your thou and thee to an Englishman?, and as though he had lost all self-control, shaking his head in a rage and uttering frightful threats, he was off in a trice. And that was how this honourable citizen gave him the slip, richly deserving another attack of his complaint. I laughed at the story, but it was a bitter laugh when I thought how unfairly my friend had been let down, and I was astonished at such surpassing ingratitude. Lions return thanks for help given them in peril, serpents remember kindness done them;[1] between man and man, friend and friend, when such a service has been rendered that no return could be adequate, an insult is the only recompense. I say this to show my hatred of the deed, not my dislike of the doer's countrymen; for it is unfair to judge all Englishmen from this one worthless specimen. The adage is recorded in a Greek epigram: 'So they say, even a mouse will fasten its teeth in a rascal.' But the author whoever he was (his name is uncertain) turns the proverb upside down, saying that good men get bitten by the merest mouse, while before bad men even dragons dare not show their teeth: the innocent always suffer, because there seems to be no risk in attacking those who will not retaliate.

1 Aulus Gellius *Attic Nights* 5.14.5–28 for Androcles and the lion; Pliny *Natural History* 8.61 for Thoas and the serpent

I ix 10
Flere ad novercae tumulum / To weep at your stepmother's funeral

Stepmothers have traditionally, if unfairly, been seen as interlopers into the family; for classical perceptions, see Patricia A. Watson, Ancient Stepmothers: Myth, Misogyny, and Reality *(Leiden 1995). Erasmus first wrote this up for* Collectanea *(786). He found a Greek form of the proverb from Diogenianus 6.34 and, as mentioned in the essay, added to it from Publilius Syrus H 19. For another proverb on stepmothers, see below at II ii 95*.*

Πρὸς τὸν μητρυίης τάφον δακρύειν, To shed tears at the grave of your stepmother, is to make a great show of grief when you really are delighted. It is not consistent for a stepson to feel distress at his stepmother's death; but all the same he sometimes weeps at her funeral out of a sense of duty. The same phrase will be used neatly enough of a rich man's heirs, about whom there is a well-known and very elegant moral maxim ascribed to Publius: 'The heir in mourning laughs behind a mask.'

I ix 12
A mortuo tributum exigere / To exact tribute from the dead

This is one of the longer essays of social criticism from the 1515 edition. In the 1508 text, the essay ended with the second sentence ('... even from the dead'). Beginning with a fairly minor proverb (from Diogenianus 1.9) it becomes a sustained attack on usury and taxation.

Ἀπὸ νεκροῦ φορολογεῖν, To exact tribute from the dead, was applied to those who accumulate wealth from any source by fair means or foul. Aristotle[1] in the second book of his *Rhetoric* quotes 'He levies taxes even on the dead,' and explains that it was used of men who sought to make a disreputable profit from any and every source, even from small things and sordid things, as Vespasian[2] did from urine; or from disgraceful activities such as pimping and prostitution; or by extorting money from no matter whom, from friends, from the poor, from beggars, and in the last resort even from the dead. It was thought discreditable[3] in leading Romans when they dug beneath the ancient monuments of Corinth and removed the Corinthian bronzes which they found, a special word being coined to express the meanness of what they did; for things stolen in this fashion were called *Necrocorinthia*, Corinthian grave-goods. In Attic Greek *phoros* means a commission levied or exaction taken from any source, including money. Those who collect such ill-gotten gains are called *phorologi*, a class of men universally hated and deservedly so. *Phoros* is derived from the word *pherein*, the same as the Latin *ferre*, to bring in, from which Latin in the same way gets the word *foenus*, usury – a word not used in early times except of the fruits of the earth, which sometimes like a grateful debtor would repay the seed sown a hundredfold.

For it is contrary to nature, as Aristotle[4] says in the *Politics*, for money to breed money. But today this is so much taken for granted among Christians that they despise the husbandman, the most innocent kind of man and the most essential to the community, and reckon usurers almost among the pillars of the Church, although usury was condemned in those very early times, controlled and repressed even by the laws of the gentiles, absolutely forbidden by Jewish law, abominated and attacked with every weapon by the decrees of the Holy See. Not that I am personally hostile to usurers, whose skill can, I am aware, be properly justified, had it not been condemned long ago by the authority of the Fathers. Especially if you consider the standards of our own time, I would accept a usurer sooner than this sordid class of merchants who use tricks and falsehoods, fraud and misrepresentation, in pursuit of profit from any source, buying in one market in order to sell for twice the price in another, or fleecing the wretched public with their monopolies; and yet these men who do nothing else all their lives are almost the only class we think honourable. I take this proverb to be identical, or at least very closely akin, with one I have recorded elsewhere:[5] 'The very statues he implores for flour.' Flour is put here humorously for tribute, because everything in the end comes down to food, and statues were put up as a memorial to the dead; and thus the man who rakes in profits even from this source can be said to exact it from the dead.

Among the ancients the right of sepulchre was deeply respected, and burial-places were exempt from all obligations. But now our mad passion for property has gone so far that there is nothing in the wide world, sacred or profane, from which something like usury cannot be extorted, and this not only by princes but even by priests. In the old days, even under tyrants, who however did not yet know their business nor fully understand the nature of tyranny, some things were actually held to be common property – seas, rivers, highways, wild beasts. Now a few nobles, as though they alone were men, or rather gods, claim everything as theirs. The wretched seaman is obliged to alter course, whatever the danger, and 'to do and suffer anything'[6] to satisfy the whim of some insolent pirate, as though the poor man had not enough trouble facing winds and waves without the addition of such storms as these. A harbour offers, and a fee is extorted from you; you have to cross a bridge, and you must pay; ferry over a river, and you are made to feel the privilege of princes; you have a piece of baggage, and you must pay these sacrilegious wretches to relinquish it; and what is much more cruel than all this, people in the humblest walk of life are robbed of their simple pleasures, and these countless tithes and taxes take the bread out of the mouths of the poor. It is not lawful to bring in the grain from your fields unless it has been tithed. You may not grind it nor bake it until someone has had a second bite at it. No wine can be imported without paying repeated tithes; you cannot store it in your cellar unless you cut off half the whole value, or at least a quarter, for these rascally harpies. In some places more than half the ale, as they call it, is put on one side for the prince. You cannot kill a beast without paying the taxman; you cannot resell a horse, which you bought with your own money, unless you pay out. When I was staying in the country near Bologna, after Julius[7] had taken possession of the city, I saw country people in the depths of poverty, whose whole property consisted of a yoke of oxen, by whose labours they had to support their entire household, paying a whole ducat for each ox. In some places it is impossible for a man to be legally married unless he has paid his dues. But why should I attempt to go through every detail? These men's rapacity strains the resources of language. There is nothing in the world from which they cannot squeeze some advantage. There is no limit to it and no end;

they invent new systems of extortion every day, and when a precedent has found its way in through some chance opportunity, they maintain it tooth and nail. These exactions are hateful enough in themselves, and since the insolence of the officials who practice them is still more hateful, they rouse no mean resentment against princes; but princes think nothing beneath them which will bring in money, in other words, which will make the poor go even hungrier and support the luxury of great men, or rather, great robbers. Nor is there any shortage of people who make no inconsiderable profit out of the misdeeds of the guilty, with the law as their fishing-net. Is there indeed any public office, any position, any post in government, which is not for sale in most parts of the world? Last but not least, when all these expedients have failed to fill that great jar with holes[8] in it, the prince's exchequer, war is the excuse put forward; the generals all play the same game, and the unfortunate public are sucked dry to the marrow, exactly as though to be a prince was simply to run an enormous business venture.

And yet, disgusting as it is to see Christian princes in this field more inhuman than any pagan tyrants ever were, yet this is a little less outrageous than the fact that among our priests also, in whose eyes all money ought to be quite worthless and whose duty it is freely to share the endowments they have so freely received, everything has its price, nothing is free. Think of the storms they raise over those famous tithes of theirs, how hatefully they oppress wretched common people! You cannot be baptized, which means that you cannot become a Christian, unless you pay cash; such are the splendid auspices under which you enter the portals of the Church. They do not authorize your marriage, unless you pay cash; they do not listen to your story in the confessional except in hope of a reward. They are hired to offer the sacrifice; without pay they sing no psalms; there is no praying without pay, no laying on of hands without pay. They will barely lift a hand to bless you from a distance, unless you have made it worth their while. Not a stone, not a chalice is hallowed without a fee. Even the duty of instructing the people, the true duty of a bishop, is defiled by the love of gain. Not least, they do not give you your share in the body of Christ, unless you pay cash. To say nothing for the moment of the harvest they reap from suits at law, from dispensations as they call them, from pardons known to common people as indulgences, from the conferring of priestly office and the confirmation of bishops and abbots. What could be given free by the hands of men who make you pay for the right of burial even in ground that is not theirs? In pagan times a public place of burial was established for the common people, for the poor; there was a place where you could bury whom you would without paying. Among Christians the dead cannot even be laid in the ground unless you have hired that little scrap of space from a priest, and the size and splendour of the place you are given will be in proportion to the price. A large sum in ready money will buy you the right to lie and rot in church near the high altar; a modest offering, and you will lie out of doors in the rain among ordinary folk. It would be a disgrace if they accept the price you might choose to offer; but now they call it their legal right, and it is astonishing how obstinately they exact it. Hebron[9] was a barbarian and a gentile, but he made Abraham, an unknown guest, the free offer of a burial-place, and could scarcely be induced by entreaty to accept the money proffered in return; how can we priests sell the right of sepulture in ground that is not ours? Or rather, how can we lease public property for money as though it were ours? And none reap this kind of harvest more greedily than those who never plant one seed for the public good, but live entirely for themselves or at least for their prince. Others spin us the old rigmarole, 'The labourer is worthy of his hire,'[10] for all the world as if there were no difference between a bishop and a hired soldier or farm-labourer. The work of menials is recompensed by a reward; princes and priests have an office so exalted as to be beyond price.

1 *Rhetoric* 2.6 (1383b25)
2 *Vespasian* 23.2 in *Lives* (Vespasian collected a tax on receptacles for urine, and on being reproached for this retorted that the money had no smell)
3 From Strabo 8.6.23
4 *Politics* 1.10 (1258b7)
5 *Adages* III ii 89
6 'to do and to suffer' from Horace *Odes* 3.24.43
7 Pope Julius II entered Bologna in triumph on 11 November 1506.
8 'great jar with holes,' a reference to the story of the Danaids, daughters of King Danaus of Argos, who killed their husbands on their wedding nights, and

were condemned to fill with water a jug riddled with holes (cf *Adages* I iv 60)

9 Genesis 23:11 (the name is Ephron)
10 Luke 10:7

I ix 14
Parturiunt montes, nascetur ridiculus mus / The mountains labour, forth will creep a mouse

A proverb still with us, kept in circulation for a long time because of Horace's famous line in the Art of Poetry. *It was known in Greek (Diogenianus 8.75) and Latin (Otto 1173), and came into English (Tilley* M *1215). Erasmus first cited it in* Collectanea *no 491.*

Ὤδινεν ὄρος, εἶτα μῦν ἀπέκτεκεν, The mountain laboured, then produced a mouse. A proverbial iambic line, customarily used of boastful characters who are all display, and rouse wonderful expectations by their munificent promises and the magisterial air of their expression and costume, but when it comes to the point they contribute mere rubbish. Lucian[1] uses this adage in the essay called *How History Should Be Written*; for he says that when a Cupid dressed up as Hercules or a Titan, he was greeted by shouts of 'The mountain laboured.' Athenaeus[2] in his *Doctors at Dinner*, book 14, records that Tachas king of Egypt directed a jibe of this kind against the Spartan king Agesilaus, who had come to offer him assistance during a war: 'The mountain laboured and Jupiter was in a fright, but it has brought forth a mouse,' Agesilaus being very small in build. He took great offence, and retorted, 'One day you will take me for a lion.' Later on there was a rebellion in Egypt and the king, not having the support of Agesilaus, was obliged to take refuge in Persia. In Greek it seems to be an anapestic line. Horace[3] too uses it in *The Art of Poetry*: 'How will our boaster match these mighty words? / The hills will travail; out will creep a mouse.' Porphyrion thinks this arose from a fable of Aesop's, which runs as follows. Once upon a time, some inexperienced rustics saw the earth on a mountain-side lifting and shifting, and gathered from the country round to such a terrifying sight, expecting the earth to bring forth some new and formidable portent, since a mountain was in labour; the Titans, they thought, would break out once more to renew their war against the gods. At length, after they had waited a long time in suspense and terror, a mouse crept out of the ground, and soon they were all roaring with laughter.

1 *How History Should Be Written* 23
2 Athenaeus 14.616d
3 *Art of Poetry* 138–9 (Porphyrion is one of the ancient commentators on Horace; the story in Aesop is 520 Halm and Phaedrus 4.24)

I ix 34
Leonem ex unguibus aestimare / To know a lion by his claws

Erasmus seems to have picked up this proverb from Diogenianus 5.15, as he did others in a sequence that follows: I ix 35 'The fox is given away by his brush,' 36 'I judge the fabric from its border,' 37 'I know by the taste,' 38 'I judge an Ethiopian by his face,' and 39 'I know the tree by its fruit' (from Matthew 12:33), all in Collectanea *no 22. 'To know a lion by his claws' was circulated in sixteenth-century England (Tilley L 313); it was parodied in the satirical drama* Return from Parnassus, Part 1 *(c 1600): 'I am one that can judge according to the proverb,* bovem ex unguibus' *– in which the speaker ironically substitutes* bos *(or ox) for the lion.*

Ἐκ τῶν ὀνύχων λέοντα γινώσκειν, To know a lion by his claws, is to form an idea of an entire object from one single inference, to infer much from little evidence and great results from small indication. The adage seems to take its rise from the sculptor Phidias who, as Lucian[1] tells us in his *Sects*, having seen nothing but the claw of a lion, formed an idea of the size of the whole lion and reproduced the whole beast on the evidence of one claw. Plutarch[2] in his essay 'On the Obsolescence of Oracles' appears to refer it to Alcaeus, for he writes: 'Not, as Alcaeus has it, painting the lion from a single claw,' inferring, that is to say, great things from one small one. Philostratus[3] in his *Life of Apollonius*: 'Such as I see you already to be from the claw.' Basil the Great[4] writing to the philosopher Maximus: 'A man's words are truly a reflection of his soul, and so I learnt to know you from your writings, as they say one knows a lion from his claws.' This is done by using mathematical ratios (as Vitruvius[5] tells us in book 3) in such a way that even from the smallest limb the dimensions of the whole body can be inferred. It was by this method that Pythagoras[6] calculated the dimensions of Hercules' body from the stadium at Pisa, which he had laid out by stepping it himself. In the same way physicians judge the state of a man's health at all points from the pulse in one artery, and one can infer the whole of a man's life from his hair, his waistline, or the movement of his eyes; in this way we assess the whole of a man's education from a single letter, and from one reply form an idea of his whole stock of wisdom.

1 *Hermotimus* 55 (a dialogue also called *The Sects*)
2 'On the Obsolescence of Oracles' in *Moralia* 410C citing Alcaeus frag Z 115 Lobel-Page (Mynors points out that Alcaeus, the poet, is earlier than Phidias the sculptor, and Erasmus would have known this, yet missed the inconsistency)
3 *Life of Apollonius* 1.32
4 St Basil of Caesarea *Letters* 9.1 (*PG* 32.268C)
5 Vitruvius *On Architecture* 3.1.2 (this author mentioned only twice in the *Adages*)
6 From Aulus Gellius *Attic Nights* 1.1.2

I ix 55
Illotis manibus / With unwashed hands

Like many ancient proverbs, this one, from Diogenianus 1.43 (see also Otto 1046), picks up a religious taboo and elevates it to a generalized secular wisdom. Erasmus applies the proverb to biblical interpretation at the end of the essay: the interpreter must approach the text well prepared for the sacred task of interpretation. It is related to the modern phrase 'to dirty one's hands' (Tosi 1542); see also Tilley H 125. *Erasmus first recorded it in the* Collectanea *no 504. It follows immediately after 'To enter with unwashed feet'* (I ix 54), *referred to below in the quotation by Gregory, and in relation to St Jerome and scriptural interpretation.*

Ἀνίπτοις χερσίν, With unwashed hands, is recorded by Diogenianus in the sense of irreverent and ill-prepared. This too is a metaphor from ritual purity. Hesiod[1] in the *Works and Days* forbids the offering of a libation to Jove in the morning with hands unwashed: 'Never with hands unwashed in the early light of morning / Offer the glinting wine to Jove and the other immortals.' He also forbids anyone to enter a stream or spring without washing his hands. Hence the frequent mention of the *chernips* in Homer,[2] a word which by its sound precisely conveys the sense of 'hand-washing,' with which the ancients always made a propitious start to religious ceremonial, and also to dinners which have a ceremonial element in them. Gregory the Theologian,[3] as they call him, in the apology for his flight into Pontus, connects both phrases: 'With unwashed hands, as the saying goes, and uninitiate feet they force their way into most sacred things.' Gaius in the first book of the *Pandects*,[4] title *De origine juris*, writes: 'If it is thought indecent, if I may so put it, for counsel presenting a case in court to set out the facts before the judge with no introduction, how much more improper it will be for those who offer an interpretation to overlook the early stages and make no search for origins, but with unwashed hands, if I may so put it, to proceed at once to the subject-matter of their interpretation.'

Either proverb will properly be used of those who plunge into some undertaking full of self-confidence or ignorant of what they ought to know; for instance, anyone who assumes the office of a prince with no equipment of virtue or wisdom or experience of affairs, or sets out to interpret Holy Scripture untaught and unpractised in Greek, Latin, and Hebrew and indeed in the whole of antiquity, without which it is not only foolish but impious to undertake to treat of the mysteries of theology. And yet, outrageous as it is, this is now common practice. Equipped with a few frosty syllogisms and some childish sophistries, where (Heaven help us) do they draw the line? Where do they not lay down the law? What problems are insoluble? Could they but see the merriment, or rather, the sorrow that they cause to those with some experience of the ancient tongues and of antiquity, could they see the monstrosities that they produce and the shameful errors into which they fall continually, they would surely be ashamed of their headlong incompetence and return even in old age to the rudiments of a liberal education. Many men come to a right conclusion unaided by the laws of dialectic, to say nothing of the quillets of sophistry. There was sense and wisdom among mortals, even before the idol of these people, Aristotle, was born. No one ever understood another person's meaning without a knowledge of the tongue in which that meaning was expressed. And so St Jerome, when he had decided to interpret Holy Scripture and was determined not to take up such a task with unwashed feet, as the saying goes – I ask you, did he equip his mind with sophistic rubbish? With Aristotelian principles? With nonsense yet more nonsensical than this? Not he. How did he start then? With incalculable efforts he acquired a knowledge of the three tongues. The man who is ignorant of these is no theologian, he treats divine theology with outrage, and with both hands and feet in very truth unwashed he does not take up this most sacred of all subjects, he profanes it and defiles it and outrages it.

1 *Works and Days* 724–5 and 737–9
2 The word brings together *cheras*, hands, and *niptein*, to wash, and is found throughout Homer.
3 Gregory of Nazianzus *Oratio* 2.8 (*PG* 35.416B)
4 *Digest* of Justinian 1.2.1

I X 13
Canis in praesepi / Dog in the manger

The proverbial tale of the dog in the manger does not appear in the early collections of Aesop, and is derived from the reference in Lucian as Erasmus gives it below (also appearing in Suidas K *2729 and Apostolius 17.20a). The story was expanded in Renaissance fable collections and only then became part of the Aesop corpus (it is number 702 in Ben Edwin Perry's listing of all the Aesop-related proverbs at the end of his Loeb edition of Babrius and Phaedrus). The proverb is common in English (Tilley* D *513).*

Ἡ *κύων ἐν τῇ φάτνῃ*, The dog in the manger, is said of those who neither enjoy something themselves nor allow other people to get any benefit from it; for instance if a man were to keep valuable manuscripts tightly locked up, which he never opens himself nor allows anyone else to read them, just like a dog in a manger that does not eat the barley itself and prevents the horse from eating it. Lucian[1] *Against an Ignoramus*: 'But you behave like the dog that lies in the manger, neither eating the barley itself nor making way for the horse that could eat it.' He uses it again in his *Timon*. It is cited by Suidas[2] in his article on the proverb Nothing to do with Dionysus, but no source is named: 'You bring the dog to the manger, and bring forward nothing to do with Dionysus,' that is, you adduce something quite off the point, and of what was relevant to the point at issue you adduce nothing. Athenaeus[3] in book 6 reports something similar of a tribe of Galatians called the Cordistae: they abominate gold and do not import it into their own country, but none the less do not cease to seize gold from other people. This tribe is said to be the remnant of the Gauls who ravaged the oracle at Delphi under their leader Brennus, who were pursued and dealt with mercilessly by their leader Bathanatus. Hence their hatred of gold, for the sake of which they have suffered so much; and yet they grudge it to anyone else.

1 Lucian *Against an Ignoramus* 30 and *Timon* 14
2 Suidas O 806
3 Athenaeus 6.234a–b (in the original Bathanatus did not *pursue* the Gauls, but *settled* them on the land; not *ediôken*, but *edioikisen*)

I X 25
Summum ius, summa iniuria / Extreme right is extreme wrong

This proverb has almost the force of a legal principle, and it is often used in the context of the law (Otto 884, Tosi 1094). It appears in English writers both in the Latin and as 'Extreme right is extreme wrong' (Tilley R 122).

Extreme right is extreme wrong means that men never stray so far from the path of justice as when they adhere most religiously to the letter of the law. They call it 'extreme right' when they wrangle over the words of a statute and pay no heed to the intention of the man who drafted it. Words and letters are like the outer skin of the law. The folly of some pedantic interpreters of the law is fully and brilliantly shown up by Cicero[1] in his speech *Pro Murena*. Terence:[2] 'But the saying is, Chremes, that extreme right is often extreme injustice.' Cicero[3] in the first book of the *De officiis*: 'Hence came that proverb which is now so familiar, Extreme right is extreme wrong.' Columella[4] in book one of his *Agriculture*: 'Nor for the matter of that should we always exact whatever we have a right to; for our forefathers thought that extreme right was extreme torment.' Celsus too as a young man is reported in the Pandects,[5] book 45, title *De verborum obligatione*, in the chapter *Si servum Stichum*, as saying: 'For this is a question of justice and equity, a field in which dangerous mistakes are frequently made under authority from the science of the law.' Paulus too in book 50, in the title *De regulis juris*: 'In all things, but in the law especially, regard should be had to equity.'

Seneca[6] uses a similar metaphor, *summo animo*, in the first book of his *On Anger*, where he says: 'If you understand that the wickedness is not deep-seated, but resides, as they say, in the surface levels of the heart.'

1 *Pro Murena* 11.25
2 *Heautontimorumenos* 795–6
3 *On Duties* 1.10.33
4 *Res rustica* 1.7.2
5 *Pandects* in Justinian's *Digest* 45.1.91.3 and 50.17.90
6 The metaphor from Seneca *On Anger* 1.19.5 seems out of place and perhaps was intended to go with another adage such as I X 46 'Listen to a man who speaks from his heart.'

I X 59
Aut mortuus est aut docet litteras / He must be either dead or teaching school

An amusing, if somewhat depressing, proverb. The source is Zenobius 4.17 (often called 'Zenodotus' by Erasmus).

Ἢ τέθνηκεν ἢ διδάσκει γράμματα, He must be either dead or teaching school. An iambic line current as a proverb, and used in old days to convey that a man was in great misfortune, though it was not clear what he was doing. This passed into common speech, as Zenodotus tells us, on the following occasion. The Athenians, under command of Nicias, had on one occasion fought and lost a battle against the Sicilians; they suffered heavy casualties, and many prisoners were taken and carried off to Sicily, where they were compelled to teach Sicilian children their elements. And so the few who escaped and returned to Athens, when asked what so-and-so was doing in Sicily, used to reply with the line I have quoted above: 'He must be either dead or teaching school.'

I x 60

Oportet testudinis carnes aut edere aut non edere / When you're offered turtle-meat, either eat or do not eat

There is no direct English equivalent, despite the antiquity of the proverb (Zenobius 4.19, Suidas H *85), though there are striking parallels: 'Fish, or cut bait' or the cruder 'Shit, or get off the pot'* (OED *'Pot' 12 l)*

Ἢ δεῖ χελώνης κρέα φαγεῖν ἢ μὴ φαγεῖν, Eat, or don't eat, your turtle: you must choose, is a proverbial iambic line, directed against those who, having taken up some piece of business, go through with it slowly, neither finishing nor giving it up. Some think the saying derives from an author called Terpsion; and among them is Athenaeus,[1] book 8, who says he was the first to lay down rules about eating, and published a code which made clear what one ought to abstain from and what one ought to eat, in which was this rule about turtle, 'eat or don't eat.' They say further that turtle-meat eaten in moderate quantities causes griping of the bowels, which is relieved by larger amounts; very much what Pliny[2] tells us about lettuce. It amounts to a way of saying: Make up your mind. Either go to war or don't go to war; either study or don't study. Remember how many activities there are which are admirable if you throw yourself into them, and do harm if you are lukewarm; or which do not admit of mediocrity, like music and poetry. Again, there are some things of which a taste is sufficient, to which class the study of philosophy was assigned by Neoptolemus in Ennius[3] and Callicles in Plato.[4] It is not far from that text in the Apocalypse:[5] 'I would thou wert hot or cold.'

1 Athenaeus 8.377b citing Terpsion, fourth-century BC author of a *Gastrology*

2 Pliny *Natural History* 20.64

3 Ennius Sc 376 ed Vahlen quoting Neoptolemus
4 Plato *Gorgias* 454C, citing Callicles
5 Revelation 3:15

II i 1
Festina lente / Make haste slowly

This proverb begins the second series of a thousand proverbs. It is one of the longest essays, a fascinating mix of research, speculation, and personal history, greatly expanded from a tiny note in Collectanea *no 196, and worked on in successive editions of the* Adages. *It was also seen by Erasmus as a form of mock eulogy. In* Foundations of the Abundant Style *(the* De copia*) he describes this essay in part as a rhetorical performance of playful 'cleverness': 'Thus Favorinus eulogized fever, Synesius baldness, myself folly (in my* Moriae encomium*), and I also extolled Aldus' anchor in the* Adagia*' (CWE 24 659). Aldus, or Aldo Manuzio (c 1450–1515), was a brilliant Venetian scholar-printer who produced many beautiful editions of the classics as well as of contemporary works. See pp xiii–xiv. The image of the dolphin and anchor had appeared in the* Hypnerotomachia Poliphili, *printed by Aldus in 1499 (Erasmus seems to refer specifically to this text below; see illustration on p 138), had a long tradition in emblem literature and, because of Aldus, is still famous as a printer's mark. In the English-speaking world, it was used by British publisher William Pickering in the early nineteenth century and in the twentieth century by Dent in the Everyman series and by the U.S. publisher Doubleday. The adage (Tilley H 192) was very popular in its Latin and Greek forms, was also varied in the medieval collections, and has moved into other European languages (listed in Tosi 1581, who mentions the modern German* Eile mit Weile, *a rhyming oxymoron). An interesting counter-sentence from the Renaissance is Friar Laurence's too cautious 'Wisely and slow, they stumble that run fast' (*Romeo and Juliet *2.3.94).*

Σπεῦδε βραδέως, Make haste slowly. This proverb has at first sight an agreeable touch of the riddle about it, made up as it is of contradictory words. It must therefore take its place in a particular class which I pointed out at the beginning of this work – those which are expressed by *enantiosis*, the contrast of opposites, of which δυσδαίμων εὐδαιμονία, *Infelix felicitas*, Unhappy happiness, would be an example.

ERASMI ROTERODAMI ADAGIORVM CHILIADES TRES, AC CENTVRIAE FERE TOTIDEM.

ALD. STVDIOSIS. S.

Quũ nihil aliud cupio, q̃ prodesse uobis Studiosi. Cum uenisset in manus meas Erasmi Roterodami, hominis undecunq; doctiss. hoc adagiorũ opus eruditum. uarium. plenũ bonæ frugis, & quod possit uel cum ipsa antiquitate certare, intermissis antiquis autorib. quos paraueram excudendos, illud curauimus imprimendum, rati profuturum uobis & multitudine ipsa adagiorũ, quæ ex plurimis autorib. tam latinis, quàm græcis studiose collegit summis certe laborib. summis uigiliis, & multis locis apud utriusq; linguæ autores obiter uel correctis acute, uel expositis erudite. Docet præterea quot modis ex hisce adagiis capere utilitatem liceat, puta quẽadmodum ad uarios usus accõmodari possint. Adde, q͛d circiter decẽ millia uersuum ex Homero. Euripide, & cæteris Græcis eodẽ metro in hoc opere fideliter, & docte tralata habẽtur, præter plurima ex Platone, Demosthene, & id genus aliis. An autem uerus sim, ἰδοὺ ῥόδος, ἰδοὺ καὶ τὸ πήδημα. Nam, quod dicitur, αὐτὸς αὑτὸν αὐλεῖ.

Præponitur hisce adagiis duplex index. Alter secundum literas alphabeti nostri. nam quæ græca sunt, latina quoq; habentur. Alter per capita rerum.

Make haste slowly The title page of the 1508 edition of the *Adages*, with the anchor and dolphin mark of Aldus Manutius. Aldus' short address to the studious reader praises the labour that has gone into the book and ends wittily with two Greek proverbs: *Here's Rhodes: let's see you jump* (III iii 28) and *He is his own flute-player* (II v 86). (Houghton Library, Harvard University)

And I should think it a reasonable guess, were someone to suppose that it started from that phrase in the *Knights* of Aristophanes[1], 'Make haste with speed,' σπεῦδε ταχέως, that is, *propera propere*, the man who alluded to it [in the corresponding expression], whoever he was, having substituted an *enantiosis* for the *anadiplosis*, the forcible doubling of the same idea. This effective use of the contrast, and the neatness of the allusion, acquire not a little further grace from such apt and utter brevity, which seems to me somehow to have a special value of its own in adages, as in seal-rings, and makes them all the more admired and valued. If you consider the vigour and wealth of meaning embodied in these few brief words, so pregnant, so authoritative, so wholesome, so widely applicable to the whole range of human life, you will easily agree with me that in this great company of proverbs no other so richly deserves to be inscribed on every pillar, written up over the gate of every church (yes, and in letters of gold!), painted on the great doors of princes' courts, graven on the seal-rings of prelates and figured on the sceptres of kings – it should, in a word, be brought before the eye on all public buildings everywhere and become widespread and familiar, as something which ought ideally to be always present in every man's mind and never very far from men's eyes. For there is no mortal creature who would not greatly profit by it, and especially princes and those to whom, if I may borrow Homer's words,[2] 'peoples are given in trust, and many the cares that beset them.' For men of humble station, if they are idle and fail to do something, or headstrong and make a mistake, do far less damage and any unfortunate results are more easily set right. But one fit of idleness in a prince, one rash decision – just think what storms it sometimes raises and what ruin it can bring with it into the affairs of men! If on the other hand to make haste slowly is not forgotten, which means the right timing and the right degree, governed alike by vigilance and patience, so that nothing regrettable is done through haste, and nothing left undone through sloth that may contribute to the wellbeing of the commonwealth, could any government be more prosperous, more stable and firmly-rooted than this? – though this prosperity is by no means limited by its actual boundaries, but spreads everywhere far and wide among neighbouring peoples, so that nowhere is there more truth in that remark of

Hesiod's:[3] 'An evil neighbour is as great a bane / As a good one's a boon.'

And so my personal opinion is that if ever a proverb truly deserved the name of royal, this is the one, not only for the reasons I have given but because the spirit of princes seems especially close to these two faults. The favour of fortune, great possessions, every incitement to luxury ready to hand, complete liberty to do as one pleases; above all, the plaudits of the toadies that are so corrupting, and the approval, the applause and congratulations that await everything they do or say whatever it may be like – it is not surprising, I say, that all this and more of the kind makes some princes lazy, most of all if this soothing treatment is lavished on youth and youth's constant companion, inexperience. Conversely, it happens sometimes that the inborn vigour natural to a prince, and his lion-like spirit, if I may so express it, increased by ample resources, stimulated by success in great enterprises, fired perhaps by anger or ambition or other such desires and sharpened by bloodthirsty counsellors – all this sometimes sweeps them off their course and carries princes themselves and the whole mass of their dominions to the edge of the abyss. Though if one must make a mistake in one direction or the other, it will be much better for a king to be too slow than to be over-hasty. Homer seems to have given his Agamemnon some reprehensible kind of soft-heartedness, which is the 'slowly' of our proverb, so that no valiant deed or show of spirit is reported of him, except for his anger when Chryseis was taken from him, and his seizure of Briseis who belonged to Achilles. On the other hand he makes Achilles too rash and headstrong, in fact gives him our 'Make haste'; unless anyone thinks it was 'making haste slowly' when he drew his sword in the council and made for the king, and had to be restrained by Pallas,[4] who told him to confine his anger to abusive words. And yet to go even that far showed a complete lack of self-control – in a crowded session of the princes to break out with such a flow of curses and open abuse against the man who held supreme command. Achilles seems to have served as a model for Alexander the Great, who indeed outdid him; for he was driven so headlong by his passions that he drew his sword even against his dearest friends. Sardanapalus[5] imitated Agamemnon, and so successfully that he far surpassed him. In fact it is possible to find an infinite number of each kind, reproducing the sloth of one or the ferocity of the other; but you would discover very few who have followed our proverb and found the right mixture of well-timed speed and wise deliberation. One man perhaps may stand for many, the famous Fabius Maximus[6] who was actually nicknamed Cunctator, Old Steady-does-it, who not only won immortal glory for himself but by his 'slow, slow tactics saved the Roman state,'[7] which the ill-advised haste of other generals had by then brought into the greatest jeopardy.

I can see therefore that it was not without reason if our 'Make haste slowly' appealed so much to two Roman emperors – and those two easily the most highly thought of among them all – Octavius Augustus and Titus Vespasian. There was a lofty spirit in them both beyond the common run, coupled with a remarkable gentleness and easiness in personal relations, such that, after winning all hearts by their friendly and gracious demeanour, none the less, when the situation called for a strong man, they rapidly solved the greatest problems. Augustus in consequence was so devoted to this saying, as Aulus Gellius[8] tells us in the *Attic Nights*, book 10 chapter 1, followed by Macrobius[9] in book 6 of the *Saturnalia*, that he used it freely in his daily conversation and often included it in his letters, using these two words as a spur to encourage 'the concurrent application to business of rapid energy and meticulous care.' Gellius thinks this is expressed in Latin by a single word *matura*, ripe. For we call things 'ripe' that happen neither prematurely nor later than the proper time, but just when they should: and Virgil[10] used the word in this sense when he wrote in the first book of the *Aeneid* 'The time is ripe to flee.' Though in general this word *maturare* is used in good authors in the sense of *festinare*, to hasten, subject to the proviso that, hasten though you may, you do not anticipate the proper time; for you could rightly call things done prematurely *festinata*, but not *maturata*. This agrees with what Suetonius[11] tells us in his life of Augustus: 'He thought nothing more out of place in the finished general than to be hasty and rash, and often used to repeat the familiar words Σπεῦδε βραδέως, ἀσφαλὴς γάρ ἐστ' ἀμείνων ἢ θρασὺς / στρατηγός.' So says Suetonius. It is a line of verse, trochaic tetrameter catalectic, taken from some poet,[12] I suppose, to which Caesar added the last word out of his own head. The sense is 'Make haste slowly. For he who achieves a result slowly and without a mistake is better than someone rash and self-confident.' What is foreseen and planned at leisure is safer than what is done in a hurry and planned in haste. Again, Vespasian's approval of our maxim can easily be inferred from very ancient coins issued by him, one of which I was allowed to inspect by Aldo Manuzio.[13] It was struck in silver from ancient dies clearly of Roman date, and he said it had been a present to him from Pietro Bembo, a Venetian patrician, a young man who was not only a scholar of distinction but a most industrious explorer of the whole field of ancient literature. The design of the coin was as follows. One side showed the head of Vespasian with an inscription, the other an anchor, the central shaft of which had a dolphin coiled round it. Now the only meaning conveyed by this symbol is that favourite maxim of the emperor Augustus 'Make haste slowly'; and this we learn from the ancient texts relating to hieroglyphics.

Hieroglyphics is the name given to those enigmatic designs so much used in the early centuries, especially among the priest-prophets and theologians in Egypt, who thought it quite wrong to express the mysteries of wisdom in ordinary writing and thus expose them, as we do, to the uninitiated public. What they thought worth knowing they would record by drawing the shapes of various animals and inanimate things, in such a way that it was not easy for the casual reader to unravel them forthwith. It was necessary first to learn the properties of individual things and the special force and nature of each separate creature; and the man who had really penetrated these could alone interpret the symbols and put them together, and thus solve the riddle of their meaning. For example, when the Egyptians wish to denote their god Osiris, whom they identify with the sun, 'they represent a sceptre and draw on it the outline of an eye,' to indicate of course that Osiris is a god, enjoys a king's exalted power, and can see everything, because the ancients used to call the sun Jove's eye. Something of the sort is recorded by Macrobius[14] in the first book of his *Saturnalia*. The year they represented like this: they drew a serpent coiled into a ring so that it held its own tail in its mouth, suggesting how with the same changing round of seasons the year always returns upon itself. Hence (so Servius[15] maintains) the Greeks gave the year the name *eniautos*, and Virgil[16] had this in mind when he wrote 'Round its old track returns the rolling year.' Though Horus the Egyptian,[17] author of two

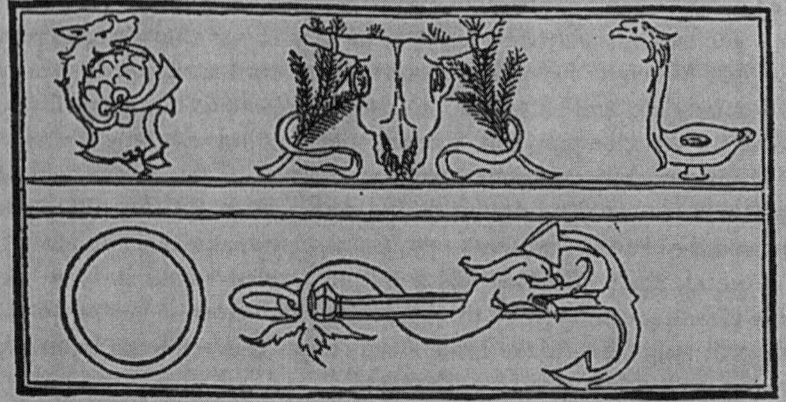

Make haste slowly This image of the anchor and the dolphin, discussed by Erasmus at II i 1*, appeared in a description of hieroglyphics by Francesco Colonna in the *Hypnerotomachia Poliphili* (*Poliphilus' Strife of Love in a Dream*), here in the edition published by Aldus Manutius in 1499 (sig d7r). The signs at the top represent patience and the combined form at the bottom is interpreted, as Erasmus tells us, as *aie speude bradeôs*: always (circle) hasten (dolphin) slowly (anchor). (Houghton Library, Harvard University)

books which still survive on symbols of this kind, tells us that the serpent-image represents time and not the year; the symbol for a year is sometimes an image of Isis and sometimes of a phoenix. The same question was considered by Plutarch[18] in his essay 'On Osiris,' and among the Greeks by Chaerêmon, according to Suidas,[19] from whose works are excerpted, I suspect, the records of this sort of thing which I have seen lately. These included among other things a design to this effect: a circle to begin with, then an anchor, the middle of which, as I have said, has the twisted body of a dolphin twined around it. According to the explanation which was attached, the circle as having neither beginning nor end represents eternity. The anchor, which holds back and ties down the ship and binds it fast, indicates slowness. The dolphin, as the fastest and in its motions most agile of living creatures, expresses speed. If then you skilfully connect these three, they will make up some such principle as 'Ever hasten slowly.' What is more, this kind of symbolic expression is not only of venerable antiquity, it has a charm of its own for anyone who, as I said above, has fully mastered the properties of things; and this result is achieved partly by the careful examination of things and their natural causes, and partly by acquiring a good knowledge of the humanities.

Suppose for example that one were to obtain from that book of Aristotle's[20] which he called his *Lectures on Physics* a firm grasp of the existence of some relation and resemblance between magnitude, motion, and time, because each of these three exists equally in the same object. Just as time is inseparable from motion, so motion is inseparable from magnitude. What a point is in magnitude, a moment is in time, and an impulse in motion (if I may use that word provisionally for the smallest quantum of motion, which is indivisible; for we need not trouble ourselves about names, provided we are agreed on the thing). Suppose then that you were to consider magnitude in a straight line; you will find two points, one of which is solely the beginning and the other exclusively the end – the points from which, as it were, length starts to run and in which it stops. Now set up motion in that same straight line, and you will equally find two impulses, with one of which the motion begins and in the other it finishes. It is basic to these that the initial impulse is nothing except the beginning of that motion, and the concluding impulse is nothing except its conclusion.

Motion must of necessity be associated with time; for time is as it were the measure of it, and if you were to contemplate its nature in abstraction you can find two moments (if I may so put it), one of which is the beginning of that space of time and the other its end. But now suppose that in the same line you consider the points of magnitude, the impulses of motion and the moments of time which lie between the beginning and the end: you can see that each of them has a sort of dual nature. Considered in reference to the beginning, they are ends; considered in relation to the end, they are beginnings. Moreover, when the magnitude comes to an end, at the same place and time the motion ends and the time also must be ended. But a magnitude which has a beginning of such a kind that it cannot also be the end, and an end of such a kind that it cannot be considered as a beginning, must be finite; and this we find in all shapes except that of the circle or the sphere. In this there is no definite point which can properly be called a beginning, and nothing which can be called an end in the sense that it is the only thing so called; and in the same way there is no moment and no impulse of which this can be true. Hence it follows that in this shape there is no finite magnitude, no finite motion, and no finite time. Again, when any point of magnitude you like to take is at the same moment a beginning and an end, magnitude must of necessity be unlimited. And by the same reasoning, when an impulse you choose can be either a beginning of motion or an end, there motion is clearly unlimited. Finally, when any moment you choose can be simultaneously either a beginning of time or an end, there time must be unlimited. But time unlimited we call eternity, and this corresponds to eternal motion; eternal motion requires magnitude which is also eternal or infinite. These considerations do not apply to any magnitude that is not spherical or circular. Hence certain philosophers have inferred the eternity of the universe, because they observed that the heavens as a whole and the heavenly bodies are spherical in shape, and their motion also is spherical. And so not only does the principle of the circle agree with magnitude of this kind; but the motion inherent in it is also a kind of circle. Likewise the time by which this motion is measured can be called circular, as Aristotle also avers in the fourth book of his *Lectures on Physics*. Anyone therefore who has mastered all this and more of the same kind from the study of philosophy will easily form an idea why it was that the Egyptians chose a circle to represent everlasting time.

Now let us briefly consider the significance and nature of the dolphin. The authorities tell us that with its incredible speed and amazingly vigorous movement it leaves all other living creatures far behind. Thus Oppian[21] in his second book on the nature of fishes compares dolphins, not with birds of any ordinary kind, but with the eagle:

As in the fowls of the air there is no king but the eagle,
Over carnivorous beasts the monarch of all is the lion,
Just as in things that crawl the mastery lies with the viper,
Even so by his onrush the dolphin is lord of the fishes.

He also compares it to a projectile: 'For they fly through the sea like an arrow,' and even finally with the wind, or rather, with a whirlwind or hurricane: 'Sometimes it darts through the deep sea-wave like a whirlwind.' Pliny[22] in his *History of the World*, book 9 chapter 8, accepting the view of Aristotle, gives an account which at no point differs from this. The dolphin, he says, is the fastest of all living creatures, and not only among those which live in the sea; it is faster than any bird and has a higher velocity than any missile. And its exceptional speed can be inferred from one piece of evidence in particular: the fact that, though its mouth is a long way from its snout – in fact, half way down its belly, which must necessarily be a considerable handicap to it in catching fish, for it cannot seize them unless it turns over on its back – yet hardly any fish is fast enough to get away from it. Nor is the creature itself unaware of this natural gift; but as though to secure admiration, or to amuse itself, it sometimes races ships in full sail. For the dolphin is exceptionally fond of man (some say of boys in particular), and it is therefore a mortal enemy of the crocodile, which is more hostile to man than any other animal. And so it does not fear man as something alien, but comes to meet vessels and plays exultantly round them – races them even and passes them, however great their spread of canvas. Moreover, when chasing mullet in Lake Laterna, it gives a splendid exhibition of its speed and skill, and also of its goodwill towards mankind. And how can I describe its thrust, which almost defies belief? When, spurred on by hunger, it has pursued a fleeing fish down to the bottom and has held its breath for some time, it rushes up to breathe like an arrow shot from a bow, and leaps out of the water with such force that often it will clear a ship's canvas swollen by the wind at a single bound. To express that eager and tireless spirit, what symbol could be more appropriate than the dolphin?

To convey the idea of slowness and hesitation the fish they call *echenēis*, the Latin *remora*, was not unsuitable;[23] but its shape was thought too difficult to recognize (for apart from its small size, it has no distinguishing mark), and so for this purpose the anchor was preferred as an emblem, which, if sailing is rendered dangerous by high following winds, ties down the ship's excessive speed and holds it fast.

It is clear then that this saying, Make haste slowly, arose in the secret heart of ancient philosophy; whence it was called into their service by two of the most highly esteemed of all Roman emperors, one of whom used it as a device and the other as an emblem, so well did it agree with the character and disposition of both. And now it has passed to Aldo Manuzio, citizen of Rome, as a kind of heir in the third generation, 'for so methinks heaven's power and purpose held.'[24] It is he that gives fresh celebrity to the same device that was once approved by Vespasian. And it is not only most familiar, it is also highly popular among all those everywhere in the world to whom sound learning is either familiar or dear. Nor do I think this symbol was more illustrious then, when it was stamped on the imperial coinage and suffered the wear and tear of circulation as it passed from one merchant to another, than it is now, when in every nation, even outside the limits of any Christian empire, it spreads and wins recognition, it is held fast and prized in company with books of all kinds in both the ancient languages, by all who are devoted to the cult of liberal studies. I think especially of those who despise the barbarous and uncouth learning of our own day and aspire to that true knowledge stemming from antiquity, for the restoration of which this man was surely born – was made and modelled, so to say, by the fates themselves. Such is his burning devotion to this single end, such is his tireless zeal, so great his readiness to shoulder any burden, so that their supply of texts may be restored, complete and genuine and uncorrupted, to all intelligent men of good will. How great the influence he has already exercised in this direction, although with fate (I would almost say) against him, the facts are there to prove. And if only some deity that favours good literature would give a fair wind to the noble, the positively royal ambitions of my friend Aldus – 'if only hostile powers give leave'[25] – I can promise students a great future in the next few years. Everything in the way of good authors in four languages – Latin, Greek, Hebrew, and Chaldaean – and in every field of study will be at their disposal, complete and correct, through this one man's efforts, and none of them will any longer feel the lack of any part of his literary heritage. And when that moment comes, it will then be clear what a wealth of good manuscripts is still lying hid, either concealed by neglect or kept secret by some men's ambition, whose only motive is the wish to have an apparent monopoly of knowledge. Then at length it will be recognized what prodigious blunders disfigure the text, even of those authors who are now thought to be in a pretty good state. Anyone who wishes to form an idea of this from one sample should compare the letters of Pliny,[26] as they will shortly appear from the Aldine press, with the current copies, and what he will find there he may expect in other authors. A labour indeed worthy of Hercules,[27] fit for the spirit of a king, to give back to the world something so heavenly, when it was in a state of almost complete collapse; to trace out what lies hid, to dig up what is buried, to call back the dead, to repair what is mutilated, to correct what is corrupted in so many ways, especially by the fault of those common printers who reckon one pitiful gold coin in the way of profit worth more than the whole realm of letters. And another point: however loudly you may sing the praises of those men who by their valour protect or even extend the boundaries of their country, they are active at best in worldly things and constrained within narrow limits. But he who restores a literature in ruins (almost a harder task than to create one) is engaged on a thing sacred and immortal, and works for the benefit not of one province only but of all nations everywhere and of all succeeding ages. Last but not least, this was in old days the privilege of princes, among whom Ptolemy[28] won special glory, although his library was contained within the narrow walls of his own palace. Aldus is building a library which knows no walls save those of the world itself.

I cannot believe this modest digression to be without its point. Let it encourage all who wish to learn to give these symbols more serious support and to take more pleasure in them, now that they know from what distinguished precedents they descend, and understand what they mean, and while they bear in mind the blessings which that dolphin promises, if only some deity is at hand to bless these splendid efforts.

I will resume[29] the thread of my discourse after this diversion; but first I must set out my grievance against certain printers, who do a great disservice to the cause of literature. The complaint itself is not new; but never was it more justified than in these latter days, in which I was preparing the fourth edition, if I am not mistaken, of this work. It was in the year 1525. The city of Venice, with its many claims to distinction, has none the less become distinguished through the Aldine press, so much so that any books shipped from Venice to foreign countries immediately find a readier market merely because they bear that city's imprint. And yet the attraction of the name of Venice is so misused by certain sordid printers, that scarcely any city sends us more shamelessly corrupt editions of the standard authors, and those no ordinary names but the very first, Aristotle for instance and Cicero and Quintilian, to say nothing of religious books. It is provided by law that no man should sew a shoe together or make a cupboard, unless he has been approved by his trade guild; yet these eminent authors, to whose works we owe religion itself, are published to the world by men so ill-educated that they cannot so much as read, so idle that they are not prepared to read over what they print, and so mercenary that they would rather see a good book filled with thousands of mistakes than spend a few paltry gold pieces on hiring someone to supervise the proof-correcting. And none make such grand promises on the title-page as those who are most shameless in corrupting everything. The authority of the law gives a right of redress against a man who sells cloth as dyed scarlet, if it is discovered that no berry of the scarlet oat has been added in the dying, and a man can be fined heavily who has practised deception in such goods as these. And is he to enjoy his profits, or rather, the proceeds of his thieving, who at one stroke imposes on so many thousands of his fellow-creatures? In the old days the copying of books by hand was subject to standards no less high than are now demanded of notaries public and sworn attorneys, and they ought certainly to have been higher; nor has there been any more portentous source of textual confusion than the entrusting of so sacred a responsibility haphazard to obscure nobodies and ignorant monks and lately even women. Yet how little is the damage done by a careless or ignorant scribe, if you compare him with a printer! And on this the law of the land has gone to sleep. Punishment waits for the man who sells cloth dyed in England for cloth dyed in Venice, and he is left free to profit from his impertinence who markets mere textual corruptions, intellectual colic, under the label of good authors. You may say, it is not the seller's business to guarantee the buyer against any and every defect. Perhaps: but at least it should be so here, if the title-page promises diligent accuracy and the book is stuffed with blunders. And some are errors which even good scholars cannot at once detect. It is the innumerable crowd of printers that now throws all into confusion, especially in Germany. The first comer is not allowed to set up as a baker; printing is a source of profit from which no mortal being is excluded. You may not draw what you like, or say what you like, without some risk; you may print anything.

Is there anywhere on earth exempt from these swarms of new books? Even if, taken out one at a time, they offered something worth knowing, the very mass of them would be a serious impediment to learning from satiety if nothing else, which can do far more damage where good things are concerned, or simply from the fact that men's minds are easily glutted and hungry for something new, and so these distractions call them away from the reading of ancient authors; than whom we have nothing better to show, though I do not deny that the moderns can make some discoveries which have escaped them. A man may exist, for example, who can teach us something that was hidden from Aristotle, but I do not think one will arise who can give us a body of philosophy more complete than what we owe to him. In theology likewise there may perhaps be someone who can see things that were hidden from Chrysostom or Jerome; but I do not think there will be anyone to do for us, taken as a whole, what they did. Now those great men are virtually outdated, and we waste our time on indiscriminate rubbish, while honourable fields of study are neglected with their standard authors, and the authority of legislatures, councils, universities, lawyers, and theologians falls in ruins. If things go on as they have begun, all power will in the end be concentrated in a few hands; we shall see in our midst the same sort of barbarous tyranny that exists among the Turks. Everything will be subject to the whim of one man or of a few; no traces will remain of civilian government, all will be subject to the violence of a military junta. All honourable fields of knowledge will become a desert, and one law alone will be in force, the will of the dictator. As for the princes of the Church, they will be of no account whatever; and if they have any resources left or any influence, they will be held entirely at the good will and pleasure of masters who will control everything as the fancy takes them and not by reason. How much better for mankind if society followed the pattern of nature! – where one element is so balanced against another that all is held together in an eternal concord. Thus every element in the body politic would retain its own legitimate authority: the common people would enjoy their rights, the senate and magistrates would be granted all the privileges that learning, law, and equity would allow them, bishops and priests would still be honoured as they deserve, nor would monks be denied what is their due. This universal harmony in discord, this variety all tending towards one end, would preserve the system of the body politic far more faithfully than happens now, when everyone tries to get his claws into everything. No household can hold together for long unless the husband yields part of his sphere of action to the wife, unless there is some distinction between freemen and slaves, and unless slaves in their turn are treated not as beasts of burden but as human beings; last but not least, unless there is some distinction between one slave and another, such that those who serve in the spirit of free men get more indulgent treatment and as a prize for their service can expect their freedom.

At this point someone will say 'Hey, home-made prophet, what has all this to do with printers?' Because no small part of the trouble is introduced by the failure to punish their licence. They fill the world with pamphlets and books – I will not call them worthless, for it may be I write that sort myself but foolish, ignorant, malignant, libellous, mad, impious, and subversive; and such is the flood that even things that might have done some good lose all their goodness. They fly out in swarms, some of them with no author's name or, what is more criminal, with a forged one. When caught out, the printers reply 'Give me something to buy food for my household, and I will cease to print books like this.' You might get the same answer, but with rather more excuse, from any thief, any confidence-trickster, the keeper of any brothel: 'Give me something to live on, and I will abandon my crafty ways.' Or is it perhaps a lesser crime to make secret assaults on another man's purse than openly to deprive him of his reputation? To prostitute your own body or another person's for gain without using violence, than to attack someone else's way of life and the reputation that is dearer than life itself? But enough, and more than enough, of these complaints: I must suggest a remedy. This evil will be much reduced if princes and magistrates will be at pains, so far as they can, to keep out the men without work, whose source, more than anything, is the use of mercenary troops in war. Secondly, if those rascals who are restrained by neither reason nor decency can be shown by the laws, that a big stick awaits them unless they mend their ways. Thirdly, that those who embark on schemes for the public good should be assisted, if their resources fail them, by grants either from princes or from bishops and abbots or from the public treasury. To expect such a public service from business men, most of whom are devoted to Mammon, would perhaps be asking too much. Take those who build an altar or a monument, who hang a picture or set up a statue, and promise themselves a name among posterity: how much more durable the reputation they would secure by the method I suggest! Out of many possibilities I will offer one example. In the interpretation of Holy Scripture scarcely anyone has shown more skill than St John Chrysostom, nor is any author more suitable reading for those who prepare themselves for their duties in the pulpit. And he left a large output, a good part of which we still have, in versions of varying merit, but the majority corrupted, and also mixed with some things that have no Chrysostom about them. Think of the light that would be shed on sacred study, if we had such an important author complete, in Greek, and in a corrected text! – or if we had him at any rate speaking as good Latin as he speaks Greek. I will not put on record here how many ways our magnates have of wasting money, how much is absorbed by gaming, wenching, drinking, needless travel, pageants, wars sought deliberately, ambition, favourites, players, and fools. Of all this at least that is spent to their shame let them divert some portion either for the public benefit or for their own glory or for both.

When Aldus was attempting such things, was there a scholar who did not support him? Who did not make some contribution to help a man overburdened by so great a task? How often were ancient copies sent him unsought from Hungary and Poland, and complimentary presents with them, that with all needful diligence he might publish them worldwide! And what Aldus was attempting in Italy – for he himself has breathed his last, although the press still enjoys the goodwill of his honoured name – that Johann Froben attempts across the Alps, with no less zeal than Aldus and not wholly without success but, it cannot be denied, with less than equal profit. If you ask why, of many possible reasons I think this is the one, that in our country men's minds are not so open as they are in Italy, at least in the literary field. For I am not afraid to speak from my own experience. When I, a Dutchman, was in Italy, preparing to publish my book of *Proverbs*, all the learned men there had offered me unsought authors not yet published in print who they thought might be of use to me and Aldus had nothing in his treasurehouse that he did not share with me. Johannes Lascaris did the same, so did Battista Egnazio, Marco Musuro, Frate Urbano.[30] I felt the benefit of kindness from some people I knew neither by sight nor name. I was bringing nothing to Venice with me except the confused and unsorted materials for a book that was to be, and that material was confined to published authors. With the greatest temerity on my part, we both set to work together, I to write and Aldus to print. The whole business was finished inside nine months more or less, and all the time I was coping with an attack of the stone, a trouble in which as yet I had no experience. Just consider what advantages I should have lost, had not scholars supplied me with texts in manuscript. Among them were Plato's works in Greek, Plutarch's *Lives* and also his *Moralia* which began to be printed when my work was nearly finished, the *Doctors at Dinner* of Athenaeus, Aphthonius, Hermogenes with notes, Aristotle's *Rhetoric* with the scholia of Gregory of Nazianzus, the whole of Aristides with scholia, brief commentaries on Hesiod and Theocritus, Eustathius on the whole of Homer, Pausanias, Pindar with accurate commentary, a collection of proverbs under Plutarch's name and another ascribed to Apostolius to which I was given access by

Girolamo Aleandro.[31] There were other small things too whose names escape me or are not worth recording. Not one of these had yet been printed.

And now in turn let me describe the generous behaviour of a friend of mine from across the Alps; one of my special friends I thought him, and still do, for one should 'know one's friends' weaknesses but hate them not.'[32] When I was preparing the Venice edition, I happened to have seen in his possession a Suidas[33] which had the proverbs marked in the margins. It was an immense work, and meant a great deal of reading. Hoping therefore to spare myself trouble, I asked him to lend me the volume, even if only for a few hours, while my servant transcribed the notes into my copy. I asked him repeatedly, and he always said no. After bringing every form of pressure to bear on him without success, I asked him whether he had a mind to publish the proverbs himself, for if so I would most gladly get out of the way of a man who would do the job much better than myself. He swore he had no such intention. 'Then what' I asked him 'are your motives?' And at last, like a man who confesses under torture, he said that everything is now becoming public property from which scholars hitherto had been able to secure the admiration of the common people. 'Hence all those tears.'[34] There lie hid in the colleges and monasteries of Germany, France, and England very ancient manuscripts which their owners are so far from making available of their own accord (with few exceptions) than when asked to do so, they either conceal them or deny their existence or charge an exhorbitant fee for the use of manuscripts which they value at ten times their true worth. In the end these books, so beautifully looked after, are either destroyed by damp and worms or are removed by thieves. And our grandees are so far from helping the cause of good literature by their generosity that they think no money so irretrievably wasted as what is spent on such good purposes; nor do they approve of anything at all from which they get no pecuniary return. If only the princes on our side of the Alps encouraged liberal studies in the open-handed way one finds in Italy, the Froben serpents[35] would not be much worse off than the Aldine dolphin. Aldus, making haste slowly, has acquired as much gold as he has reputation, and richly deserves both. Froben holds his staff always upright with no purpose in view except the public good, he never swerves from the innocency of his doves, and expresses the wisdom of serpents more in his badge than his behaviour; and so he is richer in reputation than in coin. But it is time to put a stop to these digressions.

I must now return[36] to the exposition of the adage. It will be possible to use the proverb in three ways. The first is when we wish to point out that one should give prolonged thought to a piece of business before starting on it, but when one's mind is made up one should finish it with speed, so that the anchor symbolizes delay in considering and the dolphin speed in finishing. That remark in Sallust[37] comes in here: 'You should take counsel before you start; and when you have thought, then act quickly and have done.' The same opinion is reviewed by Aristotle[38] in book 6 of the *Ethics* as one widely held: 'They say' he remarks 'that what you have thought about should be despatched quickly, but you should take time to consider things.' For this Laertius[39] tells us that Bias is the authority, for he used habitually to advise a slow start in any business, but steady perseverance once it is begun. There is a moral maxim due, I suspect, to Publianus,[40] which is not far from this: 'Prepare for war at leisure, that you may more quickly win,' as well as that other one: 'Weigh well what's right; there's safety in delay.' To which one can add the proverb[41] 'Night is the mother of counsel.' And that phrase of Sophocles[42] in the *Oedipus Tyrannus*: 'Quick thinkers are not safe.' With these one should put a saying of Plato's which I have quoted elsewhere:[43] 'He who is in too much of a hurry to start is slow to arrive.' Rather different, but to be classified under the same head, is Quintilian's[44] view that children of precocious gifts do not easily come to much good; also the current saying that those who are wise in childhood, and as it were before their time, make foolish old men. This is, I think, confirmed by Accius, who is reported by Gellius[45] as saying that the minds of the young are like unripe fruit. He thought a certain tartness acceptable in both, because it showed the only ones that would ripen. They will be sweet all in good time when they are ripe; while all the rest go off before ripening.

There will be another way of using this, when we wish to point out that the emotions must be reined in, as it were, by the reason. Plato,[46] having divided the soul of man into three parts, reason, impulse, and desire, thinks philosophy can be summed up in this, that the emotions should obey the reason as their king, and considers that for this very purpose the seat of the reason is located in a kind of citadel in the brain. The Peripatetics, with Aristotle as their standard-bearer, consider that nature has endowed us with emotions, which are a kind of moving force in the mind, to be a kind of stimulus to rouse us to the practice of virtue; although this is rejected by the Stoics, and in particular by Seneca[47] in the books *On Anger* which he addressed to Nero. Their view is that emotions of this kind make no contribution to virtue, and in fact are an obstacle; though they do not deny, any more than anyone else, that in the heart of their theoretical wise man there remain original impulses which normally forestall the reason and which you would find it impossible to root out altogether. But to prevent their proving acceptable, they are promptly rejected by the reason. This is what Homer[48] alludes to when, in the first *Iliad*, Pallas stands behind Achilles and restrains him when he puts his hand to the hilt of his sword. And so you would be right to call those powerful impulses the dolphin, and the anchor the wisdom that controls them. Seneca[49] has said nothing is the better for delay, except anger, but whenever our desires or dislikes are immoderate, there delay is a good thing. Plutarch[50] in his 'Sayings of Romans' tells how the philosopher Athenodorus, having obtained leave from Octavius Augustus to retire to his own home on grounds of age, recommended to him that when angry he should never do or say anything until he had repeated to himself the names of the twenty-four letters of the Greek alphabet. Whereupon the emperor replied that he still needed Athenodorus, to teach him the art of silence as well as speech, and on this pretext he retained him for a whole further year. There is a line in Terence[51] to the same effect: 'Be careful; this may be a little too hot.' Some people by nature need the spur, and some the bridle; and so those men in ancient times were quite right who liked to see a dolphin twisted round an anchor, because the two things should be balanced one against the other and always coexist, so as to produce a permanent habit of mind like that which Plato[52] thinks can be engendered by the equal practice of 'music' and 'gymnastic.'

A third method of use will be when we wish to point out that in all business one should avoid the headlong haste which in some people is by nature a besetting fault and in everything makes them think a delay however short is too long. This kind of hurry is usually accompanied by error and repentance, as in that well-known Greek line[53] 'Haste is for many men a cause of trouble.' One must keep on dinning into such people that famous remark of Cato[54] 'Soon enough if well enough,' which is recorded by St Jerome, when he writes to Pammachius in these words: 'That's a good remark of Cato's too: "Soon enough, if well enough," which made us laugh when we were young and heard it said by a finished orator in some brief preface. I expect you remember how we both went wrong, when the whole lecture-hall rang to the students' shouts of "Soon enough, if well enough."' Those were Jerome's words. It will be suitable also for those who pursue a reputation in a hurry, and would rather have a great name easily come by than one which is solid and will last. What blooms too early quickly withers; what grows slowly will endure. Horace:[55] 'Marcellus' glory grows as grows the oak, / By secret lapse of time,' and Pindar[56] in the eighth of his *Nemean Hymns*: 'But valour grows as grows the tree, fed with fresh dews, rising among wise men and just towards the limpid sky.'

All those, in a word, who go astray either from idleness or from undue haste should call to mind Octavius Caesar's motto 'Make haste slowly' and that famous emblem, once Vespasian's, that now belongs to Aldus: let them remember the dolphin and the anchor.

1 *Knights* 495
2 *Iliad* 2.25
3 *Works and Days* 346
4 *Iliad* 1.206–14
5 Sardanapalus was a king of Assyria.
6 The dictator whose delaying tactics held back Hannibal
7 Ennius *Annals* 370 (Vahlen)
8 *Attic Nights* 10.11.5
9 *Saturnalia* 6.8.9
10 *Aeneid* 1.137
11 'Augustus' 25.4 in *Lives of the Caesars*
12 Euripides *Phoenissae* 599 (Mynors observes that Erasmus claims not to know the source, though he quotes the play often in the *Adages*)
13 The dolphin and anchor coin was first issued by the Emperor Titus in AD 80; Pietro Bembo (1470–1547), who gave the coin to the Venetian printer Aldo Manuzio, was a humanist scholar who later became cardinal.
14 *Saturnalia* 1.21.12
15 Servius' commentary on *Aeneid* 5.85 (the Greek word means 'turning back on itself')

16 *Georgics* 2.402
17 Horapollo *Hieroglyphics* (a book purporting to explain the Egyptian writing) was published by Aldus in 1505.
18 *Moralia* 351–84
19 x 170
20 *Physics* 4.10–11 (218ff)
21 *Halieutica* 2.539–42, 535–6, 587
22 *Natural History* 9.20–9
23 The *echenêis* or remora is a mythical creature, a kind of suckerfish that when attached to the hull could slow down a ship; it is described in Pliny (also D'Arcy W. Thompson, *A Glossary of Greek Fishes* [Oxford 1947] 68–70).
24 Virgil *Aeneid* 6.368
25 Virgil *Georgics* 4.7
26 The edition appeared in 1508, the same year as the *Adages* printed by Aldus, and was based on a sixth-century manuscript.
27 Cf III i 1*
28 The first Ptolemy (fourth century BC) founded in Egypt what became known as the Library of Alexandria.
29 The next five paragraphs were added in the edition of 1526; the edition Erasmus mistakenly calls the 'fourth' is actually the sixth.
30 Janus Lascaris (1445–1534), Giambattista Egnazio (1478–1553), Marcus Musurus (1470–1517), and Urbano Valeriani (c 1443–1524) were all scholars who taught in Venice.
31 Girolamo Aleandro (1480–1542), a scholar, later a cardinal; despite the early friendship he became an enemy to Erasmus.
32 Publilius Syrus A 56, the basis of adage II v 96
33 The friend who owned the marked-up copy of this important collection of proverbs is not known.
34 See I iii 68*.
35 Froben's printer's mark was a caduceus, a rod entwined with two serpents, on the tip of which perched a dove.
36 See note 29.
37 *Cataline* 1.6; *Adages* II iii 70
38 *Nicomachean Ethics* 6.10 (1142b4)
39 Diogenes Laertius 1.87
40 Publilius Syrus D 3, D 6
41 II ii 43
42 *Oedipus the King* 617
43 III v 60 from *Republic* 7.528d
44 *Institutes of Oratory* 1.3.3
45 *Attic Nights* 13.2.5
46 *Republic* 4.441e
47 *On Anger* 1.9–10, 1.17 and 3.3
48 *Iliad* 1.206–14
49 *On Anger* 2.29.1
50 *Moralia* 207C
51 *Eunuch* 380
52 In many places in Plato, eg *Republic* 3.412a
53 Menander *Sententiae* 631
54 *Dicta memorabilia* 80 Jordan, quoted in the *Letters* of Jerome 66.9.2
55 *Odes* 1.12.45–6
56 *Nemean Odes* 8.40–2

II i 19
Naribus trahere / To lead one by the nose

'To lead by the nose' is found in most European languages (Tosi 419); though this is the most common form, there is also a variant in English, 'to lead one by the ear' (Tilley N 233, ODEP 449).

Τῆς ῥινὸς ἕλκεσθαι, To be led by the nose, is to be carried in any direction at another man's will and pleasure without any choice of one's own. The image is borrowed from oxen, creatures which have a ring inserted in the tip of the nostril, and so can be led about as horses are governed by the bit. Though horses too sometimes have a piece of wood or metal fitted with teeth inserted in the nostril, or even in the mouth, to curb their bad temper. This instrument, says Nonius,[1] is called a *postomis*. Lucian[2] in a dialogue between Juno and Jupiter: 'As for you, he is indeed your master, and drags you hither and thither, leading you as they say by the nose.' And again in *The Sects*: 'Nothing will stop you from being led by the nose by each one in turn.' To be dragged by the scruff of the neck is used of people who are forced to do something whether they will or no. Philostratus[3] in his life of Heliodorus seems to have used 'to lead by the chin' in the same sense: 'But he carried him off into court, unwilling as he was, dragging him by the chin.' This is a metaphor from horses, which their grooms lead by the lower jaw until they can put the bridle on them.

1 Nonius is a fourth-century AD lexicographer, compiler of *De compendiosa doctrina*.

2 *Dialogues of the Gods* 9.(6).3 and *The Sects* (or *Hermotimus*) 68

3 *Lives of the Sophists* 626 (Erasmus has 'chin' for what appeared in Philostratus as 'beard')

II i 21
Rara avis / A rare bird

A widely circulated proverb (Otto 232, Tosi 671) that appears in both English and Latin as a catchphrase, rather than as a proverb (not in Tilley or ODEP), except as 'As rare as a black swan' (Tilley S 1027). Interestingly, the phrase is listed in the OED *not under 'rare bird' but under* 'rara avis,' *citing Juvenal and Persius, with the first English citation dated 1607. It first appeared in Erasmus as* Collectanea *no 235.*

A rare bird was a proverbial expression for anything new and very seldom to be found. Persius:[1] 'Should something good emerge ... however rare the bird.' Juvenal:[2] 'Rare bird the wide world o'er, your true black swan,' and elsewhere: 'rarer than white crow even.' As for the rarity of the phoenix, it became proverbial.[3] The image is derived from outlandish unfamiliar birds, which sometimes find their way to our country by chance or are imported as something marvelous. Hence the phrase often repeated in Aristophanes:[4] 'Whatever bird is this?' of a foreigner and a person unknown.

1 *Satires* 1.46
2 Juvenal 6.165 and 7.202
3 For the proverbial 'phoenix' see *Adages* II vii 10 'As rare as the phoenix.'
4 *Birds* 270

II i 43
Ne in Melampygum incidas / Mind you don't fall in with Blackbottom

'Mind you don't fall in with Blackbottom' is the kind of obscure proverb for which commentary is absolutely necessary. The proverb never seems to have transferred to English, though a hairy ass may be seen as a traditional sign of gross brutality. Erasmus found it in Zenobius 5.10 and Diogenianus 6.38. The correction of the mistranslation of Herodotus by Lorenzo Valla is typical of the kind of thing Erasmus seemed to pick up on the fly.

Μὴ τῷ Μελαμπύγῳ περιτύχοις, Mind you don't fall in with Blackbottom. Suitably addressed to licentious men who do wrong to others, for it is the language of one who threatens them that they may one day happen upon somebody strong enough to punish their misdeeds. This adage is used by Philostratus[1] in his life of Apollonius, book 2: 'This was perhaps what they mean by falling in with Blackbottom.' Aristophanes[2] in the *Lysistrata*: 'Hence came that hairy man Myronides; / Blackbottom he in truth to all his foes.' He uses the word as though it meant one who will avenge and punish. Blackbottom in Greek indicates in any case one whose posterior is black, and this was given to Hercules as a nickname, because he did not pluck the hair from that part of his person as they did in Lydia, nor was it white as in effeminates, but shaggy and thick with black hairs. For effeminate and unwarlike men and those who lead a dissolute and luxurious life are called in Greek bright-rumped and whitebottomed, and conversely they had a habit of calling strong and valiant men blackbottoms, as we learn from the scholiast[3] on Lycophron. He tells us that this proverb is also found expressed in these words: Οὔπω Μελαμπύγῳ τετύχηκας You have not yet fallen in with Blackbottom. They think the proverb must be derived from some story such as this, which I will append here, partly from Suidas[4] and partly from the explanatory notes on Gregory of Nazianzus.[5] Once upon a time there were two brothers, who ranged far and wide, inflicting outrages of every kind on their fellow-men, from which they earned names to match their monstrous behaviour; for one of them was called Passalus[6] and the other Achemon or, as other sources have it, Achmon. Their mother, whose name was Sennonis, when she saw the wicked crimes they committed everywhere, told them to be careful in case one day they should fall in with Blackbottom. Later one day it happened that Hercules was lying asleep under a tree, against which he had leaned his weapons. The brothers, Cercopes or Perperi (for both names are found), came up and tried to attack Hercules as he slept with his own weapons. He at once detected their stealthy approach, seized them and bound them, and hung them from his club like a couple of dead hares, to carry them around like that behind his back. As they hung with their heads downwards, they had a good view of Hercules' backside, all shaggy and rough with black hair; this recalled their mother's warning, and they spoke of it one to the other. The moment Hercules heard what they said, he was delighted with his new nickname, roared with laughter, and set them free and sent them away. Plutarch[7] alludes to this story in the essay 'How to Tell a Flatterer from a Friend,' where he says that Hercules was amused by the Cercopes. Herodotus[8] also mentions it in book 7, where he speaks of the place called Blackbottom Stone, and the home of the Cercopes; a passage where a notable mistake has been made by Lorenzo Valla,[9] because he either did not know this story or at any rate did not recall it. Plutarch[10] in his essay 'On the Education of Children' records this among the other riddles of Pythagoras: 'Taste not of anything with a black tail,' and explains this as meaning that one should have nothing to do with wicked and disreputable people – though this is rather different from the proverb.

1 Philostratus *Life of Apollonius of Tyana* 2.36
2 *Lysistrata* 801–3
3 The 'scholiast' was the Byzantine scholar John Tzetzes commenting on *Alexandra* (line 91) by the obscure Greek poet Lycophron (early third century BC).
4 Suidas M 449
5 The commentary on Gregory of Nazianzus, one of the early Greek fathers, by Nonnus (*PG* 36.1006)
6 'Passalus ... Achmon' from Suidas K 1405 on the Kerkopes
7 Plutarch in *Moralia* 60C
8 Herodotus 7.216
9 Lorenzo Valla, who translated Herodotus just before his death in 1457, mistook *Melampygum* in this passage literally as *nigrum fontem* ('black spring'), as Erasmus says, not recognizing that this was a place name.
10 Plutarch in *Moralia* 12E (cited by Erasmus in I i 2).

II i 54
Lynceo perspicacior / More clear-sighted than Lynceus

The proverb first appeared in Collectanea *no 653 and was widely known in antiquity (Otto 1003). Lynceus was one of the Argonauts, fabled for his eyesight. The English word 'lyncean' has a double meaning 'lynx-like' and 'sharp-eyed'* (OED)*, the animal and the mythical figure collapsed into one word.*

Lynceus' piercing sight was proverbial. Pliny[1] in the *Natural History*, book 2 chapter 17: 'That the last of the old moon and the new moon can be both seen on the same day or in the same night, in Aries the Ram and in no other sign; and few mortals have this gift. Hence the fable of Lynceus and his eyesight.' Some say[2] that Lynceus was the first man who discovered mines for metals, copper silver and gold, and that this was the origin of the widespread myth that he could even see things underground. The scholiast on Lycophron[3] is a witness to this, and Plato[4] mentions it in one of his *Letters*. Aristophanes[5] in the *Plutus*: 'I'll make you see clearer than Lynceus' self.' Lucian[6] in the *Hermotimus*: 'But you seem to us more clearsighted than Lynceus, for apparently you can pierce the breast and see what is within.' And again in the *Icaromenippus*: 'How have you now suddenly become a second Lynceus, able to see everything?' Horace[7] in his first *Epistle to Maecenas:* 'You may not see as clear as Lynceus could, / Yet for sore eyes a salve you'd not refuse.' Cicero[8] writing to Marcus Varro: 'Who is such a Lynceus that in such great darkness he never stumbles, never runs into anything?' Apollonius[9] writes in the *Argonautica* that this man Lynceus was so clear-sighted that his gaze could pierce the earth itself and watch what was going on in the Nether Regions:

> Lynceus, whose eyes most piercing were of all,
> If fame speaks true, which says that easily
> E'en things hid deep in earth he could espy.

Plutarch[10] in the essay which he called 'Against the Stoics' assures us that Lynceus had the reputation of being able to see even through rocks and trees, his sight was so penetrating. Pausanias[11] in his account of Corinth records that Lynceus succeeded to the throne after the death of Danaus. Pindar[12] in the tenth hymn of his *Nemeans* mentions Lynceus who, he says, from Mount Taygetus could see Castor and Pollux lying hid under the trunk of an oak, and wounded one of them with a javelin. The scholiast on Pindar cites the History of Cyprus, Aristarchus and Didymus.

1 *Natural History* 2.78
2 'Some say' as in the *Corpus* of Greek proverbs (Appendix 3.71 and Apostolius 10.79)
3 The scholia on Lycophron *Alexandra* 556
4 *Letter* 7 (344A)
5 *Plutus* 210
6 Lucian *Hermotimus* 20 and *Icaromenippus* 12
7 *Epistles* 1.1.28–9
8 *Letters to His Friends* 9.2.2
9 *Argonautica* 1.153–5
10 *Moralia* 1083D
11 *Description of Greece* 2.16.1
12 The ancient scholiast on Pindar *Nemean Odes* 10.60–70 refers to the *Cypria*, a lost Homeric poem (frag 9 Kinkel).

II i 55
Quod in animo sobrii, id est in lingua ebrii / What is in the heart of the sober man is in the mouth of the drunkard

This proverb is closely related to I *vii 17* 'In vino veritas' or 'Wine speaks the truth' (Tosi 734). This more elaborate form is also found in English (Tilley* H *333).*

Τὸ ἐν τῇ καρδίᾳ τοῦ νήφοντος ἐπὶ τῆς γλώττης ἐστὶ τοῦ μεθύοντος, What is in the heart of the sober man is in the mouth of the drunkard. A proverbial maxim, recorded in the collection of Diogenianus.[1] Plutarch[2] uses it, expressly as a proverb, in the essay called 'On Garrulity.' Nor should that thing in Herodotus[3] be overlooked: 'Down goes the wine, up float the words.' For men while sober are restrained by fear or shame from blurting out things which they think it better to keep secret; but wine puts shame to flight and drives out fear, and the result is that men in their cups 'cannot suppress words which in the end will cut their throats.'[4] Pindar[5] in the *Nemeans*: 'And words wax brave over the mixingbowl,' either because wine brings with it confidence, or because boasting has no dangers at a drinking-party, or because he who has won a victory is praised deservedly and without risk.

1 Diogenianus 8.43
2 *Moralia* 503F
3 *Histories* 1.212
4 'cannot suppress words': a reference to Pliny *Natural History* 14.141
5 *Nemean Odes* 9.49

II i 65
In foribus urceum / The water-jar on the doorstep

This is an unusual essay, because it shows that Erasmus hasn't been able to figure out the proverb. It was explained by Sir Roger Mynors in CWE *33 (note on p 358): 'A person who has "laboured in vain" or found that "there's many a slip between the cup and the lip" can be typified by a girl who has brought home a full pitcher from the well, only to drop and break it on her own doorstep; the "water-jar on the doorstep" therefore denotes the safe and successful conclusion of a venture.'*

Ἐπὶ θύραις τὴν ὑδρίαν, The pitcher on the doorstep (this is Plautus' word[1]). Aristotle[2] in the first book of the *Rhetorica*: 'But the end is good. Hence those phrases "And praise for Priam" and "'Tis shame to wait so long," and the proverb "The water-jar on the doorstep".' Some commentator[3] (I was provided with the book by my very learned friend Battista Egnazio, and has no author's name) says that this means something despicable and worthless; for things are neglected which can be found everywhere and are easily accessible to all. Thus no one troubles to pick up a water-jar on his own doorstep – it is too easy; pearls stored safely in chests are more sought after. Plutarch[4] in 'On Having Many Friends' says that brambles which cling to one by nature are thought nothing of and passed by, while vineyards and olive-trees are coveted; he is reviewing the aphorism 'Choose not that which is very easily obtained.' Again, in Seneca's *Letters*:[5] 'Many men pass over what is accessible, and search diligently for what is hidden and obscure. Padlocks attract the thief; what is open is thought worthless, the housebreaker overlooks what is exposed to view. This is typical of the multitude, and of the uneducated in general; they long to break into a secret.'

Apart from that, the proverb seems incomplete and mutilated; for Aristotle often reproduces things in that state, as though they were already well enough known from other sources. This is clearly half of an iambic trimeter, borrowed from some writer of comedy.

1 Plautus *Circulio* 312 uses *aqualis* for 'pitcher.'

2 Aristotle *Rhetoric* 1.6.22 (1363a5) citing Homer *Iliad* 2.160 and 298 (the *Rhetoric* supplied Erasmus with over seventy adages)

3 'Some commentator,' referring to the notes ascribed to Gregory of Nazianzus in an edition Erasmus consulted while in Venice preparing the 1508 *Adages*, a book given to him by Battista Egnazio (1478–1553), a Venetian scholar (*Contemporaries* 1:424–5); see also II i 1*.

4 Plutarch 'On Having Many Friends' in *Moralia* 94E

5 Seneca *Letters* 68.4

II ii 4
Asinus portans mysteria / An ass that bears the mysteries

As a proverb this appears in Diogenianus 6.98, who cites Apuleius Metamorphoses *8.24ff (the scene in which Lucius has been turned into an ass and is in the service of priests). The image was widely known; it appears for instance in Spenser's* Faerie Queene *at I vi, when the fauns and satyrs try to worship Una, but when she refuses them they worship instead the ass that carries her. The popularity of the tale, which offers a different reading of the events than given by Erasmus, is due to the Greek writer Babrius, who wrote up the story as part of his collection of Aesopic fables (Halm 324; Perry 182 [Loeb]), a source strangely not mentioned by Erasmus, who had the proverb in the early* Collectanea *no 648. The fable was adapted by Andrea Alciato as Emblem 7, 'Not for you, but for religion' (see accompanying figure), and he gives the traditional version thus:*

> *A doltish little ass carried a figure of Isis, having the revered mysteries upon its curved back. Everyone near the goddess reverently adored her, and on bended knees sent forth their holy prayers. But the ass believed such honour was being shown to him, and swelled up, filling entirely with his pride – until the driver, who restrained him with whips, said, 'You are not a god, little ass; rather, you bear a god.'*

Ὄνος ἄγων μυστήρια, An ass that bears the mysteries, was said of a man who occupied a more important office than he deserved – someone, for example, of no education made head of a library. Aristophanes[1] in the *Frogs*: 'God knows, an ass that bears the mysteries / Am I; but I'll not carry them much longer.' The scholiast declares that the adage took its rise from the practice of loading an ass with the objects that had in the old days to be taken to Eleusis for the celebrations. It will also suit those who labour solely for the advantage of other people, while they themselves get nothing but trouble meanwhile, a man for example who carries food for others of which he is not allowed to partake himself. It looks as though Apuleius[2] were alluding to this when he makes himself out to be an ass carrying the goddess Ceres round the district. Suidas[3] adds that Demon referred it to the upper millstone, which is called *onos*, donkey, in Greek, because it was a

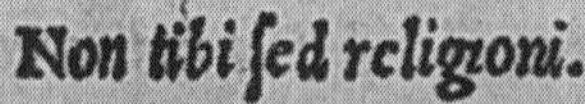
Non tibi ſed religioni.

Iſidis effigiem tardus geſtabat aſellus,
Pando uerenda dorſo habens myſteria.
Obuius ergo Deam quiſquis reuerenter adorat,
Piaſq; genibus concipit flexis preces.
Aſt aſinus tantum præſtari credit honorem
Sibi, & intumeſcit admodum ſuperbiens,
Donec eum flagris compeſcens dixit agaſo,
Non es Deus tu aſelle, ſed Deum uehis.
C iiij

An ass that bears the mysteries A picture from Andrea Alciato's *Book of Emblems* (emblem 7, from the edition of Paris 1540, p 39). Erasmus used the same source material for his adage II ii 4*. (Thomas Fisher Rare Book Library, University of Toronto)

Greek custom at festivals to decorate their grain-mills with garlands. So to divert this to men who enjoy honours they do not deserve will have an elegant effect, as for instance when ignorant men are given the title, bonnet, and ring of a doctor, and similar distinctions.

1 *Frogs* 159–60
2 *Metamorphoses* 8.24ff (perhaps in turn due to Diogenianus 6.98)
3 Suidas O 382–3 citing Demon, an early collector of Greek proverbs

II ii 36
In canis podicem inspicere / To look into a dog's anus

One of a small number of crude proverbs. Erasmus, who here holds his nose as he does his work, returns to the theme at IV ii 20 E canis podice, *'From the anus of a dog.'*

Aristophanes[1] in the *Ecclesiazuae*: 'I told him to go and look into a dog's anus.' The scholiast informs us that this was commonly applied to near-sighted people, and he adds a trochaic line about peering up the breech of a bitch and three vixens. He alludes to it again in the *Acharnians*: 'Blow up the dog's arse on your pipes of bone.' The line is too obscene to give much pleasure to the translator. In fact, I could hardly bring myself to write out such rubbish, were I not determined to perform my allotted task at all points and, having received this Sparta[2] as my portion, to do my best for her.

1 Aristophanes *Ecclesiazuae* 255 (with a note provided by an ancient scholiast) and *Acharnians* 863
2 This is II v 1*, one of many instances of an adage being used in the *Adages*.

II ii 40
Ollas ostentare / To make a display of pots

Mock encomia were common in classical antiquity and were greatly admired in the Renaissance – praises of baldness, of the flea, and so on. See headnote to

II i 1, another adage which Erasmus described as a mock encomium. 'To make a display of pots' is a justification for his* Praise of Folly. *Though the first few lines of the essay appeared in 1508, most of it (from the third sentence 'Not that it would invite ...' onwards) was added in 1515, four years after the* Praise *was published, and in response to the many criticisms of it. This essay is closely related to the letter to Marten van Dorp (Ep 337) in which Erasmus also vigorously defends his own work.*

Χύτρας ἐπιδείκνυσθαι, To make a display of pots, is to produce something sordid and contemptible in itself as though it were of great importance. Plutarch[1] in his essay 'On How to Study,' criticizing the sophists for their practice of dressing up unseemly topics in the language of panegyric, vomit for instance and fever and Busiris and others of the kind, says 'making, if you please, a display of pots.' Not that it would invite immediate disapproval if a man were to amuse himself with this sort of subject for practice or as a relaxation, provided there was style and knowledge in his levity and something profitable as well as entertaining; for 'to speak truth with a smile no rule forbids.'[2] The result in fact is that truth makes its way without offence into the minds of mortals and finds a warmer welcome, when it has attractions of this kind to recommend it. So true is this that Aulus Gellius[3] has no hesitation in preferring Aesop's amusing fables to all those sour-faced doctrines of the Stoics that came down from heaven. Plutarch[4] himself took to humorous writing in his 'Gryllus,' which is amusing enough to be sure, but with the limitation that one can always recognize the philosopher in playful mood rather than the professional humorist.

I wrote a humorous work myself some years ago, my *Praise of Folly*. I spent seven days' work on it at most, and did so without the help of any books, for at that time my baggage had not yet arrived. Whatever the merits of that small book, I observe that it is thought very well of by fair-minded men and those who have been properly grounded in the classics; and apart from its gaiety and humour, they maintain that there are a number of things in it which do more to raise the standard of human behaviour than Aristotle's *Ethics* or *Politics*, for his teaching in this field, pagan as he was, is of a level one would not expect from a pagan. And yet I hear that some people take offence; but they are few in number, and the sort who approve of nothing except what is barbarous, tasteless, and innocent of all commerce with the Muses. They themselves read Juvenal, sworn foes as they are of other forms of poetry, in order to nourish the attacks in their sermons on the vices of princes, priests, merchants, and particularly women; and they often describe those vices in language which might provide a lesson in obscenity. For my part, though my chosen subject was not incompatible with it and such a wide field lay before me in all directions, I attack no individual in particular except perchance myself, I leave unmoved that loathsome Camarina[5] of crimes and vices, and touch on a few points with more fun in them than filth. But you criticize bishops, they say, bishops and theologians and princes. But, for one thing, they fail to notice the moderation, the freedom from all spite, with which I do what they say; and then again they fail to bear in mind that principle so often urged on us by St Jerome,[6] that in a general discussion of vice no slur is cast on any individual, and no one gets a black mark as an offender, but everyone is put on notice not to offend. Or is their point really that all princes are wise, all theologians faultless, all bishops and pontiffs are what Paul and Martin[7] were, all monks and priest so many Anthonys and Jeromes? Then they take no account of a cardinal principle in dialogue, that the words must suit the speaker, and imagine it is Erasmus speaking and not Folly. Just as though, if one were to compose a discussion between a pagan and a Christian, it would be anathema for the pagan to say anything that did not square with Christian teaching. Last but not least, even despots laugh at what they hear said by their jesters, and think it uncivilized to take offence at their remarks; and it is surprising if these men, whoever they may be, cannot listen to a single word spoken by Folly herself, as though anything said in any context about vices must inevitably be to their address. But on this topic I have already said more than enough; we must return to our pots.

Thus this proverb is related to one of which I have spoken elsewhere: You are decorating a cooking-pot.[8]

1 Plutarch 'On How to Study' in *Moralia* 44F; Busiris was praised by Isocrates, even though this mythological king of Egypt slaughtered all foreigners coming to his shore.

2 Horace *Satires* 1.1.24–5

3 Aulus Gellius 2.29.1

4 Plutarch in *Moralia* 985D–92E (his 'Gryllus' was a disputation between Odysseus and one of his companions who preferred to remain a pig after being so transformed by Circe)
5 Camarina is a city in Sicily, proverbial for that which should be left untouched (*Adages* I i 64).
6 Jerome *Letters* 125.5
7 Martin is St Martin of Tours, whom Erasmus admired.
8 I iv 66

II ii 48
Ignis mare mulier, tria mala / Fire, sea, and woman, here be evils three

The 'proverbial line' is Menander Sententiae *323. Anti-feminist proverbs have a long tradition and this proverb has a number of variations (Tosi 1379).*

Here is another proverbial line which circulated in Greek: Πῦρ καὶ θάλασσα καὶ γυνὴ, κακὰ τρία. Nothing is more terrifying than a house on fire, and the sea too is full of perils, so that Aeschylus[1] writes in the *Persae* of 'the sea's unconquered waves.' That women are something very like them is the meaning of the proverb. In fact, the view that every woman is bad was very neatly conveyed by a certain Lacon who, after marrying a very diminutive wife, used to say that of evils one should choose the least. Medea too in Euripides[2] admits that the female sex are a bad lot: 'We're what we are, we women; I'll not say / An evil.' Euripides, quoted by Planudes in his life of Aesop, assigns the first place among all evils to womankind:

> Constant the fury of the ocean wave,
> Of raging rivers and hot streams of fire
> Frightful is poverty and much else besides,
> But naught so frightful as a wicked woman.

1 Aeschylus *Persian Women* 90
2 Euripides *Medea* 889–90 and frag 1059 Nauck cited by Maximus Planudes, the Byzantine scholar, in his *De Aesopo* 247.12 Eberh

II ii 74
Proteo mutabilior / As many shapes as Proteus

Though the essay does not make the connection, it may be considered in the light of Erasmus' own theories of composition and interpretation (see headnote to I i 93 'Adopt the outlook of the polyp'). It first appeared as* Collectanea *no 590, where the main source was the Latin poet Horace (for other Latin sources, Otto 1478); in the revised version, the Greek satirist Lucian is now the principal authority. The proverb also found its way into English (Tilley S 285), probably kept alive from the vivid and well-known scenes in Homer's* Odyssey *or Virgil's* Georgics. *Neither of the two variants given by Erasmus have had an afterlife.*

Πρωτέως ποικιλώτερος, As many shapes as Proteus, fits any cunning fellow and jack-of-all-trades. Lucian[1] in his *Sacrifices* says Jove has as many shapes as Proteus himself, because he was always turning himself into different things. Plato[2] in the *Ion*: 'But just like Proteus, you take all sorts of shapes, and twist yourself back and forth.' Horace,[3] of people who easily change their opinions: 'With what knot am I to bind / This Proteus, constantly changing his mind?' And in another passage: 'But Proteus (curse him!) will evade these bonds.' By Proteus he means one who twists and turns, for whom Greek has a word *dysphôratos*,[4] hard to pin down. As for the story of Proteus, it is, I think, too well known to need retelling here. It can be found in Homer[5] in book 4 of the *Odyssey*, and in Virgil's[5] *Georgics*, also in the fourth book.

Using a similar image, one could also say Versatile as Vertumnus. He is another god who changes into every kind of shape, whence he gets his Latin name. Horace:[7] 'Vertumnus in all shapes frowned on his cradle.' Ovid[8] tells of him, and describes how, as he wooed the goddess Pomona, he assumed one form after another.

There is also Εὐμεταβολώτερος Ἐμπούσης, As changeable as Empusa. She is spoken of by Lucian[9] in his essay *On Dancing*: 'So you will see them all at the same moment suddenly changing their shapes, recalling Proteus himself; or one should compare them to Empusa, who could change herself into a thousand different forms.' She is referred to by Aristophanes[10] in the *Frogs*:

– But look! Great heavens, I see a monstrous beast!
– What's it like?
– Terrible, and changes shape, Now ox, now mule. Now it's a pretty girl.
– Where is she? Let me get at her!
– No, no: No more a girl, 'tis now a barking dog.
– I know: it's an empusa.

The scholiast adds that an empusa is a sort of spectre sent by Hecate to be visible to misery and disaster; and its habit is to show itself in constantly varying forms. Some think that its custom is to appear around the middle of the day to those who are sacrificing to the dead. I am not sure, however, that it may be rightly connected with that phrase in the Hebrew Psalter:[11] 'From strange meetings and from the demon that walketh in the noonday.' Some are sure this is Hecate in person; for they say that it is seen to have only one foot, which makes them think the name *empusa* comes from the Greek words for 'one' and 'foot.' Demosthenes[12] says that Aeschines' mother, whose name Aeschines himself had changed to Leucothea, was called Empusa, because she was prepared to do anything, and have anything done to her, for money.

1 *Sacrifices* 5
2 *Ion* 541E
3 *Epistles* 1.1.90 and *Satires* 2.3.71
4 *dysphôratos* from Plutarch *Moralia* 51D means 'hard to detect.'
5 *Odyssey* 4.456–8
6 *Georgics* 4.440–2
7 Vertumnus was a Roman god of crops; *vertere* means to turn or change.
8 *Satires* 2.7.14
8 *Metamorphoses* 14.622–97
9 *De saltatione* 19
10 *Frogs* 288–93
11 Psalm 91:6
12 Demosthenes 18.130

II ii 95
Odium novercale / Stepmotherly hatred

This proverb may be compared with I ix 10 above, also on the stepmother. As he and his contemporaries (and we too!) so often do, Erasmus translates a social behaviour – here, conflict in a reconstructed family – into innate and* *even natural behaviour; indeed in some places, Nature is herself a stepmother (see III vii 1* n 40 and IV i 1* n 16). Proverbs encourage this kind of thinking. This one was familiar to the Romans (Otto 1239).*

We use a similar image[1] when we speak of stepmotherly hatred, for innate in every stepmother is a sort of predestined and irreconcilable hatred for her stepchildren, as is made clear in a stylish Greek epigram which I shall give myself the pleasure of transcribing. It has come down to us under the name of Callimachus,[2] and is not unworthy to have him as its author. Though I knew myself unable to match the elegance of these lines, I have rendered them as best I could to make them easier to understand. 'A boy once set a garland on his stepmother's tomb – it was but a small piece of marble – thinking she had parted from her ill-nature as she had from his life. The tomb in which she lay fell on him and killed him; children, beware your stepmother's tomb, dead though she may be.' Euripides[3] in the *Alcestis*: 'To the earlier children a stepmother is an enemy merciless as any viper.'

1 The preceding adage was 'Hate worthy of Vatinius,' an 'excessively bitter and deadly hatred.'

2 Callimachus was not the author of the quoted epigram, which is from *Greek Anthology* 9.67.

3 *Alcestis* 309–10

II iii 2
Siculus mare / The Sicilian and the sea

*In one of his letters, consoling the father of a suicide, Goethe makes an unusual statement: 'After the nocturnal storm one gains the shore again, the drenched survivor dries off, and the next morning, when the brilliant sun begins to shine on the sparkling waves, the sea already is hungry for figs again.' Figs? The allusion is explained by Erasmus, probably Goethe's source, or so argues Hans Blumenberg (*Shipwreck with Spectator: Paradigm of a Metaphor for Existence *trans Steven Rendall [Cambridge, Mass, 1997] 56–7). Goethe was an enthusiastic reader of the* Adages, *and recommended them to Schiller (ibid, 116). As Erasmus says, the adage appears in the standard Greek collections*

(Zenobius 5.51, Diogenianus 7.6, and Suidas o *686). It is also a fable in Aesop (Halm 370, Perry 207, though the story tells of a shepherd, not a Sicilian, and dates, not figs).*

Σικελὸς θάλασσαν, The Sicilian and the sea (we must understand that he is gazing out over it), is used of those who are tempted to expose themselves to some risk a second time. It is said to be derived from a Sicilian who had been shipwrecked when sailing with a cargo of figs. Later he was sitting on the shore surveying the sea, which was so calm and tranquil it seemed to be inviting him to repeat his voyage; and he is reported to have said 'I know what you want: you want some more figs.' This is recorded by almost all the collectors of Greek proverbs.

II iii 5
Ficus ficus, ligonem ligonem vocat / He calls figs figs, a spade a spade

Despite Erasmus' learned account, there is actually no classical proverb that says 'To call a spade a spade.' In the 1515 text, Erasmus seems to have mistaken the Latin scapha, *a small boat (from Greek* skaphê, *a dugout boat, a wash-tub, or kneading-trough, or bowl) for a tool for digging, and changed* scapha *to* ligo, *a spade (the Greek* skaptein *means to dig, so the error is understandable). Our proverb in English (Tilley* S *699 and F.P. Wilson* Shakespearian and Other Studies *[Oxford 1969] 147) is the direct result of Erasmus' retranslation. See also Tosi 301.*

Τὰ σῦκα σῦκα, τὴν σκάφην σκάφην λέγων, Calling the figs figs, calling a spade a spade, is an iambic line from the comedies of Aristophanes[1] adapted for use as an adage. It suits a man who speaks the truth in a simple and countrified style, who tells of things as they are, and does not wrap them up in ornamental verbiage. The technical writers on rhetoric describe figures of speech which enable one to clothe obscenities in seemly language, to make rude things sound gentle and proud things modest, and to say biting things so as to win approval. Men of more homely mother-wit speak more crudely and more plainly, and call things by their true names. Lucian in the *Jupiter tragoedus*: 'For I'm a rustic fellow, as it says in the comedy, and call a spade a spade.' Again, in his *How History Should Be Written*, he thinks a writer should be uncommitted and incorruptible, reporting things as they really happened, and calling figs figs and a spade a spade. It is also found in another form:[2] I call figs figs and a dough-trough a dough-trough. Aristophanes[3] in the *Clouds*: 'I'd never give a man a ha'penny / Who called a *kardopos* a *kardopê*.' *Kardopos* means a trough for making bread in. The poet makes Socrates a great quibbler, maintaining that one ought not to use the form *kardopon*, as used by Cleonymus, but *kardopên*, as (says he) 'you speak of Sostraten.'

1 Aristophanes does not seem to provide this source and perhaps the comic writer is Lucian, who is here referred to several times, *Jupiter tragoedus* 32 and *How to Write History* 41, citing Menander frag 717.

2 'another form' in Apostolius 16.10

3 The reference to Aristophanes confuses two scenes in *Clouds* 118 and 670–80. The point is that the genders have been confused, so that the *kardopê* is clearly not the *kardopos*.

II iii 48
Homo bulla / Man is but a bubble

Erasmus found this common proverb in Varro, and first used it in Collectanea *(no 702). The topos was well known to the Romans (Otto 275) and is found in many European langages (Tosi 511), including English (Tilley M 246), where it was very popular with writers of the Renaissance (eg, Francis Bacon's variation 'The world's a bubble, and the life of man / Less than a span'). The essay concludes with a brief but thematically appropriate panegyric on the death (1506) of Philip, archduke of Austria, son of the Emperor Maximilian.*

Πομφόλυξ ὁ ἄνθρωπος, Man is but a bubble. The lesson of this proverb is that there is nothing so fragile, so fleeting and so empty as the life of man. A bubble is that round swollen empty thing which we watch in water as it grows and vanishes in a moment of time. Thus

Marcus Terentius Varro[1] in the preface to his book on agriculture: 'Bearing in mind' he says 'that I must make haste; for if, as they say, man is but a bubble, much more is this true of an old man. My eightieth year reminds me to pack my baggage, before I bid farewell to life.' Lucian[2] too in his *Charon* makes men's lives something very like this kind of bubble: some vanish at once as soon as they are born, some last a little longer, but all of them at very brief intervals take the place of others. Nor could one think of anything, in fact, which would give a better picture of the utter nothingness of this life of ours. Consider first what risks we run when we see the light of day. How destitute, how much exposed to great perils is our infancy! How fleeting is our adolescence! How our prime hastens by! Aristotle[3] in the *Politics* and again in book 3 of the *Rhetoric* states that a man's bodily powers begin to fade about his thirty-fifth year and his mental powers about his forty-ninth. Hippocrates brings the peak of a man's life to an end at forty-nine; and if you deduct childhood and old age from the sum of life, just think how little will be left, and that little beset with such great emergencies. Unnumbered kinds of sickness threaten us every day, and no fewer are the mishaps to which we are exposed, collapsing houses, poison, shipwreck, war, earthquakes, landslides, lightning, anything. One man is suffocated by swallowing a grape-pip, another strangled by drinking a hair in a cup of milk. There are cases of men meeting sudden death, when an icicle hardened by frost has fallen from a roof. And this is the same creature that sets such commotions afoot, and for whose appetites this world is too narrow.[4]

I cannot refrain from transcribing at this point a passage from book 7 of Pliny,[5] where he skilfully depicts the frailty and shortness of our life. 'Fragile truly and uncertain is this gift, such as it is, that nature gives us; brief and niggardly is our portion, even for those who get the most generous share, at any rate if we consider the whole span of time. In fact, if we take account of the nights spent in slumber, each man is alive for no more than half of his allotted term, and an equal portion is spent in a state like death, or is punishment if one cannot sleep. Nor does this take account of the years of infancy, which have no sense, nor of old age when long life is a punishment; all the dangers of many kinds, the sickness, fears, anxieties, the appeals to death, so frequent that it is the most common object of prayer. Nature indeed has given men nothing more precious than shortness of life. The senses fail, the limbs are tormented, our sight hearing and walking before we fail ourselves, and so do our teeth and the organs by which we feed. Yet all this time is counted as a part of life.'

The comparison with bubbles finds a parallel in Homer's famous image[6] of the leaves falling from the tree. These are the words of Glaucus in Homer, in the sixth *Iliad*:

Like leaves upon the tree, the life of man:
One race of leaves the wind strews on the ground
And another the wood puts forth at the call of spring.

These lines, so Diogenes Laertius[7] tells us, were a particular favourite with Pyrrho the Academic philosopher. Homer[8] again, in *Iliad* 21:

Like leaves, they now are green and flourishing,
Eating earth's plenty, and now they fall and die.

And in another passage, I forget where: 'For earth breeds nothing less robust than man.' Menander,[9] cited by Plutarch in his 'Consolation Addressed to Apollonius':

Hear the whole tale in brief: you are a man.
No creature climbs so quickly to the heights,
Changes, and sinks again into the depths
And rightly so for, weakest as he is
Of living things, he takes great tasks in hand.

Euripides,[10] cited in the same author: 'Happiness is not steadfast; it lasts but for a day. One day tears down what yesterday exalted, and raises the low on high.' In that same passage Demetrius of Phalerum[11] is said to have criticized the poet, otherwise renowned for the elegance of his style, on the ground that instead of 'one day' he ought to have written 'a point of time.'

Pindar[12] outdid even the image used by Homer, for he called mankind not 'leaves' but 'a shadow in a dream.' The passage will be found in the eighth hymn of the *Pythians*: 'Creatures of a day, what is anyone?

What no one? Man is a shadow in a dream.' Nothing is as empty as a shadow, for it appears to be something, and is nothing; but he has found what is emptier even than that, a shadow in a dream. As a result, no one can say 'This man is somebody,' or its opposite, 'This man is nobody'; for so sudden are the changes in human affairs that the man who seems to be something the next moment is nobody, and he who seemed to have perished is in a moment somebody. Aeschylus,[13] in a fragment preserved by Stobaeus, makes man's life like the shadow of smoke: 'The seed of man thinks thoughts that last a day, / No more to be trusted than the shadow of smoke.' Sophocles[14] too in the *Ajax*: 'Man is but wind and shadow, nothing more.'

Pindar[15] in the eleventh hymn of the *Nemeans*: 'If a man is rich, and in bodily grace surpasses others, and if by victory in the games he has shown heroic strength, let him remember that the limbs he bears round with him are mortal, and that he must be clad in earth, the end to which all men come.' This truth might properly be written up in the courts of princes, on their drinking-cups and in their tapestries and their banners, rather than such boastful words as 'He can that will' and 'Further yet' and other things of the kind.

But nothing can be more exquisite than the well-known comparison between roses, which open so quickly and so quickly grow old and die, and the life of man. A poem survives under Virgil's name[16] which, though it does not particularly recall Virgil's style of writing, is yet so full of elegance and charm that it clearly stems from some author who was not only a polished scholar but, whoever he was, a very gifted man.

Here too belongs that myth beloved of poets, which depicts all mortals as suspended from threads spun by the Fates, and when those threads are cut, down they fall forthwith. Some too hang from white threads and some from threads of a mornful hue, some hang high in air and some near the ground, but all have the same lot: the moment Atropos, who hears no man's prayer, snaps a thread with her thumb, down falls the man who hung from it, nor is any distinction made except that the man who hung higher makes more disturbance when he falls. You may smile, and think is a mere fable, a game that poets play. A game it may be, but pitiless and cruel is the game played by the Fates. And if they would but confine it to ordinary ineffectual men who are covered by Homer's phrase[17] 'a useless burden on the earth,' and would not take from us before their time men gifted by heaven and the very best of our princes! It is not merely that they do not refrain from playing their unprincipled game even with such as these; they seem to lie in wait for them of set purpose as though they were jealous of their power and meant to leave no doubt that this is within its range, and to make it clear that every mortal, whoever he may be, is equally nothing but a bubble.

What a loss the world of letters lately suffered, when early death snatched from us Paolo Canal,[18] patrician of Venice, a young man scarcely yet twenty-five years old but, in heaven's name, so gifted, so prolific, with such keen judgment, such ready utterance, such knowledge of every language and of every subject! Inexorable Fate thought it not her business if she inflicted such a loss on humane studies, to which he had already begun to contribute so effectively, or if she left such a sense of bereavement in the devotees of good literature by suddenly cutting off that great harvest and the high hopes of scholars everywhere.

And now there is the unexpected death of my Prince Philip[19] of which I cannot speak, so bitter is my sorrow for his loss, yet it is not right for me, prompted by such a context, to say nothing of one who showed me such outstanding generosity. Of all the princes upon whom the Sun ever shone he was unique, the best, the greatest, the most gifted. Fortune gave the world a glimpse of him, and, alas, it was only a glimpse and she snatched him away. Whether natural endowments or the splendours of exalted rank, what can heaven give to mortals which was not his in highest excellence and greatest plenty? Physically of heroic stature, how noble, and yet how winning, was his air, and how bright his eye! His was a happy disposition, vigorous health and strength, a noble stance and bearing. Of his distinguished ancestry why need I speak? Kings, emperors, famous captains are to be found in it in such plenty, that nothing could be imagined so grand, so illustrious and so noble. With these there went some secret heaven-sent power, which acted like a magnet, and won him instantly the affection of kings and peoples, of his own nation and of foreigners and, in a word, of all mankind, so that not merely to see him or to talk with him, but even the sound of Philip's name, somehow aroused exceptional goodwill. And could the greatest prince hope for a happier gift than that? This charm, which was part of his destiny, was enhanced by his singular courtesy and flexibility of manner, such that all kings and all nations were remarkably unanimous in their affection for him, and even those who were at war not long before, were equally zealous, once they had laid down their arms, in doing honour to Prince Philip. Such were the universal peace and concord, the gratitude and joy, wherever he had sown the light of his countenance. Well might the generals of antiquity and classical triumphs seem of no account to anyone which all those kings, princes and nations – France, Savoy, Spain, Germany, England – competed with one another in contributing to those two expeditions into Spain. Anyone who had contributed anything to Philip's glory felt that he had much enhanced his own. On all this my *Panegyricus* is there to testify. Then there is the wife[20] who has borne him a family, his children all alive and well, his father (to put limitless glory in a single word) Maximilian. There are all those kings closely bound as well by ties of kinship; the greatness of the empire in which he was born and the wealth of the kingdom to which he was summoned, the succession to his father's majesty, and all the great hopes inspired by the gifts, the destiny and the character that were his – hopes that were sure and certain, had heaven been willing to allow any certainty in mortal affairs. The success he had already enjoyed was very great, and all the greater because it did not come, as it does to most men, through violence and bloodshed and the sufferings of others; for there is scarcely any other way to acquire supreme power. Among all the elements of our Philip's achievements, not one was stained with blood, not one brought with it misery or loss for anyone else. And what the future held was offered on such terms that he would not seem to be grasping it for himself; he would be in no position to refuse it. These were the gifts, these the distinctions, the international popularity, the goodwill of so many monarchs, the just and affectionate prayers of a devoted father, the enthusiasm of his own countrymen and their unbounded hopes, the whole world's expectations – all this, as I say, was suddenly cut short by his untimely death. It was a needlessly cruel demonstration of the truth that no mortal man, however close he may come to the heavenly powers, is other than a bubble.

But it is more than time for me to leave this topic and return to the subject on which I am engaged, for I would not give anyone cause to complain that I have abandoned my adages in mid-career and turned to declamation; though I see that Pliny[21] frequently digresses on similar topics to please himself. It was grief drove me somewhat off course, and not the charm of the subject-matter.

1 Varro, *De re rustica* 1.1.1
2 Lucian *Charon* 19
3 Aristotle *Politics* 7.16 (1335b32 and following) and *Rhetoric* 2.14 (1390b9)
4 Juvenal 10.168–9, commonly attributed to Alexander the Great
5 Pliny *Natural History* 7.167–8
6 Homer *Iliad* 6.146–8
7 Diogenes Laertius 9.67
8 Homer *Iliad* 21.464–6 and *Odyssey* 18.130
9 Menander frag 740.10–14 cited in Plutarch *Moralia* 103D
10 Euripides *Phoenissae* 558 with a fragment from his *Ion* (frag 420 Nauck) in Plutarch *Moralia* 104A
11 An Athenian orator of the late fourth century BC
12 *Pythians* 8.95–6
13 Aeschylus frag 399 Nauck, in Stobaeus 4.34.44
14 Sophocles frag 12 Nauck, from the lost *Ajax Locrensis*, in Stobaeus 4.34.52
15 *Nemeans* 11.13–16
16 The *Carmen de rosis*, a 50-line poem in the *Appendix Vergiliana*, also ascribed to the late classical poet Ausonius
17 *Iliad* 18.104
18 Paolo Canal died shortly before these words appeared in the edition of 1508.
19 Philip, archduke of Austria (1478–1506), son of Emperor Maximilian and Mary of Burgundy
20 Joanna the Mad, heiress to the Spanish throne; she and Philip were the parents of Charles V
21 Pliny the younger occasionally writes about the recently dead in his *Letters*.

II iii 97
Sine Cerere et Baccho friget Venus / Without Ceres and Bacchus Venus grows cold

In the Renaissance this was an oft-quoted proverb from Terence, who himself acknowledges it as an 'old saying.' Though it passed into many European languages (Tosi 1411), including English (Tilley C 211*), it was nevertheless* *often quoted in Latin (Otto 1868). It also appeared in less obvious guise; in* Twelfth Night *(2.1.123) Sir Toby cries out to Malvolio, 'Dost thou think because thou art virtuous, there shall be no more cakes and ale?' which in this context may echo the ancient adage (Ceres/cake, Bacchus/ale). Erasmus first discussed this as* Collectanea *no 539.*

Terence[1] in the *Eunuchus*: 'How true indeed is that old saying, that without Ceres and Bacchus Venus grows cold.' This is put into the mouth of Chremes, a countrified young man, who hated courtesans when sober, but was by no means against them later when he had some drink inside him; for food and drink are the things that stimulate desire. The way he puts Ceres for food, Bacchus for drink, and Venus for sexual desire, maintaining the same form of expression throughout, is very neat. And the verb itself *friget*, grows cold, enshrines a metaphor, which Donatus says is derived from the practice of coating wine-jars with pitch, because pitch when it is cold does not stick. What a frigid and over-ingenious explanation! – with all respect to such a good scholar, if the interpretation is really his. Lovers are full of fire and things which have lost their interest are said to cool off. Horace:[2] 'Never again shall I be fired / By any other female form,' and husbands who are not especially fond of their wives are said to 'grow cool' towards them. St Jerome[3] explains Terence's aphorism on rather cruder lines: 'When the stomach is distended, the parts of the body adjacent to it are distended too; we indicate that lust is greed's boon-companion.' Wine in particular arouses sexual desire, and that is why the Pauline Epistles[4] forbid us to be 'drunk with wine, wherein is excess.' Euripides:[5] 'When wine's not present, Venus isn't there.' In the Greek collections[6] I find 'Without Bacchus and Ceres, Venus is a corpse.' A Cynic, quoted by Athenaeus[7] in book 6 of the *Doctors at Dinner*, records the same aphorism in the following words: 'In an empty stomach there's no room for love of beauty, for the Cyprian goddess is bitter to hungry men.' And he then adds a line from Euripides, said to have been borrowed by him from Achaeus the satyric poet: 'The Cyprian? Yes, when full; when empty, no.' Athenaeus in book 1 of the *Doctors at Dinner* cites a couple of lines containing the same thought: 'Cypris loves plenty, but the unfortunate / Find Venus hard of hearing to all their prayers.' In book 10 of the same work, Aristophanes[9] calls wine 'Venus' milk,' because it encourages desire: 'It's a sweet wine to drink, it's Venus' milk.' Here belongs an epigram[10] of uncertain authorship:

Hunger's the cure for love; or, if that fails,
Then time. If none of these will quench your flame,
One sole resource remains, the knotted rope.

Apuleius[11] wished to convey the same message when he represented Venus as under the influence of wine while Psyche was hungry. Though Aristotle[12] suggests that drinking wine to excess makes men unfit for coition; wine, he says dilutes the strength of the semen, and that is why Alexander the Great was sexually so ineffective: he drank too much wine. Athenaeus tells us that this was also in Theophrastus.

1 Terence *Eunuch* 732, with commentary by the ancient critic Donatus
2 *Odes* 4.11.33–4
3 *Against Jovinianus* 2.7 (*PL* 23.297A)
4 Ephesians 5:18
5 *Bacchae* 773
6 'Greek collections': Apostolius 12.2
7 Athenaeus 6.270b (a 'Cynic' is an error for Cynulcus one of the speakers); the next quotation is from Achaeus frag 6 Nauck and the quotation about Cypris is from Euripides frag 895 Nauck.
8 Athenaeus 1.28f citing the comic poet Antiphanes frag 242 Kock
9 Athenaeus 10.444d, citing Aristophanes frag 596 Kock
10 *Greek Anthology* 9.497
11 *Metamorphoses* 6.11
12 Aristotle on wine comes from the spurious *Problemata physica*, which Erasmus found in Athenaeus 10.434f–5a, as also the reference to Theophrastus.

II iv 17
Tempus omnia revelat / Time reveals all things

Robert Greene's romance of 1588 Pandosto *is subtitled* The Triumph of Time, *with the tag 'Temporis filia veritas' (Truth is the daughter of time) on the title page. This work is the source of Shakespeare's* Winter's Tale *in which a daughter, in time, teaches truth to her father. A celebrated article on the motif is F. Saxl 'Veritas filia temporis' in* Philosophy and History: Essays Presented to Ernst Cassirer *ed R. Klibansky and H.J. Paton (Oxford 1936) 197–222. The proverb is widely found in the variants given here by Erasmus (Otto 1756, Tosi 296), including English (Tilley T 324, 329a, 333). Erasmus quotes Scripture in the midst of all the classical citations, as though the ancient texts and the Bible together provide a continuous, related, and consistent wisdom. First used in* Collectanea *no 31.*

Tertullian,[1] whom St Cyprian habitually called his teacher, in his *Apologeticum against the Gentiles* says 'It is just as well that time reveals all things, as your proverbs too and moral maxims testify.' Aulus Gellius[2] in book 12 chapter 12 of his *Attic Nights* cites to this effect these lines of Sophocles: 'Hide nothing therefore, for all-seeing Time / and Time all-hearing brings all things to light.' Sophocles[3] again in *Ajax with the Scourge*: 'All things the uncountable extent of time / Brings out of hiding, and hides what could be seen.' In the same passage Gellius tells us that some ancient poet[4] called Truth 'the daughter of Time,' because though for a space she may lie hidden, yet with the progress of time she comes forth into the light. There is also a proverbial iambic line[5] to the same effect: 'But time brings out the truth into the light,' and another like it: 'All things revealing time will bring to light.' I suppose Thales[6] to have been of the same opinion when he said: 'Time is the wisest thing there is, for it discovers all things.' Pindar[7] thought the same in the *Olympians*: 'The days that remain are the wisest of witnesses.' And in another passage he calls Time the father of all things, because everything is brought about by the progress of time: 'Even Time father of all things could not undo what is once done and finished.' Pindar makes the same point in several places, and particularly in his tenth *Olympian*: 'Time that alone reveals the certain truth, and on its forward progress made the whole story clear.' Virgil[8] seems to have had this in mind in book 6: 'And drives them to confess if any in the world above, exulting in some fruitless fraud, has left the burden of his guilt unexpiated till the hour of death, too late.' Nor is there any disagreement between this and the saying in the Gospel,[9] Matthew chapter 10: 'There is nothing covered that shall not be revealed, and hid that shall not be known.' Plutarch in his 'Problems'[10] poses the question why it is that the ancients were accustomed to sacrifice to Saturn with their heads covered; and he thinks the point was that truth as a rule is covered and unknown, but is none the less revealed by time. For Saturn is fabled to be the creator and the god of time, Kronos being his name in Greek and *chronos* the word for time. Livy[11] holds the same opinion when he says in book 22: 'They say the just cause of truth is too often in difficulties, but is never extinguished.' Seneca[12] in his *On Anger*, book 2: 'We must always allow time, for day after day brings truth to light.'

1 *Apologeticum* 7.13
2 *Attic Nights* 12.11.6–7, citing a fragment in Sophocles (280 Nauck)
3 *Ajax* 646–7
4 Unidentified reference
5 Menander *Sententiae* 13 and 639
6 Diogenes Laertius 1.35
7 *Olympians* 1.33–4, 2.18–19, 10.53–5
8 *Aeneid* 6.567–9
9 Matthew 10:26
10 *Moralia* 266E
11 Livy 22.39.19
12 *On Anger* 2.22.2

II iv 60
Crocodili lachrymae / Crocodile tears

Though there is ancient authority for the proverb (reported in Apostolius 10.17), there even being a Greek verb krokodeilizein *(to act the crocodile), it was widely known in the Middle Ages as part of standard beast lore, and the expression is today found in all modern European languages (Tosi 224), including English (Tilley* C *831). The first two sentences appeared in* Collectanea *no 703.*

Κροκοδείλου δάκρυα, Crocodile tears, is used of those who pretend to be deeply affected by the distress of anyone for whose destruction they are themselves responsible or for whom they are planning some great disaster. Some writers tell us that when the crocodile sees a man in the distance, it sheds tears before proceeding to eat him. This is very close to the tears of the emperor Bassianus, of which Aelius Spartianus[1] tells, who wept whenever he heard the name or saw a likeness of his brother Geta, whom he had put to death. Others relate that it is the natural habit of a crocodile, when roused by hunger and planning some treacherous attack, to fill its mouth with water, which it sprays over the path by which it knows that other animals, or men, will come down to drink; the plan being that, when they have fallen on the slippery descent, and cannot make their escape, it will seize and devour them. Then, when it has eaten the rest of the body, it softens the head by shedding tears on it, and eats that too.

1 *Geta* 7.5 (in *Historia Augusta*)

II iv 68
Medium ostendere digitum / To show the middle finger

A proverb based on an ancient gesture that remarkably has survived into modern times. Compare 'Thumbs down, thumbs up' at I viii *46*, in which the ancient meaning is reversed, and 'To lift a finger' at* III iv *14*, in which the ancient meaning has now disappeared. Erasmus first wrote about this in* Collectanea *no 705.*

To hold up the middle finger was another way[1] they had of showing supreme contempt. Martial,[2] book 2: 'And hold up your middle finger.' For Martial calls this finger 'shameless': 'He shows a finger – and his shameless one.' Persius[3] calls it 'infamous': 'With infamous finger and purifying spittle.' Here, I think, must belong a story in Laertius[4] of which I have spoken elsewhere: how, when some visitors wanted to set eyes on Demosthenes, Diogenes pointed him out by holding up not his forefinger but his middle one, thus suggesting that he was no man and effeminate. A little later in the same passage he makes it quite clear that the outstretched middle finger conveys some obscene symbolism, when he says that those who stretch out the middle finger are thought to be of unsound mind, but that of the forefinger this is not so. So it was two adages in the same line that the satirist[5] used to express extreme contempt, when he wrote 'Bade her go hang, showed her his middle fingernail.' Both will be more stylish if bent some way from their proper use, for instance 'Tell the precepts of the philosophers to go hang; live your own life,' and 'Merchants hold up the middle finger at the rulings of divines,' that is, they simply despise and laugh at them.

1 The preceding adage is 'To bid one go hang.'
2 *Epigrams* 2.28.2 and 6.70.5
3 *Satires* 2.33
4 'Life of Diogenes' in *Lives of the Philosophers* 6.34, where the philosopher Diogenes the Cynic is pointing out Demosthenes the celebrated orator (in I x 43).
5 Juvenal ('the satirist') 10.53, the other adage being the one immediately preceding

II V 1

Spartam nactus es, hanc orna / Sparta is your portion; do your best for her

One of the major essays in the Adages. The Greek form is found in Suidas K *2141, the Latin in Otto 1679. Erasmus had only the first paragraph in 1508, and wrote most of the essay for the edition of 1515. Though he brings in some ancient sources, by the end he is concerned entirely with contemporary political figures, and his comment on the wasted life of Alexander Stewart is deeply felt. The essay should be seen as part of his continuing attempt, in so many of his secular works, to instruct monarchs and other leaders in the moral responsibilities of governance. For a general note on the anti-war essays, of which this is one, see introduction to* IV *i 1* 'War is sweet to those who have not tried it.'*

Ἣν ἔλαχες Σπάρτην κόσμει, Sparta has fallen to your lot; be an honour to her, or rule her well. The purport of this adage is that, whatever sphere of activity may chance to be ours, we should adapt ourselves to it, and live up to the standard that it sets. Cicero[1] in his *Letters to Atticus*, book 4 letter 6: 'Nothing is left but "Sparta is your portion; do your best for her." I simply can't, and can understand why Philoxenus preferred to be sent back to jail.' Again in the same collection, in book 1: 'That is why, when you say that Sparta is my portion, I shall never desert her; and what is more, if she deserts me, I shall stand by my original convictions.' The words[2] Cicero quotes form an anapaestic line from some tragedy. The scholiast on Theocritus[3] points out an allusion to this proverb in his *Wayfarers*: 'Compete from there then, and pasture your oxen from there. / Tread your own beat and keep your oaks.'

It will thus be permissible to apply the proverb to various purposes; when, for instance, we urge someone to maintain in a proper spirit the role which he has adopted. If you are a bishop, behave like a bishop, not an oriental prince. If you're a husband, mind you fulfil a husband's duties; if a courtier, then play the part of a courtier; if a judge, be no man's private friend or enemy, but be a judge. Has Fortune given you a princedom? – do your princely duty. Are you a private person? – act as a private person ought. This is very much how Aristophanes[4] uses the phrase (for his is the name attached to the comedy called *Thesmophoriazusae*): 'The poet his behaviour must adapt / To suit the play that he's obliged to write.' Equally, when we tell any individual that it is his duty to be content with the lot that has befallen him; for like an experienced ship's-captain, who shows his seamanship in any weather, a wise man acts a wise man's part in any circumstances. If you have an ample fortune, use it wisely; if the reverse, enjoy the blessings of a modest station. If you have had a good education, make it serve a good life; if not, do not repine, for godliness is sufficient to secure salvation. Plutarch[5] in his essay 'On Tranquillity of Mind,' making the point that everyone should be content with what he has, says 'Sparta has fallen to your lot; do your best for her.' In the same essay he tells us that this saying was uttered by Solon.[6] It is however cited from Euripides:[7] 'Sparta's your portion, Sparta you must rule; / Mycenae ours.' (The words seem addressed by Agamemnon to Menelaus.) This is close to Plato's[8] 'Make the best of what you have' or 'Take it in good part.' But the mass of people nowadays are more devoted to increasing what they have than to making the most of it; against which we are rightly warned by Socrates' words in Plato's *Theaetetus*:[9] 'For surely it is better to do something small well than something large inadequately.'

And so it would be right for this sentence 'Sparta is your portion; do your best for her' to be inscribed everywhere in the courts of princes; for you will hardly find one who truly considers what it means to play a prince's part, or who is content with the authority he has and does not attempt to add something to the extent of his dominions. It is a prince's duty to provide by all the means in his power for the well-being of the commonwealth, to protect public liberty, to cherish peace, to banish wrongdoing with the least possible sacrifice of his own subjects, and to see to it that he has virtuous and upright servants. And so, when he does not spare a thought for these things, but amuses himself with gaming, dancing, wenching, music, hunting, or business deals, and in a word is wholly occupied in other things, that is the time to din into his ears the adage 'Sparta is your portion; do your best for her.' Again, when he neglects the dominions which are already his and spends his time abroad, thirsting for the territory of others; when he brings his own subjects into great peril, exhausts his people utterly, and stakes alike himself and his whole fortune on the hazards of war, in order that he may add to his territories two or three petty towns; it is then he should be reminded of the adage 'Sparta is your portion.' Nothing brings a prince more credit than to take such dominions as Fortune has given him, and make them more flourishing by his own wisdom, virtue, and activity. Your lot is a small town: take Epaminondas[10] as your model, and make that small dull town far more populous and richer by your efforts. Your lot is a barbarous and intractable race of men: make it your business to tame them and render them law-abiding by degrees. Your lot may be a crown without much glory: do not challenge your neighbours, but improve what you have without inflicting loss on others. The desire for foreign dominions has very rarely turned out well. Some nations have been made separate by their character and language, like the Germans and the Spaniards; some men nature herself has isolated, the islanders by the sea, the Italians at the same time by the sea and the great mass of the Alps; some have been given their proper boundaries by chance. If every prince were to try to improve what he has been given, we may be sure all things would flourish universally; and among friends[11] of course, who are Christians, all things will be common to all. As things are, it often happens that we try to undermine the possessions of others, and entirely overthrow our own; or, even granting things go well, the blood of all those of our fellow-citizens, all that expense, such dangers and such efforts and so many childless homes, and in a word evils past counting, purchase some empty title and the smoke of a great name. Xerxes and Cyrus and Alexander the Great[12] would have lived longer and won more solid glory, had they preferred the good government of their own states to the harrassment by force of arms of states that were not theirs.

Charles, duke of Burgundy,[13] great-grandfather of the present duke, had he turned his outstanding intellectual gifts and his noble spirit to the enriching of his own dominions instead of conquering other men's, would not have met a wretched death in war, and might have been numbered among the most admired of princes. A great part of my native realm was at that time in the grip of a sort of fatal pestilence, a very foolish but uniquely disastrous civil strife; the whole population was split into two camps,[14] of which one took its name from a hook and the other from a codfish. City fought against city, village against village, house against house; often those who were united by sharing the same bed were divided by a difference of party, which broke the bonds of natural affection and rent brother from brother. Everywhere was a turmoil of robbery, strife, bloodshed, and rapine; and all the time that excellent prince, just as though this were not his business, was far away, laying siege to the walls of strangers.

Charles, king of France,[15] eighth of that name, after ranging over Italy returned to his own people; but at the price of such distress and danger for himself and them as made them repent of his success. Some even maintain that he might have reached old age, had he left Italy to the Italians.

What shall I say of Philip,[16] father of this present Charles? He set off for Spain, not to risk the hazards of war but because he was summoned to assume his share of the kingdom. There was universal peace; and yet that auspicious expedition – what tears it cost his country, plundered by unbearable taxation! He himself was more than once in great peril of death. He lost François de Busleyden,[17] archbishop of Besançon, a man without peer in every way. Somehow or other, none the less, he returned; but he was not allowed to be quit of his troubles so lightly. Once again he left his own people and, after being most cruelly tossed by a storm, he was cast up on the coast of England, which was at that time none too friendly to my countrymen. How he fared then, the treatment he received, the promises he made, on what conditions he was sent away, are subjects on which I would rather not dwell. He was the slave of necessity, of course, and I forgive him; but why was it necessary to subject himself to that necessity? Nor did he learn his lesson from these troubles and think of returning to his own country; he had to revisit Spain, and there he died, a young man born to do great things, had he not begrudged himself his own good fortune. Thus one man's death at one stroke deprived his country of an excellent prince and Maximilian[18] of an only son.

What am I to say of the Most Christian king of France, Louis XII?[19] He attacked Venice, which at that time seemed invincible, and in one conflict restored all those towns to the Roman pontiff Julius and to the Emperor Maximilian, and won so many for himself, returning, as it seemed, in triumph. But as a result what a sea of troubles[20] came flooding into France! With their own blood the French had won all those famous victories for Julius, and it was Julius' doing that with still greater bloodshed they were expelled from Italian soil. Nor was this all, and they were branded with every form of ignominy. Had Julius not been carried off by death, we should have seen that kingdom, the most properous in the whole world, utterly overthrown.

Of James,[21] most serene king of Scots, what am I to say? Prosperity and reputation, both without flaw, were his, if he had confined himself permanently within his own frontiers. He was so handsome that even from afar you could see he was a king; he had great powers of mind, incredible and universal knowledge, and unconquerable spirit, a truly royal nobility of feeling, the most perfect courtesy, the most open-handed generosity; there is, in short, no good quality that might grace a great prince in which he did not so far excel as to win praise even from his enemies. He was blessed with a wife – Margaret,[22] sister of his most serene majesty King Henry the eighth of England – of such beauty, such good sense, and such devotion to her husband, that he could not have asked heaven for a different queen. On the kingdom of Scotland, which in wealth, in the number of its inhabitants and in grandeur is thought to fall short of many others, he had shed such lustre by his own qualities, and had so exalted, so embellished it, that he deserved the true praise of an outstanding prince, if he had kept within this field of action in his quest for glory. But alas, when a king leaves his kingdom, this is never a blessing for the country, and rarely for the prince. In an excess of friendly feeling for the king of France, and in hopes of diverting the English king, who was mounting serious and active threats against the French, and recalling him to the defence of his island, he crossed the frontier of his own kingdom and opened hostilities against the English. In brief, he perished, bravely but disastrously, not so much for himself as for his kingdom, and perished while still in his prime. Long might Scotland have enjoyed such a great prince; long might Margaret have enjoyed such a husband, his son (for he had had a son by her) such a father, and he in his turn all these blessings and his own renown, had he not begrudged himself a longer life.

Killed with that valiant father was a son, a son worthy of such a father, Alexander[23] archbishop of Saint Andrews, a young man only some twenty years of age, in whom no quality that would grace a man in his maturity was lacking. Strikingly handsome and dignified, and of heroic stature, he had a very placid temperament, but none the less was very quick to acquire knowledge in every field. I once lived under the same roof in the city of Siena, at a time when I was coaching him in rhetoric and Greek. What gifts he had, in heaven's name! How quick his mind, how fertile, how ready to follow any clue, how capable of grasping many things at once! At the same time he was learning law, but did not much enjoy his lawbooks with the element of barbarism in their style and the tedious verbosity of the commentators. He used to have lessons on rhetorical theory, and declaimed on a prescribed theme, practising at the same time both pen and tongue. He was learning Greek, and every day used to return at the agreed time the exercise that had been set him. The afternoons were given up to his music teachers, in the monochord, the flute, and the zither; sometimes he also sang. Even dinner-time did not fail to contribute to his studies. The chaplain used to read continuously some improving book, the *Papal Decrees* perhaps or St Jerome or Ambrose; nor was he ever interrupted as he read, unless one or other of the two learned men between whom the archbishop was sitting had drawn attention to some point, or he himself, not fully understanding what was read, had asked some question. After dinner again there was conversation, but not for long, and it was spiced with sound learning. No part of his life in fact was exempt from study, except for what was given to divine service and to sleep. For even if there had been any time to spare (and time did not suffice for so great a variety of studies) – if in spite of this there was any time left over, he spent it on reading the historians, for history was his favourite subject.

The result of all this was that, when a youth scarcely more than eighteen years old, his achievements in every department of learning were such as you would rightly admire in a grown man. Nor was it the case with him, as it is with so many others, that he had a natural gift for learning but was less disposed to good behaviour. He was shy by nature, but it was a shyness in which you could detect remarkable good sense. His spirit was lofty, and far above the usual unworthy desires, but in a way that avoided both the disdainful and the farouche. Sensitive as he was, he often concealed his feelings, nor could he ever be provoked to lose his temper; such was his gentle nature and his fairness of mind. In wit he took great delight, but it must be educated and have no cutting edge, seasoned with the white salt of Mercury, not the black salt of Momus.[24] Had there been any domestic trouble among his household, the skill and plain speaking with which he normally dealt with it were remarkable. Last but not least, his was a very devout religious nature, without a trace of superstition; no one, in a word, was ever more worthy to be a king's son and the son of that king.

If only his devotion to his father, admirable as it was, had been equally fortunate! Resolved never to fail his father, he went with him to the war. What pray had you to do with Mars, the stupidest of all the gods of poetry, when you were already enlisted as a disciple of the Muses and, what is more, of Christ himself? With your handsome person, your youth, your gentle nature, and your fairness of mind, what could they mean to you, the trumpet-calls, the cannon, and the sword? What place has learning in the line of battle, or a bishop sword in hand? It was, no doubt, excessive filial devotion that misled you. You proved your love for your father with a courage that was too great, and unhappily fell with your father on the field of battle. Those gifts of nature, those high qualities, those splendid hopes, were all sunk in the hurricane of a single fight. Something of mine was lost there too: the pains I had devoted to teaching you, and so much of you as was made by my efforts, I claim as my share in you.

And what supreme felicity there might have been, had not some evil genius driven the king to pass the frontiers of his own kingdom and try the fortunes of war in foreign fields against a nation noted for ferocity! If only he had been willing to complete the task he had begun so admirably, of doing the best for the Sparta which was his portion! Kings find their proper and their noblest field for distinction within the frontiers of their realm. Take the commonwealth of bees: the other citizens fly hither and thither at will; only the king[25] is without a sting, and he only has much smaller wings in proportion to his body, so that he is not well-fitted for flight. The ancients used to represent Venus with her feet resting on a tortoise-shell, to convey the message that the mother of a family ought never to leave the house, since all her duties are confined within domestic walls. It was in any case much more the point for the prince to take warning from his emblem, for if he does wrong, his wrongdoing entails unhappiness, not for a single family but for the whole round world.

Has he so little business in his own country that he must look for trouble in foreign parts? Crime like a great cesspit lies everywhere, all that sacrilege and robbery, that oppression injury and insult; those fraudulent magistrates, those laws enacted by tyrants or wrested to the service of tyranny; to say nothing of the small-scale scandals, the neglected roads between our towns, the churches falling into ruin, the river-banks neglected. To heal these evils in such a way that you expend on the remedy as little as possible of your people's blood, and the commonwealth feels the benefit without feeling the expense, is surely a splendid task for any prince and earns him immortal renown. If, however, all your desire is to extend the horizon of your glory beyond the bounds of your own realm, see to it that your neighbours learn your greatness from the benefits you confer on them, not from your misdeeds. Do you burn farms and trample crops, demolish cities, drive off flocks and herds and slaughter human beings? Are these the only means by which you show your greatness? A pretty contest, had you been matched against a pirate! Hesiod[26] wrote that 'an evil neighbour is a mighty woe,' a good one on the other hand an enormous boon. Let your neighbours see this proved true in you; let them admire your greatness, in so far as your goodness wins their affection.

But I have given rein enough to my grief, and to the memory of my disciple; it remains to return to my catalogue of proverbs.

1 *Letters to Atticus* 4.6.2 and 1.20.3
2 The line is a fragment from Euripides, for which see note 7 below.
3 5.60–1
4 *Thesmophoriazusae* 149–50
5 *Moralia* 472D
6 An error of reading; Solon was actually the author of the next saying in the Plutarch essay.
7 From the lost *Telephus* frag 723 Nauck, from Stobaeus 3.39.9
8 Perhaps *Gorgias* 499C
9 *Theaetetus* 187e
10 Epaminondas, who came from the 'dull town' of Thebes, became a great military leader in the fourth century BC.
11 *Adages* I i 1*, an example of the way Erasmus uses one adage inside another
12 Xerxes was murdered, Cyrus died in battle, Alexander died at the age of thirty-three.
13 Charles the Bold died in 1477 at the battle of Nancy.
14 The 'Hoeks' and the 'Kabiljauws'
15 Charles VIII (1470–98) of France attempted to take Italy but was successfully repelled in 1496.
16 Philip the Handsome (1478–1506), father of Charles V
17 François de Busleyden died in Toledo in 1502.
18 The Emperor Maximilian I (1459–1519) was father of Philip the Handsome and grandfather of Charles V.
19 Louis XII of France (1462–1515) managed to defeat Venice in the battle of Agnadello (1509), but by 1513 had been driven out of Italy.
20 'A sea of troubles' I iii 28
21 James IV of Scotland (1473–1513) died in the battle of Flodden.
22 Margaret Tudor (1489–1541)
23 Alexander Stewart was a natural son of James IV.
24 Mercury is the patron of learning, Momus a figure of petty criticism.
25 Up through the early modern period, the hive was believed to be organized around a 'king bee.'
26 Hesiod *Works and Days* 346

II V 87
Ipse dixit / He said himself

The proverb has retained its Latin form Ipse dixit *in English and in other languages (Tosi 373), though we now refer to a final and unalterable statement as 'an ipse dixit,' which doesn't make much grammatical sense. Coleridge took the now English phrase further when he coined 'ipse-dixitish'* (OED).

Αὐτὸς ἔφα, He said himself. Whenever we wish to convey that one man's authority is so great as to justify our belief in something even with no reason given, in the way that 'He said himself' is sufficient in Holy Scripture,[1] though not in other texts. The adage took its rise from Pythagoras who, in order to achieve more respect and authority for himself and his school, used to say in his lectures 'He said himself,' just as though he were repeating not his own opinions but utterances that he had received from some oracle. The words then migrated into common speech. Such is more or less the account given by Suidas.[2] Diogenes Laertius[3] gives us to understand that the remark stems from Pythagoras of Zacynthus. All the same, Cicero[4] in the first book of his *On the Nature of the Gods* tells a different story: 'For in a discussion we should look not for authorities but for reason to sway the balance. In fact the authority of those who profess themselves teachers is often a handicap to those who wish to learn; they cease to use their own judgment, and accept as authoritative whatever verdict they find passed by the judge of their choice. Nor do I normally approve a habit I have heard ascribed to the Pythagoreans; it is said that when they asserted something in a discussion to be true, and were asked why this was so, they were wont to reply "He said so himself." The "himself" of course was Pythagoras. Such was the effect of an opinion predetermined, that authority carried the day, even with no appeal to reason.' Quintilian[5] in the *Principles*: 'For juries give a reluctant hearing to the man who takes for granted that his case is right, nor can counsel rely on finding among his opponents the principle to which Pythagoras could appeal among his disciples, He said so himself.' But this approach is sometimes more defective, sometimes less; it depends on the sort of man who uses it. Aristophanes[6] also alludes to this in the *Clouds*:

– Tell me, who's this man swinging in the basket?
– Himself. – And who's himself? – Why, Socrates.
– Who's Socrates? Call him – a good loud shout.
– No, no: call him yourself. I haven't time.

(When he says 'swinging in the basket,' I may explain in passing, this is a new and humorous idea: he wants us to understand that Socrates is contemplating the clouds, with his mind set on higher things. The *kremathra* of which he speaks is a hanging container in which the left-over remains of food used to be kept.)

The phrase is used in two ways, sometimes with its simple meaning but more often ironically; for example to someone citing Aristotle as an oracle one might reply 'No doubt he said so himself,' to show that one needed his reasons and was not satisfied with the bare authority of the writer. It will be useful too when we wish to transfer the unpopularity of some opinion, or the task of defending it, from ourselves to the man who is really responsible. Juvenal:[7] 'Such is my will and pleasure; if I please, / That's good enough for you.' Horace[8] is better: 'To no man's words in blind allegiance pledged.'

It is perhaps worth pointing out that 'He said himself' in this proverb has much the same force as 'Thus saith the lord,' so that Pythagoras might be thought to have learnt this phrase, which is familiar to us in the Prophets, from the seers in Egypt. Aristophanes[9] in the *Frogs*: 'Go, tell the girls, / His lordship has arrived – and here I am,' meaning that the master arrives in some sense, even if he only sends his servants. In the same way in the scriptural prophets[10] 'Here I am,' meaning 'your lord and master.'

Here belongs what I have said earlier on the proverb After planting the dart.[11] Thus Augustine[12] in some passage where he reviews the opinion of Manichaeus, if I remember right: 'Manichaeus said this, and departed,' his point being that he was content to have stated his view, when he should have argued it. Galen[13] too *On the Natural Faculties*, book 1: 'Having said this and more like it without preparation and without hesitation, as though what he said could not be wrong or be misunderstood, he ended by dashing off and leaving us where we were, as though we were quite unable to produce any counter argument with even a shadow of probability.'

1 Holy Scripture, as in 'Thus saith the Lord'
2 Suidas A 4523 (also Diogenianus 3.19)
3 *Lives of the Philosophers* 8.46
4 *On the Nature of the Gods* 1.5.10
5 *Institutes of Oratory* 11.1.27
6 Aristophanes *Clouds* 218–21
7 *Satires* 6.223
8 *Epistles* 1.1.14
9 *Frogs* 519–20
10 Isaiah 52.6 and 58.9
11 at I i 5
12 Passage not identified
13 *On the Natural Faculties* 1 ed Kühn 2.35

II V 93
A Dorio ad Phrygium / From Dorian to Phrygian

This learned proverb is about moving from one mode to another (musical, psychological, etc). Erasmus' learned exploration doesn't actually explain what a mode was in Greek music: it is a scale defined from other such scales by its sequence of intervals and also by its tonality. Rhythm and tempo changed from one mode to the other, but the basic difference was in the unequal intervals of progression – quite unlike our more equally divided modern Western scale. There was a significant ethical component to the music; probably the best-known discussion is in Plato's Republic *(3.398c and following), where Socrates outlines the kind of music appropriate to the young guardians, although at the same time indicating the difficulty of Greek music when he admits, 'I don't know the modes.'*

A man was said to pass From Dorian to Phrygian, Ἀπὸ Δωρίου ἐπὶ Φρύγιον, who had turned from a more abstemious way of living to a life of luxury, or who had passed from a modest situation to one of more noise and bustle. The metaphor is taken from those very familiar kinds of harmony used by the ancients, of which the Dorian was the more restrained, as Suidas indicates, quoting the following words from an author[1] whose name I do not know: 'The way of life that had fallen to his lot was moderate and far from luxurious, such as would neither blight a man's prospects through poverty or sap his energies through too much wealth; it was a middle way, well-tuned and truly adapted to the Dorian mode of fortune.' Suidas also refers to another passage,[2] suppressing, if I am not mistaken, the author's name; it is not easy to give an appropriate rendering of this without knowing what precedes or follows, but I will add my own guesswork, to serve until the passage turns up: 'It will be clear that I put forward, not the chosen language of men of rotund utterance but their actual meaning; only I shall not have from Dorian (as they say) to Phrygian.' Though in Suidas the reading is not *monon ou* 'only I shall not have,' but *monon ei*, 'only if I have.' From these words it is clear that the Dorian mode was more delicate and the Phrygian more severe. Apuleius[3] in the first book of his *Florida* makes it quite plain that the Dorian style in music was very different from Phrygian, since one aroused the mind to religious feelings and the other fired it with martial ardour. Apuleius' words run as follows: 'There was a flute-player once called Antigenidas, whose control of every note was sweet as honey, a master too in the management of every mode, whether you wished him to play the simple Aeolian, the versatile Asian, the plaintive Lydian, the solemn Phrygian or warlike Dorian.' Such are Apuleius' words; and if he is right, the Dorian, which kindles men with martial ardour, cannot be a temperate mode, unless maybe the flutes played calming music to men on their way into battle, because at that moment self-control is more use than wild enthusiasm. Whether in the passage from Apuleius we should read 'Aetolian' (*Aetolicum* or *Aetolium*) for 'Aeolian' and 'Ionian' (*Iassium* or *Iastium*, from *Ias* or *Iasti*) for 'Asian,' I leave open for the consideration of the learned. Though this does not agree properly with what Lucian[4] writes in his *Harmonides*: 'And each mode has its special character, divine force' (what Apuleius calls 'solemnity') 'in the Phrygian, Bacchic enthusiasm in the Lydian, severity in the Dorian, cheerfulness in the Ionian' (which Apuleius seems to have rendered by 'versatility'). Dion[5] on the other hand, in his essay 'On Kingship,' records that the fighting spirit of Alexander the Great was always aroused when the musician Timotheus played in the Dorian mode. Athenaeus[6] in book 14 credits the Dorian mode with 'manly severity and majesty and force,' neither languishing nor gay, but solemn and the reverse of versatile.

A later author, Boethius[7] in the preface to his work *On Music*, shows how this art has a special power of rousing our feelings, and that the feelings it rouses or calms differ from one mode to another. He adds the story of a young man, a barbarian by birth (for he came from Taormina), who had been excited by music played in the Phrygian mode, and was drunk and furiously angry; when he was already trying to set fire to the house of his mistress, who had admitted a rival, Pythagoras told the flute-girl to change to a spondaic rhythm, and so restored him to sanity. Boethius says the young man had been excited by the Phrygian mode, and returned to his senses when the mode was changed; but he does not tell us what mode replaced the Phrygian. Cicero,[8] who is quoted in this passage by Boethius, mentions neither mode, and only says that the young man was pacified by music in spondaic rhythm. If it was with the Dorian mode that Timotheus used to rouse Alexander to war, and with the Phrygian that this young man was fired to attack the house, it would seem that there was not much difference between these two modes. Lucian ascribes madness, *to entheon*, to the Phrygian, but madness of a sacred kind. Of this Plato[9] establishes three sorts: one inflicted on poets by the Muses, one on seers by Apollo, and the third on lovers by the god of love. Bacchus and Mars have their own madness too. Thus the young man in the story, when he went out of his mind, had been seized by madness of three kinds, from Bacchus, Cupid, and Mars. That a pyrrhic rhythm rouses men to battle, I have shown elsewhere[10] for this is the source of To have a pyrrhic look in the eye, used of fierce excited people; and the pyrrhic is the opposite of the spondee. Had not Boethius spoken of a change of mode, we might have accepted that the same Phrygian mode could rouse with pyrrhic rhythms and calm with spondees. And it seems possible that Boethius, in speaking of a change of mode, meant a change not of harmony but of rhythmic speed.

There is clearly a place for the proverb when there is a change of subject, when, for instance, a man starts with the principles of rhetoric and digresses to speak of theology. I myself suppose that the ancients have given us different accounts of the systems of harmony, because the system itself changed with changes in the behaviour of society. In early days the people of Asia were reputed for their discipline, before they were softened by luxury. The same happened to the Spartans, among whom were Dorians. Hence those names for mixtures of mode, hypodorian, mixolydian and hypermixolydian. Athenaeus[11] thinks the hypodorian mode is the same as the Aeolian, to which he attributes pomp and circumstance and a touch of effeminacy. Some music-scholars affirm that to change from Dorian to Phrygian is very difficult. I have shown elsewhere[12] that there was a Phrygian form of song called *skolion*, which was also commonly used in the dirges at funerals. If Dorian music is different from Phrygian, inasmuch as it arouses martial ardour, everyone must agree that it consisted of pyrrhics, since the pyrrhic is the opposite of the spondee. But there is a great deal about these kinds of harmony in Plato's *Republic*,[13] and again in the *Laches* he teaches us that the true Dorian harmony, and the true Greek harmony (neither Phrygian nor Ionian nor Lydian) is to be found when there is complete harmony in a virtuous man between his life and language. Plutarch[14] has something to say in his essay 'On Music.' For my part, I have said enough to make clear the meaning of the adage.

1 Damascius, late classical philosopher (fifth–sixth century AD), frag 50, in Suidas A 764
2 Synesius *Praise of Baldness* 4 (*PG* 66.1173C), in Suidas Δ 1461
3 *Florida* 4
4 *Harmonides* 1
5 Dion of Prusa 1.1
6 14.624d
7 *De institutione musica* 1.1
8 Frag 10.3
9 In his *Phaedrus* 244c–5c
10 III vii 71
11 14.625a
12 II vi 21
13 *Republic* 3.398e and *Laches* 188d
14 'On Music' 11ff

II v 98
Esernius cum Pacidiano / Esernius against Pacidianus

Like the preceding, a very specific proverb that does not appear in English. The opening analysis sets the scene for what turns out to be the principal subject of the essay: an account of a debate between the English Franciscan Henry Standish (d 1535) and an unnamed Italian Servite Friar. Erasmus disliked Standish, who had maligned him publicly on a number of occasions (for more, see Contemporaries *III 279–80). This essay is unusual in its focus on present-day events and unique in its attack on a single individual. Indeed, the writing here is far more typical of Erasmus' lively correspondence. Adages are used freely – typical is the reference to the 'god in the machine' (I i 68*) at the beginning of the fourth paragraph.*

There is a well-known phrase very like this[1] in Lucilius:[2] Esernius matched against Pacidianus. They too were gladiators, a well-matched pair and far more distinguished than all their contemporaries. Cicero in his book *On the Best Kind of Orator*: 'For my part, to compare small things with great, I bring onto the stage a famous pair of gladiators. Aeschines takes the part of Esernius, "no filthy fellow he," as Lucilius puts it, but a skilled and doughty fighter, "is matched with our Pacidianus, and is far / The best that ever was since men were men."'

A spectacle very like this was presented to us in these last few days in London, England, to the great delight of all those present, by two theologians. One of whom was that great figure, Standish, the archimandrite of the Franciscans who in that isle are called conventuals, a powerful speaker and tireless Scotist who knows not fear, and a man of such sinews and physical vigour that he might well have been a guardsman or a prizefighter, had he not been a theologian. The other was an Italian,[3] a member of the community commonly called the Servite Friars, the reason being (so they tell me) that, though as black as beetles, they serve the Virgin Mary as their only mistress, and have no truck with Christ or any of the saints besides. This man, however, though in learning perhaps not inferior, was quite unequal, in my opinion, in all those gifts that make a gladiator. Having retired to England shortly before Lent as his custom was, he wanted to demonstrate that the efforts he had expended in Paris for several years already on the study of theology had not been wasted, and so he proceeded to put forward a number of conclusions, as they call them, for discussion in academic circles, most of which related to commercial problems, but not the first, which was taken to cast some aspersions on St Francis. The text was something to this effect: that the Friars Minor commit sin if they accept money, whether personally or through a third party, and in consequence those who give them money also commit sin, for whoever furnished another with the opportunity to commit sin, sinned himself also.

The cause that moved a foreigner to take this bold step was as follows. This Servite was lodging with the Augustinians who call themselves Hermits, I suppose by some principle of opposites. The Augustinians in London do very well out of the merchants, Italians especially, and this made the Minorites jealous. The man Standish therefore, in hopes of diverting this source of income to his own Order, warned the congregation in a sermon to be extremely careful in the choice of a confessor; only two Orders had been authorized by the Holy Father to hear any man's confession, the Minorites and the Jacobites. As this would clearly reduce the other Orders to starvation, they put their heads together, and suborned the Servite, whose ignorance of English did not permit him to preach in public, to seek satisfaction for such an outrageous attack by a series of academic theses. Fixed up therefore on every church door and at every street corner were to be seen the 'conclusions' of which I began to tell.

The news of this spread gradually, as it usually does; and when it reached the ears of Standish, the spirit of that holy and high-hearted hero was fired with appropriate wrath. Dire were his threats, and all seemed set for some great and tragic outcome, when some god intervened, as they say, from the machine.[4] Our wise philosopher saw clearly that the affair would end in famine at Saguntum,[5] if such a proposition were even to get a hearing in public; and among themselves they reckon most saintly the man who has most coin. To cut a long story short, the Servite was forced to go and see Standish in order to apologize and pacify him. He went with great reluctance. He was a stranger, and there were plenty of people to frighten him with the news that Standish was a poisonous man, and noisy, and had an ungovernable temper; that he was thought to be something by common people, sailors perhaps and cart-drivers and cobblers, old-clothes dealers and fullers and other such leaders of society; and that he had sufficient self-confidence to stand out alone against the whole English Church in a most valiant defense of the case for immunity,[6] which had made him unpopular with all priests and bishops and a large part of those ordinary folk who wish well to the secular clergy. When the Servite was ushered into the presence, having dabbled in rhetoric as well as theology, he attempted to secure the man's goodwill by the following exordium: 'Worshipful father,' says he, 'I have come, to be sure, most reluctantly, having heard from several sources that you are ungovernably angry and, if some of my informants are to be believed, actually mad.' Having thus, fully in accordance with the rules of the art, secured his hearer's goodwill, he went on briefly as follows: 'But in any case, as these fathers have so strongly urged me to do so, I have come to hear if you have anything to say.' At this the other man exploded, and abused him roundly. His 'conclusion' was a perfect scandal; it was offensive to pious ears, it stank of heresy, it showed gross contempt of the Seraphic Order of St Francis, and its author would soon pay the penalty if he did not recant. The Servite replied, as a brave man should, that he had put it forward for discussion, and there was no call for recantation. At such godless words Standish lost all control over his emotions; he told the man to wait a moment, and rushed into the house. The Servite, who on this point also was reluctant to obey the great man, was already proceeding to depart. His opponent, rapidly summoning several of his bodyguard in their monastic habit, of whom he has a large number, as muscular and as bold as any king's, caught up with him as he retreated, seized him, and dragged him into the house feet first like a second Cacus.[7] Thereupon the poor Servite, desolate and fearing his end was near, did as men often do in an extremity: he appealed to Jesus, crying 'Jesus, Jesus' over and over again at the top of his voice. Among the Franciscans Jesus was nowhere to be found, and all the time the wretch was being dragged along; but there were some builder's workmen in the neighbourhood, who were aroused by the name of Jesus, and came running up with stones, and with the tools of their trade, and rescued the man by force from the hands of that bodyguard. And that was the first act of the play.

The next act opened with torrents of abuse on either side, as the leaders of both parties appealed to their supporters. The Servite is even said to have hung up a votive picture in gratitude to Jesus his saviour, in which the story was portrayed in colour, with an epigram appended. By now the tale had spread rapidly through the population, and had even got as far as the ears of the cardinal,[8] who is the chief magistrate and judge of that kingdom. Having a sense of humour, and thinking this might be an entertaining spectacle, he ordered both of them to appear before him. Standish delivered a severe attack, and the Servite defended himself vigorously. The cardinal decided, this being a scholastic proposition and open to debate, that immediately after Easter, on the Thursday, they should hold a public discussion in St Paul's Cathedral, which is the most famous church in the island. Neither side declined battle. The chieftains arm themselves, their soldiers get ready for the fray. The 'conclusions' are nailed up on every door, at every crossroad and on every fence; people gather even from long distances to see the fun. Men hold opposite views, but all are at one in their excitement. Not to make a long story of it, the day came that had been fixed for the battle, and with learned and unlearned the place was packed, when lo and behold, the efforts of certain people had secured an order from the king, announced by the cardinal, that things should go no further. Whereupon Standish, to secure all the credit for himself, sent some of his people separately to put it about all through the crowd that the Servite had thrown himself humbly at his feet and begged him that the dispute might not proceed. Most of them were already convinced of this, the other man being a foreigner and unable to speak English, had not some god given the Servite a bright idea. He went up into the pulpit, and addressed the crowd in these words: 'Right learned doctors, and all other honourable men, there was to have been a dispute today, but his Eminence the Cardinal for good and sufficient reason has given orders to cancel it, so do not wait in vain for something to happen.' The Minorites, seeing the prize of so great a victory torn from their grasp, fell upon the man, and would have torn him to pieces right there in the cathedral, had not the cardinal seen this coming and attached a few men to him to protect him who were known to his own household.

So the Minorites wagged their heads at him and uttered a great many threats from a safe distance, which was all they were allowed to do; and then they accused the Servite a second time before the cardinal with a lot of uproar for having dared to breach the royal prohibition and go on record before a public audience that he was prepared to defend such an impious 'conclusion.' Both parties were ordered to appear. Standish beside his bodyguard had also brought a boy in a monastic habit, who was already learning his Scotus; such is the importance of being correctly brought up from an early age. This boy he proudly displayed to the magnates of the court, as they passed through the different rooms to the cardinal's privy chamber; for Standish was known to many of them, better known than loved. He assured them that they would see the boy polish off the Servite and trample him under foot. 'We have got to the stage' said Standish 'when a boy can be pitted against him.' But the cardinal said it was improper to pit a boy against a man who was a graduate, as they call it; for the Servite was a bachelor of theology, though whether *currens* or *sedens, formatus* or shortly to become so, is uncertain. So a Minorite was put forward, this time an Italian confronting an Italian, so that one crow might pick out the other crow's eyes.[9] A number of scholars and leading members of the court stood round listening eagerly. 'Do you maintain' began the Minorite with arm outstretched 'that the Friars commit sin if they handle money?' 'Yes,' he said, 'I do.' 'Do you deny that the Pope has power to issue a privilege to make it lawful?' 'No,' he said, 'I do not.' 'But the Pope has given us a privilege.' 'I dare say.' 'So then it is lawful.' 'I have nothing against that.' 'So then your "conclusion" is a lie.' This weapon the Servite dodged like this: 'My conclusion' he said 'makes a statement about the Friars Minor. It is not lawful for them; for you, who are not Friars Minor, it is lawful.' 'But the papal bull' said the other man 'calls us Friars Minor.' 'So it does' said the Servite, 'but it adds the words "who are conventuals"; for conventual friars are Friars Minor in the same way that a dead man is a man.' This silenced the Minorite, for it was a solution he had not seen coming; and the cardinal, admired this skill in argument with a pleasant smile. When Standish saw that the first round had gone so badly, he entered the ring himself, and said with a threatening frown and outstretched arm: 'I maintain that you are excommunicated.' When the other said no, he went on 'We have a papal bull which excommunicates everyone who dares to say the the conventual Friars Minor in England commit a sin if they accept money. You have seen the bull, and you say this: therefore you are excommunicated.' At this point the Servite was fairly in trouble, had he not wormed his way out by saying that the bull spoke of conventual Friars Minor, who were not really such, while his conclusion referred to Friars Minor without qualification. The cardinal, whose object in all this had been entertainment rather than serious business, dismissed them both in such terms that it was not yet quite clear which was the stronger man. The Servite returned to Paris to enjoy his triumph there; the Standish party on the other hand put it about among themselves that he was defeated by a boy and reduced to complete silence. The 'conclusion' remains to be discussed at Oxford and Cambridge in the schools of theology.

This spectacle I found so exceedingly entertaining, dear reader, that I thought I would share my pleasure with you, so that you could lighten the tedium of your reading with this agreeable relief.

1 The preceding adage was 'Bithus against Bacchius,' on two well-matched gladiators.

2 Lucilius, an early satirist, quoted in Cicero *On the Best Kind of Orator* 6.17

3 'The Italian' has not been identified.

4 I i 68*

5 Saguntum, in southern Spain, fell to the Carthaginians in 218 BC, after a siege, the hardships of which were proverbial, as in I ix 67 'Famine at Saguntum.'

6 Act of Parliament in 1512 limiting the extent of clerical

protection

7 Cacus was a monster killed and dragged about by Hercules in Virgil *Aeneid* 8.264–5.

8 Thomas Wolsey, cardinal archbishop of York and Henry VIII's Lord High Chancellor

9 I iii 75

II vi 12

Ignavis semper feriae sunt / For sluggards it is always holiday

This proverb is built around a single source, Theocritus Idylls *15.26, though the proverb had other citations in antiquity (Tosi 958). The proverb came into English, though it is uncommon ('With sluggards every day is holiday' Tilley D 67 and S 548).*

Those who find time to do nothing are said *feriari*, to make holiday, and leisure is *feriae*, holidays, and those who enjoy it are *feriati* and these metaphors were in common use as though they were proverbial. Theocritus[1] in his *Bucolics*: 'It's always holiday for those who have no work to do.' For on holiday pagans no less than Christians abstained from worldly business.

Those who fight shy of work wish for the feast-days on which it is permitted to do nothing, and gratify your wish to eat, drink, and be merry. In antiquity a certain number of holidays were allowed to country folk with the deliberate purpose of refreshing them with play instead of work when they were tired; but there is an admixture of religion to keep the play between bounds. Today the common run of Christians misuse the holy days, devised in old days for pious purposes, in drinking, wenching, gambling, quarreling, and fighting; and at no season are more crimes committed than at those when crimes are most clearly out of place. Never do we so clearly imitate the pagans as on the days when we have a special duty to behave like Christians; and thought is is clear that a practice designed for the advancement of religion now tends to put religion itself in peril, yet on some policy I do not understand the popes daily add new holidays on top of old. It would be more appropriate to follow the practice of prudent physicians and alter remedies to suit the pattern of diseases, with no object in view except to contribute to good health. Thus, when they see that a practice wisely instituted long ago to suit the pattern of those times is now, with the changes in Christians' way of life, a menace to religion, why these scruples about changing the established order with the same end in view as that with which our fathers established it? What I say about holy days would make sense about many other things; not that I think the Christian practice of holidays should be condemned, but I would rather it did not grow to unmeasured lengths, and I should prefer to see the few festivals instituted by the authority of early times converted to the purpose for which they were invented. For to a true Christian every day is a holy day; while to the bad Christians, who form the greatest crowd,[2] holy days are not so much holy as profane.

But to return to my proverb, it will be well adapted to those who always have some excuse why they should be at leisure; those, for example, who do not enjoy reading are at one moment in poor health, at another busied with domestic cares; sometimes the cold of winter is the obstacle and sometimes summer heat or the treacherous climate of autumn, or they are called away from their books by the lovely spring weather which will so soon be gone. After dinner they say one should have nothing to do with books until one's stomach has settled down, and when they have not yet dined the pangs of hunger remove the desire to read. In daylight, they say, it is lazy to sit doing nothing indoors, and to sit up by lamplight is bad for their eyes. If they have enough to live on, they say, why bother to read? A young man says he cannot spend the best years of his life on cares which are all right when you're old; and a man in later life says he must be careful of his health.

1 15.26

2 Cf Virgil *Aeneid* 6.611

II vi 20
Vino vendibili suspensa hedera nihil opus / Good wine needs no bush

This is one of the very few proverbs in the Adages *for which Erasmus gives no classical source, and it seems that the proverb (or the practice to which it refers) is late medieval. The parallels he cites from Plautus and Horace are really quite different. In* Collectanea *no 404, where he first discussed the proverb, Erasmus followed Angelo Poliziano, the great fifteenth-century classical scholar, from his* Letters *(1.11). Poliziano may have picked it up from a medieval collection or from hearing of the practice. Placing a branch before a tavern was done in the fifteenth century in western Europe (ASD II-4, 33n) and is still followed today in some places. The proverb has had a long history in English (Tilley W 462).*

Good wine needs no bush. True excellence, in other words, needs no outside advertisement. Good things please in their own right, and feel no lack of external commendation. Evidently taken from the inn-keepers' practice of hanging an ivy-bush as a sign over their wineshops. Plautus[1] has the same idea in the *Poenulus*: 'For unsaleable goods you must go out and look for a buyer; good stuff finds its own buyer easily enough.' Horace:[2]

The salesman here no panegyric spares
To find a market for his lingering wares.

1 *Poenulus* 341–2
2 *Epistles* 2.2.10–11 (Erasmus reads *largius aequo* for *plenius aequo*)

II vi 38
Adrastia Nemesis. Rhamnusia Nemesis / Nemesis of Adrastus, of Rhamnus

The figure of Nemesis is widely found in Renaissance art and poetry. Alciato translated the same lines from the Greek Anthology *as did Erasmus, and the version in his* Book of Emblems *no doubt helped in the circulation of the figure.*

Ἀδράστεια Νέμεσις, Adrastia Nemesis – we must supply 'is at hand' or 'will be here,' or something of the sort. It will be permissible to turn this against those whose insolence and arrogance moves us to threaten them with a change of fortune, or who have been brought down from

Nec uerbo nec facto quenquam lædendum.

Aſſequitur, Nemeſisq; uirum ueſtigia ſeruat,
Continet & cubitum duraq; frena manu.
Nec malè quid facias, néue improba uerba loquaris:
Et iubet in cunctis rebus adeſſe modum.

B

Nemesis Andrea Alciato's emblematic poem (no 27) combines the same two epigrams from the *Greek Anthology* that Erasmus used in his essay on Nemesis at II vi 38*. This picture of a not terribly frightening goddess comes from the edition of Paris 1540, p 17. (Thomas Fisher Rare Book Library, University of Toronto) prosperity to a disastrous situation. This Nemesis some suppose to be a goddess, the scourge of insolence and arrogance, whose province it is to forbid excessive hopes and punish them; and her name Adrasteia comes from the negative particle *a* and *drasmos*, which means running away, because no guilty person has ever escaped the punishment he deserves, although sometimes she is slow in overtaking. Lucian[1] in the *Dialogues of Courtesans*: 'There is a goddess Adrasteia by name, and she watches over things like this.' Euripides[2] in the *Rhesus*: 'O Adrasteia, daughter of Jove, mayest thou defend our words against ill-will.' And again in the same play: 'With Adrasteia's good leave I speak.' There is more evidence for this in the *Epigrams*,[3] for instance: 'With bit and bridle Nemesis forewarns: / Do nought beyond the mean and keep a tight rein on your tongue.' And another: 'Nemesis, carry a bridle, and if you ask me why, / My warning to all men is to do nothing beyond the mean.'

Strabo,[4] in book 13 of his *Geography*, tells us that Adrasteia got her name, not from escaping, but from Adrastus, the king who first founded a temple in her honour; and he supports this with some lines from the poet Antimachus: 'There is a goddess Nemesis, a great goddess, to whom all this has been entrusted by the blessed gods. For her an altar was first set up by Adrastus on the banks of the Aesopus river, where she is honoured still, and is known as Adrasteia.' This city is mentioned by Pliny,[5] book 5 chapter 32, in these words: 'The colony of Parium, which Homer calls Adrasteia.' The goddess Adrasteia is also referred to by Plato[6] in the *Phaedrus*. Ammianus[7] in book 14: 'This, and countless other things of the same kind, are the work from time to time of Adrasteia, she who avenges impious deeds and rewards the good; and would that she always did so! – she whom we also call Nemesis, giving her two names.' She is said, in accordance with the views of the ancient theologians, to have been appointed mistress of the moon and to have possessed a general power of supervising the fates, surveying from above all human affairs as queen and arbiter of all things. She is particularly inimical toward pride. Sometimes she humbles and degrades those who are bold and arrogant, at other times she raises up good people from the depths and lifts them to the heights of success. In antiquity they also gave her wings, as a symbol of speed, and provided her with a rudder and a wheel, to signify that she speeds everywhere and has control of every single thing. Ammianus again in book 22: 'When he thus became unbearable, Adrasteia, she who watches over human affairs, plucking him (as the phrase goes) by the ear, to warn him to live a better regulated life,' and so forth.

Zenodotus[8] refers the origin of the adage to the following myth, which I for my part, though not very willingly, will give here, lest I should seem to have unfairly deprived the reader who has an appetite for such things. Eteocles and Polynices, after the death of their father Oedipus, came to an agreement about the kingdom of Thebes, that they would enjoy the government in alternate years. Eteocles however when his time was up (for it so happened that the first year had fallen to his lot) refused to hand the kingdom over to his brother, and so Polynices, thrown out, took refuge at Argos, which was then ruled by Adrastus, and arrived there by night. There by chance he fell in with Tydeus, who had gone into exile from Calydon after committing a murder, and joined battle with him; and in the resulting noise and tumult Adrastus intervened and separated the combatants. Recalling at the same time an oracle, by which he had been advised to give his daughters in marriage to a boar and a lion, he secured them both as sons-in-law, for one had a boar and the other a lion on his shield, and promised them both that he would restore each to his own country. He began by attacking Thebes in support of Polynices, but the Argive chieftains were killed, and Adrastus alone escaped. When the Thebans threw out the bodies of the slain unburied, and were not prepared to give them burial, their children took refuge at the altar of Mercy and demanded the bodies of their parents. The Athenians approached with an army, and the Thebans handed over the corpses. This was the occasion when Evadne, the wife of Capaneus, threw herself on the pyre, and was burnt with her husband's body. Thereafter the sons of the Argives who had been killed at Thebes never again won a victory fighting for their own land, but served as mercenary troops for some other power.

Diogenianus[9] gives the proverb in another form: Nemesis is at your feet. Galen,[10] finally, in book 6 of his work *On the Use of Parts of the Human Body* has 'to remember and make clear that none can escape the law of Adrasteia,' and a little further on: 'giving no thought, I suppose, to the law of Adrasteia.' He is threatening physicians who teach falsehoods instead of truth.

The goddess is also called Rhamnusia, taking the name from a place in Attica called Rhamnus, where, as Zenodotus[11] shows, she had a statue made of a solid block of marble fifteen feet high and carved by Phidias. She was at one time represented in the form of Venus, and therefore held an apple-tree in her right hand, as we learn from Eudemus.[12] This adage, although separated by Zenodotus, seemed to me to be properly joined with the preceding, since there is nothing between them but the change of name. Pliny,[13] book 28 chapter 2: 'Why do we take steps, by invoking some special patron, against the evil eye? Some invoke the Greek goddess Nemesis, who for this reason has a statue in Rome on the Capitol, although she has no name in Latin.'

1 *Dialogues of Courtesans* 12.2
2 *Rhesus* 342–3 and 468
3 *Greek Anthology* 16.223 and 224
4 13.1.13, citing the early-fourth-century epic poet Antimachus of Colophon frag 53 (ed B. Wyss [Berlin 1936])
5 *Natural History* 5.141
6 *Phaedrus* 248c
7 Ammianus Marcellinus 14.11.25–6 and 22.3.12
8 Zenobius 1.30
9 Diogenianus 6.80
10 *On the Use of the Parts of the Body* 6.12 and 13 (ed Kühn 3.464 and 466)
11 Zenobius 5.82
12 Eudemus of Rhodes, a pupil of Aristotle, compiled a *Rhetorical Lexicon* which Erasmus used sixteen times for the *Adages*.
13 *Natural History* 28.22

II vi 51
Ex arena funiculum nectis / You twist a rope of sand

'To twist a rope of sand' is to perform an impossible or useless act, the kind of task one might be asked to do in a fairy tale (Tosi 439; Otto 790). Contradiction is typical of many proverbs, and Erasmus mentions a few of them here (see headnote to I iv 50*). A similar proverb follows. Erasmus does not seem to remember that he had already written on this proverb back at* I iv 78*. There he used Aelius Aristides as a source, and here he seems to follow Suidas (*E 1536*; cf Apostolius 7.50). There is an English version, Tilley* R 174.

Ἐξ ἄμμου σχοινίον πλέκεις, You twist a rope of sand, was said of anyone who attempts some vain and foolish action, or labours to connect together things that have no connection whatever. It will be properly used of a speech, or a syllogistic argument, that does not hold together; so that it is related to Sand without lime, and Brooms untied.[1] It is used much in that sense by Irenaeus[2] in his first book. An example is the activity of those who collect centos from Homer.[3] Taken over all, it will fit anything impossible and absurd, so that it also belongs to the same category as You are washing a brick, and You are whitening an Ethiopian.[4]

1 II iii 57 and I v 95 respectively
2 *Against Heretics* 1.8.1
3 A cento, literally in Greek a patchwork cloak, was a kind of poem made up of passages taken out of various authors, including Homer, by scholars in late antiquity to make up different narratives, a practice Erasmus frowned on (in a note he made in his edition of Jerome on *Letters* 53.7).
4 I iv 48 and I iv 50*

II vi 81
Clavi findere ligna et securi fores aperire / To split logs with a key and open the door with an axe

Another near confused or contradictory action (for a related type, see headnote to I iv 50). Erasmus' sole source is Plutarch 'How to Study' in* Moralia *43C. A similar proverb is 'You shoot with a plough' (II vii 45). Erasmus' applications of the proverb show how he embeds his moral teaching in even the shortest essays.*

Τῇ κλειδὶ τὰ ξύλα σχίζειν, τῇ δὲ ἀξίνῃ τὴν θύραν ἀνοίγειν πειρᾷς, You try cleaving logs with the key and opening the door with the axe. Used of some topsy-turvy behaviour; when, for instance, a man tries fear as the way to correct his children and indulgence to win the love of his servants, or uses philosophical arguments to convince uneducated people and in learned company tries to win the day by shamelessly shouting them down. Recorded by Plutarch in the essay called 'How to Study.'

II vii 13
Sustine et abstine / Bear and forbear

The rhyming form of the adage, which was known in the Middle Ages (Walther 30937a) is kept in other languages (German Leide und meide, *Italian* Sostiente e astienti; *Tosi 1664). An older English form is 'Well thriveth that well suffereth.' It was a common phrase in Stoic philosophy, and was used, for instance, by Pascal in his* Pensées *(no 124). Alciato also employed the adage as the motto for his comic emblem 34. First listed in* Collectanea *no 443.*

Epictetus, a philosopher of the Cynic school, embraced without exception all those principles of philosophy which relate to the happiness of human life, and which other philosophers expound with difficulty in so many volumes, in two words and no more. For a long time now they have been current as a proverb among educated men, and well do they deserve to be inscribed on walls and columns everywhere, and to be engraved on every ring. They are as follows: Ἀνέχου καὶ ἀπέχου, Bear and forbear. One of them teaches fortitude in adversity; the other warns us to refrain from forbidden pleasures. They are recorded in the *Nights* of Gellius,[1] book 17 chapter 19. The following lines are recorded in Athenaeus,[2] with no mention of the author's name: 'Good should we call the man who brings good things; / Good too is he who beareth bad things well.'

1 17.19.6
2 10.458a, citing a fragment of a lost comedy (com frag adesp 228 Kock)

II viii 11
Anus saltat / An old woman dancing

This saying and Erasmus' essay show how certain types of social conventions are retained and concentrated in proverbs and made to appear as universal and eternal truth. In western culture today we might still claim that certain behaviours are appropriate for certain ages (we are still told to 'act your age'), yet this proscription is clearly no longer relevant. As elsewhere, Erasmus does not question its truth. It was also in Suidas Γ *432.*

Γραῦς χορεύει, An old woman dancing, suits a person who does something outside all propriety; if, for instance, a graybeard were to play with children's toys, or a theologian to be carried away by florid rhetoric, or a prince to follow Nero's example and give a concert. It is close to one I have already recorded above, The camel dances.[1] Horace,[2] writing of an old woman whose lecherous ways were unsuited to her years: 'The fleeces shorn near famed Lucera are fit work for you; not yours the dance-band and the red, red rose, nor the cask drained to its last dregs: you're an old woman now.' In Plutarch,[3] we read in his life of Pericles of a woman called Elpinice, who attacked people openly with indecent abuse, and got no answer except that line of Archilochus: 'Now you're an old woman, do not drench yourself with scent.' When Lapus[4] got the idea of rendering it 'You've not forgotten [*oblita*[5]] the perfume, now you're an old woman,' I cannot guess, unless perhaps instead of ἠλείφεο he read ἠλείθεο or εἰλήθεο.

1 II vii 66
2 *Odes* 3.15.13–16 (used again at III iv 65)
3 *Pericles* 28.5, citing Archilochus frag 205 West
4 Lapo da Castiglionchio (1405–38) was one of the translators of Plutarch into Latin.
5 Erasmus confused *oblitus* 'drenched' with *oblītus* 'forgetful'; according to Mynors, the Greek forms he suggests are not possible.

II viii 65
Ut fici oculis incumbent / As warts grow on the eye

A ficus *is not technically speaking a 'wart' but a varicosity near the eye. This unusual proverb, from Aristophanes and Suidas* Σ 1327, *gives material for a short but strongly felt essay on abuse of power by prince and church, on rebellion and the need to drive out the 'drones' from the social hive. Some of the material on 'the disorders that have broken out among the country people in Germany' was added in 1526, after the Peasants' Rebellion in Northern Europe. For a general note on the group of anti-war essays, see the introduction to* IV i 1*.

"Ὥσπερ τὰ σῦκ' ἐπὶ τοὺς ὀφθαλμοὺς ἔφυ, As warts grow on the eye, was said of those who relentlessly pestered others and urged some favourite piece of business. The image is taken from 'figs' (large warts), a troublesome growth that comes on the eyelid and cannot easily be removed by force without damage to the eye. Aristophanes[1] in the *Frogs*: 'It was like warts that on the eyelids grow.'

And it will be by no means pointless if adapted also to those people who, though a grievous and intolerable burden, cannot be forcibly removed without great public mischief. Would that there were not now, and never might be, princes of this sort and princes' chief ministers! Insatiable as they are in their avarice, riddled through and through with lust, cruel in their love of destruction, merciless in their tyranny, the real enemies and predators of the common good, equipped for public devastation not only with resources military and financial but with a new sort of cunning such as Dionysius and Phalaris[2] never knew; even so they cleave so close to the public, they loom over us, they have so secure a hold on it, that they can neither be tolerated nor removed by force. So true is it that there is no council, no body of magistrates, no branch of religion, no part of the body politic into which they have not thrust their roots and penetrated, as a plague spreads through every vein in the body. No doubt they have noticed – for they use their eyes and their wits solely to do harm – that the one remaining sheet-anchor of public prosperity is the restraint of despotic powers by honourable agreement between citizens and between states; the dissolution of this concord is therefore their first aim. They realize that in peace their scope is limited, when law and wise counsel are the springs of action, not cunning or armed force; and so it is their chief object, by every means to prevent the people from enjoying the blessings of peace. They see clearly that the prosperity of a country lies above all in this, that it should have a prince who is honourable, intelligent, and watchful, in a word a true prince; and so his tutors take incredible efforts to ensure that the prince shall never be a man. His chief ministers, those who batten on public misfortunes, do their best to see that pleasure makes him as effeminate as possible, and that he should know none of the things which are most appropriate for a prince to know. Villages are burnt down, fields laid waste, churches despoiled, innocent citizens butchered, things sacred and profane[3] utterly confused, while all the time the prince sits idly playing games of chance, dancing, amusing himself with court fools, hunting, womanizing, drinking. O for the line of Brutus[4] and his like, now long extinct! Where is Jove's thunderbolt, now blind or blunted? For there is no doubt that these corruptors of princes will pay God their due penalty, though we may not live to see it. And meanwhile we must bear with them, lest tyranny give place to anarchy, an almost more pernicious evil.

This has been proved by long experience of public affairs, and recently too the disorders that have broken out among the country people in Germany have taught us that the brutality of princes is in some ways more tolerable than the anarchy which reduces everything to chaos. Thunderbolts frighten everyone, but they do not strike all that many; an invasion of the sea spares no man, and all is confounded, all is swept away.

But the place of godless grandees in the state is perhaps taken in the Church by some members of what are commonly called the Mendicant Orders. I bring no charge against the religious among them, I have no quarrel with an Order; it is the bad I criticize, of whom there are great crowds everywhere. These men have so spread themselves all over the body politic, that nothing can anywhere be done without them. They lord it in the pulpit, the special prerogative of bishops; they have seized despotic power in the universities, which stand next in importance. It is they who dispense the sacraments of the Church, and it is by their leave that we are priests. It is they who, with severity too great for any censor, pass judgment on the faith a man professes: this man is a Christian, that a half-Christian, this man a heretic, that a heretic and a half. It is into their bosoms that ordinary folk pour out the hidden actions of their lives and their hearts' most secret thoughts. Nor does this content them. No treaty can be concluded between princes in which they play no part; no wedding can be solemnized without them; at contests in the theatre and public lotteries they are the judges and organizers, so far are they from any sense of shame. In fact, one cannot even die without them. Of princes' courts there is not one into which they have not wormed their way, and if princes have decided on some nefarious action, it is they who execute it. If popes set on foot some policy which is a little further than one could wish from the traditional and apostolic holiness of their office, these are the men whose services they mostly use; be it war, for instance, or civil disorder, financial exaction, or an unwise indulgence, these are the plays in which these men play the lead, and all the time the simple-minded public are deluded by their show of holiness. Priests compared with them are no priests at all; bishops trust them and sleep sound on either ear.[5] The poor abandoned public instead of living under single shepherds is torn in pieces by a double kind of wolves: their bishops rule as tyrants, nor are these men shepherds but robbers of another sort.

Let me repeat: I do not criticize the good among them, or the religious order. There are men among them of the highest integrity, who deplore the same things that I deplore. Bees can from time to time drive out their drones, however thievish, for they have no sting. These drones have sharper stings than any hornet, and neither kings nor popes could drive them out of the commonwealth without disaster to the Christian religion, so well defended are their secret gangs, so well have they secured the whole world with their fortresses and their troupes, building themselves new nests every day, on the ground, no doubt, that the religious fervour of the earlier monasteries, and the reputation for it to which those houses owed their rise in the first place, are now no more, as though the sincerity (if it can be so called) of their own religion would not soon be no more in its turn. As a result, the world is burdened with irreligious and idle flocks of monks; princes are deprived of their people, bishops of their flock, ordinary people of their shepherd, and the purity and liberty of the Christian religion is gradually slipping into Jewish ceremonial. It is hard to say which is the greater burden for the state, the agreement of bad princes among themselves or their mutual hostility, for if they go to war it costs the people dear, and if they are in league they conspire for the public detriment. Just so, one cannot tell which is the more to be desired – it would be better to say, to be detested – the agreement of these men among themselves or their mutual feuding, for both bode public evil.

I take the word *ficus* here to mean a horny swelling that grows on the socket of the eye; this is extremely vexatious, but cannot be removed without risk, being so near the eye, which is highly intolerant of interference and surgical operation. The adage is mentioned in Suidas.

1 *Frogs* 1247
2 Dionysius and Phalaris are ancient tyrants famous for their cruelty (referred to in Cicero *On Duties* 2.7.25–6).
3 *Adages* I iii 82
4 Brutus is Caesar's assassin, the most famous of the ancient tyrannicides.
5 I viii 19

II ix 72
Simul et dictum et factum / No sooner said than done

Now a common expression in English, as well as in other European languages where the parallelism is retained (Italian Detto fatto, *German* Gesagt getan, *French* Aussitôt dit, aussitôt fait; *see Tosi 930). Erasmus is interested in the Greek origins; it is found in the ancient proverb collections of Zenobius 1.77, Diogenianus 2.24, and Suidas* A *1462 (see also Otto 529). The proverb first appeared in 1508, but it was greatly expanded in 1533 by the philological discussion of* autoboei *(from 'Greek gives …' onward). As so often happens with these additions, what are technically two proverbs are discussed under a single heading. Erasmus returns to a similar phrase at* III vi 85* Dictum ac factum, *given below for comparison.*

Ἅμ' ἔπος ἅμ' ἔργον, No sooner said than done, when a man actually does without delay what he promises verbally. In Latin they say *cum dicto,* On the word, to mean immediately after the word has been uttered. Virgil[1] has 'Swifter than speech he calmed the swelling waves,' which is clearly taken from Homer,[2] who has the line 'At once the word was spoken and the deed was done.' Greek gives the same meaning in a single word *autoboei,* with the shout, which looks like a metaphor from the shouting of soldiers, by which the enemy is sometimes put to flight even before battle has been joined. It is so used by Thucydides.[3] Theopompus[4] has it in the sense of 'with all one's might,' and not from ambush. The man who lays an ambush for his enemy does so in silence; the man who trusts in his own strength charges down with shouts upon the foe. Some think it derived from *boes,* the word for oxen, so that it would look like a reference to ploughmen who, when they promise to finish a piece of work *autêmar,* on the same day, often use the word *autoboei,* with the same pair of oxen before they unyoke them. It can be adapted to the rapid performance of any action, so that it has the same value as *parachrêma* or *autothen*, immediately.

1 *Aeneid* 1.142
2 *Iliad* 19.242
3 2.81.4, etc
4 The fragment from Theopompus (of Chios, historian from fourth century BC) and the following word notes are from Suidas A 4486 and 4474.

II X 42
Lignum tortum haud unquam rectum / A twisted branch, never straight

'Bent is the branch that could have grown full straight' is the concluding moral to Marlowe's Doctor Faustus. *Marlowe, who had an excellent schooling, may well have come across the expression via Erasmus, though it was also extant in the Middle Ages (Walther 13772a). We still speak of personalities as 'bent' or 'twisted,' of getting people 'straightened out.' Erasmus would have found variants in the Greek collections by Diogenianus 6.92, Suidas Ξ 96 and* T *801, and Apostolius 12.25 (see also Tosi 110). His fussing over the correct reading of the Greek is typical.*

Ξύλον ἀγκύλον οὐδέποτ' ὀρθόν, A twisted branch, never straight. This too is half of a hexameter line. Twisted and distorted characters can hardly ever be brought to bear good fruit. When a man has once grown old in wrongdoing, it seldom happens that he returns to a right mind. Also expressed in the form *τὸ ξύλον σκαμβόν*, that is, A crooked branch, never straight. Galen[1] uses it in book 4 of his *De differentiis pulsuum*: 'Giving them no reply, but repeating to ourselves that saying in the comedy, that neither can the crooked branch be straightened nor will an old tree, if transplanted, send up new shoots.' (In this passage *ὑμᾶς* is printed for *ἡμᾶς* and *γερύανδρον* for *γεράνδρυον*; this seemed worth a mention, to prevent any corruption of the reading given here.) This latter proverb[2] I have treated of already. Horace[3] makes clear the image from which it derives, when he writes 'Though you cast out nature with a fork, it still returns,' for he shows that it comes from those who try to correct the defect of a twisted tree by supplying it with a prop. This is further confirmed by the proverbial maxim 'To change a twisted nature is not easy.'

1 *De differentiis pulsuum* 3.3 ed Kühn 8:656, a work on the human pulse, quoting a fragment from an anonymous lost ancient comedy (frag com adesp 1582 Kock); the reference to Galen was added in 1528, three years after an important edition of the collected works had appeared in Venice.
2 II vii 14
3 *Epistles* 1.10.24

II X 51
Labyrinthus / A labyrinth

The story of Daedalus and the labyrinth was probably best known to Renaissance readers from Ovid Metamorphoses *book 8, though it does not appear to be a source for this particular essay (Otto 897). The association between the labyrinth and the meandering river is an interesting addition at the end of the essay. The labyrinth was a powerful and widely used image in Renaissance poetry and art; for a history of the motif, see Penelope Doob* The Idea of the Labyrinth from Classical Antiquity through the Middle Ages *(Ithaca, NY 1990).*

Λαβύρινθος, A labyrinth, was a name in old days for any speech or course of action which was excessively complicated and hard to unravel, as for instance if one were to call the study of philosophy 'a labyrinth' because those who have once entered can never find the way out, or were to apply 'labyrinth' to the pursuit of pleasure, because the way thither is downhill but the way out very difficult. Taken from the labyrinth made by Daedalus, which according to the story was a cave in Crete so full of windings and insoluble complications that it was inextricable; there the Minotaur was confined. Suidas[1] thinks it got its name from *mê labein*, fail to obtain, and *thyran*, exit, because it had no exit, and shows that it also suits chatterboxes and people who talk a lot of nonsense, who once they are launched in their chattering can find no way out. Gregory the Theologian[2] in a letter to Eusebius of Caesarea twists it to be applicable to a cunning man: 'Since I have to do with a man who is no lover of falsehood himself, and is as quick as anyone to detect it in others, however much it is wrapped up in different cunning labyrinths.'

Not unlike this is the use of meander. A meander was a kind of painted pattern derived from the idea of the labyrinth, such as we still see even today in some pavements. Prudentius[3] uses it in a poem, of which the first words are *Cultor Dei*:

Serpent in sinuous callings rolled,
Who by your web of treacherous arts
And through meanders thousandfold
Destroy the peace of quiet hearts.

Hence too the river Maeander in Lydia got its name, from its wandering sinuous course.

1 Λ 11
2 Gregory of Nazianzus *Letters* 16.1
3 *Cathemerinon* 6.141–4 (the only quotation in the *Adages* from this late classical Christian poet of the fourth century AD)

III i 1
Herculei labores / The labours of Hercules

This has become a proverbial expression in all European languages (Otto 801, Tosi 1646). The form given in Propertius at the beginning of the essay seems to be the standard. Erasmus assumes from the start that the reader knows the story of the twelve labours, one of the most familiar of classical narratives. Hercules killed his children in a maddened frenzy caused by Hera, and as a kind of purification he was made to undertake a series of labours – overcoming the Nemean lion, destruction of the Lernaean hydra, capture of the Arcadian deer, capture of the boar of Erymanthus, sweeping out of the stables of Augeas, killing of the Stymphalian birds, capture of the Cretan bull, capture of the man-eating mares of Diomedes, taking of the girdle of the Amazon Hippolyta, capture of the oxen of Geryones, taking of the apples of the Hesperides, and bringing Cerberus back from the underworld. Though the proverb appeared in Collectanea *(no 13), the expanded essay first appeared in the 1508 edition by Aldus, whom he here mentions (see also* II i 1*) . Erasmus concentrates on the Lernaean hydra, which he begins by relating to politics, then uses to exemplify the work he has undertaken with the* Adages, *the main subject of this brilliant reflection on his own methods and expectations, and on scholarly work and methods in general. The 1523 Holbein portrait at Longford Castle shows Erasmus, his hands on a folio volume, with this proverb appropriately written on the fore-edge. Of all his essays, this may be the one most full of proverbs worked into the writing.*

Ἡράκλειοι πόνοι, The labours of Hercules, can be taken in two ways. Sometimes it means continuous and very great exertions, and such as demand Herculean strength, and it was so used by Catullus:[1] 'But to seek you' he says 'would be already a task for Hercules.' Propertius[2] too has 'Then, when you have endured to the end the fabled toils of Hercules,' and again elsewhere 'Not all Alcides' toils.' Cicero[3] in the second book of his *De finibus*: 'But while earning the gratitude of all nations, while bringing help and well-being to those in need, actually to suffer the afflictions of Hercules – for *aerumnas*, afflictions is the very gloomy name which our forefathers gave to labours from which there was no escaping, even in the case of a god – I should exact from you,' and what follows. Sometimes 'the labours of Hercules' means tasks of the kind that bring very great blessings to other people, but almost no return to the man who undertakes them, except a little reputation and a great deal of ill-will. And they think that this was somehow destined to happen to Hercules, because he is supposed to have been born on the fourth day of the new moon, as I have said in another context.[4] Homer,[5] as poets will, puts the responsibility on the goddess Atê, and on Juno. Juno, he says, hated Hercules because he was the son of her husband's mistress, and therefore she exposed him to perils of every kind.

No wonder the poets speak continually of the labours of Hercules, and even draw up lists of them; and of them all by far the greatest and most difficult was the Lernaean hydra,[6] an indomitable plague which was almost too much even for the hero who had already despatched all the rest. That the ancients used this as a symbol of ill-will is sufficiently clear from a passage in Horace's *Epistles*:[7]

He who the hydra crushed, he who subdued
With toils predestined all those famous monsters,
Learnt that ill-will is tamed the last of all.

For this most pestilent of beasts is always in attendance upon noble deeds, and follows close on outstanding excellence as a body is followed by its shadow, so that there was point in Josephus' remark[8] in his work on the fall of Judaea: 'There is no device by which he who does good can escape ill-will.' For who can avoid ill-will that follows like a shadow, unless he equally avoids the light that is cast by excellence? The two things have a close mutual connection, and that which is the best of all things has the worst of all things as its inseparable companion. And so it was clearly not without reason that Pindar[9] wrote 'One thing grieves me, that envy should be the reward of deeds well done,' for he was indignant (and it is of course a very proper subject for indignation) that noble actions should be rewarded with envy as their recompense.

And indeed the ancients of whom I speak were clearly not far off the mark when they chose the hydra as the emblem of envy. It was, for one thing, a plague that lived in a marsh; for, as we learn from those who research into natural causes, men are more liable to suffer from this disease who have a low and grovelling spirit, and these are people of a more cold-blooded type. This too is the reason why Ovid[10] says of Envy that her home

Is in the valley-bottoms sunless hid,
Where no wind blows, but gloom and sluggish chill
Fill all the place; no fire is ever kindled,
And darkness reigns.

Nor is it a simple monster that one has to face, but one armed with a hundred heads; and if a man cuts off any one of the heads, two instantly sprout in its place. Such, to be sure, is the nature of ill-will: if you strive against it, you arouse it more and more; if you try to overwhelm it by the bright light of excellence, that is the moment when it rises swelling more bitterly than ever. Cut it down in one place, and it comes up stronger in another; to put it out by stages is impossible, and it can hardly in the end be overcome. But this success has befallen very few, hardly Hercules himself. For though 'envy, like fire, makes for the summits,'[11] there is all the same something which is so perfect and so grand that it is out of reach. This is the position which Horace[12] prides himself on having attained, when he writes 'And out of reach of envy,' and in another passage 'And am no less gnawed by envy's tooth.' And indeed what is the filth with which these baneful undercover critics bespatter those who, in the attempt by their noble endeavours to do good to the world, engage in some noble enterprise, – what is it but unmixed venom and a more than deadly poison? For to generous and lofty minds their honour, which these men attack, is as a rule not a little dearer and more precious than life itself.

Remember too that what gentile mythology conveyed under the symbol of Hercules is suggested to us in Jewish history, wrapped up in the story of Joseph; for what Lerna was to Hercules, Joseph found in the jealousy of his brothers. This is how Philo[13] interprets it in the essay called *Political Life*. He thinks the figure of Joseph represents those who hold the reins of public affairs, as is indicated by the fact that, while he was still a shepherd, Joseph by well-doing both won his father's favour and aroused jealousy among his brothers. And to rule a commonwealth is surely nothing else but to play a shepherd's part. Homer[14] too, who is actually cited in Philo's work, calls a king several times 'the shepherd of his people.' No men get a more niggardly return of thanks for their good deeds than those who do a service to the common people. But what Hercules achieved by the use of Greek fire,[15] Joseph secured by the greatness of his public services and the favour of heaven – to overwhelm his rivals and to see those same men, from whose jealousy he had once suffered, kneeling before him on a later day and confessing now that they owed their lives to a man against whose life they had once conspired.

Princes therefore, who have public business in their hands, ought to be animated by this spirit, so that they follow this example and look only to the public good, not using their office, for all the world as if it were some kind of mercantile activity,[16] as a source of profit for themselves rather than other people; not trying to lay some kind of legal snares for those in whom they see a possible source of profit for themselves, but to do good service without recompense to men of good will, engaged in a continual struggle against monsters (which are the vices) and content with nothing save a good conscience as a more than adequate reward for work well done. And if public opinion grudges your actions the response that they deserve, if you hear the secret serpent-hiss of envy and that monster of Lerna assails you on every side with the poisonous breath of all its heads, be they never so many, that is when you will find one proof, and one only, of a truly lofty and unconquerable spirit: to battle on undaunted for praise that will not die, to think what you can do for others no matter how great the cost to yourself, and to reckon it the finest and greatest reward of virtue, if you can promote the greatest happiness of the greatest number, imitating in that respect, as far as any mortal can, the immortal deity. Notwithstanding that no thanks, no service on our part can reach the deity in return, yet with the fundamental goodness which is a part of his nature he lavishes his bounty, like the sun, on all men grateful and ungrateful, deserving and undeserving alike, with one sole result in view, the giving to as many men as possible some portion of himself. But not only can God receive no benefit from his generosity; no annoyance from ingratitude can touch him, while for mortals it is a common experience to be rewarded for a high degree of well-doing by a high degree of ill-will and of loss.

But if any human toils deserve to be awarded the epithet 'Herculean,' it seems to belong in the highest degree to those at least who devote their efforts to restoring the monuments of ancient and true literature. Incomparable as are the labours they undertake on account of the incredible difficulty of the subject, they arouse none the less the greatest unpopularity among the common herd; for the herd have always objected to distinction in any form, and novelty in particular has always been objectionable, not only to simple minds but even among the educated. So true is it that we are nowhere more ungrateful, more jealous of others, more difficult to please, nowhere less open-minded, than in evaluating the labours of these men, to whom, in my opinion, it is impossible to make an adequate and suitable return. The uneducated pay no attention, the half-educated regard them as a joke, the educated (with few exceptions, men of distinction indeed but few of them all the same) are jealous, some of them, and some are needlessly hard to please and critical, which makes them overlook the many merits of the writing; and if by any chance the writer has made one or two slips (and who does not slip up sometimes?), that is the only thing they notice and the only thing they remember. Here's your chance then, here's a splendid reward on offer for all those protracted nights of study, all those efforts, all those sacrifices. Cut yourself off from the pleasures of human life that all men share, neglect your worldly affairs, have no mercy on your appearance, sleep, or health. Never mind loss of eyesight, bid old age come before its time, think nothing of the life you've lost; and the result will be to arouse the dislike of very many people and the ill-will of even more, and in return for all those nights of toil to win a few snorts of contempt. Who would not be deterred by this from undertaking labour of the kind I speak of, unless he had the spirit of a true Hercules, and in his zeal to help others could 'do and suffer anything'?[17]

This train of thought, to tell the truth, has somewhat roused my feelings and, full in the course of my efforts to discharge the burden of this work, a kind of weariness comes over me as I think, of course, of the quality of men we have seen in our time, and how ungenerous the response of public opinion even when they have already been dead for some time; how irreverently they are despised by men whom you might truly call unworthy, as the saying goes, to hold their chamber-pot;[18] with what ingratitude they are criticized by the half-educated, and how few there are even among the learned who sincerely and openly give them their due. One critic discovers shortcomings, another finds something with which he disagrees; one attacks their way of life, and another praises them with such obvious distaste that abuse might have been preferable. What's more, no judges are so unjust as the half-educated, who measure a man's learning by their own, and think themselves entitled to criticize anything they have not learned themselves, or as learned men who have not yet sampled this new kind of labour. These people simply 'judge the Achaeans from the tower,' as the Greek proverb[19] puts it; they stand on shore themselves, watching at leisure the skill of a ship's captain and the risks he runs. Had they made any such attempt themselves, they would read the results of other men's work with less contempt and greater readiness to make allowances. Seeing then, as I do, that this is the fate of such great princes (heroes, rather) in the field of literature, what can I expect to happen to myself, all whose productions when compared with theirs are, as well I know, mediocre or, to speak more truly, null and void, particularly in this kind of writing which is far more laborious than anyone could easily guess who had himself never tried it – in which too, for many reasons, it is very easy to make a mistake and, last but not least, nowhere can one's shortcomings be more easily detected.

And so I do not think it will be out of the way if, now that the context itself seems to have suggested it, I say a little more on these topics, not to boast of my intelligence or advertise my own industry, but to make my reader more sympathetic. And anyone will be much less unsympathetic, at any rate, who has considered the immense labours and the infinite difficulties that this collection of adages, however crude, has cost me. Right from the start then, let my first point be the extreme antiquity of the things themselves, which can be traced not from Evander[20] or the Aborigines but, as they say in Greek, from Cannacus[21] – right from the age of Saturn himself and anything still more ancient; as a result of which the majority are, as the phrase goes, a whole diameter[22] remote from the customs of our own day, so that you must either guess the meaning of your adage and send for some sort of Delian diver,[23] or hunt for an explanation in the ancient authorities. And what sort of authorities, if you please? Not just two or three or some definite number, as normally happens in other subjects; as, for instance, if a man sets out to write on the art of oratory, he has a definite and appropriate list of authorities, and not such a long list either, to be sure, and it would be enough to follow them. But here it is all the writers that ever were, ancient and modern, good and bad alike, in both Latin and Greek and in every known subject – in short, it is the whole range of the written word that a man must, I will not say, run through, but analyse and examine with particular care and attention; for adages, like jewels, are small things, and sometimes escape your eye as you hunt for them, unless you keep a very sharp lookout. Besides which they do not lie on the surface, but as a rule are buried, so that you have to dig them out before you can collect them. And who can make an adequate estimate of the infinite labour required to seek out such small things everywhere, one might say, by sea and land?[24] One lifespan would scarcely suffice for the inspection and analysis of all those poets in both languages, those grammarians, those orators, those dialecticians, those sophists, those historians, those mathematicians, those philosophers, those theologians, when the mere listing of their titles would exhaust a man; and all this not once and for all, but as often as the context demands that like Sisyphus[25] you roll your stone up the hill all over again. Everybody, I imagine, must see this by now, everybody must agree that it is a colossal task. But, I ask you, how small a part is it of all my labours? An almost larger army of commentators lies in wait for you, some of whom by their idleness and inaccuracy and a certain number by pure ignorance (for they too must be worked through, in hopes of course of one day picking some gold off the dunghill[26]), have added not a little to the burden of my labours.

And another thing: need I now plead the prodigious corruption of the texts, which has acquired such a hold upon all our copies of both Latin and Greek authors that, whatever you touch in hopes of quoting it, you hardly ever have the good fortune not to stumble over some obvious error or suspect one below the surface? So here's a fresh field of toil: you must hunt out and get together copies of the text – and plenty of them, I assure you – in hopes of course that among so many you may have the luck to find one that is more correct, or that in comparing a large number you may discover something true and genuine by some process of divination. This too one could put up with, did it not happen nearly every time you have quoted something; and you must be quoting all the time.

To all these many counters there's another to be added which is, I think, far from negligible: the fact that the works of the ancients, which are as it were the springs from which proverbs are drawn, are in great part lost. Greek comedy, for instance, in both its forms has perished entirely except for Aristophanes, and so has tragedy in Latin, with the sole exception of Seneca. Perhaps this too might have been tolerable, if only we still had the works of the men who collected the proverbs to be found in them and provided explanatory notes. Among their number are Aristotle, Chrysippus, Clearchus, Didymus, Tarrhaeus, and other men as well of whom not the smallest fragment has come down to us. We are left therefore with some later writers, who are not only careless and uncritical but ill-informed and mutilated into the bargain, such as Zenobius, Diogenianus, Suidas; and in regard to them I have not yet made up my mind, whether they deserve our ill-will for having handed down to us, in place of such accomplished and well-supplied authorities, materials so scanty and so bald, or our gratitude for the zeal which did secure for us the survival of such fragments of antiquity as we possess. Unless, that is, one were to hold their epitomes responsible also for the neglect and loss of the originals, just as some Latin scholars commonly ascribe the loss of Livy's work to Florus, of Trogus Pompeius to Justin, of the civil law of the Empire to Justinian, and of theology to the author of the so-called *Sentences*[27] – a charge which, in my view at least, is not far from the truth. What is more, there is so little agreement among these compilers that their work is often contradictory, with the result that a further weight is added to your labours: you must not only work through various commentators on the same topic, but must also repeatedly consult, collate, evaluate, and judge between them.

And here is another thought I would put before you. In other literary work there is often scope for using one's wits, so that there is some pleasure to be gained from creative and original thought, and in any context and at any moment you may be able by nimbleness of mind to polish off some portion of your task, the rate at which you finish being directly dependent on your natural speed of thought. But here, like a slave bound to the mill,[28] you are not allowed to diverge one foot's breadth, as the saying[29] goes, from the texts. For the whole business depends almost entirely on a good supply of texts, Greek texts especially; and how scarce these are is common knowledge. This has two results. One is that you wear out your eyes on crumbling volumes covered with mould, torn, mutilated, gnawed all round by worms and beetles and, besides that, often highly illegible as well; in such a state, in short, that anyone who spends a long time on them easily develops some sort of decay and old age in his own person. The other result is that many of them belong to other people; and the importance of that simple fact is recognized at once, though I were to say nothing, by those who have made the experiment.

All this time I need hardly say that any pleasure to be derived from compilations of this kind is entirely confined to the reader; nothing comes the writer's way except the unpopular and unvarying toil of collecting, of sweeping together, explaining, and translating. Yet pleasure, as Aristotle[30] has truly said, is the one thing which makes it possible for us to remain at work for long spells of time. In other fields one can seek relaxation in flights of fancy, one can sometimes divert oneself with lively flowers of speech; there are agreeable byways in which to rest when one is tired and refresh one's mental powers. In all business, and especially in literary work, change keeps satiety at bay and does not allow weariness to raise its head. But in this task it has not been 'twice-served cabbage,' as the Greek proverb[31] has it; I have had to repeat the same things three thousand times – what does an adage mean, what was its origin, and for what purposes was it suitable – so that never was there a context more suitable than this for that hackneyed Greek adage The twirling of a pestle.[32] Last but not least, it contributes to our pleasure when we handle the sorts of things that gain in polish from the handling and confer a brilliance and fullness of their own on a writer's style. The things dealt with here are all of the sort that get their shine from daily use, not craftsmanship, and do not reveal their innate power to please until they are displayed in context like jewels in their proper setting. Separately they lose interest, and give the impression of being small and unimportant. Add to this that in other cases a work is judged by the total of what it contains, and the reader as well as the writer has to do some work. Things of this kind are read in snatches, and to each adage, no matter what, the reader brings a fresh mind, a mind at leisure, in some cases actually eager and in others the opposite, full of disdain. How unjust then, in view of all this, are the conditions in which I labour and the demands I have to meet! On every single adage I must content the leisured reader, give the hungry man what he needs, and satisfy the disdainful.

On top of all this, there is the labour of translating the Greek, which I am sure everyone will think a most difficult task except those who have never addressed themselves to turning good Greek into good Latin. Here again let me ask you to consider the great variety of authors, each one of whom should be given his particular style. Think of all the kinds of verse, of which this work confronts us with such an immense multitude (not fewer, I suppose, than ten thousand lines) that, if anyone in the space of a few months, which is all I have had for finishing this work, had produced a Latin rendering of all those verse-lines and nothing else, and a verse rendering at that, it is not altogether dear that he could be accused of idleness. Furthermore, what other men will think, I do not know; for my own part I find it also quite an achievement to bear in mind, in such an immense number of adages, what you have said and where and not to be confused by crowding materials. If a man, then, is engaged in such great difficulties that even to make a full list is the greatest of them all, is it surprising if he sometimes slips, especially if he is in a hurry? And why I have had to hurry should be explained in the sequel. After all, if Horace,[33] even in other subjects which are free from these disadvantages, is ready to pardon

> the scattered blemish born of carelessness,
> which slipped through human nature's faulty guard,

if he thinks that in a longish work sleep may be permitted to creep over one, if he does not lose patience with Homer because he sometimes nods, what reason, I ask you, can there be for us to mingle sea and sky[34] if a handful of mistakes happen to be detected in a work like this? – a work in which, over and above the common causes of error to which I have referred, you are not even left free to finish your task as you may think best, and must follow guides who are quite capable from time to time of giving you a handle for going wrong. To say nothing at this point of faults in your texts, which sometimes impose on excellent scholars; to pass over in silence the tedium which, perhaps more than anything else, is apt to dull the powers of the mind; and not to mention that complex brew, so to call it, of things of every sort and kind which distracts the mind in so many directions that it cannot always be in attendance when required.

It remains, I suppose, to say a few further words in answer to those who will, I foresee, find my collections in need of somewhat more care and diligence. Some people, I perceive, are of a disposition to measure books by their size, rather than by the learning they contain, and think a thing finished only if nothing can be added to it and much is superfluous, nothing adequate that is not greatly overdone, and fullness never achieved except where everything is repeated ad nauseam. Among these gentry, someone will say that there are points to which I might have given fuller and richer treatment. And then in reading the authorities someone will happen on a passage which may or may not contribute to a proverb, but he thinks it does; and at once he will start complaining that I have left it out. Who, I ask you to begin with, is so arrogant that he dare maintain such a thing? So unfair as to demand that in this kind of literary work no passage shall ever be passed over? Suppose you have read everything, made notes of everything, have everything ready at hand: is it all, in this vast medley of materials, instantly available, just what you needed and where you needed it? Then think what tedious pedantry it would have been to collect from every quarter all that could in any way have been adapted to the enrichment of a proverb! Think what limits and what conclusion could have been found for my volumes, had I been willing, when expounding the 'Sardonic laugh'[35] (to take this as an example), to repeat a description of the whole island of Sardinia out of the works of all the geographers, and to survey the layout of the country, and the early history and origins of the inhabitants from head to heel,[36] as the saying goes! Then to sweep together into one pile the appearance of the relevant plant[37] and its effects, and all the information about it that could be found in any work on medicine, besides combing the physicians for evidence on the mechanism of this kind of laughter, and the reasons behind its appearance in the dying! Then to do some research in all our historical authorities on the peoples among whom this form of laughter was at one time traditional; and thereafter to pile into the same heap how unbecoming such laughter is for an honourable man and whatever, in short, is to be found in moral philosophers and poets on the question of laughing properly or improperly. Last but not least, to make an exhaustive collection of everything in the way of an apophthegm or a witty comment or a memorable action, every anecdote or fable or moral maxim, anything whether sympathetic or hostile, which can somehow or other be dragged in to help explain the adage. Had this been my intention, anyone can see that each individual adage might have been given a volume to itself. How could this have been less absurd than to start my explanation of the proverb An Iliad of troubles[38] by proceeding to tell the whole history of the Trojan war, beginning (as Horace[39] puts it) 'from that twin egg,' or to illustrate An invention worthy of Ulysses[40] by unfolding the whole narrative of the

Odyssey? And then how often in this field we are met by commonplaces on death, on life, on friendship, on quarrelling, on justice and injustice! But it is foolish of me to set about listing them when they are nearly as numerous as the proverbs themselves; nor would it have been difficult to multiply them on good rhetorical principles, until each one ended up long enough to fill a volume on its own. But any such labour would not only be very foolish; it would be beyond the capacity of a man who writes in chiliads, measured by the thousand, and beyond the endurance of the reader. I have therefore thought it best in this work to seek moderation rather than fullness, and to look for a way out rather than a way forward. All the same, if, as I hurried on my way, anything came into my mind in passing which seemed at the same time worth knowing and not unrelated to my proverb, I have not been reluctant to add it as a kind of bonus. There are moreover some passages (Why should I not speak frankly?), but not very many of them, in which I myself find something lacking. These, however, I have not thought it right to pass over in silence, although I was not entirely satisfied with what I had hitherto found said of them in my authorities. It seemed best to list them, for this purpose if no other, as a means of supplying a reason for research to others who have either more leisure or a larger supply of books or a better memory and more productive learning, while I content myself with that phrase in the play 'As best we can, since as we would we may not.'[41]

I saw too that it would be possible to introduce some sort of order, if I had put forward as many headings as possible, following the principle of like and unlike, opposite and closely akin, and had assigned each proverb to some supposed proper class. But this I deliberately did not do, for several reasons. Partly because in miscellaneous materials of this kind it seemed to me somehow right and proper that there should be no order; partly because I saw that if I had crammed everything that expressed the same opinion into the same class (so to call it), the resulting uniformity would be a source of tedium for the reader, who would cry out periodically in his disgust Twice served cabbage is death[42] and Corinthus son of Jove[43] is in the book; partly because I was daunted by the size of the task. Why not tell the truth? I saw clearly that that could not be done without rewriting the whole book afresh from head to heel, and there could be no thought of publication until

I had added the proverbial colophon,[44] so that I really should need the whole of Horace's nine years.[45] As things are now, it has been possible to add even during publication anything that might turn up which did not deserve to be passed over.

Again, I can hardly bring myself to believe (though I suppose even this will happen) that any people will be so unjust as to demand eloquence, of all things, from a Hollander in the first place (something worse, that is, than a Boeotian[46]), and, joking apart, in a work entirely and properly adapted to convey information, of a kind worth having, to be sure, but so fragmented and so prosaic that it not merely makes no demands for stylistic ornament and fullness, but actually repudiates and rejects them. In such a miscellaneous jumble of materials, with such constant naming of authors even of low degree (a necessary though somewhat clumsy and prosaic part of my task of instruction), with the continual divergences into Greek and the frequent versions, what scope was there for brilliance, for elegance, for a smooth and flowing style? Cicero[47] does not demand eloquence from a philosopher; and how can anyone demand it from a collector of proverbs? Seneca[48] never finds it desirable, except when it comes cheaply, when it presents itself unbidden, so as to set forth some great subject with a touch of greatness. But to look for the stock-in-trade of the schools of rhetoric here! What more is it, I ask you, than Perfume on the lentils[49] (as the saying goes) and Fitting pygmies' limbs on a colossus,[50] to say nothing of Decorating a cooking-pot?[51] Personally, though in other fields I do not despise it, I have never been much attracted by the pursuit of fine writing; somehow I have always taken more kindly to sincerity in style rather than to ornament, provided there is nothing mean in the writing and it is adequate to convey my meaning. And had I at some stage acquired the power to write well, it would inevitably have been lost in the lengthy, miscellaneous, and disorganized leafing through of Greek and Latin authors; for, as Cicero[52] himself tells us, even a short interruption can make this readiness in writing dry up. And then, even if the matter in itself offered plenty of scope for good writing, I had in any case no leisure; all the time that there was was too short for reading all those books, noting down all those passages, and getting so many things by heart. Not but what the expression of this same material in not wholly inadequate language will be regarded,

I think, as a by no means negligible form of eloquence by anyone who has truly learned what that word means. I have no time for some people I could name, those apes[53] of eloquence as I could almost call them, who measure the virtues of a style by a sort of empty and puerile jangling of sounds and, when at length after many days' labour they have woven two or three childish blossoms into what they have written and sprinkled it with four words from Cicero and four more from Sallust, are at once persuaded that they have attained the pinnacle of Roman eloquence. After that, they dislike the style of St Jerome, Prudentius stinks in their nostrils, and everything seems tongue-tied, dumb, and inarticulate in which they have not found their four precious words from Cicero. Had these men ever made an experiment to discover what it means to devote whole books to this rubbish (as they think it), perhaps they would recognize how inarticulate they are themselves and show less impudence in despising the eloquence of other people.

Some critic, however, whom I must take seriously, may well say 'All the same, this might have been the very place for artistry, conferring a greater dimension on these small-scale topics by literary skill, giving humble material a touch of nobility, and in Virgil's words[54] "adding this honour to a lowly theme." And for this you could have found the time, if only you had separated the labours of collecting and polishing and allotted a proper space of time to each. What need was there, as Plautus[55] puts it, to suck and blow at the same time? Who compelled you to publish in such a hurry, to finish labours so immense and so elaborate, if I may use the word, in a year and a half, and having finished them to rush them into print? Had you observed Horace's rule and sat on the produce of your nightly vigils for nine years, it might have been possible to add a welcome note of eloquence and, what is more, to put out a work of greater fullness and accuracy, with nothing which you might regret or to which you might wish to add. In any case, you ought either not to have undertaken this task, or to have performed it adequately in all respects.' Here of course (for it is not my habit to fight against the truth) I must of necessity accept some part of the blame. I was not unaware that what this work needed was not someone basically a theologian who might have sampled ancient literature superficially and as it were in passing, but a man who had expended his whole life in reading, expounding, and analysing authors of that sort, and who would have been able not merely to spend his life on studies of that description but to die at his desk. I perceived quite clearly that this was no job for one man or one library or a few years' work; and I have finished it single-handed and by my own prowess, as the phrase[56] goes, in less than a year and a half with the assistance of only one library. It was of course the library at Aldus',[57] and so as rich and well supplied with good books as any anywhere, particularly Greek, being as it were the source from which all good libraries world-wide spring and increase; so it was very well supplied, I do not deny, but it was all I had.

But if I cannot escape the blame altogether, I can at least much reduce it. In the first place, I was long ago not so much urged by reason to undertake this task as led to do so by chance and egged on by the appeals of my friends, to which I never find it very easy to put up much resistance on other occasions, and in this case it was my great Maecenas, William Mountjoy,[58] distinguished among the leaders of the English court, who urged me to it, a man so generous to me and so dear that I think all else must take second place whenever I am able to comply with his wishes. And if even the doctrines of philosophy allow us sometimes to bend the rules of right and wrong to please our friends,[59] I think I should be forgiven if it was in hopes of pleasing so great a friend that I undertook a task most admirable in itself though perhaps not so well suited to me, especially since I saw no one[60] in the learned world prepared to undertake it, not (I imagine) because they thought themselves unequal to it but because they saw the immense labour involved and would not face it, especially in the knowledge that the reward in reputation would fall short of the effort.

Secondly, I saw that the nature of the enterprise was such as in itself would have no limits and therefore felt it essential to measure the scale of it not by the logic of the task but by my own commitments, spending on it not the labour it required but as much as I thought could be spared without doing wrong from my own researches. I have therefore finished my task in rather too much of a hurry, partly because in this field I felt myself to be, as it were, off my beat; partly so as to be able when this was finished to return with my whole heart to the subjects proper to my profession, which I had interrupted for some months in compliance with the wishes of a friend rather than with my own judgment. All the same, I am not too deeply moved by Horace's principle, for when he laid it down he was thinking of those who sought to win a reputation for their gifts, whereas I have never had any hopes except of being useful to the reader. He laid down a law for writers of poetry, in which, as Pliny[61] tells us, the highest degree of eloquence is needed; I am making a collection of adages. Finally, those nine years of care (which he himself, all the same, did not provide in poetry) might perhaps have been provided by someone concerned only with a hundred proverbs; but when dealing with thousands, it seems a tall order to provide it and pretty hard-hearted to expect it, for even the writing of chiliads is highly laborious, without adding the effort of so many changes, which is clearly not a little more difficult than the original. Though I myself think that the care demanded by Horace is to be measured not by the duration of time but by its intensity; and on this point I can affirm in all sincerity that I have tried with might and main to make up the time denied to the enterprise by watchful care and taking pains, so that I hope fair-minded readers will not find it wholly deficient even under this head. If you consider its length, my work was done in a hurry; consider the busy nights and days spent in unwearied toil, and it was finished in good time. And though my industry may not be in all respects equal to my task, one thing at least will be clear, that all those who have ever written on proverbs in either Greek or Latin (I speak of those whose compilations are still extant) have been far outdone by me in diligence.

Last but not least, since the work knows no limits and aims at being generally useful, is there any reason why we should not share the labour and by our joint efforts finish it? I have completed my task,[62] am tired and hand on the torch; let me have a successor who is ready to take his turn. I have supplied a mass of material on an, I think, not wholly ungenerous scale; now for men who will hew it to shape and polish it and inlay it. I have finished the part which offered most work and least reputation; I should be content to watch others adding what will be both easiest and most rewarding. It will make no difference to me whoever's name it bears, I shall not take it amiss whoever is left with the principal credit, as long as it is I who have provided the opportunity to put such a blessing in the way of all who wish to learn. Nor shall I take offence in the slightest degree if a better scholar corrects my work, a more diligent student enriches it, a more precise mind puts it in order, a better stylist makes it shine, a person with more leisure polishes it, a more successful one carries off the prize, if only this goes hand in hand with the greater convenience of readers in general; for that has been so much my one object in this enterprise that I have taken no account of myself. Otherwise I too, like most people, might have chosen a task which would have cost me far less exertion, and at the same time would have brought a far greater reward in reputation. Everyone would have thought it an outstanding and splendid achievement, had I made the whole of Demosthenes or Plato or some similar author available to Latin readers. And yet it would be hard to say how much less expenditure of time and midnight oil it would have required to finish this task compared with this collection of what seem to be such trifles. I might have chosen for myself two or three centuries out of such a large number, and used every sinew of my mind[63] at full stretch in polishing and enriching them and filing them to a fine edge, sowing a good deal less in the way of labour to secure a much heavier harvest of reputation in the future; but to do this would have been to pursue my own private ends and not the general advantage of all who wish to learn. But, in my opinion at any rate, in rebuilding the republic of letters one must display the spirit of a second Hercules, and no fear of weakness at the prospect of your own loss should discourage you from serving the common good.

But more than enough on these topics; I have been fearing for some time that my readers may find it a Herculean task to read through the discourse of inordinate length into which I have been drawn by an adage which has proved a task for Hercules.

And so I will make an end, but after adding a further point – that when this was first published I had surpassed all the labours of Hercules. For he, though he won every other battle, was unequal to a contest with two monsters at once, and so preferred to run away and leave us a proverb[64] rather than risk an engagement, thinking mockery and survival better than death and glory. I on the other hand had to engage with two frightful monsters at the same time, either of which by itself demanded so much effort that it demanded many a Hercules, so unlikely was it that a mere mortal by himself could be equal to the two. For in Basel were being printed at the same moment both the *Adagiorum Chiliades*, so much corrected and enriched that the revision cost me no less than the earlier edition which I completed in Venice in the house of Aldus Manutius, and the complete works of St Jerome, of which I had taken on my own shoulders the largest and also most difficult part, the books of his *Letters*[65] – no light task, in the Muses' name, even if one only had to read so many volumes. But, as things were, in God's name what a heavy struggle I had with monstrous corruptions, of which all Jerome was full! What an effort it was to restore the Greek words which the author mixes in from time to time, for most of them were lacking or added wrongly! And no inconsiderable nights of toil must needs be expended on the notes (such as they are) which I added with their summaries, not only because, in a field in which I was a pioneer, there was no one I could follow whose researches might be a help to me; there was another reason. Romulus,[66] they say, was as much an ostentatious publicist for his own achievements as a doer of noble deeds; and in the same way St Jerome had in his head a rich storehouse filled from subjects and authors of every kind, and no one, if I may so express it, makes a more showy display than he does in his writings of his wealth of learning. Such is the pious pride (so to call it) with which he confronts us as he thrusts forward and drives home abstruse points from the Old Covenant or the New, from mythology and history, and the finer problems in the Greek and Hebrew texts. Then again the establishment of the order, which had been confused in various ways by different people, although it earned no praise for one's abilities, was not a little tedious. Such was the load of work that a poor simple person like me had to carry – to carry single-handed, except that on certain Hebrew words, having had only a brief taste of Hebrew with the tip of my tongue as the saying goes,[67] I had some help from Bruno Amerbach,[68] a young man as modest as he is learned. Later, when he in turn was engaged on the remainder of the work, I helped him in several passages with the restoration of Greek or Latin in the text, thus repaying one good turn with another. I say nothing for the moment of the considerable work involved in identifying on definite evidence, as though by recognizable tracks,[69] what had been included among Jerome's works under a false attribution (some of them scholarly, some equally ignorant and badly written, and a few also showing obvious signs of mental derangement), and in assigning the excluded pieces each to its proper place; and then in putting together out of the works he himself left behind the life of that great saint, of which others had given such untruthful and unintelligent accounts. On top of this remember that the nature of this work is such as to be profitable and useful to the general public, while nobody feels the tedium of it except the sole individual who bears the burden of it. For the reader who runs through whole books without interruption does not observe that I was sometimes at a stop for several days over a single word; he does not understand, or if he does, at any rate he forgets, the price I had to pay in terms of problems for the easy read that he enjoys, the troubles that it cost me to save my readers trouble. And so I think sometimes that I too must have been born on the fourth of the month,[70] since for some unknown reason much more than Herculean labours have fallen to my lot.

1 55.13
2 2.23.7–8, 2.24.34 (Alcides is another name for Hercules)
3 *De finibus* 2.35.118
4 I i 77; the fourth of the month was traditionally unlucky, a point that also concludes this essay.
5 *Iliad* 19.90–133
6 I iii 27
7 *Epistles* 2.1.10–12
8 *Jewish War* 1.208
9 *Pythians* 7.18–19
10 *Metamorphoses* 2.761–4
11 Livy 8.31.7, Ovid *Remedia amoris* 369
12 *Odes* 2.20.4, 4.3.16
13 *De Josepho* 1, 4–5
14 *Iliad* 2.105
15 That is, by burning off the heads of the Hydra
16 'The position of the prince is too noble to be commercialized' in Erasmus' *Education of a Christian Prince* (CWE 27 260)
17 Horace *Odes* 3.24.43
18 I v 94
19 III ii 93, V i 38
20 Early king of Rome in Virgil *Aeneid* 8
21 Mythical king of Phrygia; see II viii 19 and IV i 46.
22 *dia dis pason*, I ii 63

23 I vi 29
24 I iv 25
25 II iv 40
26 Cassiodorus *Institutes* 1.1.8 (strangely, not an adage)
27 Compilation of patristic sources by Peter Lombard (bishop of Paris 1159)
28 Though a proverb, not included in the *Adages*
29 I v 6
30 *Nicomachean Ethics* 10.3 (1174b28)
31 I v 38*
32 II viii 2
33 *Art of Poetry* 352–3, 359
34 I iii 61
35 III v 1
36 I ii 37
37 The plant is called *sardoa*, mentioned in III v 1.
38 I iii 26
39 *Art of Poetry* 147
40 II viii 79
41 Menander *Sententiae* 273 (frag 45 Körte), and see I viii 43.
42 I v 38*
43 II iii 50
44 II iii 45
45 *Art of Poetry* 388
46 I ix 6 and II iii 7
47 *De finibus* 1.5.15
48 *Letters* 75.5
49 I viii 23
50 IV i 90
51 I iv 66
52 *Brutus* 4.16
53 'Apes' is also used in Erasmus' *Ciceronianus* CWE 28 444.
54 *Georgics* 3.290
55 *Mostellaria* 791; also *Adages* II ii 80
56 I vi 19
57 See II i 1* above.
58 William Blount, Lord Mountjoy (c 1478–1534) was Erasmus' principal English patron and the dedicatee of the early editions of the *Collectanea* and *Adages*.
59 Cicero *Laelius on Friendship* 61
60 For the earlier collection of Polydore Vergil, see editor's introduction, pp xii–xiii.
61 Pliny the Younger *Epistles* 5.8.4
62 I iii 61, I ii 38
63 I iv 16
64 'Not even Hercules can take on two at once'; see I v 39. The monsters are the hydra and the crab (from Plato *Euthydemus* 287b–c).
65 The *Letters* took the first four volumes of the folio edition of Jerome prepared by Erasmus for 1516.
66 Livy 1.10.5
67 I ix 92
68 Bruno Amerbach (1484–1519) was a member of the celebrated family of scholar printers in Nuremburg.
69 IV ii 18
70 Here Erasmus follows Angelo Poliziano (1454–94), the great scholar, who in his *Miscellanea* c 80 already staked out a claim to this unlucky birthday; see note 4 above.

III i 60
Vestis virum facit / Clothes make the man

This is an interesting back-formation of a Greek proverb by Erasmus. It is actually a medieval Latin proverb (Walther 33265a, 33268a). Because of the passage in Quintilian, the proverb appeared to come from the Greek, and Erasmus translated the proverb into what seemed to be this original Greek form. This reversal was also followed by the great classical scholar J.C. Scaliger (Tosi 221; see also Otto 476). The appropriateness of one's clothing is discussed at some length in one of Erasmus' main sources, Athenaeus Doctors at Dinner *1.21c–d, but the proverb is not there and Erasmus omits this possible ancient connection in his discussion. In English as Tilley* A *283.*

Εἵματα ἀνήρ, Clothes make the man. This is still a very popular and well-known saying in our own day: 'Apparel setteth out a man; / Clothe yourself as best you can.' Quintilian confirms this in book of his *Institutions*: 'To dress within the formal limits and with an air gives men, as the Greek line testifies, authority.' I suppose this line which Quintilian cites to be that one in Homer,[1] in *Odyssey* 6: 'From these things, you may be sure, men get a good report.' And a little later in the same book, the importance of care in one's dress as a means of improving one's appearance and standing is made clear enough, when he makes the maiden Nausicaa speak as follows about Ulysses: 'At first I thought his appearance was unseemly, but now he has the air of the gods who dwell in the wide heaven.' For Ulysses, who had previously been naked, is now dressed in shining garments and looks at once like a different person: 'Then went he and sat aloof on the sea-shore, a radiant figure handsome and full of grace.'

1 *Odyssey* 6.29–30, 242–3, 236–7 (cf Quintilian at 8 Proem 20)

III ii 33
Cera tractabilior / As pliable as wax

The notion of the pliable student is very old in educational writings. Erasmus plays with the images in his Declamation on the Subject of Early Liberal

Education for Children: 'As soon as it is born, a child aborbs with great ease everything that is characteristically human ... Press wax while it is softest; model clay while it is still moist; pour liquids only into a jar that has never been used before; and only use wool that has just arrived spotlessly white from the fuller's' (CWE 26 305). This pliability is seen in the sixteenth century as a positive quality ('Why, he's a man of wax!' says the Nurse of smoothly polished Paris in Romeo and Juliet*). Erasmus wrote the proverb essay in 1508; the second part ('and hence the practice of using it ...' onwards) was added in two stages in 1515 and 1528. Though it was common in Greek (Suidas* K *1537) and Latin (Otto 373; Tosi 689), Mynors notes that Erasmus may also have found it in a collection of adages in an Aldine edition of Aesop (1505, col 104). Compare with* II *x 42 'A twisted branch.'*

Κηροῦ εὐπλαστότερος, As pliable as wax, was said of an exceedingly docile person, or of a lively and pliable intelligence that could be led in any direction. Horace:[1] 'Pliant as wax towards vice, but to good counsel rough.' Persius[2] in his fifth satire: 'And assumes plastic features under your hand.' Horace[3] again: 'In the moist clay will copy what you will.' It is a special property of wax to grow soft when worked in the hands, and hence the practice of using it to model various shapes. There was also a type of picture made of coloured waxes, mosaics made of pieces of stone, and various woods. Yet the unformed character of a child is more like clay than wax: it can be moulded to start with while it is still soft, but once the character is hardened, it is not easily reworked into another shape but, as Plato[4] says in book four of the *Republic*, 'There is some risk at any rate that the direction in which a man sets out from childhood will dictate all that follows.'

1 *Art of Poetry* 163
2 *Satires* 5.40
3 *Epistles* 2.2.8
4 *Republic* 4.425b

III iii 1
Sileni Alcibiadis / The Sileni of Alcibiades

This essay, very short in the edition of 1508, and radically rewritten and expanded in the edition of 1515, is one of the most important in the whole of the Adages. *The Silenus figure (ugly on the outside, beautiful when opened) is a metaphor for Christ and for interpretation. In his earlier* Enchiridion *or* Handbook of a Christian Knight *Erasmus remarks that the interpreter should observe in the text being read 'both a surface meaning and a hidden one – comparable to body and spirit, so that, indifferent to the merely literal sense, you may examine the most keenly hidden ... [E]specially do the Holy Scriptures, like the Silenus of Alcibiades, conceal their real divinity beneath a surface that is crude and almost laughable' (trans Himelick 105). He returns to the Silenus figure in the* Praise of Folly, *with a new emphasis on the transformative power of metaphor: 'In the first place, it's well known that all human affairs are like the figures of Silenus described by Alcibiades and have two completely opposite faces, so that what is death at first sight, as they say, is life if you look within, and vice versa, life is death. The same applies to beauty and ugliness, riches and poverty, obscurity and fame ... you'll find everything suddenly reversed if you open the Silenus' (trans Betty Radice in* CWE *27 102–3). Daniel Kinney, who discusses these two passages in his essay 'The* Adages *of Erasmus: Midwife of Learning'* (Journal of Medieval and Renaissance Studies *11 [1981] 169–92), astutely adds 'Every proverb, in short, is a Silenus figure in its own right' (189). In his prologue to* Gargantua *(1534), François Rabelais likens his text to a Silenus figure, in turn to an apothecary's box, crude and rough on the outside, but when it is opened you find 'a divine and priceless drug.' Erasmus' essay was published separately (with notes by Johann Froben) in 1517, and went through a number of later editions and translations as an independent work. The English version appeared about 1543 as* A Scorneful Image or Monstrus Shape of a Marvelous Strange Fygure Called Sileni Alcibiadis Presentyng the State and Condicion of this Present World and Inespeciall of the Spirituallte How Farre They Be from the Perfite Trade and Lyfe of Criste.

Σιληνοὶ Ἀλκιβιάδου, The Sileni of Alcibiades, seems to have passed into a proverb among educated people; it is, at any rate, on record as a proverb in the Greek collections.[1] It will have two possible uses, either of some thing which, though on the surface and (as the saying[2] goes) at first sight looks worthless and absurd, is yet admirable on a nearer and less superficial view, or of some man whose face and bearing promise far less than what he hides in his heart. The Sileni are said to have been a kind of small figure of carved wood, so made that they could be divided and opened. Thus, though when closed they looked like a caricature of a hideous flute-player, when opened they suddenly displayed a deity, so that this humorous surprise made the carver's skill all the more admirable. Furthermore, the subject of these images was drawn from the well-known comic figure of Silenus, Bacchus' tutor and the court buffoon of the gods of poetry (for they too have their jesters like the princes of our own day). Thus in the fifth book of Athenaeus[3] a young man called Critobulus, 'who is making fun of Socrates as old and ugly, calls him "far more hideous than the Sileni."' There is a passage in Xenophon,[4] in the *Symposium,* where Socrates says 'You give yourself these airs as though you were more handsome than I,' and Critobulus replies 'Good heavens yes, or I should be the ugliest of all the Sileni in the satyr-plays.' And Alcibiades[5] in Plato's *Symposium,* who is preparing to deliver a panegyric of Socrates, draws a parallel between him and Sileni of this kind, because like them he was very different on close inspection from what he seemed in his outward bearing and appearance.

Anyone who had valued him skin-deep (as they say[6]) would not have given twopence for him. With his peasant face, glaring like a bull, and his snub nose always sniffling, he might have been taken for some blockheaded country bumpkin. The care of his person was neglected, his language simple and homely and smacking of common folk; for his talk was all of carters and cobblers, of fullers and smiths, and it was from them, as a rule, that he derived the analogies which he used in any discussion to press home his point. His means were modest, and his wife such as the low charcoal-burner would have found insufferable. He was thought to admire good looks in young men, he was thought to know the meaning of love and jealousy, though Alcibiades of all people found him a whole gamut removed from such emotions. Last but not least, that unbroken flow of humour gave him the air of a buffoon. While that was a period when the ambition to advertise one's own cleverness reached manic heights among the foolish, nor was Gorgias[7] the only man who boasted that there was nothing he did not know, but all the world was filled with know-alls of this kind, Socrates[8] was alone in declaring that there was only one thing he knew, which was that he knew nothing. For all the duties of public life he was clearly unfitted, so much so that one day, when he attempted to make a speech on some subject before the public assembly, he was laughed out of court. Yet, had you opened this absurd Silenus, you would have found, you may be sure, a divine being rather than a man, a great and lofty spirit worthy of a true philosopher, one who despised all the things for which other mortals run their races, sail the seas, toil, go to law, and fight in wars; a man above resenting any injury and over whom fortune had no power at all; so far from any fear that he despised even death, of which all men are afraid – so much so that he drank the hemlock with the same air with which he would drink wine, and even in the moment of death joked with his friend Phaedo, telling him to pay a vow on his behalf by sacrificing a cock to Aesculapius,[9] for all the world as if after drinking the fatal dose he already felt the benefits of returning health because he was leaving the body, the breeding-ground of all the countless ailments of the spirit. Small wonder then, though the world of those days was full of professional wits, if this buffoon was the only man declared wise by the oracle, and he who knew nothing was judged to know more than those who boasted there was nothing they did not know – was in fact judged to know more than the rest for that very reason, that he alone of them all said he knew nothing.

A Silenus of this sort was Antisthenes,[10] who with his staff, his satchel, and his cloak surpassed the wealth of the greatest kings. A Silenus of this sort was Diogenes,[11] commonly regarded as a dog; but in this dog something of the divine must have been detected by Alexander the Great,[12] of all princes (as it seemed) the chief, the alpha, when in admiration of his nobility of mind he declared that he would wish himself, were he not Alexander, to be Diogenes, whereas he ought to have wished for the spirit of Diogenes all the more because he was Alexander. A Silenus of this sort was Epictetus,[13] a slave and penniless and lame, as his epitaph declares, but at the same time (and this is the greatest of blessings) dear to the heavenly powers in a way that only integrity of life combined with wisdom can secure. Such, to be sure, is the nature of things really worth having. Their excellence they bury in their inmost parts, and hide; they wear what is most contemptible at first glance on the surface, concealing their treasure with a kind of worthless outward shell and not showing it to uninitiated eyes. Vulgar, unsubstantial things have a far different design: their attractions are all on the surface and their beauties are at once displayed to all and sundry, but look inside and you will find that nothing could be less like what was promised by the label and the outward view.

And what of Christ? Was not He too a marvellous Silenus (if one may be allowed to use such language of Him)? And I for my part do not see how any who proudly call themselves Christians can escape the duty of reproducing this to the utmost of their power. Observe the outside surface of this Silenus: to judge by ordinary standards, what could be humbler or more worthy of disdain? Parents of modest means and lowly station, and a humble home; poor Himself and with few and poor disciples, recruited not from noblemen's palaces or the chief sects of the Pharisees or the lecture-rooms of philosophers, but from the publican's office and the nets of fishermen. And then His way of life: what a stranger He was to all physical comforts as He pursued through hunger and weariness, through insults and mockery the way that led to the cross! It was this aspect of Him that the mystic and poet contemplated when he described Him in the words[14] 'He had no form nor comeliness; we beheld Him and there was nothing to look upon, and we desired Him, despised as He was and the least of men,' and a great deal that follows to the same effect. And now, if one has the good fortune to have a nearer view of this Silenus, open – if, in other words, He shows Himself in His mercy to anyone, the eyes of whose soul have been washed clean – in heaven's name what a treasure you will find, in that cheap setting what a pearl, in that lowliness what grandeur, in that poverty what riches, in that weakness what unimaginable valour, in that disgrace what glory, in all those labours what perfect refreshment, and in that bitter death, in short, a never-failing spring of immortality! Why are those men so much revolted by this picture of Him who boast none the less that they bear His name? It would of course have been easy for Christ to have taken over the monarchy of the whole world: to possess what the Roman emperors of old aspired to in vain, to outdo any Xerxes[15] in the number of His followers, to surpass any Croesus[16] in wealth, to silence all the philosophers and strip them of their pointless plaudits. But this was the only system which He chose to set before His disciples and His friends – before us Christians. This above all was the philosophy of His choice, worlds away from the principles laid down by philosophers and from the reasoning of the world, but the one and only way to achieve the end which others pursue by differing means, that is, true felicity.

Sileni of this sort were in old days the Prophets, wandering in exile in the wilderness, contriving to live among wild beasts, their food the poorest greenstuff and their garments the skins of sheep and goats. But he had seen the inside of these Sileni who said[17] 'of whom the world was not worthy.' A Silenus of this sort was John the Baptist, who was clothed in camelhair with a leather girdle round his loins,[18] yet far surpassed kings with their purple and their precious stones, and who lived on locusts and yet outdid the luxury of all the princes. What treasure lay hidden beneath that rustic cloak was discerned, of course, by Him who summed up all his merits in that memorable phrase[19] 'Among them that are born of women there bath not risen a greater than John the Baptist.' Sileni of this sort were the Apostles, poor, unkempt, illiterate, of humble birth, weak and rejected, exposed to insults of every kind from every quarter, mocked, hated, cursed, almost the whole world's public target at once for loathing and for laughter. But pray open the Silenus, and what tyrant could enjoy such power as theirs? – as they control evil spirits with a command, calm raging seas with a gesture, and call the dead back to life with a word. Compared with them any Croesus would seem a pauper, as they bestow health on the sick merely by their shadow, and by a simple touch of the hand convey that spirit that comes from heaven. Aristotle himself would seem a foolish and ignorant dilettante, when compared with these men who have drawn from the true fountain-head that heavenly wisdom, against which all human wisdom is mere folly. In so saying I must ask pardon of those who think it impious and wicked to weaken the authority of Aristotle in any way. He was, I grant you, an exceptionally learned man; but all the same what light can shine so bright that when compared with Christ it is not darkened? In those days the kingdom of heaven really was 'like a grain of mustard-seed,'[20] in appearance tiny and negligible, in power immense; and, as I have said, it differs utterly and what they call[21] diametrically from the system of this world.

A Silenus of this sort was that object of contempt and mockery, Bishop Martin.[22] Such were those early bishops, exalted in their lowliness, rich in their poverty, and famous because they took no thought for fame.

Even today there are some good men who are hidden Sileni; but, alas, too few! A goodly number of men reproduce Silenus inside-out. Anyone who looked thoroughly into the driving force of things and their true nature would find none so far removed from real wisdom as those whose honorific titles, learned bonnets,[23] resplendent belts, and bejewelled rings advertise wisdom in perfection. So true is this that you may not seldom find more real and native wisdom in one single ordinary man, who in the world's judgment is an ignoramus and a simple-minded fool, more or less, whose mind has been educated not by the subtle Scotus[24] (as they call him) but by the heavenly spirit of Christ, than in many of our pompous theologians, Professors three and four times over, stuffed with their favourite Aristotle and swollen with a plethora of doctoral definitions, conclusions, and propositions. I would not say this of them all, but of, alas, far too many. In the same way, in no one would you find less true nobility than in those braggart Thrasos,[25] who boast a noble lineage of the highest class with their ancient pedigrees, golden collars, and resplendent titles; nowhere men further remote from true courage than among those whose rashness and brutality have earned them a reputation as courageous and invincible; no slaves more abject and more servile than the men who think themselves next the gods (as the saying is) and lords of all; none in such trouble as those who seem most successful; none so poor in the full sense of the word as those whom public opinion adores as rich; none less truly bishops than those who among the bishops are in the first rank. (With all possible emphasis I beg you, dear reader, not to think that this is said in order to bring discredit on any individual; it is the practice, not the persons, that I criticize. I wish there were no one living whom this cap fits. And if there are no such people now – and I pray Christ it may be so – there have been such before now, and in the future perhaps there may be more. I only wish that this too may be untrue, that those men are very often furthest removed from true religion who make a show of religious perfection in title, in costume, and in ceremonial.)

So true is it in things of every sort that what is excellent is least conspicuous. Look at the trees: their flowers and leaves appeal to every eye, and their great bulk is inescapable, whereas the seed which contains the vital force of the whole – what a tiny thing it is, how well concealed, how far from appealing to the eye, how little given to self-advertisement. Gold and jewels are hidden by nature in the deepest bowels of the earth. Of the elements, as we call them, the greater the excellence of each, the further it is removed from the senses, air for example and fire. In the animal kingdom the best and most active parts are hidden deep inside. In man, the part which more than the rest is divine and immortal is the one part that cannot be perceived. In things of every kind the matter, which is less valuable, is most fully open to perception, while the principle, the moving force active for good, is perceived through the value of that activity, and yet is itself far removed from perception. Again, in the make-up of our physical body, while phlegm and blood are familiar to the senses and visible, that which make the largest contribution to life is by no means visible, I mean breath. In the universe, finally, the things that are greatest are not seen, for instance what they call the separate substances,[26] and among them that which is highest of all is farthest of all remote from perception, I mean God Himself, so much so that He is beyond the imagination and the understanding, for all that He is the sole source of everything.

And no less in the sacraments of the Church you may find some sort of reflection of the Sileni. (Let no man misinterpret what I say.) You see the water, you see the salt and the oil, you hear the words of consecration, and this is like seeing a Silenus from the outside; the power from heaven you neither hear nor see, in the absence of which all the rest would be mere mockery. After all, Scripture too has its own Sileni. Pause at the surface, and what you see is sometimes ridiculous; were you to pierce to the heart of the allegory, you would venerate the divine wisdom. Let us take the Old Testament. If you looked at nothing beyond the story; if you heard how Adam was made out of clay and his poor wife taken secretly out of his side while he slept, how the serpent tempted the woman with an apple as his bait, how God walked out to take the air, and how a great sword guarded the gate to prevent the exiles from returning later, would you not think this was a fable that issued from Homer's workshop? If you read of Lot's incest, the whole story of Samson which St Jerome,[27] judging it by the outside, calls a fable, of David's adultery and the girl who slept in his embrace when he was old and cold, or of Hosea's marriage to a prostitute, would not anyone with a reasonably sensitive ear reject the whole thing as an improper story? Yet under these wrappings, in heaven's name, how splendid is the wisdom that lies hidden! The parables in the Gospels, if you judge them by their outward shell, would be thought, surely, by everyone to be the work of an ignoramus. Crack the nutshell and of course you will find that hidden wisdom which is truly divine, something in truth very like Christ Himself. But I must not go on too long in the pursuit of details. It is in fact the same in nature and in the mysteries of religion: the more excellent a thing is, the more deeply it is hidden, and far removed from uninitiated eyes.

It is the same with knowledge: the real truth of things is always most profoundly concealed, and cannot be detected easily or by many people. The stupid multitude, judging things as they do upside down, and using of course as their criteria for every purpose what is most clearly obvious to the bodily senses, constantly make mistakes and go astray, are misled by phantom images of good and bad, and keep their admiration and respect for any Silenus that is inside out. I am speaking of bad men; the good I will not hurt, nor the bad either, for that matter for, after all, the discussion of faults in general has no connection with attacks on any individual. How I wish there were fewer people to whom these strictures could apply! When you behold the sceptre, the insignia, the bodyguard; when you hear the titles, 'Most Serene,' 'Most Merciful,' 'Right Glorious,' can you fail to revere a prince, and suppose yourself to see some earthly deity, something greater than a human being? Open this inside-out Silenus, and you will find a despot, sometimes an enemy of his citizens, one who hates the public peace and is skilled in sowing the seeds of discord, who oppresses men of good will, perverts the laws, overthrows cities, despoils the Church, lives by robbery and sacrilege, a lecher and a gambler – in a word, what the Greek proverbs[28] call 'an Iliad of evils.' Some men by their titles and their outward show advertise themselves as governors and guardians of the commonwealth, while in truth they are wolves and pirates preying on the community. There are some whom, if you saw only their shaved heads, you would respect as priests; but look inside the Silenus and you will find them worse than laymen. It may be that you will find even some bishops in whom, if you observe their solemn consecration and run your eye over their new attributes of honour, the mitre glittering with jewels and gold and the crozier equally studded with gems – in a word, from head to foot[29] all that mystic panoply – you would no doubt expect to find some heavenly character, some man more than human. Turn your Silenus inside out, and you will sometimes find nothing but a man of war, a merchant, even a despot, and you will now decide that all those splendid trappings were just play-acting. There are some men (and how I wish one did not meet them everywhere!), whom anyone prepared to judge them by a forest of beard, a pale face, a cowl, a stiff neck, a belt, a proud brow, and a savage expression, would think were as good as any Serapion or Paul;[30] but if you open them, you will find mere buffoons, squanderers, impostors, gluttons – robbers in a word and despots (but of another sort and one I rather think more pestilential inasmuch as it is more concealed), and your treasure, as the saying goes, will be simply coals. Once again I give notice that no one should take offence at what I say, for no person is identified by name. Anyone who is not of the kind I describe should reflect that none of this concerns him; if he recognizes his own faults, let him consider that the warning is meant for him. One of the two can congratulate himself, and the other owes me thanks.

Finally, in every class of mortal men everywhere there are those of whom you would say, were you to inspect their outward bodily form, that they are human beings, and distinguished beings too; open the Silenus, and inside you will find maybe a pig or a lion, a bear or a donkey. Your experience will be the converse of what we are told in the fables of the poets about Circe's magic spells.[31] Her victims had the shape of animals but the mind of a human being. Those I speak of conceal something worse than a beast beneath a human shape. There are, on the other hand, some whom from their outward shape, as I have said, you would judge to be hardly human, while in their inmost hearts they hide an angel. In this therefore we find a difference between the worldly man and the Christian. The one chiefly respects and follows all that is most coarse in texture and immediately presented to the eye; things of other kinds he either overlooks altogether, or at least rates them in the lowest place. The other, from the opposite point of view, picks out what is least visible to the eye and what is furthest removed from the nature of corporeal things, and these alone he pursues, either passing over all the rest or using them with a measure of contempt, because he draws his principles of judgment entirely from what is within.

Among the good things, as Aristotle[32] calls them, which do not as a property belong to man, the lowest is wealth; but among common people, and indeed almost universally, that man is most highly thought of who possesses wealth by some means or other, and wealth is pursued by everyone 'through rocks, through fire.'[33] The next place is held by noble lineage, which without other qualities is nothing but a mockery, an empty name. A man is thought to be a demigod who can trace his ancestry to Codrus[34] the Athenian or to Brutus the Trojan, who I rather think never existed, or to the mythical figure of Hercules; and is he of low degree who has won himself a reputation by literary gifts and force of character? A man is noble if his great-great-great-great-grandfather proved himself on the field of battle a doughty murderer; and is he a plebeian without pride of ancestry who by his intellectual gifts has been a blessing to the world? In a third class are physical advantages, and anyone who happens to be blessed with a body that is big, healthy, handsome, and of great strength is not eliminated from the list of the fortunate, but on the principle that, all the same, riches must take first place and noble birth second, while the mind is the last thing they consider. And if, with St Paul,[35] you divide this one man into three parts, body and soul and spirit (for I will use his own words), it is the lowest of the three, the most clearly visible and the one which the apostle entirely condemns, which is a favourite with the multitude. The middle one, of which he approves only when it is joined with the spirit, finds favour with a good many. But the spirit, the best part of ourselves, which is as it were the spring from which flows all our felicity, and through which we are joined with God – on this they set so small a value that they do not ask even whether it exists or what that spirit is on which, in spite of all this, Paul insists so often. And thus the judgment of the multitude is topsy-turvy: What ought to be put first is, like the Megarians,[36] of no account, and the objects they should have pursued with might and main they think quite contemptible. Thus gold is more valued than sound learning, ancient lineage more than integrity, bodily endowments more than intellectual gifts; true religion takes second place to ceremonies, Christ's commandments to the decrees of men, the mask to the true face; shadow is preferred to substance, artificial to natural, transient to solid, momentary to eternal.

And then these topsy-turvy opinions give rise to topsy-turvy names for things. What is lofty they call lowly, what is bitter they call sweet, what is precious they call worthless, and life they call death. Let me select a few particular examples in passing. To 'love' a person, in common parlance, is either to corrupt by over-indulgence or to lay schemes against both chastity and reputation, hostile actions which it would be hard to surpass. 'Justice' is their name for outdoing evil with evil and one crime with another, and when you are wronged, to repay the wrong with interest. A man is said to be 'prejudiced against' matrimony, who demands that it should be unsullied, as close as possible to celibacy and as far from the life of the brothels. They call a man a traitor and an enemy to his prince who wishes a prince to have no power above the laws and outside what is right, who wants him, that is, to play the part of a true prince and be as unlike as possible to the picture of a tyrant, the most savage beast there is. He on the other hand is called a counsellor, friend, and supporter of princes, who corrupts them with misguided education, infects them with foolish ideas, deludes them with adulation, eggs them on by bad advice to incur the hatred of their subjects, and involves them in wars and in the frenzy of civil discord. They say that a prince actually gains in majesty when he acquires a tincture of the tyrant – the greater part, that is to say, of the worst thing of all. He who would like to see some reduction in the taxes extorted from the public has an eye, they think, to his own profit. The fact is that a prince has three special good qualities, in which he reflects God, who is the only true king: goodness, wisdom, power. How can that man pass for a prince's friend, who strips him of two of these special attributes, goodness and wisdom, and leaves him only power – sham power at that and, what is more, not even really his? For power that is not united with wisdom and goodness is tyranny and not power, and the public will, which gave it to him, can equally take it away, while all the time, if he is driven from his throne, goodness and wisdom, as his personal possessions, keep him company. To insult a prince's escutcheon is an offence punishable with death; is there to be a reward for those who corrupt his heart, who turn a good man into a cruel brute, a wise man into a fox, and a powerful man into a tyrant? A single death is not enough for the criminal who has tried to put poison in a prince's cup; and shall he win a prize who corrupts and poisons his mind with most pestilent opinions, who taints, as it were, the public water-supply of the community and inflicts the greatest harm on the whole world? A prince's duty, they say, is to rule; whereas in truth to be a prince is nothing but to organize the common good. The dynastic marriages and their constantly changing alliances, they call the cement of Christian peace, although we can see them as the causes from which spring nearly all wars and most of the convulsions in human affairs. They speak of a just war when princes play a match of which the outcome is to exhaust and oppress the commonwealth; they speak of peace when that is the very object against which they conspire among themselves; they reckon that dominions are enlarged when a prince has acquired the title to one or two wretched towns, bought at the price of all those citizens despoiled, of all that bloodshed, of wives left husbandless and children without fathers.

In the same way they give the name of 'the Church' to priests, bishops and supreme pontiffs, though they are in truth nothing but the Church's servants. No, it is Christian people who are the Church, whom Christ himself calls 'greater,'[37] in the sense that bishops ought to serve them as they sit at the table, taking a lesser place in the service they render, but by another reckoning greater, if only they will follow the example of Christ, not only by taking on his duty of service but by the imitation of his character and life who, though he was in every way the lord and master of all things, took upon himself the part of a servant and not a master. Every thunderbolt is brandished over those – and they are called enemies of the Church and little short of heretics – who defraud priests' purses of a few small coins. For my part, I offer no support to the fraudulent – let no one think that is what I mean – but tell me this: if it is a good thing to hate an enemy of the Church, could the Church have an enemy more pernicious or more deadly than a godless Pontiff? When there has been some reduction in the estates or revenues of the priesthood, there is a universal outcry that this is an oppression of the Church of Christ; when the world is seething on the brink of war, when the open immorality of the clergy is putting so many thousand souls in jeopardy, no one laments the fate that has befallen the Church, although the Church is now really suffering. They say the Church is adorned and honoured, not when religion is on the increase among ordinary folk, when vices are shrinking and virtue flourishes, when sacred scholarship is in full vigour, but when altars gleam with gold and jewels – or rather, when the altars are neglected and it is land, servants, luxury, mules, horses, the costly construction of houses (more like palaces) and all the other noise and bustle of life that puts priests on the level of Eastern potentates. To such an extent does this seem right and proper that even the official documents of the papacy contain words of praise like these: 'Whereas such-and-such a cardinal by maintaining in his household so many horses and so many men in purple adds such outstanding glory to the Church of God, we grant him the dignity of a fourth episcopal see.' And for the Church's greater glory bishops, priests, and clergy are bidden to array themselves in purple and silk. What a marvellous distinction for the Church! What next, now that we have corrupted even our words of moral approval? For I do not choose to mention at this moment those who lavish their clerical income on sinful purposes, causing great offence to ordinary people. If anything further comes their way, we wish them joy of it, we say that the Church of Christ has made a step forward, although the one true profit that the Church can make lies in progress in the Christian life.

They call it blasphemy if a man speaks with less than perfect reverence of Christopher or George, and fails to set all the stories of all the saints on the same level as the Gospel. Yet Paul[38] calls it blasphemy whenever as a result of Christians' irreligious behaviour the name of Christ is discredited among the Gentiles. What can we expect the enemies of Christianity to say, when in the Gospel text they have seen Christ urging us to despise riches, to reject pleasure, to take no thought for reputation, and on the other hand have observed even the chief and leading men among those who profess Christianity living in such a way that in the race to acquire wealth, in love of pleasure, in splendour of life, in cruelty of battle and in almost all other forms of wrongdoing they actually outdo the gentiles? The intelligent reader will understand how much I do not say on this point, to spare the honour of the name of Christian, and how I sigh within my heart.

What peals of laughter do you suppose they raise when they see that Christ in the Gospel did not distinguish His followers by cult and ceremonies and rules of diet, but wished Christians to be identified by the mark of mutual charity binding them together, and then observe us enjoying so little agreement among ourselves that never did gentiles of any kind indulge in disputes more disgraceful or more destructive? Prince makes war on prince, one city fights another; two universities, two religious bodies (as they now call them) cannot agree; wrangling and faction and strife fill the whole world. This and this alone is the true blasphemy, and the people responsible are those who provide it with a just excuse.

They call it heresy if someone has said or written something which disagrees in some way, be it only on a point of grammar, with the petty pronouncements dear to our master-doctors in theology; and is he no heretic who[39] extols as a principal part of human felicity what Christ Himself on all occasions taught us to despise; who introduces a way of life so very different from the precepts of the Gospel and the principles of the apostles; who, contrary to Christ's teaching,[40] arms the apostles, as they set out to preach the gospel, not with the sword of the Spirit which alone, by cutting away all earthly passions, can make the sword unnecessary, but with steel to defend themselves against persecution (nor is there any doubt that under the word sword he means us to understand crossbows and cannon, siege-engines and all other munitions of war); then burdens them with a wallet in which to carry their money, no doubt that they may never run short of anything, and under the word wallet wants us to understand all that pertains to equipment for this life? And he who teaches this is cited among our great theologians!

It is sacrilege beyond expiation, if someone has stolen anything from a sacred building; and is it regarded as a trifling crime to fleece poor people and widows, the living temple of God, and cheat them and oppress them? – a normal practice with princes and great nobles, and sometimes too with bishops and abbots. It is profanity to pollute a sacred edifice by fighting or by an emission of semen; and should we not load with curses a man who with soft speech and gifts and promises and flattery debauches a pure and virtuous young woman, a temple of the Holy Spirit, and corrupts and pollutes her? And he who does this is commonly spoken of as an elegant man of fashion. I am no supporter of wrongdoing, as I have said before; my point is that public opinion sets much more store by what they see for themselves than by things that are all the more real, the less they are exposed to view. The consecration of a stone-built place of worship is before your eyes: the dedication of a soul you cannot see, and so you ignore it. The ornaments of a church you fight to protect; to protect integrity of character no man draws the sword of the spirit, which Christ in the gospel tells us to acquire even at the cost of selling our last shirt. It is called the height of piety, if in order to defend or increase the power and cash-resources of the priesthood one were to take up arms and confound things sacred and profane[41] in the tumult of war. And all the time in defence of the coin in a mass-priest's pocket, surely a thing of a very small importance, what a vast cataclysm is let loose upon every sort of religion, when we let loose a war! For is there any form of evil which war does not bring in its train?

But all this time, maybe, the reader's unspoken thoughts will be protesting: 'To what purpose all this rancid stuff?'[42] he says; do you want a prince to be like what Plato[43] makes his guardians in the Republic? You strip priests of their absolute power, their dignity, their splendour and their riches: would you recall them to the wallet and staff of the apostles? Steady, steady! I strip them of nothing; I merely enrich them with things far more precious. I do not turn them out of their possessions; I challenge them to do better. Answer me this: which of us has the more exalted idea of kingly excellence? – you, who wish him to be allowed to do just as he pleases, who want him to be a despot rather than a prince, who surfeit him with pleasures, who abandon him to luxurious living, who make him the servant and bond-slave of his appetites and wish him no more sense than any random member of the crowd, who burden him with the very things which even gentiles always thought it noble to despise? Or I, who desire to see a prince as like as can be to God, whose image in some sort he bears, surpassing all other men in wisdom, which is the merit peculiar to kings, and far removed from all base desires and all distempers of the mind that carry away the common herd; I, who want him to admire nothing common, to rise above riches, to be in short in the commonwealth what the soul is in the body and God is in the universe? Which of us sets a truer valuation on the dignity of a bishop? – you, who weigh him down with worldly wealth, entangle him in mean and sordid cares, and involve him in the storms of war? – or I, who long to see a vicar of Christ and guardian of His heavenly spouse perfectly free from all earthly contagion and, as far as may be, closely similar to Him whose place and service he fulfils? The Stoics say that no man can be good except him who is free from all infections of the spirit, and they give the name of infections of the spirit to desires or feelings. Much more is it the duty of Christians to be free of them, and most of all, the duty of princes; and again, more than all others, of a prince and father of the Church, that is, the heavenly ruler of that heavenly commonwealth. I like to see a priest who reigns, but your earthly power I judge unworthy to burden a man whose business is with heaven. I like above all things to see a pope in triumph, not in these bloodstained triumphs which cursed Marius and impious Julius[44] held, so worthless that they are greeted with scurrility and satire – and had the famous Democritus[45] watched one, I think he would have died with laughter – but in triumphs genuinely magnificent and worthy of an apostle, such as Paul[46] describes, a warrior and commander far more glorious than Alexander the Great, when he says, as though singing his own praises 'In labours very many, in prisons more abundant, in blows above measure, in deaths often. From the Jews five times I received forty stripes save one, thrice was I beaten with rods, once I was stoned, thrice I suffered shipwreck, a night and a day I have been in the deep; in journeys often, in perils of rivers, in perils of robbers, in perils of my countrymen, in perils of gentiles, in perils in the city, in perils in the wilderness, in perils in the sea, in perils among false brethren, in labour and in pain, in many a sleepless night, in hunger and thirst, in fasting often, in cold and nakedness; besides those things which press upon me from without, my daily care of all the churches. Who is weak, and I am not weak? Who is offended, and I burn not?' Again a little earlier he says 'In all things showing ourselves as the ministers of God, in much patience, in afflictions, in necessities, in distresses, in scourgings, in imprisonments, in tumults, in labours, in vigils, in fastings, in purity, in knowledge, in long-suffering, in kindness, in the Holy Spirit, in love unfeigned, in the word of truth, in the power of God, by the armour[47] of righteousness on the right hand and on the left, by honour and dishonour, by evil report and good report, as deceivers and yet true, as unknown and yet well known, as dying and behold we live, as chastened and not killed, as sorrowful and yet always rejoicing, as poor yet making many rich, as having nothing and yet possessing all things.' Such are the feats of battle, the victory and the triumph proper to an apostle! This is that glory by which, as if it were something holy, Paul sometimes swears; these are the noble deeds for which he is confident there is laid up for him a crown of immortality. Those who claim for themselves the place and the authority of the apostles will find it no hardship to follow in the footsteps of the apostles.

I desire that pontiffs should be very rich – but rich with the pearl of which the gospel speaks, rich with that heavenly treasure of which they themselves will enjoy more abundance the more freely they lavish it on all men; nor will there be any risk that generosity may prove its own undoing. I would like to see them as well defended as can be – but with the armour spoken of by the Apostle: the shield of faith, the breastplate of justice, the sword of salvation which is the word of God. I would like them to be warlike – but against those true enemies of the Church: simony, pride, lust, ambition, anger, impiety. These are the Turks against whom Christians must be always watchful, always on the offensive; this is the sort of warfare in which a bishop should lead and inspire. I would like to see priests most highly respected, not for the noise and bustle of a tyrant's court but for their high standard of sacred learning and their outstanding virtues. I would like them to be revered – but for their integrity and strict way of life, not merely for their titles or their grandiose costume. I would like them to be feared – but as fathers, not as tyrants; I would like them to be feared – but only by the wicked, or rather I would like them to be the sort for whom bad men feel awe rather than fear or hate. In a word, I wish them a life full of pleasures, but rare pleasures, far more enjoyable than those known to common folk.

Would you hear what are the riches of one who is truly a Supreme Pontiff? Listen to one who is very close to the Prince of pontiffs:[48] 'Gold and silver have I none, but such as I have give I thee: in the name of Jesus rise up and walk.' Would you hear what is the glory of the name 'apostle,' which outshines all honorific titles, all statues and triumphal arches? Listen to St Paul,[49] that truly famous man: 'We are unto God a sweet savour of Christ in every place.' Would you hear of his more than royal power? 'I can do all things' he says[50] 'through Him who strengthens me.' Would you hear of his glory? 'My joy and my crown you are in the Lord.'[51] Would you hear titles worthy of a bishop, ornaments of a true pontiff? That same Paul[52] paints him for you: 'sober, accomplished, prudent, modest, given to hospitality, apt to teach, not given to wine, not violent, but humble, not quarrelsome, not greedy of filthy lucre, not a novice, having a good report of them also which are without, lest he fall into reproach and into the snare of the devil.' Consider the ornaments with which Moses decorates Aaron[53] the high priest, the wealth with which he equips him, the colours in which he paints him, the various jewels gleaming like stars with which he adorns him, the glittering gold with which he glorifies him. If you have learned the meaning of these from the interpretation of Origen and Jerome,[54] you will of course understand with what vestments bishops will be equipped who are truly great.

Whom should popes reproduce in their lives rather than those whom they reproduce on their leaden seals, whom they recall in their titles, whose office fulfil? Is it more appropriate for the vicar of Christ to model himself on the life of Julius and Alexander, of Croesus and Xerxes, great robbers all of them, than on Christ, the Church's sole general and commander-in-chief? Whom could the successors of the apostles more justly imitate than the prince of the apostles? Christ openly denied that His kingdom was of this world, and can you think it proper for Christ's successor not merely to accept an earthly rule but even to seek it as desirable, and in order to secure it to leave, as they say,[55] no stone unturned?

In this world there are, as it were, two worlds, which fight against each other in every way, one gross and corporeal, the other heavenly and already practising with all its might to become what it one day will be. In one of these, first place is taken by him who is as far as possible removed from what is truly good and burdened with what is falsely so called. A pagan king, for instance, who outdoes all men in lust and luxury, in violence, in pride and pomp, in riches and rapacity, and is accounted first only if the greatest share of this filth has flooded down to him, and as little as can be in the way of wisdom, temperance, self-control, justice, and the other qualities that are truly good. With him who is the greatest it is the opposite: he is the least contaminated by those gross plebeian blessings, and at the same time most richly blessed with those true and heavenly sources of wealth. Why therefore do you wish a Christian prince to be what pagan philosophers too have always condemned and despised? Why locate his majesty in those very attributes which it is most honourable to despise? Why load an angel of God – for so a bishop is called in Holy Scripture – with these burdens, which are unworthy even of a good man? Why estimate him by the wealth which makes robbers rich and tyrants formidable? There is something heavenly about a priest, something more than human; nothing is worthy of his exalted position except what is heavenly. Why do you degrade his dignity with common things? Why stain his purity with this world's dirt? Why not let him be strong with the power that is really his? Why not allow him to be powerful with his own authority, exalted in his own glory, venerable in his own majesty, rich in his own wealth? This is the man chosen out of the heavenly body, which is the Church, by that heavenly Spirit for appointment to the highest place. Why do you drag him down into the raging rivalries of rajahs? Paul boasts that he has been 'separated':[56] Why do you plunge my prelate deep in the filth of the lowest rabble? Why degrade him to the anxieties of usurers? Why drag down a man touched with divinity to business barely worthy of a man? Why measure the felicity of Christian priests by these of all things, at which Democritus[57] laughed for their foolishness and Heraclitus wept because they were so pitiable, which Diogenes[58] scorned as frivolous and Crates threw away as burdensome, while saints have always fled from them as pestilential? Why gauge the value of Peter's successors by the wealth which Peter himself boasts that he does not possess? Why wish that princes who follow the apostles should show their greatness by those trappings which the apostles trod under foot, and thus showed how great they were? Why call something 'the patrimony of St Peter' which Peter himself boasted that he did not possess? Why do you think the vicars of Christ should be ensnared in riches which Christ Himself called thorns? Why do you overwhelm him whose proper and principal duty is to scatter the seed of the divine word, with wealth, which is the best thing there is with which to stifle the seed he sows? Why do you wish the teacher of equity and the judge to be enslaved to the mammon of injustice? Why do you make the dispenser of heavenly mysteries into a steward of all that is most worthless? The Christian world looks to him for its food of sacred learning, it looks for the counsel that leads to salvation, for fatherly consolation, for a pattern by which to live. Why thrust one destined and dedicated to such noble purposes into a prison-cell of vulgar cares, at one stroke robbing a bishop of his proper dignity and leaving the people fatherless without a bishop?

Christ has His own kingdom, and it is too fine a thing to deserve pollution by a gentile kingdom or, to speak more accurately, tyranny; He has His majesty, His wealth, His pleasures. Why do we mingle things that are so much at war with one another? Why do we confound earthly with heavenly, lowest with highest, pagan with Christian, profane with sacred? So many and so great are the gifts of that at once most rich and most generous spirit, gifts of tongues, of prophecy, of healing, of knowledge, of wisdom, of learning, 'the discerning of spirits,'[59] exhortation, consolation: these sacred endowments why do you associate (I will not say annihilate) with the profane world's gifts? Why try to join Christ and Mammon, and the spirit of Christ with Belial?[60] What has a mitre in common with a helmet, a sacred vestment with a soldier's breastplate, consecrations with a cannon, a merciful shepherd with armed robbers, priest's orders and order of battle? How does he come to overthrow towns with siege-engines, who holds the keys of the kingdom of heaven? How can it be proper for him to start a war who greets the people with words fraught with peace? How can he have the face to teach ordinary Christians that wealth is a thing to be despised who grounds his position, stem to stern,[61] in money? How can he have the effrontery to teach what Christ taught by precept and example, and what is so often stressed by the apostles, that we must not resist evil but must overcome the wickedness of evil men with goodness, repay an injury with kindness, and overwhelm an enemy with good deeds - how can he teach this who, to secure the lordship of some poor town or the revenue from salt, upheaves a world with the hurricane of war? How can he be a leader towards the kingdom of heaven (for so Christ describes His Church) who is wholly absorbed in the kingdom of this world?

But suppose you are highly pious, and wish to make the Church more glorious by adding all this to her other riches: I would approve, did not this programme bring with it, together with small advantages, such a mass of evils. When you gave him absolute rule, you gave him at the same time all the troubles of accumulating wealth, a tyrant's bodyguard, troops in full armour, scouts, horses, mules, trumpets, warfare and carnage, triumph and tumult, treaties and battles – in a word, all the things without which absolute rule cannot be exercised. Granted that he has the spirit to act, when will a man have the leisure to perform his apostolic office who is pulled in different directions by all those thousand cares? There are troops to be mustered, treaties to be drawn up and torn up, pressure to be applied to those reluctant to obey while those on the lookout for changes are retained in their allegiance, enemies to be driven out, fortresses to be strengthened, plans to be given a hearing, secular envoys to be treated with, foreign potentates to be entertained at dinner, friends to be promoted to high office while those ordered to give place to the more fortunate are put out of the way – all this, and other things happen which I do not choose to mention, and yet happen they must. Does that man seem to you to understand the dignity of pope and cardinals who thinks they should be degraded to this mass of filth from prayer, in which they converse with God; from holy contemplation, in which they enjoy the society of angels; from the flowery meadows of Holy Scripture, in which they wander blissfully; from the apostolic office of preaching the gospel, in which above all they resemble Christ? Does he seem to you to wish them well who would like to divert them from such great felicity and the peace of life they once enjoyed to this hard labour and this state of turmoil?

For a kingdom by its own nature demands infinite exertions, and at the same time is far less successful in the hands of priests than of laymen; and for this there are perhaps two reasons. For one thing, the common mass of people are more ready in this field to obey secular rulers than ecclesiastics, partly because laymen, expecting as they do to bequeath the kingdom to their children, do their best to make it flourish, while clerics on the other hand are called to rule late in life and usually when old men already, and so, ruling as they do for their own benefit and not for an heir, plunder their charge rather than enrich it, just as if it were a windfall that had come their way rather than a responsibility. Besides which, a secular ruler, when he comes to power, has perhaps only one struggle for his kingdom, one stage of promoting and enriching his princely favourites; but in the other case, there is a fresh struggle from time to time, as those whom he had previously promoted are turned out of their places, and then a succession of new men have to be enriched at the public expense. And another point is not without importance: the people bear much more readily the rule of a man to whom they have become accustomed, even though he is more severe and, though he dies, he seems to survive in the son who succeeds him, and the common folk imagine that they have not changed their prince for another, but acquired a new version of the old. It is normal too for children to reproduce in some way the character of their parents, especially if trained by them. On the contrary, when absolute rule is entrusted to clerics dedicated to God's service, there is usually a sudden change in all respects. Add to this that your lay ruler comes to the seat of power after some thought, and an education that started in his cradle. Supreme power often falls to the other man contrary to all expectation, so that it is a man born by nature to tug at the oar who is exalted by a freak of fortune to the throne. Last but not least, it can hardly happen, as with Hercules[62] and his two monsters, that one man should be capable of administration in two very difficult fields. To play the part of a good prince is of all things most difficult; but it is far finer, and at the same time far more difficult, to be a good priest. And what, pray, of both at once? Is it not inevitable that those who accept both tasks do justice to neither? And in this way, of course, it comes about, if I am not mistaken, that while we see the cities of secular kings go from strength to strength in riches, buildings, and manpower, the towns of priests are chill and crumbling.

What then was the need of these additions, which bring such great drawbacks in their train? Are you afraid that Christ with His own resources will have too little power, unless some secular tyrant gives him a share of his own force? Do you think he will look dowdy unless some worldly warrior allows him to share the gold brocade, the white carriage-horses and the bodyguard – infects him, in other words, with a touch of his own pomp? Is his glory inadequate unless he is allowed to flaunt the insignia which Julius,[63] that most ambitious of men, rejected for fear of their unpopularity? Do you reckon him of no account unless he is burdened with secular powers which, if used for his own benefit, will make him a tyrant, and if for the public good, will load him with overwork? Leave worldly things to men of this world; in a bishop what is lowest surpasses the summit of a whole empire. The more you add of the good things of this world, the less will Christ give him of His own good things. The more completely he is purged of the one, the more lavishly will he be enriched with the other.

You can see, I imagine, how wholly different the outcome is if you turn your Silenus inside out. Those who seemed the greatest supporters of a Christian prince you find to be the prince's greatest betrayers and enemies. You understand that those whom you would have called pillars of the papal dignity in fact defile it. Not that I would say this because I think priests should be stripped of anything that has come to them by any channel in the way of power or wealth, for no devout man ought to approve of revolution; but I want them to be aware and mindful of their greatness within limits: these plebeian, not to say pagan, distinctions they should either reject of their own accord and abandon to their inferiors, or, while retaining, should at least despise them and in Paul's words[64] 'so have them as though they had them not.' In a word, I wish them to be so adorned with the riches of Christ that whatever else they have acquired out of the glory of this world will be put in the shade by the light of better things, or even seen to be sordid in comparison with them. The result will be to make them happier, because less anxious, in the possession of it; for they will not be tormented by fear that someone will snatch it from them, nor will they suffer the great tumult of fighting for transitory and worthless things, if they lose any part of it. Last but not least, they will not be deprived of blessings that are theirs, in exchange for the joy of growing rich on those that belong to others, nor will they lose the gospel pearl while they pursue the glassy jewels of the world, to say nothing for the moment of the fact that the very things which I wish them to despise will come to them in greater measure if they have been despised, and will bring greater honour if they follow those who avoid them than if seized by those who pursue them. How indeed did the Church's wealth begin if not from contempt of wealth? Whence came its glory if not from giving glory no thought? The laity will be more ready to give these things, if they see them rejected by those whom they think wiser than themselves.

Sometimes perhaps we should endure even wicked princes; some respect should be paid to the memory of those whose places they are seen to occupy and some concession made to the title they bear. We should not attempt a remedy which, if unskilfully attempted, may well prove, I suspect, a greater disaster. But in what poor state all this time are human affairs, if those whose whole life ought to be a public marvel are such that the worst of men applaud and the good sigh and groan, men whose high position is entirely owed to the support of the wicked, the cowardice of men in middle station, or the inexperience of simple folk, or rather, who are made impregnable by public failure to agree, who are made great solely by civic disputes, and whose felicity is fed by the infelicity of the people at large.

If priests in setting a value on things would only follow a right course, the acquisition of a secular jurisdiction brings with it such great drawbacks that it should be refused even when freely offered. They become slaves of princes and of the Court, they are the targets of sedition, they are involved in wars in which from time to time they breathe their last; the result, in short, is that monarchs have honourable men in their service, but where all this time are the fathers of a Christian people? Where are the shepherds? And what are we to make of the way abbots and bishops buy titles of this kind from monarchs for large sums? An abbot does not seem respectable unless he is also a count; a man is thought to have added to the dignity of the priesthood if he has added the title of duke by purchase. Fine pairing of words, these – abbot and satrap, bishop and warrior! And yet it is much more absurd that in this department they should play heroic parts, and in the field which was their proper sphere of action they are mere shadows. They have hands and swords with which to kill men's bodies (only let this be in the cause of justice), and at the same time have no tongue with which to heal the spirit. An abbot knows how to draw up a line of battle, and is ignorant of the way to lead men to religion; a bishop is well enough informed how to conduct an engagement with arms and cannon, but when it comes to teaching, exhortation, consolation he is speechless. Well-armed with javelins and catapults, he finds no sort of weapon in the Holy Scriptures; and yet all the time whatever in the way of recompense or reward is owed to pious abbots or to saintly bishops is exacted by them to the nearest penny from their underlings – indeed, not so much what is owed to them as what they choose to ask. The Lord will reward the patience of His people, who endure such masters from a love of peace, but I fear that for this very reason those masters will find God a harsher judge. All this turmoil in the world, what other message has it for us, loud and clear, except that God is angry with us all? And what remains except for all of us, alike the greatest and the least, both sacred and secular, with humble hearts to take refuge in the Lord's mercy? How much wiser this would be than for each of us, not recognizing his own fault, to put the blame on others, thus provoking still more the anger of the Deity, and not healing but making still more severe the wounds we have ourselves inflicted on one another! The people are resentful against their princes, the princes have no mercy on things secular or sacred, the mob fart in the face of priests.[65] And yet it happens not seldom that God, losing patience with His people's crimes, sends them rulers of the kind that they deserve. Up to now, with our complaints, our cruelty, our quarrelling, our turmoil, we have got nowhere; all that remains is a communal act of confession by us all, that God may have His mercy in readiness.

But whither has the flood of my language carried me away, so that I, who profess myself a mere compiler of proverbs, begin to be a preacher? Of course it was Alcibiades in his cups, and his Sileni, that drew me into this very sober disputation. But I shall not be over-penitent for this error if what does not belong to an exposition of proverbs does belong to the amendment of life, if what does not contribute to learning contributes to religion, and if what in the light of the task I have undertaken may seem a sideline and 'nothing to do with Dionysus'[66] may prove not ill-adapted in the light of the life we have to live.

1 Actually the proverb does not appear in any of the collections. Reference to it is found in a letter of 1485 by Giovanni Pico della Mirandola to Ermolao Barbaro (first noted by Dr Silvana Seidel Menchi in her *Adagia: sei saggi politici* [Turin 1980]).

2 I ix 88
3 5.188d
4 Xenophon *Symposium* 4.19
5 Plato *Symposium* 215a
6 I ix 89
7 The ancient rhetorician, at the beginning of Plato's *Gorgias*, claims there is no question he cannot answer.
8 Plato *Apology* 21 (proverbial as in Tilley N 276 'I know nothing except that I know not')
9 Plato *Phaedo* 118a
10 A pupil of Socrates, one of the founders of the Cynic school (see Diogenes Laertius 6.1–19); the staff, satchel, and cloak are traditional signs of the beggar.
11 Most famous of the Cynics, flourished in fourth century BC (Diogenes Laertius 6.20–81); he was called 'dog' or *kunos* by his contemporaries and thus the name of the philosophical school.
12 Diogenes Laertius 6.32
13 The famous Stoic philosopher of the first century AD
14 Isaiah 53:2–4
15 The five-million-man army of Xerxes is described in Herodotus 7.186.
16 The mythical wealth of Croesus was proverbial: I vi 74.
17 Hebrews 11:38
18 Matthew 3:4
19 Matthew 11:11
20 Matthew 13:31
21 I x 45
22 St Martin of Tours, described as being dishevelled and quite unprepossessing to those bishops called upon to elect him as one of their own, in the life by Sulpicius Severus 9.3 (ASD II–5, 167n)
23 Worn by university professors as part of their academic regalia
24 The great medieval scholastic Duns Scotus (c 1266–1308), in Erasmus' time still an important figure in academic philosophy
25 The braggart in Terence's *Eunuchus*
26 Ie, angels
27 *Commentarii in epistolam ad Philemonem* (*PL* 26.645)
28 I iii 26
29 I ii 37
30 Very holy Egyptian hermits
31 Homer *Odyssey* 10
32 *Politics* 7.1 (1323a40); *Rhetoric* 1.5 (1360b5ff); cf Cicero *De finibus* 4.18.49.
33 Horace *Epistles* 1.1.46
34 II viii 33 and IV iii 21 (Brutus led a mythical expedition to England after the fall of Troy)
35 1 Thessalonians 5:23, Galatians 5:17
36 II i 79
37 Luke 22:24
38 Romans 2:24
39 Nicholas of Lyra, the scholastic philosopher, so named in the text of 1515, though the name was removed in a revision of 1523
40 Compare Luke 22:35ff.
41 I iii 82
42 Horace *Satires* 2.7.21
43 *Republic* 5.473d, 6.502ff
44 Marius, the Roman general, celebrated three triumphs; Julius Caesar celebrated a fourfold

triumph in 46 BC; the 'pope in triumph' is Julius II, whose entry into Rome Erasmus witnessed in 1507.
45 Traditionally, the 'laughing philosopher' (see below, note 57)
46 2 Corinthians 11:23–9, 6:4–10; cf 2 Timothy 4:8.
47 Ephesians 6:14–17
48 Acts 3:6
49 2 Corinthians 2:15
50 Philippians 4:13
51 Philippians 4:1
52 1 Timothy 3:2-3, 6–7
53 Exodus 28, Leviticus 8:7–9, 16:4
54 Origen *Homilies on Exodus* 13.2; Jerome *Letters* 53.8
55 I iv 30
56 Romans 1:1
57 The contrast between Democritus, the laughing philosopher, and Heraclitus, the weeping philosopher, was almost proverbial (cf Juvenal 10.28ff).
58 Two Cynic philosophers
59 1 Corinthians 12:8
60 Cf 2 Corinthians 6:15.
61 I i 8
62 I v 39
63 Julius Caesar refused a crown (Suetonius 'Julius Caesar' 79.2 in *Lives*).
64 1 Corinthians 7:29
65 II vii 76* 'To fart in someone's face'
66 II iv 57

III iii 38
Domus amica, domus optima / A loved home is the best home

Our modern 'home, sweet home' is a partial equivalent to the proverb described here, though the closest English version in Erasmus' time was 'Home is home, be it never so homely' (Tilley H 534). The sentiment is found in many languages (Tosi 1047). Erasmus examines the legal and moral aspects of the proverb, but the story of the tortoise gets the analysis started.

Οἶκος φίλος οἶκος ἄριστος, A loved home is always the best home. Nowhere can a lucky man live in more convenience, more freedom, and more comfort than at home. Some people[1] with humorous distortion apply this to the tortoise, of which the following tale[2] is told. Jupiter once invited animals of all kinds to attend his wedding, and all the others came, but not the tortoise. He was much surprised, and when she turned up (which was not until the feast was over), he asked her what the reason was of this delay. And she replied 'A loved home is the best home.' Jupiter was angry, and gave orders that wherever she went in future, she should carry her home about with her. Hence the tortoise is described by Cicero[3] in the second book of his *On Divination*, with deliberate and humorous obscurity, as 'Earth's tardigrade, home-carrying, bloodless creature.' (For we must, I take it, read *terrae*, earth's, for *terrigenam*, earth-born.)

Besides which, the privacy of home has the support of the civil law. Thus Gaius[4] in the *Pandects*, book 4, title *De in jus vocando*: 'It has been commonly held that no man may be summoned to court from his own home, because each man's home is his safest refuge and place of resort, and he therefore who should summon him to court from his home was thought to commit a violent assault.' Similarly Paulus in book I, title *De regulis juris*. Cicero[5] alludes to the fable in one of his letters, writing to Dolabella: 'This place is pretty, or at any rate remote, and if you have something to write, free from interruption. But somehow "a loved home," you know; and so my feet are all set to carry me to my house at Tusculum.' This corresponds with one I have placed elsewhere:[6] 'He for whom all goes well should stay at home,' for to him alone a loved home is the best home. Otherwise, to the man whose home contains a quarrelsome wife and nothing to eat, home is a prison. On the other hand, Plutarch[7] has a word for this idle sort of man who is happy indoors and in the shade, and loves to be always sitting motionless at home. He calls them *oikouroi*, home-keepers. And in his essay 'On Tranquillity of Mind' he disapproves of this stay-at-home lack of activity. Again in his 'Advice to Bride and Groom' he records that Phidias made a statue of Venus for the people of Elis with her foot on a tortoise, as a tacit suggestion that wives should stay at home and hold their peace. Plutarch also tells of a custom in Egypt that newly wedded wives should not wear sandals, to prevent them of course from ever leaving the house. All the same, this ideal would have little chance of acceptance by our own countrywomen, as they flit busily round all the markets and all the wine-shops and everywhere on earth by land or sea.

This seems the place to add a remark recorded by Plutarch in his life of Titus Flaminius. When seeking to persuade the Achaeans that they should not lay claim to the island of Zacynthos, 'They would' he said 'run risks like tortoises, if they struck their heads out beyond the Peloponnese.' Livy[8] has something very like this in book six of his *Macedonian War*, where Quinctius speaks as follows: 'If I thought that the possession of that island was of any value to the Achaeans, I would recommend the Roman government to let you have it. But I have my eye on the tortoise: gathered into its shell, it is safe from all attacks, but when it puts out any part of itself, whatever it exposes is at risk and defenceless. It is much the same with you Achaeans: you are enclosed on all sides by the bounds of the sea, and what lies within the Peloponnese, you can add to your own, and easily defend what you have added; but if once you exceed these limits in your greed for further acquisitions, all your overseas possessions are naked and exposed to all attacks.'

1 Collection of proverbs ascribed to Plutarch (ASD II-5, 209:53n), *Prov Alex* 11, Crusius p 9 (this form also in Apostolius 12.39)
2 Aesop ed Halm no 154
3 *On Divination* 2.64.133 (also in Athenaeus 2.63b)
4 Justinian *Digest* 2.4.18, to Paulus, 2.4.21 and 50.17.103
5 *Letters to Atticus* 15.16A (not a letter to Dolabella)
6 II i 13
7 *Moralia* 776E, 792B, 465–6 ('Tranquillity of Mind'), 142D and C ('Advice'), 'Titus Flaminius' 17.2 in *Lives*
8 36.32.5–7

III iii 41
In occipitio oculos gerit / He has eyes in the back of his head

Widely circulated in sixteenth- and seventeenth-century English (Tilley E 236 *'He has an eye behind';* ODEP 235*), this is still a very common proverb in English and other languages (Tosi 1572). As with many proverbs in this section of the* Adages, *Erasmus found it in Apostolius (12.94); see also Otto 1263.*

Ὄπισθεν κεφαλῆς ὄμματα ἔχει, He has eyes in the back of his head. Used of cunning and wary people, and those whom it is by no means easy to deceive. Men of this sort are called by Persius[1] Januses: 'What a Janus you are! No stork can peck you from behind.' And Homer[2]

The big fish eat the little fish Erasmus alludes to this proverb in his essay on 'A serpent, unless it devours a serpent, will not become a dragon' (III iii 61*). The engraving (made in 1557) is based on a drawing by Pieter Bruegel the Elder, whose famous 1559 painting *Netherlandish Proverbs* (at Berlin) depicts scores of proverbs, a small number of which may have come from the *Adages*. (Harris Brisbane Dick Fund, Metropolitan Museum of Art, New York)

demands of a prince that he should have eyes 'both before and behind.' Plautus[3] in the *Aulularia*: 'She has eyes in the back of her head as well.'

1 1.58 (Janus being the god of two faces)
2 *Iliad* 1.343
3 *Aulularia* 64

III iii 61
Serpens ni edat serpentem, draco non fiet / A serpent, unless it devours a serpent, will not become a dragon

Erasmus picked this up from Apostolius 13.79. In a curious turn, the little proverb swallowed up inside this proverb essay became the better known one – 'The great fish eat the small' appeared in English (Tilley F 311*) as early as 1509, though Erasmus' version also made it into English (Tilley* S 228*). Aristotle made the observation about big fish devouring smaller ones in his* History of Animals *8.2 (591b16) and there is a very dramatic illustration of that proverb by Pieter Bruegel the Elder (see accompanying figure).*

Ὄφις ἢν μὴ φάγῃ ὄφιν, δράκων οὐ γενήσεται, A serpent, unless it devours a serpent, will not become a dragon. The powerful grow at the expense of others, and the fortunes of the nobility would not increase as they do, had they no victims whom they can suck dry. Just so, among fish and beasts, the larger live by butchering the smaller. Though in my opinion this is another saying that smells of the dregs of the population.

III iii 63
Phallus deo / A phallus for the god

The proverb appears in the standard Greek sources (Apostolius 13.81, Diogenianus 7.22; see also Suringar 169). The adage referred to at the end, II vi 47 *'A chickpea Bacchus' means something contemptible, a kind of beer made from the chickpea or other legume; at the end of that adage Erasmus has further citations on the carrying of the phallus in ancient processions. In some of these processions small flowers were hung as a comic gesture 'to represent the male organ,' and this comic reference to a diminutive organ may yield another sense of the expression 'chickpea Bacchus.' The adage discussed here never made it into English, perhaps because it relies too much on a knowledge of the pagan ritual.*

Ὁ φαλλὸς τῷ θεῷ, A phallus for the god. Used by custom when something is paid by way of tribute which is not very respectable but highly apt, like saying[1] 'to make water in a chamber-pot.' Plutarch[2] in his essay 'On Love of Wealth' makes it clear that in ancient times a procession at the solemn games went as follows. In the first place was carried an amphora of wine and a clematis (which is a kind of bean); next, a goat was led by somebody, and then another man carried a basket of nuts; in the last place was borne the *phallus*. This was a representation of the male sexual organ, and the reason why it was incorporated in the mysteries is given by Plutarch[3] in his 'On Isis and Osiris.' Columella[4] in the book he wrote in verse calls Priapus himself Ithyphallus: 'But in the rough-hewn trunk of some old tree / Venerate Ithyphallus' deity.' And Pompeius makes it clear that Ithyphallus is a name for the male sexual organ. Hence it is that even in our own day the Italians use that word to show disapproval of someone they despise. Something on the phallus will also be found in the second book of Herodotus.[5] I have spoken elsewhere[6] of the phallus as belonging to Bacchus – on the proverb A chickpea Bacchus.

1 I v 68
2 *Moralia* 527D
3 'Isis and Osiris' in *Moralia* 365B
4 Columella 10.31–2 (the commentary is that of Pomponio Leto, an Italian humanist scholar)
5 2.48
6 II vi 47

III iv 1
Chamaeleonte mutabilior / As changeable as a chameleon

This essay was modified a number of times by Erasmus from 1508 onwards. He began with the proverb from Apostolius 18.9 (Latin versions *are in Otto 381 and Tosi 564). He did not expand the essay further, even though it concerns the theme of transformation, to which he returned often in the* Adages *(see headnote to I i 93* 'Adopt the outlook of the polyp'). It appears in English as Tilley C 221 'As changeable as a chameleon' and C 222 'The chameleon can change to all colours save white.'*

Χαμαιλέοντος εὐμεταβολώτερος, As changeable as a chameleon. The chameleon is recorded among animals which change their colour. Aristotle[1] describes its appearance carefully in the second book of his *Historia animalium.* As far as the changing of colour is concerned, he reports as follows: 'Its colour changes when it is breathed on. This becomes at one time black, not unlike that of crocodiles, at another pale, like that of lizards, at yet another a spotted black such as that of leopards. This sort of change of colour occurs over the whole body. Even the eyes and tail end up becoming the same colour as the rest of the body. This animal's movement is sluggish, very much like that of the tortoise. It turns pale when it is dying. This same colour persists after death.' That is what Aristotle has to say. Quite compatible with these remarks is what Pliny[2] reports, in book 8 chapter 33, with the addition that this animal imitates with its whole body whatever colour it is near, except red and white. The adage therefore can be applied to the man who is a dissembler,[3] or who is inconstant and adopts any appearance to suit the time. Plato[4] says in the *Ion*: 'But you change into every possible shape, absolutely like Proteus, as you twist back and forth.' In the first book of the *Nicomachean Ethics,* Aristotle[5] uses the word 'chameleon' to describe the vice of inconstancy.

1 *History of Animals* 2.11 (503a–b)

2 Pliny *Natural History* 8.33.121–2

3 Latin *versipellis* means 'one who changes his skin,' sometimes a werewolf.

4 *Ion* 541e (added in 1523 to *Adages* II ii 74 'As many shapes as Proteus')

5 *Nicomachean Ethics* 1.10.8 (1100b6), though Aristotle actually said that we should have to suppose the happy man to be a sort of chameleon, if the definition of happiness depends on fortune

III iv 2
Suus cuique crepitus bene olet / Everyone thinks his own fart smells sweet

Apostolius 6.98 calls the proverb 'vulgar,' yet it moved into other languages, including English (Tilley F *65). Erasmus comments shrewdly that the proverb is probably not true, except in a comparative sense – a reflection that could be made about many proverbs. He makes further comments on the subject in* III *vii 1* 'A dung-beetle hunting an eagle' – 'As a matter of fact man is peculiar in that he finds the smell of his own excrement offensive' (note 131).*

Ἕκαστος αὑτοῦ τὸ βδέμα μῆλον γλύκιον ἡγεῖται. Everyone thinks his own fart smells as sweet as apples; there is no one, in other words, to whom his own faults do not seem to be his best qualities. Aristotle[1] in the ninth book of the *Nicomachean Ethics*: 'For most things are not valued at the same price by those who possess them and by those who wish to acquire them. For to everyone his own goods, and what he gives, seem to be of great value.' This passage was better suited to the proverb[2] What is one's own is beautiful, but that page had already passed out of my hands. I suspect this proverb about the fart was drawn by Apostolius[3] from the dregs of the common people, for I have never yet heard of anyone to whom his own fart smelt sweet. It is true that men shrink from other men's excrement and farts more violently than from their own.

1 *Nicomachean Ethics* 9.1 (1164b16)
2 I ii 15
3 6.98

III iv 14
Tolle digitum / Lift a finger

For us, to 'lift a finger' is an idiomatic phrase, not quite a proverb, and has quite a different meaning from what Erasmus gives here. Though it is listed as a Greek proverb in the old sources (Apostolius 1.75, Suidas AI *281), Otto 554 believes the Greek form is derived from the Latin. For other physical gestures, see* I *viii 46* 'Thumbs down, thumbs up' and* II *iv 68* 'To show the middle finger.'*

Αἶρε δάκτυλον, Raise your finger, means Confess yourself beaten, for this was the signal by which the man who had been worsted in a contest admitted his defeat. Persius[1] in his fifth satire: 'Has reason made no concessions in your favour? Lift a finger: you're wrong.' Related to one of which I have spoken in another place,[2] To proffer grass. Saint Jerome,[3] if I am not mistaken, had this in mind in his *Dialogue between a Luciferian and an Orthodox Christian*, when he says 'See, I put my hand up, I give in, you've won.' Athenaeus[4] in book 6 quotes these lines from Antiphanes on tragic poets:

> When they can think of nothing more to say
> And are quite stuck in working out the plot,
> Up goes the machine, not the finger!

It seems to have been used in somewhat different sense by Cicero[5] in the sixth book of the Verrines: 'But the guardians come running to the rescue; Junius his uncle raises his finger.' For here it seems to be a gesture of approval, or of someone who indicates that he is buying or leasing something, since in the old days this was also the way of giving one's vote or expressing readiness to buy or lease a lot in auction.

1 5.119
2 I ix 78
3 *Dialogus contra Luciferianos* 14.5 (*PL* 23.168B)
4 6.222b, quoting a fragment from Antiphanes (fr 191, 14–16), for which see also I i 68* 'God from the machine'
5 *Second Verrine* 1.141

III iv 96
Inter caecos, regnat strabus / Among the blind, the cross-eyed man is king

The proverb came into English in the sixteenth century in the form 'In the kingdom of the blind, the one-eyed man is king' (Tilley E *240;* ODEP *428),*

and that it is how it is found in other European languages. Erasmus picked up an uncorrected form of the Greek from Apostolius 7.23 (see also Tosi 978).

Ἐν τοῖς τόποις τῶν τυφλῶν λάμων βασιλεύει. In the country of the blind the one-eyed man is king. Among the uneducated, the one who is half-educated is considered very learned. Among beggars, the one who has a few pennies is a Croesus. The proverb smacks of the common dregs.

III v 95
Scindere glaciem / To break the ice

Erasmus included this one in his Collectanea *(no 374); there he gave his source as Francesco Filelfo, the Italian humanist (probably* Epistulae *12.45 which has* glaciem fregi, *I have broken the ice). Unlike almost all his other adages, this expression is not found in classical literature, though it is now common in English (Tilley I 3 and* ODEP *83), often with reference to relations with others, especially strangers.*

To break the ice, is to open the way and to be the first in beginning a task. A figure derived from boatmen who send one of their number ahead to break up the ice on a frozen river and open the way for the others.

III vi 17
Post bellum auxilium / Help when the war is over

A remedy that comes after the event is expressed by the English proverb 'to close the barn door after the horse has gone' or, in its sixteenth-century form, 'to shut the stable door after the steed is stolen' (Tilley S 838). Erasmus has another analogy in I i 28 'The Phrygians learn wisdom too late.'

Μετὰ τὸν πόλεμον ἡ συμμαχία, Support when the war is over. Whenever a remedy comes too late. It is recorded by Suidas.[1] It originated with, or at least was used by Diogenes the Cynic. Laertius[2] tells a story about

him like this: A young man was being rather boastful about the wife he had recently taken and put the following inscription on his house: 'The son of Jupiter, victorious Hercules, / lives here. Here let no evil enter.' Diogenes wrote after this: 'Help when the war is over' meaning, that is, that evil had already been received into the house, when the man, evil himself, moved in. It belongs with that expression of Plato which I have recorded elsewhere:[3] 'To arrive after the war is over.' Brutus[4] in the letter to the Lycians: 'Your machines have been brought in, as the proverb has it, when the war is over.' Likewise in the letter to the Myrians:[5] 'For delay in war is the same as doing nothing at all; what is done late is done in vain.' In his 'Declamation on Feeding a Dead Body' Quintilian[6] has two phrases rather like this proverb: 'Is not medicine for the dead too late? Does anyone pour water onto ashes?' This is how he denotes a remedy that comes too late; since for the mortally sick a doctor comes too late. And it is too late to pour water on a building reduced to ashes.

1 Suidas M 739
2 6.50, added in 1526 as well to II ix 52, where Erasmus appears to confuse the two Diogenes, and a similar anecdote 6.39, added in 1526 to III iii 60
3 *Adages* II ix 52 'That's the way to take part in a battle, when it's all over.' A reference to the opening line of Plato *Gorgias* 447a
4 *Epistulae* 23 (*Epistolographi graeci* ed Hercher p 181); cf *Adages* III i 17.
5 *Epistulae* 45 (*Epistolographi graeci* 185)
6 *Declamationes* 12.23

III vi 19
Piscem natare doces / You are teaching a fish to swim

Erasmus found this proverb in Diogenianus 5.33 (it is also Apostolius 9.19 and Suidas I *780). A parallel first appeared in* Collectanea *as 'You teach an eagle to fly' (no 499). The similar 'You are teaching a dolphin to swim' is* Adages *I iv 97. The English is Tilley* F *323.*

Ἰχθὺν νήχεσθαι διδάσκεις, You are teaching a fish to swim. This is just as if you were to say 'You are teaching the learned.' Very close to one

we have recorded elsewhere: 'You are teaching a dolphin to swim.' Which is also expressed thus: 'You are giving advice to a dolphin on how to swim.' The authority is Diogenianus.

III vi 79
Anguillas captare / To hunt eels

Erasmus' source is really Suidas E *174 from a set of ancient notes (or scholia) on Aristophanes* Knights *865 (Tosi 236). The reference to 'certain princes,' added in 1517, follows the kind of political commentary also found in* III *iii 1* 'Sileni of Alcibiades,'* I *ix 12* 'To exact tribute from the dead,' and* III *vii 1* 'A dung-beetle hunting an eagle.' See also* I *iv 95* 'You are holding an eel in a fig-leaf.'*

Ἐγχέλεις θηρᾶσθαι. People are said 'To hunt eels' when they stir up trouble for the sake of a private advantage. The metaphor arises from the fact that those who hunt eels catch nothing if the water remains still, only when they stir the water up and down and thoroughly muddy it do they catch them. It will be suitable for those for whom there is no profit when the nation is in a peaceful state. Therefore they are glad if rebellions arise whereby they can turn the state's public disaster to their private advantage. The proverb is found in Aristophanes' *Knights*:

> For your case is like those who hunt for eels.
> When the fen remains still, they come away with no fish,
> but if they stir the mud up and down,
> they make catches; thus you yourself make catches when you make public trouble.

This art, alas, is understood only too well by certain princes who because of their desire for power sow discord between states or stir up war on some pretext so that they can more freely tax the wretched common people and satisfy their greed by starving absolutely innocent citizens.

III vi 85
Dictum ac factum / Said and done

This is a virtual repeat of a proverb already discussed, though the essay moves in a different direction. It first appeared in Collectanea *no 559. See the note at* II *ix 72*.*

Ῥεχθὲν καὶ πραχθέν, Said and done. A proverbial figure which signifies that nothing has been omitted in taking care of an affair. Terence:[1] 'I have carried it out, said and done.' (Donatus,[2] in his commentary on the *Andria* asserts this is a proverb for speed: 'He will have found some cause, no sooner said than done.' Again in the *Self-Tormentor*: 'Clitipho went in there, no sooner said than done.'[3]) And how familiar is this figure of speech in the Greek poets:[4] 'Neither said nor done,' for what is in no way true. In the *Iliad* book 1 Homer[5] has: 'Neither a good word nor a deed has ever come from you.' Euripides[6] in the *Hecuba*: 'As for you, do not stand in my way / Either by word or by deed.' In the opposite sense, those who are skilful and energetic in every respect are said to be strong 'in words and deeds.' According to Homer[7] Phoenix taught Achilles thus: 'To be both a speaker of words and a doer of deeds.' Likewise Pindar[8] in the first *Nemean Ode*: 'But your character has the use of one and the other.' This was preceded by: 'For strength displays itself in action, but intelligence in counsel.'

1 *Heautontimorumenos* 760 and 904. Erasmus translated the Latin back into Greek and incorrectly put *rhechthen* (done) instead of *rhêthen* or *rhethen* (said) (ASD).

2 Donatus, the ancient commentator, on Terence *Andria* 381, ed Wessner (Teubner) I, 139

3 Although the Latin in all these cases is 'dictum ac factum,' they would seem to be more appropriate examples for *Adages* II ix 72*.

4 'No sooner said than done'; cf *Odyssey* 15.375

5 *Iliad* 1.108

6 *Hecuba* 372–3

7 *Iliad* 9.443; trans A.T. Murray

8 *Nemean Odes* 1.29–30 and 1.26–7

III vii 1
Scarabaeus aquilam quaerit / A dung-beetle hunting an eagle

This is one of the famous long essays against war. For these, see the introduction to IV i 1. Erasmus first wrote about the proverb in* Collectanea *no 581. It appeared in his Greek sources, Diogenianus 2.44 and Zenobius 1.20, and was a well-known fable in Aesop (no 3). Erasmus expanded the note into some thirty lines in 1508, though the real expansion took place in the edition of 1515. The subject of the essay fits into his more general program of the education of the Christian prince. The essay might be interpreted as a plea for a kind of populist revolt against the unpopular tyrant, yet the beetle is no democrat. He is just as warlike as the eagle. The Erasmian irony never gives up. This essay is a remarkable display of learning: the notes show how far he ranges beyond Aristotle and Pliny, his two basic sources for the animal lore. The essay was published separately by Froben in 1517, and became well known independently of the* Adages.

Κάνθαρος ἀετὸν μαίεται, A dung-beetle hunting an eagle. When a weaker and less powerful person seeks to do harm to a far more powerful enemy and lays an ambush for him. There is another reading and one which in my judgment is more correct: Ὁ κάνθαρος ἀετὸν μαιεύεται, The dung-beetle is midwife to the eagle. The meaning is almost the same whether you read *maietai* or *maieuetai*, for the adage is applicable to a weak and insignificant man who plots harm to someone far stronger by means of malicious traps and secret wiles. Aristophanes[1] in the *Lysistrata*: 'I am furiously angry with you; when you the eagle lay your eggs, I shall be the dung-beetle serving as your midwife.'

On this subject there is a rather neat Greek fable by Aesop according to Lucian,[2] since he says in *Icaromenippus* that Aesop related how once upon a time the beetles and the camels went up to heaven together. As far as the story of the beetle and the eagle is concerned it goes like this: For a long time there has been, between the race of the eagles and the whole tribe of beetles an old hostility, a long-standing, absolutely deadly feud; in fact what the Greeks call a 'war without truce.'[3] For they hate each other more than people hated Vatinius;[4] so much in fact that not even Jupiter himself, 'who has the supreme power'[5] and 'at whose nod all Olympus trembles,'[6] has been able to settle the matter between them and put an end to their strife – if the fables tell the truth.

In short, there was no more agreement between them than there is between our palace gods and humble, obscure folk nowadays. But perhaps someone, ignorant of Aesop's fables or unfamiliar with them, will wonder what business a beetle could ever have with an eagle, what kinship, what similarity, what affinity there could be between two such different creatures; for it is between those who have close ties that enmity usually arises, especially between rulers. Besides, whatever could be the cause of such a terrible hatred? And where then did the beetle find courage enough to undertake without second thought a war with the eagle folk? What outrage offended the 'haughty spirit'[7] of the eagle so deeply that he did not treat such a petty enemy with contempt and reckon it unworthy even of his hatred? Clearly this is a vast subject, the injury is of long standing, the subsequent history long and tangled too, and the whole matter is beyond human eloquence to explain. But if the Muses, who were not reluctant at one time to dictate to Homer the 'Battle of the Frogs and Mice,'[8] will condescend to leave Helicon for a moment and come to me, I shall try to give a summary account of the matter to the best of my ability. For nothing is too difficult for men to dare if the Muses help. But to provide a clearer light on the subject before I come to the story itself, I shall describe in as few words as I can the habits, the appearance, the character, and the capabilities of the two protagonists.

First, then, it occurs to me to wonder what came into the heads of the Romans – sensible people in other respects – to treat the eagle the way they do. Having taken this bird as their symbol, they extol themselves above all other peoples and count themselves closest to the gods, they win so many victories under its auspices and hold so many triumphs, yet far from being grateful to the well-deserving bird, they show an intolerable contempt for it. For this bird, of all birds the most masculine and most vigorous, they emasculate and castrate,[9] turn it into a sort of Tiresias,[10] thereby making themselves less masculine, for in Greek *aëtos* is certainly masculine. And this, if I am not mistaken, is much more fitting for one to whom the supreme father and king 'of men and of gods'[11] 'Gave dominion over the wandering birds, for Jupiter had found him / trustworthy in the matter of flaxen-haired Ganymede.'[12] He alone dares hand to angry Jove his 'triple bolt'[13] while the other gods keep their distance, not frightened by the proverb which says 'Away from Jove and from the thunderbolt.'[14] With good reason, I think, from among so many nations of birds and so many tribes the eagle was thought to be the most suitable candidate for the monarchy, not only by the *phratrai*[15] of the birds but by the unanimous vote of the 'senate and people' of the poets. Insofar as the judgment lay with the birds, many were inclined to entrust the supremacy to the peacock; for kingship seemed to be its due because of its beauty, magnificence, exalted character, and quite regal loftiness. And the voting would have gone that way immediately if some birds with long experience, like the rooks and the crows, had not foreseen that, if they put the peacock in charge, things would turn out as we have seen for some years past in certain monarchies, namely that he would be king in name only and by the noise he made, and the eagle would rule just the same without the popular vote. As for the poets, the wisest of men, I believe they realized that no better image to represent the conduct and life of kings could be conceived. I am speaking of most kings, not all – for in any field there always has been and always will be a scarcity of good people, and different times bring different men.

But let me, if I may, briefly put two parts of the argument. In the first place, if there is anything to be divined from a name (and there certainly is) the eagle is aptly called *aëtos* in Greek, from *aïssô* which roughly means to rush violently along, to plunge rapidly. Some birds are quiet by nature and gentle, whilst some are wild but can be tamed and quietened by skill and training. The eagle alone is neither amenable to training nor can be tamed by any effort. It is simply driven headlong by the force of instinct, and whatever it has conceived an appetite for it demands to be given. Would you like to see a picture of a chick of really aquiline spirit? It has been graphically painted by Horace:[16]

> Like a winged servant of lightning ... Once youthfulness and inborn drive impel him, unaware of hardships, from the nest, and the spring winds, sweeping away the clouds, teach the startled bird their unaccus-

tomed ways, then a swift dive sends him down to attack the sheep-folds, then love of feast and battle makes the writhing snakes his prey.

This enigmatic simile is better understood by territories that have experienced the many evils which such unbridled violence in young rulers has cost them. It is philosophers who control their appetites and follow the guidance of reason in everything. 'But,' says the satirist,[17] 'there is nothing more open to violence than the ear of a tyrant.' He is always ready with the words: 'This is what I want; this is what I order; let my will be your reason.'[18] Secondly, while there are six kinds[19] of eagle known, they all have in common a sharply hooked beak and no less sharply hooked claws, so that, from its physical characteristics you can see the bird is a carnivore, an enemy of peace and quiet, born for fighting, rapine, and plunder. And as if it were not enough to be carnivores, there are some which are called bone-crushers[20] – and so they may be.

But at this point, dear reader, I hear immediately your unspoken question: what has this picture to do with a king whose proper source of glory is to be merciful, to wish harm to no one, despite being all-powerful, to be the only bee in the hive without a sting[21] and to devote himself entirely to the well-being of his people? This is so true that when the wise Niloxenus[22] was asked what was the most helpful of all things he replied 'A king,' signifying thereby that the proper quality of a true ruler is to harm no one as far as in him lies, to benefit everyone, and to be the best rather than the greatest. However, there is no way in which he can be the greatest other than by being the best, that is by being the most beneficent to all. For my part I admire the model ruler skilfully portrayed by philosophers, and I rather think the princes who administer Plato's state are of such a kind. However in the chronicles you will scarcely find one or two whom you would dare to compare with this portrait. Moreover if you consider the rulers of more recent times, I fear you may discover at every point they deserve the terrible reproach that Achilles hurls at Agamemnon in Homer: 'people-devouring king.'[23] (Hesiod[24] uses the expression 'gift-devouring' – *dôrophagoi* – though he should have said 'all-devouring' – *pamphagoi*.) Aristotle[25] distinguished between a king and a tyrant by the very obvious sign that the latter thinks of his own private advantage and the former consults the good of his people. To the early and really great rulers of Rome the title of 'king' seemed excessive and one to be avoided for fear of envy, yet to some it is hardly enough unless it is accompanied by a long train of the most resounding lies: they must be called 'divine' when they are scarcely men; 'invincible' when they never came out of a battle except defeated; 'majestic' when they are petty-minded in everything; 'most serene' when they shake the world with the storms of war and mad political struggles; 'most illustrious' when they are enveloped in a black night of ignorance of all that is good; 'catholic' when they have anything in mind but Christ. And if these gods, these famous men, these victors[26] have any leisure left from dicing, drinking, hunting and whoring, they devote it to truly regal considerations. They have no other thought but how they may organize laws, edicts, wars, treaties, alliances, councils, and courts ecclesiastical and lay in such a way that they sweep the whole wealth of the community into their own treasury[27] – which is like collecting it in a leaky barrel[28] – and like the eagle cram themselves and their young with the entrails of innocent birds. Come now, if some honest reader of faces will take a careful look at the features and the mien of the eagle, the greedy, evil eyes, the menacing gape, the cruel eyelids, the fierce brow, and most of all the feature which Cyrus the Persian king found so pleasing in a ruler, the hook nose,[29] will he not recognize a clearly royal likeness, splendid and full of majesty? Add to this the very colour, mournful, hideous, ill-omened, a filthy, dark grey. Hence anything dark or approaching black is called *aquilus*.[30] Then there is the harsh voice, the frightening, paralysing, threatening screech which every species of living thing dreads. Now this symbol is immediately recognized by anyone who has endured or indeed has seen the frightening nature of princes' threats, even when uttered in jest, and how all things tremble when this eagle's voice screeches out: 'If they do not give it, I shall come and help myself to your prize, or that of Aias; or I shall walk off with Odysseus'. And what an angry man I shall leave behind me!'[31] Or this which is no less 'kingly': 'Sit there in silence and be ruled by me, or all the gods in Olympus will not be strong enough to keep me off and save you from my unconquerable hands.'[32] At this screech of the eagle, I declare, the common folk immediately tremble, the senate huddles together, the nobles become servile,[33] judges become obsequious, theologians are silent, lawyers assent, laws give way, and established custom yields: nothing can stand against it, not right, not duty, not justice, not humanity. However many eloquent, however many musical birds there are, however various are their voices and their tunes, which may even move stones, more powerful than all these is the harsh and unmusical screech of the eagle. But there is one species of eagle which Aristotle[34] approved of particularly, perhaps because he may have wanted Alexander, his own chick, to be like it: no less predatory and greedy than the other species, but still a little more modest and quiet, and certainly having a little more compassion, because it rears its own chicks – others do the same as undutiful parents who abandon their young, though even tigers look after their cubs. And for this reason it is called 'true-bred' and 'natural.'[35] Homer[36] saw this species, blind as he was; for he calls it 'black-backed' and 'a hunter,' words which would fit very well such rulers as Nero and Caligula and very many others. But some of these are much more like the true eagle, God knows, more 'aquiline' if I may say so; although close to the gods because of their sceptre and the images of their ancestors,[37] yet sometimes they stoop to flatter even the common people and as it were play the sponger if they can expect some worthwhile plunder.

We are told in literature that the eagle is long-lived. When it reaches extreme old age it desires no other drink but blood and by this means it prolongs a life which is universally hated; in fact the 'upper beak grows so long' that it cannot eat flesh. This is the source of that very well known adage[38] 'An eagle's old age,' applied to old men who become addicted to wine, because all other birds of this genus which have hooked talons either do not drink at all or do so very rarely, if we are to believe Aristotle.[39] When they do drink however, they drink water. Only the eagle thirsts for blood. So, by deforming the beak, nature, who is certainly not always an unkind stepmother,[40] seems to have taken thought for other animals and put some limit to this insatiable greed. For the same reason she has provided that the eagle should not be permitted to lay more than three eggs or to rear more than two chicks. In fact if were are to believe the line of Musaeus[41] which Aristotle quotes as authority: 'It hatches two, lays three, and rears one.' And during the days in which it sits on its eggs – as it does for about thirty days – nature's providence ensures that 'it has no food' by keeping the claws withdrawn, so that 'it cannot snatch the young of all the other wild creatures.' During that time 'their feathers become white through lack of food,' and therefore they come to hate their own young.[42] (One can only wish for this constraint in the case of the Roman eagles,[43] for it does not happen; they observe neither limit nor measure in pillaging the common people. Their thirst for spoil increases with age and they never oppress more heavily than when they have hatched a chick. Then indeed the population is struck with one tax after another.) As well as all these characteristics, nature gave this one bird many enemies, about which we shall say more later. And no one will wonder at this careful provision of nature if we accept as true what Pliny[44] relates: this extraordinary evidence of insatiable voracity, perhaps credible even on the testimony of Democritus,[45] and even though Plutarch,[46] one of the most serious of authors, tells it as established and acknowledged fact. Namely that even the feathers[47] of eagles, if mingled with the plumes of other birds, eat them away and in a short time reduce them to almost nothing – such is the power of their innate greed. Indeed I believe the same would happen if the bones of tyrants were mingled with the bones of common people, and that their blood can no more be mixed than that of the aegithus and the florus.

Now just tell me whether this does not apply quite well to certain rulers. (I am not talking about the ones who are pious and good; and having said this once, I should like the reader to remember it at all times.) One pair of eagles needs a large tract of land to plunder, and they allow no other predator in the area, so they mark the limits of their territories. And among our eagles too, what sovereignty is not circumscribed? What concern to enlarge endlessly the kingdom! What sparring with neighbouring eagles or hawks about the limits of the kingdom, or rather of the area to be plundered! Perhaps the comparison is not quite exact in that this bird, however rapacious, does not plunder its neighbour, probably for fear that the harm it does will sooner or later fall back on its own head, but brings its plunder to the nest from much farther away. Tyrants however do not spare even their own friends, or keep their greedy claws off their closest relatives or their servants; indeed one is more exposed to this danger the closer one is to the prince, as if close to Jupiter and his thunderbolt. This ingrained greed for plunder, inherited from the parents, is much increased by upbringing too. For it is said that the eagle pushes its young out of the nest to hunt when they are barely able to fly, so that straight away and 'from the time their claws are soft,' as they say,[48] they are accustomed to robbery and to living by their own talons. And in the case of many rulers, ye gods, how many incitements are added to this rapacity! In addition to a thoroughly corrupt upbringing, such a swarm of flatterers, so many unprincipled officials, corrupt advisors, stupid friends, and profligate companions who take delight in being able to do the public harm, even without provocation. Add to these pomp, pleasures, luxury, and entertainments which no plundering can ever suffice to pay for; add silliness and inexperience, the most intractable of all evils if it is combined with wealth; and since even the most promising minds can be corrupted by these factors, what do you think will be the result if they are infused in a greedy and worthless nature like oil poured onto a fire?[49]

But the eagle would not be equipped in kingly fashion if it were armed only with hooked beak and hooked talons to carry off its prey; it had to have in addition eyes sharper than those of Lynceus,[50] able to look unblinking at the brightest sunlight. It is said they use this ability as a test to decide whether their young are genuine.[51] So the prey they intend to attack they can observe from a great distance. However the king of birds has only two eyes, one beak, a limited number of claws, and one stomach. But our eagles, wonderful to relate, have goodness knows how many Corycaean ears,[52] spies' eyes, officials' claws, governors' beaks, judges' and lawyers' stomachs with utterly unquenchable appetites, so that nothing can ever satisfy or be safe from them, not even things that are kept in the most private chambers or most secret drawers.

Nevertheless the eagle would perhaps not be so dangerous if its physical weapons and powers were not reinforced by a cunning mind, if, so to speak, the steel, deadly enough in itself, were not tipped with poison. It retracts its claws when it walks in order not to blunt their points and make them less effective in hunting, something which it has in common with the lion.[53] And it does not attack at random, but only if it believes itself to be the stronger. Nor does it swoop suddenly down to the ground like other birds as it attacks but descends gradually so that the prey is not startled by a violent movement and frightened off. It will not attack even a hare, its favourite prey, unless it sees that it has moved down onto level country. It does not rove about at all times, so that it cannot be caught out through weariness, but flies out hunting from breakfast time to noon, and sits idle for the rest of the time, until men gather again to do their business.[54] Then it does not immediately devour what it has killed on the spot, lest a sudden hostile attack catch it off guard on its prey, but first tests its strength[55] and, once it has recovered, then carries off its prize to its nest which is its fortress – I shall relate shortly the means by which it takes a stag, so much stronger than itself. One proof of its intelligence is particularly memorable: when it has caught a tortoise, it flies high, picks out a suitable place, and drops the tortoise on a stone, so that it can eat the flesh from the broken shell. However, in the case of Aeschylus,[56] the eagle which killed the poor man by dropping a tortoise on his shiny pate thinking it was a stone was scarcely 'eagle-eyed,' and for this one very good reason has attracted the hatred of all the poets; and it still goes on doing it as if by right. In fact the eagle first tricked the tortoise, persuading it that it would take the trouble to teach it to fly.[57] Then when the tortoise allowed itself to be carried up with this hope into the sky, the eagle dashed it down on a stone so that, in the typical way of tyrants, it converted the tortoise's misfortune into its own pleasure. Nevertheless, anyone who considers the multifarious devices, the numerous tricks, schemes and juggling tricks that dishonest rulers make use of to despoil the common people – levies, taxes, false titles, sham wars, informers, alliances through marriage,[58] – will declare the eagle is almost unworthy to be taken as an example of monarchy.

It remains for us to describe in a few words what enemies this noble predator usually has to deal with. For it is true what the proverbs say: the eagle does not hunt flies,[59] or look for worms.[60] It disregards any prey which seems unworthy of its royal claws, unless there are some eagles related to Vespasian[61] who thought 'profit smells good whatever it comes from.'[62] There are some degenerate eagles which live on fish and which have no shame in taking carcasses left by others. But the more noble ones, like tyrants, leave something for the pirates and the robbers, from whom they are no different, as that noble pirate said in the presence of Alexander of Macedon,[63] except in that tyrants ravage and plunder most of the world with their larger ships and greater forces; they can leave small fry to hawks and sparrow-hawks[64] while they do battle with the four-footed beasts. This they do, not without danger to themselves, but on the other hand not without hope of victory, as befits an enterprising leader. Among the quadrupeds, as I have said, the eagle hunts particularly the hare; whence one species has been given the additional name 'hare-hunter,' just as you might give a leader the title 'Africanus' or 'Numantinus.'[65] It does not scorn unwarlike enemies, but hunts them as food, so that even if it gains little glory from the victory, it gets much benefit from it. Sometimes it is caught the very moment it is hunting a hare, struck by a feathered arrow, and it may well utter the proverb we owe to it: 'We are shot with our own feathers.'[66] It dares to do battle even with the stag,[67] but is likely to be the loser if it does not 'put on a fox's skin.'[68] For it makes up with craftiness what it lacks in strength. When it is about to engage in battle it first rolls in dust, then, alighting on the stag's antlers, it shakes the dust collected on its feathers into the stag's eyes and beats on its face with its wings until the stag is blinded and crashes into rocks. But with the snake the eagle has a fiercer, much more uncertain battle which may even take place in the air. The snake hunts for the eagle's eggs with deadly cunning, whilst the eagle seizes a snake whenever it sees one.

Now it will be no surprise that there is an irreconcilable feud[69] between the eagle and the fox to anyone who has heard how royally the one treated the other in days gone by. The eagle had formed a close friendship with her neighbour the fox, but when she was sitting on her eggs and had no food, she stole her neighbour's cubs and took them up to her nest. When the fox, on her return, saw the mangled remains of her brood, she did the only thing she could, which was to call on the gods and particularly on Jupiter *philios*,[70] avenger of violated friendship. And some god seems to have heard this prayer. A few days later the careless eagle chanced to deposit in its nest a live coal which was stuck to some meat it had snatched from a sacrifice. When the eagle was away the wind fanned the fire and the nest began to burn. The chicks were terrified and threw themselves out, all unfledged as they were. The fox seized them when they fell, took them to its hole, and ate them. From that moment no agreement of any sort has been possible between the eagle and the fox, although at great cost to the latter. I rather think they deserve this, for at one time they refused help[71] to the hares who sought an alliance against the eagle. This story is told in the chronicles of the quadrupeds, from which Homer took his 'Battle of the Frogs and Mice.'

Then again[72] there is bitter enmity between the eagle and the vulture which uses the same methods and competes in greed; although the eagle is both more cruel and more noble because it eats only what it has killed and does not, out of laziness, settle on carcasses killed by others. It has reason to hate the nuthatch which tries with marvellous cunning to break the eagle's eggs. And it fights with herons, for this bird, relying on its claws,[73] is not afraid to attack it sometimes, fighting so fiercely that it dies in the struggle. Nor is it surprising that there is little accord between the eagle and swans, truly birds of poetry; what is surprising is that they often get the better of such a warlike creature. The race of poets has not been too popular with kings who have a bad conscience, because they are free and talkative, and because sometimes, like Philoxenus,[74] they prefer to be sent back to the quarries rather than keep silence. For if something pains them, they write it down in their black books,[75] and divulge the secrets of kings to their own succesors. Eagles have little liking for cranes too (I think because the latter have a strong preference for democracy,[76] so hated by monarchs). Yet cranes are more intelligent, for when they migrate from Cilicia and are about to cross the mountains of Taurus, which are the haunt of eagles, they carry large stones in their beaks to muffle their cries and fly in silence at night, thus deceiving the eagles and passing safely.[77] But the eagle has a particular hostility toward the wren (*trochilus*),[78] as it is called, for no other reason, as the old rambler[79] thinks, than that it is also called king-bird and counsellor, most commonly among the Latins. The eagle pursues it with extreme hate as a pretender to power, although this is not an enemy whose strength the eagle might fear, for the wren is weak and inclined to flee, but being skilful and intelligent it hides in thickets and holes so that it cannot easily be caught even by a more powerful enemy. And once, when it accepted a challenge to fly a race with the eagle, it won more by cunning than by strength.[80] Finally the eagle wages war to the death with the *cybindus*[81] so deadly that they are often caught locked together. The *cybindus* is a nocturnal hawk, and no kind of man is more hated by tyrants than those who do not conform in any way with commonly held opinion and can see all too clearly in the dark.

But would I not be very foolish to try and enumerate all the enemies of a creature that is at war with everyone? Among the other species of living things there is sometimes war between them and sometimes friendship. The fox has many enemies, but it has a friend in the raven, who gives it help when the merlin[82] harasses its cubs. It has a friendly relationship with snakes too, because they both like using rabbit-warrens.[83] The crocodile has an enemy in the Nile rat, but a close intimacy with the crocodile-bird, so close that the bird is allowed to get right between the animal's jaws without harm.[84] The eagle alone has no friendship with any animal at all, no kinship, no comradeship, no intercourse, no alliance, no truce. It is everyone's enemy and everyone is its enemy. Indeed it cannot but be the enemy of all, for it lives and gets fat by the misfortune of all. Therefore, well aware of its guilt, it does not nest on the plain but on broken and lofty rocks, sometimes in trees, but only in the tallest, like one who repeats over and over to himself the tyrant's motto: 'Let them hate, as long as they are afraid.'[85] And so, while storks[86] are so sacred for the Egyptians that it is a capital offence to kill one, while geese were sacred for the Romans, while among the Britons no one will harm a kite,[87] the Jews will not kill pigs, the ancients would not hunt dolphins[88] (it was not permitted to harm one and, if anyone did harm one by mistake while hunting, he was punished with a few lashes of the whip like a boy). For the eagle there is the same law among all nations as for the wolf and the tyrant, there is a reward for the one who kills the common enemy. Therefore the eagle has no love for nor is loved by any animal, any more than bad rulers are loved when they rule their empires for themselves and to the great harm of the state. Perhaps such affections are for private individuals; great satraps are so remote from them that sometimes they do not even love their own children, except for the gain they may bring, and often hold them in suspicion and hatred.

Almost everyone believes that an animal as savage as the lion[89] could remember with gratitude a man who deserved well of it and saved his life because he had healed its paw. Many believe in the snake[90] which rescued the man who had fed it and came swiftly at the call of his familiar voice. There are some who believe the story told by Philarchus of the viper[91] which used to come every day to a certain man's table; when it learned that its host's son had been killed by one of its own young, it killed its child to avenge the outrage to hospitality by its own offspring and out of shame never returned to that house. Then there is a story of a panther which Demetrius Physicus[92] thought worth writing down and Pliny took the trouble to recount: because a man had rescued her cubs from a pit she obligingly led him out of the desert and back to a road where people were to be found. Aristophanes the grammarian, who loved a girl of Stephanopolis, had an elephant as a rival; Plutarch[93] recorded this as something well known to all and much talked about. He also speaks of a snake passionately in love with an Aetolian girl.[94] The dolphins' love for man is generally acknowledged:[95] it saved the life of Arion,[96] it carried Hesiod to the shore, saved the girl from Lesbos[97] and her lover, and gave a boy rides out of sheer friendliness.[98] But even those who believe all these things do not believe that a virgin could be loved by an eagle. You may judge how ill-omened this creature is and what hatred it has for man by the fact that it was chosen to be the tormentor on Mount Caucasus of Prometheus,[99] of all the gods the one who loved man the most. And yet with so many vices there is one thing we can approve. These most rapacious of creatures are not at all given to drink[100] or lust.[101] For when the eagle abducted Ganymede,[102] it did so for Jupiter and not for itself. But you will find many of our eagles' who do commit abductions for themselves, and not just one Ganymede, but they abduct girls for themselves, they abduct married women for themselves, so that in this respect they are almost more insufferable than in their pillaging for which they are already absolutely intolerable.

So, there are innumerable species of birds, and among them some are admirable for their rich and brilliant plumage like peacocks, others are remarkable for their snowy whiteness like swans, some, by contrast, are a beautiful shiny black like ravens, others are of extraordinary physical size like ostriches, some are famous for legendary miracles like the phoenix, some are praised for their fertility like doves, or appreciated at the tables of the great like partridges and pheasants;

some are entertaining for their talk like parrots, or marvellous for their song like nightingales, some are outstanding for their courage like cockerels, others are born to be men's pets like sparrows. Yet of all of them the eagle alone has seemed to wise men to be a suitable image of the king, not beautiful, not melodious, not good to eat, but a carnivore, a raptor, a predator, a plunderer, a warmonger, solitary, hated by all, a universal bane, capable of the maximum of harm, yet seeking to do even more. On the same basis the lion is adjudged monarch of the quadrupeds, for there is no beast which is fiercer or more noisome.[103] Dogs are useful for many purposes, and in particular for guarding people's property. Oxen till the soil. Horses and elephants go to war. Mules and asses are useful for carrying loads. A monkey can play the scrounger. Even the snake[104] is useful in that it showed the value of fennel for improving the eyesight. The lion has no quality but that of tyrant, enemy and devourer of all, whose survival depends only on its strength and the fear it inspires, a right royal animal just like the eagle. This seems to have been understood by those who emblazoned their noble shields with lions with jaws agape and with claws spread to catch their prey – though it seems Pyrrhus,[105] who liked to be called an eagle, understood this better than Antiochus, who rejoiced in the nickname of the Hawk. But it is no surprise that the lion should rule over the four-footed kinds, since even among the gods invented by the poets it was Jupiter who was considered to be best fitted to exercise rule: undutiful son who castrated and drove out his father,[106] incestuous husband of his sister, distinguished by so much debauchery, so many adulterous affairs, so many rapes, and yet despite this 'with sable brow' and 'flaming bolt'[107] striking terror into everyone. For even if many praise the state system of the bees, in which the king is the only one who may not bear a sting, no one imitates it, any more than Plato's.

But I come back to the eagle; for the truly royal qualities which I have described and the extraordinary services it has rendered to every kind of animal the 'senate and people' of the poets has unanimously declared firstly that it should receive the title of 'universal king' and even be called *theios*, that is 'divine.'[108] Secondly they gave it quite important place among the constellations and decorated it with a few little stars. Finally they gave it the divine task of alone bringing to angry Jupiter the arms with which he makes the whole world tremble. And so that it can do this with impunity, they also gave it the power, alone among living creatures, to be unafraid of the thunderbolt and not to be harmed by it,[109] but to look on a flash of lightning with the same stare that it turns directly on the sun. To these attributes those very wise and uncorrupted[110] Romans added this, that the eagle should have first place among the standards of their legions, that it should be, as it were, the ensign-bearer of all their standards, taking precedence over wolves, the nurses of the Roman nation, over Minotaurs and boars, not animals of the greatest rapacity, finally even over horses. For standards decorated with these four creatures followed the eagle in those times. In a short while, it would not allow them even to accompany it but, leaving them behind in camp, went forth to battle alone.[111] This bird alone, I repeat, they considered worthy to be the ornament on everything belonging to the monarch of the whole world: sceptre, banner, shield, house, clothing, cups and livery, although, if I am not mistaken, it was on an augury given by vultures,[112] not by eagles, that Roman rule was founded. The college of augurs added this: that if an eagle should perch on anyone's house, or drop a cap[113] on his head, it was a portent that he would rule.

So much for one of these leaders; I come now to the dung beetle. It is an animal – perhaps scarcely even an animal since it lacks some senses – belonging to the lowest order of insects, which the Greeks call by the notorious term *kantharos*[114] and the Romans *scarab*, nasty to look at, nastier to smell and nastiest of all in the noise it makes; its wings[115] are covered by a scaly sheath. Indeed it would be more exact to say this whole scarab is nothing but a shell. It is born in excrement, that is in the droppings of animals, and it is in these that it lives, makes its home, delights and revels. Its chief occupation is to make balls as large as possible, like pastilles, not out of sweet-smelling materials but with dung, especially goat's dung which smells to the beetle like marjoram.[116] These it rolls backwards with tremendous efforts, thrusting upwards with its back legs, which are extra long, and with its head touching the ground. If, as happens sometimes, when they push their burden uphill, the balls slip away from them and run back down the slope, you would think you were watching Sisyphus[117] rolling his stone. They never tire, they never rest, so eager are they to pursue their labour until they have got the ball down into their hole. They themselves were born in these balls, and they bring up their new-born in the same way,[118] and continue to keep them warm in these nests against the winter's cold while they are young. Now I know the dung-beetle is well known to everyone, for it is to be found everywhere, except perhaps where there is no dung. But they are not all of the same species; for there are some whose shell is a sort of shiny greenish black, and several are a repellent filthy black.[119] Some are larger, armed with extra long two-pronged horns with serrated tips like pincers; with these they can grip and squeeze to bite at will. Some are reddish, and these are very large; they dig in dry ground and make their nests there. There are some which make a terrible loud buzzing noise as they fly and give quite a fright to the unwary.[120] There are others which differ by their shapes. But this they all have in common: they are born in dung, they feed on dung, their life and their delight is in dung.

Now I imagine there will be some eager supporter of Roman generals who will deplore the lot of the eagle, such a regal bird, destined to fight such a humble and low-born enemy, whom it is no glory to conquer, by whom it would be utter disgrace to be defeated, and who may gain enormous credit by confronting the eagle even if he is beaten. According to the poets,[121] Ajax was ashamed to have such an unwarlike opponent as Ulysses; is the eagle to be obliged to contend with the beetle? On the other hand another person will wonder rather where this basest of insects found such courage, such daring, that it was not afraid of beginning a war with this by far the most bellicose of birds. And where did it find the resources, the strength, the means, the allies to be able to carry on the war for so many years? But in truth, if anyone will open up this Silenus[122] and look more closely at this despised creature, in its own setting as it were, he will see it has so many uncommon gifts that, all things well considered, he will almost prefer to be a scarab rather than an eagle. But let no one cry out or contradict me before he knows the facts.

First of all, even the dung-beetle has an advantage over the eagle in this that every year it casts off its old age and immediately regains its youth. This in itself is such an advantage that I imagine even certain Roman pontiffs, who may go straight to heaven because they have the keys, would nevertheless prefer, when they reach an unlovable old age which obliges them to renounce all pleasures, to slough off their old shell[123] like the scarab sooner than accept a sevenfold crown in place of the triple one. Second, what strength of heart it has in such a small body, what heroic mental powers, what energy in attack! Homer's fly[124] is nothing compared to the dung-beetle! This is why, if I am not mistaken, some beetles are called bulls.[125] And since not even lions will rashly attack bulls, it is still less likely that eagles will. It is also endowed with no ordinary intelligence – or are we are to think the Greek proverb 'As cunning as Cantharus,'[126] which seems to assign to the beetle a quite unusual and unrivalled wisdom, arose and became universally known for no good reason?

It makes no difference to my argument if some one objects that the beetle is poorly lodged in an ugly house. As far as physical beauty goes, if we only keep our judgment free of vulgar prejudice, there is no reason to despise the scarab. For if the philosophers[127] are right when they say that the shape they call a sphere is not only the most beautiful but in every way the best, and that the demiurge found this the most pleasing for the shape of the heavens, by far the fairest of all things, why should the scarab not seem beautiful which comes far closer to this shape than the eagle? If a horse is beautiful among its kind, and a dog among its own, why should a beetle not have its own beauty? Or must we measure the beauty of all other things by our own, so that whatever does not conform to human beauty will always be judged ugly?[128] The colour of the scarab, I think, no one will denigrate for it has the quality of jewels. The fact that it uses the droppings of animals for its own purposes is a matter for praise, not accusation. As if doctors do not do exactly the same, not only making ointments with a variety of animal and even human excrement, but prescribing it in medicines for the sick. Alchemists,[129] obviously godlike men, are not ashamed to use dung in the search for their 'fifth essence'; nor farmers who were at one time the most honoured sort of men to feed their fields with manure. There are some peoples who use dung instead of gypsum to plaster their walls. This same material, pounded and dried in the sun, is used to keep fires going instead of wood. The Cypriots[130] fatten their cattle with human dung, and not only fatten them but doctor them even.

But, you say, this stuff, however putrid, smells sweet to the beetle. Well, it would be stupid to expect the beetle to have the nose of a man. As a matter of fact man is peculiar in that he finds the smell of his own excrement offensive; this is not the case with any other creature. So the beetle is not dirtier than us, it is better off. But it is also true that men are offended not so much by excrement itself as by the current view of it; to the earliest mortals this substance was not so disgusting as it is to us, for they called it by the very auspicious name of *laetamen*,[131] and they had no hesitation in giving the god Saturn the nickname of 'Sterculeus,'[132] and this was a compliment if we believe Macrobius. According to Pliny,[133] Stercutus the son of Faunus acquired not only a name from this source, but even an immortal memory in Italy. Further, in Greece the same substance brought fame to two kings: Augeas who devised the task and Hercules[134] who made it famous. Then there is the unforgettable story of the regal old man whom Homer[135] pictured for posterity (as Cicero[136] tells in his Cato) fertilizing his fields with his own hands and with the very substance which is the beetle's delight. The stench of urine did not trouble a certain Roman emperor[137] if there was money attached to it. And why should a beetle be frightened away from a thing of so many uses by such a slight inconvenience? – if it is an inconvenience at all. Finally, seeing that the beetle in the midst of dung remains clean and always keeps its shell shining, whilst the eagle stinks even in the air, which of the two, I wonder, is the cleaner? Indeed I think the name is derived from this; it is called *cantharos* as if it were *catharos*, clean, pure (unless one prefers the derivation of *cantharus* from *Centaurus*).[138] For you should not think, because it is of a squalid nature, that the beetle despises luxurious living; it has an extreme fondness for roses and covets them above all else – if we believe Pliny.[139]

These qualities may seem slight and commonplace, but there is one which no one will deny makes the beetle great, a real feather in its cap:[140] in ancient times it was given first place among sacred images and in sacred rites as the most apt symbol of the eminent warrior. Plutarch[141] tells us in his essay on 'Isis and Osiris' among the hieroglyphic images of the Egyptians the picture of the king was an eye placed on a sceptre, signifying watchfulness combined with just government of the state; in those days, I believe, kings were of this nature, very different from eagles.[142] He says that at Thebes[143] there were preserved images without hands representing judges, who must distance themselves as far as possible from all bribery by gifts; among these images there was one without eyes also which signified the president of the court because he must be entirely without preference, and consider only the case itself without thought of the person. There too, not like 'blue pimpernel among the vegetables' as the proverb[144] says, but among the sacred images, was the scarab, carved on a seal. And what pray did those wisest of theologians intimate to us by this new symbol? Not something banal at all, but a great and undefeated general. This too is in Plutarch,[145] in case anyone thinks I have made it up, as some ignorant theologians sometimes contrive allegories.

But some uninformed person will ask 'What has a beetle to do with a military general?' In fact they have many points in common. In the first place you can see that the beetle is covered with gleaming armour and no part of its body remains unprotected by scales and plates; Mars does not seem to be better armed when Homer equips him in his fullest panoply. Then there is its aggressive approach with terrifying, unnerving thrum[146] and truly warlike voice. For what is harsher than the blare of trumpets, what is more cacophanous[147] than the roll of drums? The sound of trumpets, which delights kings so much nowadays, was intolerable to the Busiritae[148] of old, because it seemed to them like the braying of an ass, and the ass was one of the things that nation considered detestable. Then there is the beetle's patient labour in rolling its burdens along, its unconquerable courage and its disregard for its own life. Add to this that it is claimed no female scarabs are to be found but that all are males.[149] What, I ask, could be more apt for a strong leader? Indeed it is also fitting, as Plutarch also reports, that they use those dainty balls I have described to give birth to, nurture, feed and bring up their offspring; their birthplace is their food. Do not think this esoteric aptness is easy for me to explain. It could be better explained by military commanders who know what it is 'to be the guest of one's shield,'[150] to sleep 'on the ground,' who have endured hard winters in the open during sieges and often harder famines, who have dragged out a grim life by eating not only roots of plants but rotten food, who have spent months at sea. If you consider the squalor of this life, the beetle will seem pure;

if you consider its poverty the beetle is to be envied. This, in case anyone should sneer at it, is the lot and the condition of the most brilliant generals. On the other hand, it is permissible to wonder why our sabre-rattlers[151] prefer to have in their coats of arms, which they think are the foundation of their whole title to nobility, leopards, lions, dogs, dragons, wolves or some other animal which either chance has thrown in their way or they have adopted themselves; whereas their proper symbol is the beetle, which is both the most appropriate and is attested and consecrated by that very antiquity which is the sole begetter of nobility.

Finally no one will think the dung-beetle is entirely despicable if they consider that wise men and doctors obtain remedies from the creature for the worst human ills. For example the horns of the stag-beetle, or lucanian beetle as this species is called, are not only carried in purses, but hung around the neck, sometimes set in gold, as a protection against all childhood diseases.[152] Shall not the beetle be granted equal power with the eagle for offering the most effective cures, and hard to believe too if it were not for the authority of Pliny?[153] I mean that formidable type[154] of scarab which is carved on an emerald,[155] for as the proverb says, you can't carve a Mercury out of any and every wood;[156] the scarab does not consider every gem worthy of itself, but carved on the emerald, the brightest of all gems, if it is hung from the neck as I said (but only with the hair of an ape or at least a swallow's feathers), it affords an immediate remedy against all poisons,[157] and no whit less effective than the moly which Mercury once gave to Ulysses.[158] It is effective not only against poisons, but is an uncommon asset for anyone seeking an audience with a king,[159] so this sort of ring should be worn especially by those who have it in mind to ask the king for some fat benefice or archdeaconry or bishopric as they are called.[160] Likewise it prevents headaches – not a minor ill, by heaven, especially for drinkers. As far as these quite remarkable curative powers are concerned, wise physicians make no distinction between the eagle and the scarab. So who would scorn this beetle whose very image carved on a stone has such power? The mention of gems suggests to me that I should add this too: if the eagle takes pride in a gemstone called 'eagle-stone,'[161] the scarab yields nothing to it in this respect either. For to the scarab the cantharias[162] owes its name, presenting a wonderfully complete picture of the animal, so that you would say it is not a picture but the real living beetle set in the stone. To conclude with something which is perhaps also to the point, this beetle, born in dung, is distinguished by no fewer proverbs than the eagle, king of birds. If some supporter of the eagle's party should say that in this respect the scarab is not to be compared with it because the eagle used to be considered one of the divinities by those loutish fellows the Thebans,[163] I shall not deny it; but let him remember that this sort of honour is shared by the eagle with crocodiles and long-tailed apes, together with onions and the rumblings of the stomach, inasmuch as all these portents were honoured as divine among the Egyptians.[164] And if the word 'divinity,' meaningless in this assemblage of things divine, is worth anything on this argument,[165] many attributed divinity to the scarab also.[166]

Now we have painted both sorts of leaders, such as they are. It remains for us to examine the causes of such a ferocious war. Once upon a time[167] on Mount Etna an eagle was pursuing a hare; it had raised its claws and was so close to grasping its prey, that the hare, timid by nature and terrified by the eagle's hot breath, fled for refuge into the nearest beetle's hole. So it is at a critical moment, when things are desperate, we look and hope for shelter wherever we can. However, this scarab was, in Homer's[168] words, 'good and great'; for on that mountain the scarab nation was considered to be of a particularly healthy stock, so that the 'Etna beetle'[169] has become proverbial, probably because of its exceptional physical size. So the hare took refuge in this hole and threw itself at the beetle's feet begging and praying that his household gods should protect him against this cruellest of enemies. Now the beetle was not a little pleased by the very fact that someone existed who, first, was willing to owe his life to him and believed that such a great thing was in his power; and who, second, found his hole, which all men passed by cursing and holding their noses, suitable as a place in which to hide for safety like a sacred altar or the king's statue. Without delay therefore the scarab flew to meet the eagle and sought to mollify the angry creature with these words: 'The greater your power the more becoming it is that you should spare the harmless. Do not defile my household gods with the death of an innocent animal. In return, may your nest be always safe from such disaster. It is the mark of a noble and kingly spirit to pardon even the unworthy. One who has committed no crime should have the right to respect for his home, which should be safe and inviolate for everyone, as justice wills, the law allows, and custom approves. If the suppliant has no authority, at least let his zeal speak for him.

> For though you may despise our race and scarabean arms,
> Yet be certain the gods are mindful of good and ill.[170]

If you are not worried that your own hearth may be violated – a fate which will befall you one day – at least respect supreme Jupiter, whom you will offend in three ways with the same deed. This is my guest, so you will offend against the law of hospitality; he is my suppliant and thereby he is also yours, so you will offend against the law of supplication; finally I am a friend supplicating for a friend, so you will offend against the law of friendship.[171] You know how sure is the wrath which Jupiter conceives when he is angered, how sharp is his revenge when he is provoked, you who bring him his weapons when he rages. Not everything is allowed to his people, nor is everything condoned for those he loves.' The beetle was about to say more, but the eagle beat him with her wings and threw him contemptuously to the ground. The hare pleaded in vain; the eagle slew it with the greatest cruelty before the beetle's eyes, tore it to pieces and carried the mangled remains away to her savage nest. Neither prayers nor threats from the beetle had the slightest effect on her. But she would not have scorned the beetle in this fashion if her good sense had been equal to her audacity and strength, nor if it had occurred to her that once upon a time a lion[172] in immediate peril of its life had been saved by a mouse; the king of all the quadrupeds was given at the right moment the gift which was almost beyond the power of the gods by such a weak and despised little beast. Or she might have remembered that the ant[173] was inspired by a kindness received and saved the life of the dove by biting the heel of the bird-catcher. In truth, none is so humble, so lowly, that he cannot on occasion be a beneficent friend or a dangerous enemy even to the most powerful. But at that time none of this occurred to the eagle, who was concerned only to take the present booty and to enjoy it. This outrage sank deeper into the heart of the generous scarab than anyone would have believed. His lofty and titanic soul was roused by shame that his authority had been worth little in such a just cause, by pity that a harmless and peaceful animal had been so savagely torn to pieces, and by grief that the eagle's savage contempt for him could be unpunished when, as it seemed to him, he deserved no contempt at all. For personal dignity is no slight matter to anyone. Already it occurred to him that the whole race of beetles would be put to shame if the eagle's deed should go at all unpunished. At that moment the beetle, though powerless to take his revenge, showed an altogether regal quality, the one which Calchas[174] spoke of with respect to Agamemnon and other kings: 'Even if the king swallows his anger for the moment, he will nurse his grievance till the day he can settle the account.'

And so he pondered all sorts of arts and tricks. It was no common punishment but extermination and utter destruction[175] he contemplated. But he considered it too dangerous to risk war directly with such a fierce enemy as the eagle, not only because his forces were inferior, but because Mars is a stupid and frenzied god, as blind as Plutus[176] himself, or Cupid, and usually backs the wrong cause. For even if their forces were exactly equal, even if those who had right on their side were to win, he saw there was a way to torment the eagle more and to satisfy his hatred with greater vengeance, if she was deprived of descendants and suffered a slow death while still alive and fully aware. There is no means by which parents can be tormented more than through their children; those who can ignore the cruellest tortures of their own bodies cannot endure the sufferings of their children. He had seen asses plunge through fire to save their colts with marvellous disregard for their own lives, he had seen examples of this courage in many living creatures. He believed the eagle was no stranger to these common feelings. Finally he judged it would be safer for his species if he destroyed the very stock,[177] as they say, of such a tenacious enemy. I think he had heard that well known proverb[178] 'He is a fool who kills the father and spares the children.' He was also tickled by a certain alluring hope that, if the act succeeded and the eagle were overthrown, he might himself take power. And since grief not only gives strength and courage but wisdom too he looked industriously for the place where his enemy had hidden her hope of posterity. When he had found it he went to Vulcan, who was something of a friend of his because of their similarity in colour. He begged him to forge armour for him which, without being too heavy for a flying creature, would protect him against an attack of moderate force. Vulcan armed the scarab from the top of his head to his hindmost heels[179] with the armour that he still wears (for before that he was unarmed, like a fly). The eyrie was far away from there, on a high, broken crag, hedged around and defended with lots of branches and brushwood. Whether our extraordinary beetle flew there forthwith or crawled there is not clear, but he did reach it. Some say when he was struck by the feathers of the eagle he clung to them in secret and was carried unwittingly by her up into the nest. And so the beetle found a way into a place where not even man, who is more cunning and more ingenious at doing harm than any other creature, had been able to reach. He lay in ambush, hidden among the brushwood, and grasping his opportunity, pushed the eggs out of the nest,[180] one after the other, until not one was left. They were smashed by the fall, and the still unformed chicks were dashed pitifully on the rocks, deprived of life before they had any consciousness at all.

With even this cruel punishment the beetle's grief was not satisfied. There is a precious stone, one of the noblest, called by the Greeks from the name of the eagle *aetites*; it is not unlike an egg, and there is a male and female form, for in the female form you can find a foetus enclosed rather like a chicken. It has a marvellous power to induce delivery at birth,[181] and for this reason it is placed on women in labour still nowadays to speed delivery. So the eagle, who would otherwise never be able to lay eggs and certainly not to hatch them, usually places a couple of these stones in its nest.[182] It was this great treasure that the scarab threw out of the nest, thereby destroying all power of bearing offspring; the stones were shattered into fragments as they struck the pointed rocks. Yet not even this was enough to assuage the beetle's anger; he thought it would be too slight an outrage unless he could enjoy the enemy's grief and lamentations, and so he hid again in the twigs. The eagle returned, perceived the calamity which had just struck her offspring, saw their mangled and torn entrails, and the incalculable loss of the noble stone. She moaned, she cried, she howled, she shrieked, she wailed, she called on the gods, and searched around with those eyes of hers, already sharpened even more by grief, for the enemy with such power. And as she thought anything and everything came into her mind rather than the despised beetle. Terrible were her threats, terrible her curses on whoever was the author of this outrage. Imagine what delight meanwhile the beetle felt in his heart as he listened to this. What could the wretched eagle do? She had to fly off again to the Fortunate Isles to find another pair of eagle-stones, for they are not to be obtained anywhere else. The nest she removed to another much more isolated and lofty place. Once again she laid eggs, and here again, just the same, the unknown enemy penetrated; everything was destroyed and the whole preceding tragedy[183] played again. Once again the eagle moved to a safer refuge, laid more eggs, obtained more eagle-stones. And once again the beetle was there.

There was no limit to flight and no end to pursuit until, exhausted by so many disasters, the bird decided to 'let go the sheet anchor,'[184] to stop trusting in her own powers, and flee to the gods for protection. She went to Jupiter and explained the whole drama of her misfortune: how her enemy was powerful and, worst of all, anonymous, so that however much she suffered, she had no means of revenge. She added that this calamity of hers concerned Jove himself, for the imperial office which he had bestowed would cease to exist and he would have to change his armour-bearer, if the enemy continued to do what he had started; there was some value in using known and established servants, even if the novelty of Ganymede's appointment had turned out well. Jupiter was moved by the danger in which his attendant stood, especially as the recent service of the abduction of Ganymede was still in his mind. He commanded the eagle to lay her eggs, if she wished, in his very own bosom. There they would be absolutely safe, if nowhere else. The eagle complied and laid the last hope of her race in the bosom of supreme Jove, entreating him by the blessed eggs which Leda bore him long ago to guard her own faithfully. What can deep-seated grief of mind not do? I fear the story may seem to some beyond belief. Up to the very stronghold of supreme Jove flew the unconquerable beetle, helped, I rather think, by some divine power. Into his bosom he dropped a ball of dung specially made for the purpose. Jupiter is not used to squalor for he lives in the purest region of the world, separated from earthly contamination by a very wide space. Offended by the filthy smell he tried to shake the dung out of his bosom and carelessly dropped the eagle's eggs, which perished as they fell from that great height even before they hit the ground. So at last the author of so many deaths became known; and this was the culmination of the beetle's joy, for he had the pleasure of being acknowledged. On the other hand, for the eagle – she learned the whole story from Jupiter himself – there was the very heavy additional grief that the author of her calamity was such a contemptible creature. (It is no small consolation for misfortune if one is beaten by a noble enemy.) Hence the pitiless war broke out anew between them: the eagle harried the beetle race with all her strength wherever she found it, carrying them off, trampling them down, destroying them; the beetle for his part strained every nerve to ruin the eagle. And so it seemed 'there would never be pause or rest,'[185] nor any end to predation, ambush, and slaughter, except by the complete and equal destruction of both races – a Cadmean victory,[186] you might say – such was the gladiatorial spirit with which they attacked each other.[187] The eagle could not be defeated; the beetle did not know the meaning of surrender.

In the end Jupiter thought he should intervene in such a dangerous state of affairs and tried to settle the matter between them privately. The harder he tried the more violent their hatred became, the hotter their anger, the fiercer their battles. He was himself, without a doubt, more inclined to the eagle's side; on the other hand, he was influenced by the fact that a very harmful example was set if anyone were to be allowed to hold the laws of supplication, friendship, and hospitality in contempt. So he did what he usually does at critical moments; he called a council of the gods. After making a few preliminary remarks he explained the course of the affair. Through his herald Mercury, opinions were asked and given.[188] Their inclinations were divergent. Almost all the lesser gods supported the beetle, and even among the greatest Juno was strongly on his side, being hostile to the eagle's cause out of hatred for Ganymede.[189] Finally they agreed to the decree proclaimed in a clear voice by Mercury and carved in bronze by Vulcan: that the scarab and the eagle should wage eternal war as they wished; that if either suffered harm, he could not complain in law, it must be considered the fortune of war. Whatever each one seized, he held by right of conquest. Nevertheless the gods did not desire the extermination of either race. For this reason there was to be a cessation of fighting and a truce was to be observed for the thirty days in which the eagle sits on her eggs. The beetle was forbidden to appear in public during that time so that the eagle should not be burdened with the fatigue of war as well as fasting and the labour of caring for her brood. Because of his partiality Jupiter also declared, despite the protests of not a few: 'It is fair that a small corner of this vast world should be a refuge for my attendant, where she may be safe from the scarabs' attacks. I am not creating a precedent. There are places where there are no wolves, where no poisons can enter, where moles cannot live.[190] I myself will measure out an area of a certain number of acres in Thrace near Olynthus in which it shall be a capital offence for the beetle to set foot, deliberately or not, willingly or not; he shall not leave if once he has entered, but shall live in torment there until he die. The name which is given to this place is Beetlebane, so that, warned by this name, the beetle may know that it will be the end of him if he dares to intrude into that place against our decree. The eagle is banished from Rhodes[191] lest anyone should think it cruel that the beetle is shut out of Olynthus.'

> Thus he spoke and made all Olympus tremble at his nod.[192]

The whole assembly of the gods murmured their assent. The decree holds good to this day and always will. War to the death continues between scarabs and eagles; during the days when the eagle sits on her eggs, the descendants of the beetle are nowhere to be seen. The place which Jupiter designated is carefully avoided; any beetle taken there dies at once. This is a fact, and if anyone asks, Pliny is witness to it in book 11 chapter 28,[193] as is Plutarch,[194] a weightier author, in his essay 'On Tranquillity of Mind.'

But I know well enough, dear reader, that you have been thinking for some time 'What is this fellow thinking of, chattering on to us with so much nonsense about nothing and making, not exactly an elephant out of a fly as they say,[195] but a giant out of a beetle? Has he not made enough work for us to go through all the pages of these thousands of proverbs without tormenting us as well with these never-ending fables.' But let me say a word. Everyone has his own opinion, and some will think that my explanations of these adages are pinched and starved, for they think that the really grand thing is to expand a volume to an immense size. I wanted to show these people certainly that I have chosen to be brief in the rest of the book; otherwise I would not have been short of matter to enrich it if I had thought more of showing off my eloquence than of giving pleasure to the reader. But let us come back to the business of proverbs: the comic poet Aristophanes[196] recalls this tale in his *Peace* in these lines:

– It is said in Aesop's fables
To be the only creature with wings that ever reached the gods.

– O Father, Father, that's an incredible story,
That a filthy stinking brute should reach the gods.

– Yet once he did get there, I say, because of the bitter feud
He had with the eagle, rolling out her eggs
And seeking revenge upon his enemy.

The fable teaches us that no one should despise an enemy however humble. There are some little men, of the meanest sort but malicious nevertheless, no less black than scarabs, no less evil-smelling, no less mean spirited, but by their obstinately malicious spirit (since they can do no good to any mortal) they often make trouble for great men. Their blackness is terrifying, their noise is disturbing, their stench is an annoyance; they fly round and round, they cannot be shaken off, they wait in ambush. It is preferable by far sometimes to contend with powerful men than to provoke these beetles whom one may even be ashamed to beat. You cannot shake them off nor fight with them without coming away defiled.[197]

1 *Lysistrata* 694–5
2 *Icaromenippus* 10 (and Aesop 7 Halm)
3 *Adages* III iii 84
4 Roman tribune and later consul, attacked by Cicero in one case, but defended in another; cf *Adages* II ii 94 'Hate worthy of Vatinius,' based on Catullus 14.3.
5 Homer *Odyssey* 5.4, *Iliad* 2.118 and

9.25

6 Virgil *Aeneid* 9.106 and 10.115

7 Homer *Iliad* 12.300, referring to a lion

8 *Batrachomyomachia* (in Loeb edition of Hesiod)

9 Because Latin makes *aquila* feminine

10 Ovid *Metamorphoses* 3.323–31

11 Virgil *Aeneid* 1.229

12 Horace *Odes* 4.4.2–4

13 Ovid *Ibis* 469

14 *Adages* I iii 96

15 brotherhoods, clans

16 *Odes* 4.4.1, 5–12

17 Juvenal 4.86, quoted from memory ('What is more open ...')

18 Juvenal 6.223

19 The following account of eagles and their habits, down to 'its fortress,' is based on Aristotle *History of Animals* 8(9).32–4 (618b18–620a12) and Pliny *Natural History* 10.3.6–4.15, who often follows Aristotle quite closely. The comments on the characteristics of the bird, as opposed to the zoological facts, are Erasmus' own.

20 Pliny *Natural History* 10.3.11 gives *ossifrage* merely as the name of a variety of eagle.

21 The tradition that the king (ie, queen) bee's lack of a sting, or reluctance to use it, is a symbol of royal clemency derives from Pliny *Natural History* 11.17.52–3 and Seneca *De clementia* 1.19.3.

22 One of the participants in Plutarch's 'Dinner of the Seven Wise Men' *Moralia* 153A. Erasmus' memory is at fault. The story is told by Niloxenus; it concerns questions put to the king of Ethiopia by Amassis, king of Egypt, and the answer to this question is not 'a king' but 'god.'

23 Homer *Iliad* 1.231

24 *Works and Days* 39 and 264

25 *Nicomachean Ethics* 8.10.2 (1160a37–1160b2)

26 Cf *Institutio principis christiani* (CWE 27 249) and *Adages* III iii 1*, III vi 95.

27 Cf *Adages* I ix 12 'To exact tribute from the dead,' and *Institutio principis christiani* (CWE 27 260).

28 Cf *Adages* I x 33 'A great jar that cannot be filled.'

29 Erasmus has misunderstood Plutarch *Moralia* 172E or 821E–F, where the Persians are said to be enamoured of hook-nosed persons because Cyrus had a nose of that shape (ASD).

30 There is no similarly derived word in English which refers to colour; Paulus Diaconus *Epitome* Festus p 22 M (ASD).

31 Achilles in *Iliad* 1.137–9; trans E.V. Rieu

32 Zeus to Hera in *Iliad* 1.566–7; trans E.V. Rieu

33 *observit nobilitas*: the verb *observio* is not found in classical Latin.

34 *History of Animals* 8(9).32 (618b26–31 and 619a27–29); Aristotle does not explicitly state a preference.

35 Aristotle *History of Animals* 8(9).32 (619a8)

36 *Iliad* 21.252, to whom Erasmus refers directly, not to Pliny's citation (10.3.7)
37 The Romans used the *imagines familiae*, images of ancestors, kept on altars in their houses and paraded in funeral processions, as symbols of nobility.
38 *Adages* I ix 56
39 *History of Animals* 7(8).3 (593b29), 18 (601b1)
40 Cf *Adages* I viii 64 which quotes Pliny *Natural History* 7.1. Pliny in the same way says he is not sure whether nature shows herself more often as a stepmother or as a mother, considering the way she produces so many poisons and at the same time so many remedies. Erasmus returns to this below at IV i 1* (see n 16).
41 B Frag 3 Diels 1.22, in Aristotle *History of Animals* 6.6 (563a19)
42 Erasmus is following and quoting fragments of Pliny *Natural History* 10.4.13; for the thirty-day hatching time, 10.79.165.
43 From 1515 to 1530 this read 'our eagles,' a plainly contemporary reference to imperial troops. The change to 'Roman eagles' in 1533 barely disguises this since the verbs remain in the present tense. According to James D. Tracy, *The Politics of Erasmus*, chap 2 n 110, this is a reference to a subsidy demanded by Maximilian when Charles was emancipated (January 1515).
44 *Natural History* 10.4.15
45 Erasmus' comment. Democritus is usually cited as untrustworthy: see *Adages* I iv 82, II iii 62, IV iv 43.
46 'Table-talk' in *Moralia* 680E
47 Cf *Colloquies* (CWE 40 1042).
48 *Adages* I vii 52, where it is described as deriving from puppies and applying to people. Cf *Institutio principis christiani* CWE 27 209.
49 *Adages* I ii 9
50 *Adages* II i 54
51 Pliny *Natural History* 10.3.10, speaking of the sea-eagle, uses the words *adulterinum*, bastard, and *degenerem*, not true to stock; curiously, he then goes on to say that sea-eagles have 'no breed of their own, but are born from cross-breeding with other eagles'; cf *Adages* I ix 18.
52 *Adages* I ii 44
53 Pliny, *Natural History* 8.17.41, talks of 'lions and similar animals'; it is Erasmus who makes the comparison.
54 Aristotle, 8(9).32 (619a15–18), and Pliny, 10.4.15, say the reverse. The muddle is due to Erasmus' use of Gaza's translation.
55 Both Aristotle and Pliny follow the first part of this statement by speaking of testing the weight of the prey; Erasmus has presumably misunderstood the Greek.
56 Pliny 10.3.7, Valerius Maximus 9.12 ext.2; cf Aelian *On the Nature of Animals* 7.16.
57 In the fable of Aesop 419 Halm the tortoise asks the eagle to teach

it to fly.

58 Cf *Adages* I ix 12 'To exact tribute from the dead.'

59 *Adages* III ii 65

60 *Adages* I ix 71

61 Suetonius *Vespasian* 23.3

62 *Adages* III vii 13, from Juvenal 14.204–5

63 Cf Erasmus *Apophthegmata* IV Alexander Magnus 63, following Augustine *City of God* 4.4; cf Cicero *On the Republic* 3.14.24.

64 Here 'Nisus,' the legendary king of Megara who was changed into this bird (Virgil *Georgics* 1.404–9)

65 Titles of two members of the Scipio family

66 *Adages* I vi 52 and Aesop 4 Halm

67 Pliny *Natural History* 10.5.17

68 *Adages* III v 81

69 Aesop 5 Halm

70 Jupiter, god of friendship

71 Aesop 236 Halm

72 Cf Aristotle *History of Animals* 8(9).1 (609b7–610a1).

73 *unguibus freta*, which M.M. Phillips translates as 'even while it is being carried away in the eagle's claws.' According to ASD Erasmus has misunderstood Aristotle (who says the heron is at war with the eagle 'which seizes it' – trans D.M. Balme).

74 Cf *Adages* II i 31 'To the quarries'; *Apophthegmata* VI.

75 ASD: the expression *chartis illinunt atris* is a contamination of Horace's *quodcunque semel chartis illeverit*, 'whatever he has once scribbled in his books' (*Satires* 1.4.36) and *quem versibus oblinat atris*, 'whom he may besmear with black verses' (*Epistles* 1.19.30).

76 Pliny *Natural History* 10.30.58 says that cranes 'agree when to start' and 'choose a leader.'

77 Plutarch 'On Loquacity' in *Moralia* 510A and B, and 'Cleverness of Animals' in *Moralia* 967B, where Plutarch talks of geese not cranes. Not consistent with *Adages* III vi 68 'Cranes that swallow a stone,' where Erasmus followed Pliny for the explanation

78 Aristotle *History of Animals* 8(9).11 (615a18), Pliny *Natural History* 8.36.90; both appear to use the word for the Egyptian crocodile-bird, or Egyptian plover, and for the wren.

79 *deambulator*, a humorous reference to Aristotle as peripatetic

80 Aesop 434 Perry, cited in Plutarch *Praecepta gerendae republicae* in *Moralia* 806E

81 Pliny *Natural History* 10.10.24. Erasmus declines the word incorrectly because he is following the Venice edition of 1496 or 1507. The correct form of the word is *cybindis*. Cf *Colloquies* (CWE 40 1040) where he reproduces the alternative Greek form *kymindis* given by Aristotle *History of Animals* 8(9) (615b6).

82 *aesalon*, 'merlin' in the translation of Aristotle by D.M. Balme, *History of Animals* 8(9).1 (609b32). Pliny *Natural History* 10.95.205 uses *aesalon*.

83 Aristotle *History of Animals* 8 (9).1 (610a12) says 'because they both live in holes.'
84 Pliny *Natural History* 8.36.88 and 8.37.90; Aristotle 8(9).6 (612a20)
85 *Adages* II ix 62
86 Plutarch 'Isis and Osiris' in *Moralia* 380F. Plutarch is speaking of the Thessalians, not the Egyptians.
87 ASD suggests an allusion to the English predilection for falcons in the time of Henry VIII.
88 Plutarch 'Dinner of the Seven Wise Men' in *Moralia* 163A
89 Aulus Gellius *Attic Nights* 5.14; the story of Androcles and the lion
90 Pliny *Natural History* 8.22.61
91 Pliny 10.96.208
92 Named by Pliny 8.21.59; Demetrius of Apamea was an ancient physician who wrote treatises *On Affections* and *On Signs*.
93 'Cleverness of Animals' in *Moralia* 972D; cf Pliny 8.5.13.
94 Plutarch *Moralia* 972E
95 Pliny 9.8.24–28, Aulus Gellius *Attic Nights* 6.8
96 Herodotus 1.23–4, Ovid *Fasti* 2.79–118, Plutarch 'Dinner of the Seven Wise Men' in *Moralia* 161A, Aulus Gellius *Attic Nights* 16.19
97 Plutarch 'Dinner of the Seven Wise Men' in *Moralia* 162D and 163A
98 Pliny the Younger *Letters* 9.33
99 Hesiod *Theogony* 506–616, but the place is given by Lucian *On Sacrifices* 6 and *Dialogues of the Gods* 5.205.
100 Aristotle *History of Animals* 7(8).4 (593b29) and 7(8).18 (601b1) of crook-taloned birds in general
101 Aristotle *On the Generation of Animals* 3.1 (749b10); cf *Adages* III vi 21
102 Cf Xenophon *Symposium* 8.28–30.
103 Pliny *Natural History* 8.18.46; cf Aristotle *History of Animals* 7(8).5 (594b18–28)
104 Plutarch 'Cleverness of Animals' in *Moralia* 974B; Pliny 8.41.99
105 Plutarch *Moralia* 975B
106 This is a slip on Erasmus' part. At least in the commonest version of the myth it was Cronus who castrated Ouranous, not Zeus who castrated Cronus.
107 Homer *Iliad* 1.528 and *Odyssey* 22.330; trans E.V. Rieu
108 Aristotle *History of Animals* 8(9).32 (619b6)
109 Pliny *Natural History* 2.56.146 and 10.4.15
110 The Latin reads *casci*; cf Ennius *Annals* 22 Skutsch, Cicero *Tusculan Disputations* 1.27, Varro *On the Latin Language* 7.28, and Jerome *Letters* 8.
111 Pliny 10.5.16, who refers to the second consulate of Gaius Marius (104 BC). The personification in the last sentence is Erasmus' adaptation, which makes the eagle appear to follow the usual autocratic course of a tyrant.
112 Livy 1.7.1
113 According to Suetonius, an eagle

perched on Augustus' tent (96.1) and on the house of Tiberius (14.4); Tarquin was marked by the cap, according to Livy 1.34.8; cf Cicero *On the Laws* 1.4.

114 Suidas K 310

115 The zoological data are from Pliny *Natural History* 11.34.97–9. Much of it is repeated in *Adages* IV viii 94.

116 Cf *Adagia* I iv 38 'A pig has nothing to do with marjoram.'

117 Cf *Adagia* II iv 40 'To roll a stone.'

118 In addition to Pliny, cf Plutarch 'Isis and Osiris' in *Moralia* 355A and 381A.

119 Cf *Adages* III ii 39 'As black as a beetle.'

120 Cf *Adages* III ii 45 'Shades of a dung-beetle.'

121 Ovid *Metamorphoses* 13.1–20

122 Cf *Adages* III iii 1* 'The Sileni of Alcibiades.'

123 The 'slough' of a snake or cast shell of a beetle; cf *Adages* I i 26 'As bare as a snake's sloughed skin' and I iii 56 'As blind as a sloughed skin.'

124 *Iliad* 17.570–4; cf *Adages* III viii 95 'The depravity of the fly.'

125 Pliny *Natural History* 30.12.39

126 *Adages* III ii 42, in which 'Cantharus' is considered first as a proper name, then as the word for 'beetle,' with reference to Aesop, no 7 Halm.

127 Plato *Timaeus* 33B

128 Cf Cicero *On the Nature of the Gods* 1.27.77.

129 Cf Erasmus *Colloquies* 'Alchemist.'

130 Pliny *Natural History* 28.81.266, who says that oxen treat themselves by eating human excrement, and *Adages* I x 95

131 manure (Palladius 3, Servius on Virgil *Georgics* 1.1); from the same root as the verbs *laeto* and *laetifico* (used in the story of Laertes below), which mean both to make happy and to enrich or fertilize. Compare the comments here with III iv 2* 'Everyone thinks his own fart smells sweet.'

132 Macrobius *Saturnalia* 1.7.25

133 *Natural History* 17.6.50

134 Apollodorus 2.5.5

135 *Odyssey* 24.226–31. The old man is Laertes, Odysseus' father. Erasmus' text is much closer to the passage in Pliny just quoted (trans H. Rackham).

136 *On Old Age* 15.54

137 Vespasian according to Suetonius (see note 61)

138 Derivations, apparently not very serious, invented by Erasmus to oppose to Suidas (see note 114)

139 *Natural History* 11.115.279

140 In *Adages* I viii 69 'To raise one's crest' is described as a sign of eagerness and pugnacity in birds, and the military crest as something 'insolent and stupid,' rather than as a sign of legitimate pride. There may be irony or a playful use of materials here.

141 *Moralia* 354F; for the king,

Plutarch says specifically Osiris.

142 Cf *Institutio principis christiani* (CWE 27 241).

143 *Moralia* 355A 'the statue of the chief judge had its eyes closed' (trans F.C. Babbitt).

144 *Adages* I vii 21

145 'Isis and Osiris' in *Moralia* 355A: 'The military class had their seals engraved with the form of a beetle.'

146 *Panico bombo*: cf *Adages* III vii 3 'Onset of panic.'

147 Cf *Adages* II vi 18 'Strangers to the Muses.'

148 Plutarch 'Isis and Osiris' in *Moralia* 362F

149 Plutarch *Moralia* 355A and 381A, Aelian *On the Nature of Animals* 10.15

150 Cf *Adages* II vii 75 'Like a hero to entertain in my shield.'

151 Pyrgopolynices (Sabre-rattler) is the boasting soldier and principal character in Plautus' play *Miles gloriosus*.

152 Pliny *Natural History* 11.34.97 and 30.47.138

153 *Natural History* 37.40.124

154 Cf *Adages* III i 56 'A formidable man.'

155 Pliny explicitly rejects the following claims made for emeralds carved with scarabs (nn 166 and 168) as an insult to humanity.

156 *Adages* II v 47 'Do not make a Mercury out of any and every wood'

157 Pliny 37.40.124

158 *Odyssey* 10.305

159 Pliny 37.40.124

160 Latin terms *archidiaconatus* and *episcopatus* are found respectively in St Gregory (the Great) *Letters* 2.14 and Tertullian *On Baptism* 17.

161 *aetites*, Latin *aëtites* or *aëtitis*, the hollow nodule of argilaceous oxide of iron having a loose nucleus, fabled to be found in eagles' nests (Pliny *Natural History* 10.4.12, 36.39.149, 30.49.130, and 37.72.187)

162 Pliny 37.72.187

163 Diodorus Siculus 1.87.9

164 See Juvenal *Satires* 15.1–10 who mentions all these portents except rumblings of the stomach.

165 *quo calculo*: cf *Adages* I v 55 'To take back a move (or counter).'

166 Pliny *Natural History* 30.30.99 states that 'the greater part of Egypt' worships the scarab.

167 Aesop 7 Halm. Erasmus sets the location on Mount Etna, following the scholiast of Aristophanes *Peace* 73.

168 A common attribute of his heroes; see *Iliad* 2.653.

169 *Adages* II vi 65 (of things which are large and filthy)

170 A parody of Virgil *Aeneid* 1.542–3

171 Jupiter is 'hospitable,' he is approached by 'supplication,' and he is a 'friend,' all epithets in Lucian *Timon* 1.

172 Aesop 256 Halm
173 Aesop 296 Halm
174 Homer *Iliad* 1.81–3; trans E.V. Rieu
175 Cf *Adages* I x 27 'Root and branch.'
176 *Adages* III iii 6, I vii 84
177 Cf *Adages* II iv 86, in the last sentence but one.
178 *Adages* I x 53
179 Cf *Adages* I ii 37 'From head to heel.'
180 Aesop 7 Halm
181 Pliny *Natural History* 30.44.130 and 36.39.151 speaks rather of preventing abortion and miscarriage.
182 Pliny 36.39.149
183 Cf *Adages* IV iii 40.
184 Cf *Adages* I i 24, meaning to fall back on one's final resource.
185 Cf Virgil *Georgics* 3.110, *Aeneid* 5.458, 12.553.
186 *Adages* II viii 34
187 Cf Terence *Phormio* 964 and *Adages* I iii 76.
188 Cf Lucian *Parliament of the Gods* 1.
189 Lucian *Dialogues of the Gods* 8 (5)
190 Cf *Adages* III vi 16.
191 Pliny *Natural History* 10.41.76
192 See note 6.
193 That is, 11.34.99
194 *Moralia* 473E
195 *Adages* I ix 69
196 *Peace* 129–34
197 The lesson drawn in this last paragraph, unchanged from the version of 1508, does not quite fit with the preceding essay on tyranny.

III vii 5
Citius quam asparagi coquuntur / As quick as asparagus is cooked

Though it seems never to have come into English, 'as quick as asparagus is cooked' would make a fine proverb; the source is principally Suetonius' life of the emperor Augustus (Otto 195).

Cooked as quick as asparagus. Said of something done with great speed. There are certain proverbial expressions which were particular favourites of Octavius Augustus, and among them this one is recorded by Suetonius, who writes that he used to talk of the speed of some rapid action by saying: Cooked as quick as asparagus.[1] Augustus often uses it in his letters too. Asparagus is a prickly type of grass,[2] a useful medicine[3] and pleasant food as well; before it grows hard, the top is cooked lightly, but only enough to take away the rawness. It is called asparagus because, as Athenaeus says, the finest types do not grow from seed.[4] Scholars tell us that there is a similar expression about pickled fish, 'Cooked as quick as pickled fish,' because some sorts of fish which have been preserved in salt or dried in smoke or the open air are also eaten raw or lightly cooked, but I have not found the proverb in Athenaeus[5] whom they give as their source. It is very close to a proverb[6] which will be given elsewhere: 'Whitebait on the fire.'

1 Suetonius 'Augustus' 87 in *Lives of the Caesars*
2 Pliny *Natural History* 21.54.91 (in English, through a false etymology in the seventeenth century, 'asparagus' became 'sparrow-grass,' then simply 'grass')
3 Pliny 20.42.108–43.111 and Athenaeus *Doctors at Dinner* 2.62E–F
4 Athenaeus is not talking of etymology, but Erasmus takes his 'not grown from seed' as meaning *a-spartos* 'not sown, grown wild.'
5 Athenaeus 3.119E ('Broiled salt-fish, if it but see the fire ...' [Loeb])
6 *Adages* II ii 12 (whitebait, a fish, cooks extremely quickly; 'proverbial for things which perish or are consumed rapidly'); 'will be given' because Erasmus forgot to correct this passage; in the edition of 1508 this proverb on asparagus appeared earlier.

III x 88
Aethiops non albescit / The Ethiopian cannot become white

This is a virtually similar discussion to I iv 50 'You wash the Ethiopian' and is a good example of the way Erasmus could repeat an adage, sometimes using the same information as in another essay, sometimes slightly modifying the information, as in this instance with the addition of the lines from the Greek satirist Lucian. This adage became widely known not from Erasmus so much as from the emblem by Alciato (no 59), which gave a Latin version of Lucian's poem with a picture (see figure on p 80).*

Αἰθίοψ οὐ λευκαίνεται, The Ethiopian cannot become shining white. Usually said about those who will never change their nature. For an inborn trait cannot easily be changed. There is a fable of Aesop[1] about a man who bought an Ethiopian and thinking that the colour of his skin was not natural but had come about because of the neglect of a former master, scrubbed his face for so long that he even made him ill, whilst the colour was no better than it had been before. There is also an epigram attributed to Lucian:[2] 'You wash the Ethiopian in vain; why not give up the task? / You will never manage to turn black night into day.'

1 13 Halm, the same story as in I iv 50*

2 *Greek Anthology* 11.428; Erasmus added the epigram in 1533 from *Selecta epigrammata graeca* (Basel: Bebelius 1529) p 144; Andrea Alciato translated the epigram into Latin as the basis of his emblem 59 entitled 'Impossibile' (see figure on p 80).

IV i 1

Dulce bellum inexpertis / War is sweet for those who have not tried it

Erasmus wrote this long and powerful essay for the edition of 1515 along with five other commentaries on social and religious issues: I i 31 'Trouble experienced makes a fool wise'; I iii 1* 'One ought to be born a king or a fool'; II v 1* 'Sparta is your portion; do your best for her'; II viii 65* 'As warts grow on the eye'; and III vii 1* 'The beetle pursues the eagle.' These works collectively are Erasmus' most eloquent condemnation of war, a subject that had been central to his thought from 1503 onwards, the year he wrote the* Panegyricus, *that strange mixture of flattery and anti-war advice to Philip, archduke of Austria and duke of Burgundy, and son of Emperor Maximilian. By 1515–16, Erasmus was ready to speak out confidently against war in a number of sustained commentaries: these essays in the 1515* Adages; *an extensive section of* The Education of a Christian Prince *(1516) devoted to 'the arts of peace'; and the* Complaint of Peace *(1516), a monologue spoken by Peace against all war. The scandalous and hilarious dialogue* Julius Excluded, *in which Peter turns the warrior Pope Julius away from heaven, also dates from about the same period (though Pope Julius had died in 1513); most scholars are sure this anonymous work is by Erasmus.*

For Erasmus, war is wasteful, destructive of community, and an indulgence by the rich and powerful. In this adage essay he argues his case using the full range of his rhetorical skills. The proverb 'War is sweet' is commonly found in antiquity (though cited in Diogenianus and Stobaeus and elsewhere, it did not appear in Suidas and Zenobius). Erasmus presented the proverb in a single sentence in the Collectanea *of 1500, but expanded it into the longest essay in the* Adages *in 1515. A first attempt at the essay appears in a letter of March 1514 written to Antoon van Bergen (Ep 288). The proverb is found in English (Tilley W 58 'Wars are sweet to them that know them not'), but it is not a proverb one often encounters, even though Erasmus' essay appeared many times as a separate publication in many European languages from the sixteenth century onwards. The first English translation was in 1534.*

This is one of the choicest of proverbs and is widely used in literature: Γλυκὺς ἀπείρῳ πόλεμος War is sweet for those who have not tried it. In book 3 chapter 14 of his *Art of War* Vegetius[1] puts it this way: 'Do not put too much trust in a novice who is eager for battle, for it is to the inexperienced that fighting is attractive.' From Pindar we have:[2] 'War is sweet for those who have not tried it, but anyone who knows what it is is horrified beyond measure if he meets it in his heart.' You can have no idea of the dangers and evils of some aspects of human affairs until you have tried them.

> It is pleasant, for those who have never tried, to seek the favour of a powerful friend,
> But the experienced dread it.[3]

It seems fine and glorious to move among nobles at court and to busy oneself with the affairs of kings, but old men who know all about the business from experience willingly deny themselves this pleasure. It seems delightful to be in love with girls, but only to those who have not yet tasted the bitter in the sweet.[4] The adage could be applied in the same way to any affair carrying great risk and attended by suffering such as no one would face unless he were young and inexperienced. In his *Rhetoric* Aristotle[5] suggests that youth is bolder and age is diffident because the former are given confidence by their inexperience and the latter are made diffident and hesitant by their long acquaintance with suffering. If there is any human activity which should be approached with caution, or rather which should be avoided by all possible means, resisted and shunned, that activity is war, for there is nothing more wicked, more disastrous, more widely destructive, more persistently ingrained, more hateful, more unworthy in every respect of man, not to say a Christian.

Yet it is remarkable how widely these days, how rashly, for what trivial reasons war is begun, how cruelly and barbarously it is waged, not only by pagans, but by Christians, not only by laymen, but by priests and bishops, not only by the young and inexperienced, but by older people who have known it already so many times, not only by common folk and the naturally fickle mob, but especially by princes whose duty is to restrain with prudence and reason the rash impulses of the foolish majority. And there are plenty of lawyers and theologians who add fuel to the fire of these outrages and, as the saying[6] goes, sprinkle them with cold water. Because of this war is now such an accepted thing that people are astonished to find anyone who does not like it; and such a respectable thing that it is wicked – I might almost have said 'heretical' – to disapprove of this which of all things is the most abominable and the most wretched. How much more reasonable it would be to marvel at what evil genius, what plague, what excess, what madness[7] first put into the mind of man something hitherto confined to beasts – so that this gentle animal, which nature created to be peaceful and well disposed to its fellow creatures, the only one she intended for the preservation of all the others, should plunge with such savage insanity, such mad clamour, into mutual slaughter. This will cause even more wonder to anyone who has rejected popularly accepted opinions and turned his thoughts to discerning the real meaning and nature of things, looking with a truly philosophical eye on the one hand at the image of man and on the other at the picture of war.

First, then, if we consider just the condition and appearance of the human body, is it not apparent at once that Nature, or rather God, created this being not for war but for friendship, not for destruction but for preservation, not for aggression but to be helpful? For she gave every other living thing its own weapons. She armed the charging bull with horns, the raging lion with claws; she fitted the boar with murderous tusks; she protected elephants not only with their hide and their size but with their trunk as well. The crocodile is armour-clad at every point with plate-like scales, dolphins are equipped with flippers as weapons, porcupines have the defence of quills, the ray has a sting, the cock is equipped with spurs. Some Nature fortified with a shell, others with a hide, others with a scaly covering. There are some whose safety she provided for by giving them speed, like the doves; again there are others to whom she gave poison as a weapon. To these features she added hideous, savage appearance, fierce eyes and harsh voices, and implanted inborn enmities. Man alone she produced naked, weak, delicate, unarmed, with very soft flesh and a smooth skin. No part of his body seems to be intended for fighting and violence; not to mention the fact that other animals are capable of protecting themselves almost as soon as they are born; only man is born in such a state that he must be long dependent entirely on the help of others. He cannot speak, he cannot walk, he cannot feed himself, he only wails for help, so that we may conclude that this creature alone was born entirely for friendship which is formed and cemented most effectively by mutual assistance. It follows that Nature wanted man to owe the gift of life not so much to himself as to the kindness of others, so that he should learn that his end was thankfulness and brotherly love. So the appearance she gave him was not hideous and terrifying, as with the others, but mild and gentle, bearing the signs of love and goodness. She gave him friendly eyes, revealing the soul; she gave him arms that embrace; she gave him the kiss, an experience in which souls touch and unite. Man alone she endowed with laughter, the sign of merriment; man alone she endowed with tears, the symbol of mercy and pity. To him alone she also gave a voice which was not threatening and fierce as with the beasts, but friendly and caressing.

Not content with these gifts Nature gave to man alone the use of speech and reason, the thing which would serve above all else to create and nourish good will, so that nothing should be managed among men by force. She instilled a dislike of solitude and a love of companionship. She implanted deep in his heart the seed of goodwill. She arranged that what is most salutary should also be the most pleasant. For what is more agreeable than a friend, and at the same time what more necessary? So, even if it were possible to lead a comfortable life without the society of others, still nothing would seem pleasant without a companion – unless one were to put off human nature altogether and sink to the level of a wild animal. Further she added the pursuit of learning and the desire for knowledge, the most effective means of drawing the mind of man away from all savagery, just as it has special power in forming friendships. For neither close family nor blood relationships bind souls together with stronger or firmer chains of friendship than does a shared interest in worthwhile studies.

In addition to these she distributed among mankind a wonderful variety of gifts both intellectual and physical, so that everyone could find in everyone else something to love and respect for its excellence, or to pursue and prize for its usefulness and necessity. Finally she implanted in man a spark of the divine mind so that, even with no prospect of reward, he would take pleasure in deserving well of everyone. For this above all is the property and nature of God that by his benefits he has regard for all. Otherwise, what is that exquisite pleasure which we feel in our souls when we learn that we have been the means of someone's salvation? And this is why one man is dear to another, that he is bound by some great benefit bestowed. Therefore God placed man in this world as an image in some sense of himself, so that he should, like a sort of earthly divinity, take thought for the salvation of all. Even the brute beasts feel this, for we see not only the gentle ones, but leopards and lions and animals fiercer than these fly for help to man when in great danger. He is the final refuge for all creatures, he is the most hallowed sanctuary for all, he is the anchor which all regard as their sheet anchor.

We have sketched some sort of portrait of man. Now let us compare with this on the other hand, if you will, a picture of war. Imagine now that you see the barbarous cohorts that inspire terror by their very faces and the sound of their voices. On both sides iron-clad battle lines, the fearful clash and glitter of arms, the hateful roar of a great multitude, the threatening looks, harsh bugles, the terrifying blare of trumpets, the thunder of bombardons, no less frightening than real thunder but more harmful, the mad uproar, the furious clash of battle, the monstrous butchery, the merciless fate of the slain and those who kill, the slaughtered lying in heaps, the fields running with gore, the rivers dyed with human blood. Sometimes brother falls on brother, kinsman on kinsman, friend on friend, as the general madness rages, and plunges his sword into the vitals of one who never harmed him even by a word. In short a tragedy like this contains such a mass of evils that the heart of man is loath even to remember it.

I refrain from recounting other evils, common and trivial by comparison, such as crops trampled far and wide, farms burnt out, villages set on fire, cattle driven away, virgins raped, old men dragged off in captivity, churches sacked, robbery, pillaging, violence and confusion everywhere. And I say nothing of the consequences of even the most successful and just war: peasants plundered, land-owners oppressed; so many old men left desolate, more tormented by the slaughter of their children than if the enemy had killed them and taken away the knowledge of their grief; so many old women left destitute, condemned to a crueller death than by the sword, so many wives left widows, children left orphans, homes filled with mourning, rich folk reduced to poverty. As for the harm it does to the way people behave, what use is it to speak of that when everyone knows that general moral standards are ruined once and for all by war? It is the cause of contempt for duty, disregard for law, readiness to dare any sort of crime. It is the source of the huge teeming flood we have of mercenaries, robbers, despoilers of churches, and assassins. Worst of all, this deadly pestilence cannot be contained within its original limits, but, having begun in one quarter, it infects not only neighbouring regions like a contagious disease but even, through the effects of trade, of family or political alliances, drags remote ones into the general uproar and turmoil. In fact war is born from war, a real war from a counterfeit one, a huge war grows from a tiny one, and it is not unusual to see the same thing happen in these cases as the fables tell us about the Lernaean monster.[8]

It was for these reasons, I believe, that the ancient poets, who penetrated with great discernment into the significance and nature of things and also created the most suggestive images, said that war was sent into the world from the infernal regions through the Furies. Not just any Fury was suitable for this work – it was the most deadly one of all that was chosen:[9] '... she who has a thousand names, a thousand ways of causing harm.' Armed with countless serpents she blows her hellish horn. Pan fills the universe with mindless tumult. Bellona[10] cracks her furious whip. Godless Rage, breaking all his knotted chains, flies out with gory mouth, hideous to see.[11] This has not escaped grammarians[12] either, some of whom would have it that war is called *bellum* by antiphrasis because it has nothing good or beautiful (*bellum*) about it; *bellum* is the word for war for the same reason as the Eumenides (the Kindly Ones) is the name for the Furies. Other grammarians prefer to think it is derived from *bellua* because it is an act of brute beasts not of men to come together to destroy each other. But to me it seems worse than savage, worse than brutish, to resort to armed conflict. In the first place, most animals live in harmony and good order with their own kind, moving in herds and ensuring mutual protection. Not even all wild animals are fighters by nature (some are quite harmless, like deer and hares), only the most savage like lions, wolves, and tigers. But even these do not make war on each other as we do. Dog does not eat dog-flesh,[13] lions do not inflict their ferocity on each other,[14] snake lives in peace with snake, between venomous creatures there is an understanding. But for man no wild beast is more dangerous than man. And then, when they do fight, animals fight with their own weapons; we equip men to destroy men with unnatural instruments devised by the art of devils.

And animals do not become fierce for trivial reasons, but when hunger drives them mad, or when they feel they are being hunted, or when they fear for their young. But, God in heaven, we humans, what tragic wars we stir up, and for what frivolous causes! For the emptiest of territorial claims, out of childish anger, because some woman we intended to marry has been denied us,[15] for reasons even more ridiculous than these. And then among animals combat is always one to one, and very brief, and however bloody the fight may be, as soon as one or the other is wounded, it is broken off. When did anyone hear of a hundred thousand animals falling dead together after tearing each other to pieces, as men do everywhere? Remember too that just as some animals have a natural hostility for others of a different species, so conversely with some they have a real and permanent friendship. But between man and man, any man and any other, warfare is perpetual, and no treaty is capable of holding between any mortals – so true is it that anything which has departed from its own nature degenerates into a species worse than if nature herself had implanted the vice. Do you want to know what a savage, foul thing war is, how unworthy of man? Have you ever seen a lion forced to fight a bear? What grimaces, what roaring, what growling, what ferocity, what tearing of flesh! It strikes horror in any one who sees it even from a safe distance. But how much more loathsome, how much more savage, is the sight of a man fighting a man armed with so many weapons and so many missiles. I ask you, who would believe these were human beings if familiarity with the evil had not taken away our sense of wonder? Their eyes burn, their faces grow pale, their step speaks madness, the voice grates, the shouting is mindless, the man is entirely turned to iron; their weapons clang, their cannons spout flashes of lightning. It would be more humane if man devoured man for food and drank his blood; some indeed have even gone this far, doing out of hatred what custom or necessity would have rendered more excusable. But now the same thing is done in a crueller way, with poisoned darts and hellish machines. There is no trace of man in it anywhere.

Do you think Nature herself would recognize here what she created? And if anyone were to point it out to her, would she not be right to curse her deed as wicked, saying: 'What outrage is this I see? What hell has produced this monster for us? There are some who call me a harsh stepmother[16] because in the whole grand total of things I made a few poisonous creatures – although even these were meant to yield benefit to man – because I made a few animals that were not gentle – although no beast is so savage that it cannot be tamed by skill and kindness. The art of man can make lions tame, serpents gentle, and bears obedient. Who then is this, worse than a step-mother, who has given us this new beast, a plague to all the world? There was one creature I brought forth made entirely for kindly actions – peaceful, friendly, helpful. What has happened to make him degenerate into a beast like this? I recognize nothing in him of the man I created. What evil genius has degraded my work? What sorceress has conjured away his human mind and put an animal's in its place? What Circe has changed his native shape? I would order the unhappy creature to look at himself in a mirror; but what can the eyes see when the mind is gone? But look at yourself, you raging warmonger, if you can somehow come to your senses. Where did you get that threatening crest on your head, that glittering helmet, those iron horns, those winged elbow-pieces, those scales, those brazen teeth, that plate-armour, those deadly arrows, that more than savage voice, that more than bestial face, that thunder and lightning more terrifying and more deadly than Jupiter's own bolt? I made you a creature in some sense divine; what came into your head to change yourself into a brute so monstrous that no beast will be called a brute in future if compared to man?' I think Nature, the great maker of all things, would say all this and much more.

This then is how man is constituted, as we have shown, and this is what war is like, as we experience it all too often; so it seems a matter for some wonder what god, what sickness or what chance first put it into the heart of man to plunge a deadly sword into human vitals. It must have been by many stages that he descended to such an extraordinary madness. 'No one ever fell all at once to the worst depths of shame,' as the satiric poet[17] says, and the greatest evils have always crept into lives of men in the shadow and semblance of good. Long ago therefore when the first primitive men lived in the forests, naked, without fortifications or homes, they were sometimes attacked by savage beasts. It was with these that man first had to go to war, and a man was considered brave and made a leader if he had driven off attacking beasts from his fellow humans. Moreover it seemed entirely just that slayers should be slain and butchers should be butchered, especially when they suffered no harm from us and attacked our kind without provocation. Since such deeds won high praise – this was the reason Hercules was deified – spirited young people began to hunt wild animals everywhere and to show off the skins as trophies. Then, not content with having killed, they dressed themselves in the skins against the cold of winter. Such were the first murders and the first spoils.

After this they went further and dared to do a thing which Pythagoras[18] deemed thoroughly wicked and which might seem unthinkable to us if custom did not tell us otherwise. Custom has such force everywhere that among certain peoples it was considered a matter of duty to beat up an aged parent, throw him into a pit and so deprive of life the one who had given it;[19] it was thought pious to eat the flesh of one's intimate friends; it was held to be a fine thing that a virgin should become a common prostitute in the temple of Venus; and there were many other things more absurd than these that would be shocking to anyone if they were so much as mentioned here, so true is it that nothing is too villainous, or too cruel to gain approval if custom vindicates it. So, what was the crime they dared to commit? It was that they did not shrink from taking the carcasses of slain animals for food, to tear dead flesh with their teeth, to drink the blood and suck the juices, 'to stuff their entrails with other entrails' as Ovid[20] says. That crime, however monstrous it might seem to gentler minds, was nevertheless sanctioned by usage and convenience. It even became a pleasure to see carcasses served as delicacies. Meats were covered under crusts like buried corpses, they were flavoured with spices, an inscription was placed on them: 'Here lies a boar,' 'This is the grave of a bear' – What carrion pleasures! And they went further: from dangerous beasts they moved to harmless animals. There was a general onslaught on sheep, 'a creature without trickery or guile.'[21] There was an onslaught on the hare, whose only crime was to be edible. Nor did they refrain from eating the domestic ox who had supported the ungrateful family for so long with his labours; no species of bird or fish was spared, and this tyranny of greed reached the point that no animal was ever safe from the the cruelty of man. But custom also induced them to believe that this was not cruelty to any species providing it was not men they slaughtered.

Vice however is like the sea: we may have the choice of shutting it out, but to let it in and then contain it, no one has that power; once admitted, neither is controlled by our will but is driven by its own momentum. After they had had some practice in killing with these beginnings, anger convinced them that man should assault man with clubs or stones, or their fists. At least, up till then it was with such weapons that they fought, I imagine, and by killing beasts they would have learned that a man too can be slaughtered with very little trouble. But this kind of barbarity remained for a long time a matter of fighting between individuals. When one was defeated, the war was over; sometimes both fell, but then both were unworthy to live. Moreover there was some appearance of right in having stood up to an enemy, and it began to be a matter for praise if one killed some violent or pernicious man, such as Cacus and Busiris[22] were said to be, and freed the world of such monsters. We see such titles to praise among the achievements of Hercules. The next step was that numbers of people banded together according to kinship, neighbourhood, or close connection, and what is now called brigandage was then called war. Up till then it was a matter of stones and stakes with fire-hardened points; a stream in the way or a crag or some such obstacle would put an end to the fighting. Meanwhile, as savagery increased with habit, as anger rose and ambition became more and more inflamed, ingenuity provided weapons to match their violence. Men invented arms to defend themselves and missiles to destroy the enemy. Now they began to make war everywhere, in greater numbers, and with weapons. But this obvious madness had its own code of honour: they called it *bellum* (beautiful/war), and sought to make it a virtue if a man defended children, wife, herds, or places of retreat from enemy attacks at the risk of his own life. And so malice grew gradually side by side with civilization; city began to declare war on city, region on region, kingdom on kingdom, although there still remained at this time, in something which was excessively cruel in itself, traces of the humanity of the earliest times. Priests were sent to demand satisfaction,[23] they called the gods to witness, they skirmished with words before they came to blows. The battle was fought with ordinary weapons, and courage, not trickery. It was a crime to strike the enemy if the signal for battle had not been given; it was forbidden to go on fighting when the general had ordered the retreat to be sounded. In short, it was a contest in bravery and honour rather than an orgy of killing.

And as yet there was no resort to arms except against foreigners, who because of this were called *hostes*, enemies, a word like *hospites*, strangers. From these beginnings empires were born – and no nation ever ever achieved empire without great shedding of human blood. Since then there have been continuous changes resulting from wars, as one man drives another out of the seat of empire and seizes it for himself. Subsequently, as power had fallen into the hands of the most criminal sorts of mortals, armed attacks were made on anybody at will, and it was not the evildoers but the wealthy who began to be most exposed to the dangers of war, and the aim of fighting was no longer glory but filthy lucre or something even more base than that. I have no doubt that Pythagoras,[24] wisest of men, foresaw when he sought by his philosophical teaching to deter the inexperienced multitude from slaughtering flocks. He could see that some one who, without any provocation or injury, was accustomed to shedding the blood of harmless animals, would not hesitate to kill a man when angry or roused by insults. What is war anyway but murder and brigandage committed by many, all the more criminal because it is more widespread? But these ideas are laughed at as the ravings of schoolmen by the boorish lords of our own time, who have nothing human beyond the appearance of men but think themselves gods.

And yet from these beginnings we find the madness has reached such a point that life consists of nothing else. We are continually at war, nation clashes with nation, kingdom with kingdom, city with city, prince with prince, people with people and, as even the heathen admit is wicked, relative with relative, kinsman with kinsman, brother with brother, son with father; finally, worse in my opinion than all these, Christians with fellow men, and worst of all, I must add reluctantly, Christians with Christians. And men are so blind in their thinking that no one is surprised at this, no one denounces it. There are some who applaud it, make a glorious parade of it, call it 'holy' when it is worse than hellish, and inflame rulers already crazed with fury, pouring oil on the fire, as they say.[25] One uses the sanctity of the pulpit to promise pardon for all sins committed by those who fight under his prince's flag. Another declaims 'Invincible prince, if you only continue your present support of religion, God will fight on your side.' A third promises certain victory, and distorts the words of the prophets to mean something wicked with his quotations of 'You will not be afraid of the terror by night nor of the arrow that flies by day, nor of the demon of midday,' and 'A thousand may fall at your side, and ten thousand on your right,' and 'You will walk upon the asp and the basilisk, and tread underfoot the lion and the dragon.'[26] In short, the whole of this mystical psalm is perverted to apply to profane things, to fit the case of this or that ruler. There were plenty of such prophets on both sides, and plenty of people to applaud such prophets. We have heard bellicose sermons of this sort from monks, theologians, and bishops. So it is the decrepit who make war, priests make war, monks make war, and we involve Christ in something so diabolical! Two armies advance on each other and both carry the standard of the cross, which in itself could teach them how appropriate it is to conquer Christians. Under that heavenly banner, which represents the complete and ineffable union of all Christians, they rush to mutual slaughter; and of this wicked deed we make Christ the witness and the author. Where is the kingdom of the devil if it is not in war? Why do we drag Christ into this when he would be more at home in any brothel than in a war? Paul the Apostle considers it unworthy that any dispute should arise among Christians which needs a judge to settle the case. What if he could see us making war the whole world over, for such trivial reasons, more savagely than ever pagans fought, more cruelly than any barbarians? What if he could see that this is done with the authority, encouragement, and help of representatives of the pope, who is the peacemaker, the unifier of all things, of those who greet all people with the sign of peace? I am not deaf to what has long been shouted at me by the Carians[27] who reap their profit from public misfortune. 'We did not want war! We were forced into it by the crimes of other people! We are taking our rights! Whatever evil war brings, the responsibility lies with those who gave cause for it.' But let them keep quiet for a moment; I will refute their special pleadings and remove this cosmetic we have used to hide our disease.

Just as I have contrasted man and war, that is, the most peaceable of animals with what is by far the most inhuman thing, so that the horror of it should be clearer, let me now contrast war and peace, the most wretched and wicked of things with the happiest and best; it will then be clear what madness it is to resort to war with so much clamour, so much effort, so much expense, so much danger, and so many disasters, when concord could be bought at much less cost. In the first place, what is there in the whole world better and sweeter than friendship? Absolutely nothing. But what is peace if not friendship among many people? On the other hand, war is likewise nothing but hatred between large numbers. It is the characteristic of good things that the more widespread they are the more advantage they bring. Therefore since friendship between one person and another is such a pleasant and salutary thing, how great the happiness will be if kingdom is united with kingdom and nation with nation in bonds of friendship. Conversely it is in the nature of evils that the wider they spread the more they deserve their appellation. Therefore if it is deplorable, if it is criminal for a man to attack another with the sword, how much more destructive it is, how much more criminal for the same deed to be done by so many thousands of men? In concord, small things grow; in discord, even great things decline.[28] Peace is the mother and the nurse of all that is good. War immediately, and once and for all, buries, extinguishes, and destroys all that is joyous and beautiful, and pours out a veritable Lerna of evils into the lives of men. In times of peace it is just as if a fresh spring sun begins to shine on human affairs; fields are cultivated, gardens turn green, flocks graze contentedly, farms are established and towns rise, fallen buildings are restored, others ornamented and enlarged, wealth increases, pleasures are nurtured, law is enforced, statecraft flourishes, religion is fervent, justice reigns, goodwill prevails, artisans practise their crafts with skill, the earnings of the poor are greater and the opulence of the rich more splendid. The study of the most noble subjects thrives, youth is educated, old age enjoys a peaceful leisure, girls are happily married, 'Young mothers are praised for children who resemble their fathers.'[29] Good men prosper, bad men are less bad. But as soon as the raging storm of war erupts, ye gods, what a monstrous sea of troubles rushes in, flooding and overwhelming everything. Flocks are driven off, crops trampled, farmers slaughtered, farms burned, flourishing cities built over so many centuries are overturned by a single onslaught, so much easier is it to do harm than good! Citizens' wealth falls into the hands of damnable brigands and assassins; homes are filled with mourning; fear, grief, wailing, and lamentation are everywhere. The skills of craftsmen grow cold, the poor must starve or resort to wicked means. The rich either mourn the wealth they have lost or tremble for what they have left, much to be pitied in either case. There are no weddings for girls, except in sadness and mourning. Deserted wives remain childless in their homes, the laws are silent, goodwill is mocked, there is no place for justice, religion is a subject of scorn, there is no distinction between sacred and profane. Youth is corrupted with every sort of vice, the old weep and curse the length of their days. Study and learning are without honour. In short, we find more evils in war than any man's words can express, still less any words of mine.

Perhaps it would be more bearable if wars only made us miserable and not malevolent and wicked too, if peace only made us happier and not better too. But it is a wicked man who resorts to war. There are already, alas! too many evils which never cease to worry hard-pressed mortals whether they will or no, wearing them down and consuming them. About two thousand years ago there were some three hundred names of illnesses noted by physicians[30] not including sub-types, the new diseases that develop every day, and old age itself, the malady with no cure. We read of whole cities in one place destroyed by an earthquake, set on fire by lightning in another, solid areas of ground in yet another swallowed up by a gaping hole, towns undermined by diggings and collapsing, not to mention the vast number of people carried off by events so common as to be ignored: tidal waves and rivers flooding, avalanches and collapsing buildings, poisonings, falls, attacks by wild animals, eating, drinking, sleeping. One person chokes on a hair while drinking milk, another on a grape-seed, a third on a fish-bone stuck in his throat. Some have died of sudden joy; though to die of great sorrow is less extraordinary. Then there are the fatal epidemics which rage quite commonly everywhere. There is no part of the world where human life, in any case so brief in itself, is not in danger. It is prey to so many woes that Homer[31] was right to declare man the most wretched of living creatures. But these woes cannot easily be avoided and do not happen by our own fault, so they make us wretched but not guilty. What is it that makes creatures exposed to such a multitude of calamities go looking for further trouble as if they had none already? And looking not for just any trouble but the most terrible of all: so destructive that it alone beats all the others, so fertile that it alone contains all the others, so deadly that it makes people as wicked as they are tormented, utterly wretched yet not to be pitied, except those who want war the least and suffer from it the most. Add to all this that the advantages of peace spread very widely and most people have a share in them. In war, if anything turns out happily – though heavens knows whether anything in war could be called happy! – it affects only a few, and unworthy ones at that. The salvation of one is the ruin of another; one man's wealth is the spoils taken from another; this man's triumph is that man's grief. If failure is bitter, success is inhuman and bloody. Most often both sides weep over a Cadmean victory[32] as it is called. I wonder whether any war has ever ended so successfully that a sensible victor did not regret having undertaken it. So, since peace is of all states both the best and most joyful, and since war, conversely, is the most wretched and most unjust, how can we believe that people are in their right mind when they can ensure peace with little trouble yet prefer to resort to war, even at the cost of the greatest difficulties?

What an unpleasant thing it is in the first place, that first rumour of war. And then what resentment the ruler must face as he strips his subjects bare with frequent taxes, how much trouble in raising and keeping extra troops, in bringing in foreign troops and mercenaries. What trouble and expense too fitting out ships, building and repairing fortresses and camps, furnishing tents, constructing and moving machines, weapons, missiles, baggage, transport, provisions. What labours must be put into raising walls, digging trenches and underground passages, in setting watches, posting sentries, holding manoeuvres. I am still saying nothing of alarms and dangers – for what is not to be feared in war? Who could possibly tell how many hardships these idiots of soldiers put up with in their camps – and they deserve worse just for being willing to put up with these. Food that would turn the stomach of a Cyprian ox,[33] sleeping quarters that would be scorned by a dung-beetle, few hours of sleep and those not of their own choosing. A tent which lets in the wind from every direction, or no tent at all. They have to endure an open-air life, sleep on the ground, stand in their arms, bear hunger, cold, heat, dust, rain. They have to obey their commanders, they have to bear floggings with rods; for no slave's bondage is more humiliating than soldiers' service. Add to this that when the fatal signal is given you have to go and face up to death, either to kill mercilessly or to fall miserably. We undergo all these woes in order to achieve the most wretched state of all. We afflict ourselves first with these countless woes, just in order to inflict them on others.

If we will only do the arithmetic and weigh up in honest terms the cost of war and the cost of peace, we shall soon discover that the latter can be bought for a tenth part of the worry, effort, distress, risk, expense, and bloodshed that war involves. You lead forth into danger a huge host of men to demolish some town; but with the labour of these men, and with no danger at all, you could have built another town, and a far finer one! But you want to harm the enemy. That alone is inhumane, but just think: could you harm them without first harming your own men? And it seems the act of a madman to accept such certain trouble when it is uncertain which way the dice of war will fall.

But admitting that the heathen might have been brought to this state of madness by stupidity, anger, ambition, greed, or barbarity, or, as I more readily suppose, by the Furies sent from Hell, where did we get the idea that Christian should draw a bloody sword on Christian? It is called fratricide if one brother kills another, but Christian is united with Christian more closely than any blood brother, unless the bonds of nature are tighter than those of Christ. What an absurdity that there should be almost continuous warfare between those whom the church holds under one roof, who boast of being members of the same body with the same head, who is Christ. They have one father in heaven, they are given life by the same spirit, initiated into the same mysteries, redeemed by the same blood, reborn in the same baptism, nourished by the same sacraments; they fight under the same commander, eat the same bread, share the same cup; they have a common enemy in the devil and finally are called every one to the same inheritance. Where else are there so many symbols of perfect concord? so many lessons of peace? One commandment Christ called his own – the commandment of love.[34] What could be more opposed to love than war? He greets his own with the blessed sign of peace. To his disciples he gave nothing and left nothing but peace.[35] In those holy prayers of his, he prayed to the Father particularly that, as he was one with God,[36] so his own (that is, Christians) should be one with him. As you can hear, this is something more than peace, or friendship, or concord. The prefiguration of Christ was Solomon, whose name means 'Peacemaker' in Hebrew;[37] he was chosen by God to build the temple. David, who was greatly beloved for his other virtues, was nevertheless kept away from the building of the temple because he was a man of blood.[38] But he made war at God's command usually against the wicked and that in an age which had not yet learned from Him, who came to complete the law of Moses, that we should love even our enemies.[39] When Christ was born, it was not of war or triumphs that the angels sang, but of peace.[40] Even before he was born, the mystic prophet[41] sang of him: 'And his place was made in peace.'

Search the whole of his teaching; nowhere will you find anything that does not breathe peace, that does not ring of friendship, that does not savour of love. And since he knew that peace cannot exist except when we sincerely despise the things for which this world is prepared to fight, he commanded us to learn from him to be meek.[42] 'Blessed' was his word for those who thought nothing of riches and of their daughter Pride, for he called them 'the poor in spirit';[43] 'blessed' were those who reject the pleasures of this world – he called them those that mourn; those who allow themselves to be turned out of their property knowing that this world is nothing but an exile and that the real homeland and the real treasure of the devout are in heaven. 'Blessed' are those who do good to everyone, and yet men revile and persecute them with impunity.[44] He forbad anyone to resist evil.[45] To keep the matter short, just as the whole of his doctrine teaches tolerance and love, so his whole life is a lesson in compassion. This was how he reigned, how he fought, how he conquered, how he triumphed. The apostles, who drank the spirit of Christ in its purest form and were gloriously drunk with that wine, have no other teaching.

What is the sound that rings everywhere in Paul's letters but peace, gentleness, and love? What does John talk of, repeatedly, but love? What else does Peter say? What else do all truly Christian writers say? Where does all this noise of wars come from among the sons of peace? Is it nothing but a fable when Christ calls himself the vine and his followers the branches?[46] Who ever saw a branch fighting with a branch? Is it meaningless, the figure that Paul[47] used more than once: that the Church is nothing if not one body composed of different members, joined to one head, who is Christ? Who ever saw the eye fighting with the hand, or the stomach with the foot? In this universe there is a harmony of all the very different elements. In the body of a living creature, there is peace between one member and another, and the gift which each part has it has not for itself alone but for all in common. If anything happens to one part, the whole body comes to its aid. Is the bond of nature in a perishable body more powerful that the spiritual bond uniting the mystical and immortal body? Is it in vain that we pray as Christ taught us: 'Thy will be done on earth, as it is in heaven'?[48] In the heavenly city there is complete concord, and Christ wanted his church to be no less than a heavenly people on earth living, as far as possible, in the image of that city, hastening towards it and drawing strength from it.

Let me ask you to picture now some strange visitor, from the cities on the moon where Empedocles lived or from one of those innumerable worlds that Democritus[49] imagined, who had come to this world of ours seeking to learn what goes on here. Suppose that he has learned a lot about different things and has heard that there is one animal which is a wonderful combination of a body that it has in common with the beasts and a soul that is an image of the divine mind. This creature is so noble that although it lives here in exile it rules over all other animals because, owing to its heavenly origin, it always strives towards heavenly and immortal things. He has heard that God cared for it so much that, seeing that it could not achieve what it strove for either by its own natural strength or by philosophical reasoning, he sent his only Son here to bring a new kind of teaching. Suppose then that, having learned everything about the life and teachings of Christ, he wishes to observe from some lofty observatory what he had heard about. When he observes all the other animals behaving properly, each following the laws of nature according to its own kind and seeking nothing except what nature prescribes, and one animal trafficking, bargaining, quarrelling, and warring, will he not surmise that the 'man' he has heard about is any animal but the real one? Finally when man is pointed out to him and he tries to discern the whereabouts of the Christian flock which follows the teaching of its heavenly master and offers an image of the angelic city, will he not judge that the Christians live anywhere but in those countries in which he has seen such opulence, luxury, licence, pomp, tyranny, ambition, deceit, envy, anger, dissension, brawls, fights, wars, and tumults; in short a Lerna of all those things which Christ condemns worse than any to be found among the Turks or Saracens?

Where did it come from then, this plague that has infected the people of Christ? Doubtless this evil, like most others, found acceptance gradually with the heedless. For every bad thing either slips by degrees into the life of men or insinuates itself under the pretext of something good. The first thing to creep in in this case was erudition, apparently ideal for confuting heretics, armed as they were with the writings of philosophers, poets, and orators. At the very beginning such things were not studied by Christians, but people who had to do with them before they knew Christ turned what they had acquired to pious uses. Eloquence too, at first disguised rather than spurned, was later openly approved. Then, on the pretext of overthrowing heresy, an ostentatious love of controversy crept in which was a major scourge to the church. Finally things went so far that the whole of Aristotle was accepted into the heart of theology, and accepted to the extent that his authority was almost more sacred than that of Christ. For if anything Christ said is not easily seen as fitted to the way we live we are permitted to interpret it differently, but anyone who dares to oppose in the slightest degree the oracles of Aristotle is immediately hissed off the stage. From the latter we have learned that human happiness is not complete without bodily comforts and worldly goods. From him we have learned that a state in which all property is held in common cannot flourish. We try to fuse together all his decrees and the teachings of Christ, which is like mixing fire and water.[50] We have also accepted some things from Roman law because of their obvious fairness, and in order to reconcile the two better we have twisted gospel teaching as far as we could to fit them. But Roman law allows us to meet force with force and each person to pursue his own rights; it sanctions bargaining, it allows usury, providing it is moderate, and describes war as praiseworthy, providing it is just. 'Just,' however, is defined as what has been ordered by the ruler, even if he is a minor or a fool. In fact the whole teaching of Christ is so contaminated by the writings of pagan dialecticians, sophists, mathematicians, orators, poets, philosophers, and lawyers that the greater part of a lifetime must be spent before you are free to investigate the sacred scriptures; and when you do get to them you are inevitably so corrupted with all these worldly ideas that the precepts of Christ either seem utterly repugnant or they are distorted to fit the teachings of the pagans. And we are so far from condemning this state of affairs that it is regarded as a sin for anyone to speak about Christian scriptures if he has not first crammed himself 'up to both ears,'[51] as they say, with nonsense out of Aristotle, or rather out of the sophists. As if the teachings of Christ were not truly something that could be entirely shared by all, or had any kind of common ground with the wisdom of the philosophers.

The next stage was that we were accorded much honour, but spontaneously offered; then we began to demand it as our due. That seemed quite proper. Then we were given money, but to be distributed as alms to the poor; then it was for our own use. Why not? since we have learned that this is the order of charity, that each must be his own neighbour.[52] There was no lack of excuses for this fault: it is one's duty to consider the needs of one's children, it is fair that one should prepare in advance for old age. 'Why should we refuse riches after all,' they say, 'if they can be gained honestly?' By these stages it has gradually reached the point where the richest is considered the best, and never was wealth held in greater honour among pagans than it is nowadays among Christians. What is there anywhere, either sacred or profane, which is not controlled by wealth? It seemed some power should go with these honours; and there was no lack of people willing to go along with it. This also became an accepted thing, but somewhat reluctantly and sparingly; they were satisfied with the title alone and willingly left the business to others. In the end, bit by bit, it has reached the point where a bishop does not think he is a bishop unless he has some worldly power; and an abbot who can never do what tyrants do is scarcely a proper abbot. Finally, brazen-faced, we have thrown away all shame and broken down all the barriers of modesty. Whatever sort of avarice existed among the heathen, whatever ambition, luxury, pomp, tyranny, we imitate, equal and outdo.

I say nothing of less important things, but was there ever war among the heathen as continuous and as cruel as among Christians? What storms have we not seen these past few years, what waves of war, what broken treaties, what bloodshed! What nation has not clashed swords with what other? And then we abominate the Turk; as if there could be any spectacle more agreeable to the Turks than what we ourselves provide for them daily with our massacres of each other. Madness seized Xerxes[53] when he led that huge multitude to invade Greece; does he seem sane to you, writing threatening letters to Mount Athos commanding it to move aside? ordering the Hellespont to be whipped because it did not favour him when he wanted to sail across? Madness seized Alexander the Great;[54] who denies it? That demi-god wished for several worlds, so that he could conquer them, such was the fever for glory that obsessed his immature mind. And yet these men, whom Seneca[55] does not hesitate to call raving bandits, made war more humanely than we do, made war in better faith, without such machines, without such techniques and not for such frivolous causes as we Christians. If you reread the histories of the pagans you will find many leaders who resorted to extraordinary tactics to avoid war, who preferred to bind the enemy by obligations rather than defeat them by force of arms. Some even considered it better to give up their power than to go to war. But as for us pseudo-Christians, there is nothing we do not snatch at as a pretext for war. Before pagan warriors resorted to arms, they would meet to talk. Among the Romans, when everything else had been tried, a *fetialis* was sent forward with the *paterpatratus*;[56] certain ceremonies were performed; undoubtedly, they were trying to find means of delay, so that the war fever could be cooled. And when all this was completed it was not permitted to engage the enemy until the signal was given, and this was given in such a way that the ordinary soldier would not know when it was to be given. And when it was given, anyone who was not bound by the military oath was not allowed to challenge or strike the enemy, even if he were living in the camp. Thus Cato the Elder[57] wrote to his son, who was idling in camp, to tell him either to come back to Rome or, if he preferred to remain with the army, to seek the commander's permission to engage in fighting with the enemy. Just as the signal for battle gave the power to fight only to those who were bound by the oath, so the signal by which the retreat was sounded took away from everyone the right to kill. This is why Cyrus[58] praised a certain soldier who had his sword raised to kill his enemy and, hearing the retreat sounded, forthwith let his opponent go. These practices had the effect that no one thought he had the right to kill a man unless necessity forced him to.

Nowadays if a man meets one of the people with whom he is at war by chance in a wood – not carrying arms but money, not seeking to fight but running away somewhere to avoid fighting – if he kills him, and having killed him strips him, and having stripped him buries him, this is held to be valour among Christians. 'Soldiers' are those who rush into a fight of their own accord in the hope of some small loot, and fight on either side like gladiators, even brothers against brothers, and subjects of the same ruler. Such men come home from battles like these and tell the story of their exploits like soldiers; yet they are not punished as robbers and traitors to their country and deserters of their prince's cause. We loath an executioner because he puts to death the guilty and the condemned, although he is paid by the law to do so; but men who abandon their parents, wives, and children and rush off to war of their own accord, without promise of pay but asking to be hired for some wicked butchery, are almost more welcome when they go home than if they had never been away. They think they have won some sort of nobility from their villanies. The man who has stolen a garment is infamous; the man who has robbed so many innocent people while he was on his way to join his army, while serving as a soldier, and while coming back from soldiering is considered a respectable citizen. And the soldier who has conducted himself with the most brutality of all is thought worthy to be the commander in the next war. So, if you consider the rules of military service in olden times, you will see that military service among Christians is not military service at all, but brigandage.

If you compare Christian monarchs with pagan ones, how weak our own cause is! They had no ambition but glory; they took pleasure in increasing the prosperity of the provinces they had subjugated in war; where rustic peoples were without education or law and living like wild beasts, they brought refinement and the arts of civilization; they populated uncultivated regions by building towns; they fortified unsafe places, and made men's lives easier by building bridges, wharves, embankments, and a thousand other such amenities, so that it turned out beneficial to be conquered. How many stories are told of things wisely said or soberly done by them, even in the midst of war! But the things done in wars between Christians are too disgusting and too cruel to be mentioned here. The fact is that we copy only the worst practices of the pagans, or rather we outdo them.

But it would be worthwhile to hear how we justify this great madness of ours. If it were always a sin to make war, we are told, God would not have commanded the Jews to fight against their enemies. I hear you, but you should take into account the fact that the Jews hardly ever went to war among themselves, only against foreigners and unbelievers. We Christians fight with Christians. Their reason for fighting was a difference of religion, different gods; we are drawn into it by childish anger, by greed for money or thirst for glory, often by sordid wages. They fought by divine command, but it is passion that makes us draw the sword. However, if the example of the Jews is so attractive, why do we not by the same token practise circumcision? why do we not make animal sacrifices? why do we not abstain from pig's flesh? why do we not each marry several wives? Since we condemn these practices, why is their example in war alone acceptable? Why in a word do we here follow the letter which kills?[59] War was allowed for the Jews, but like divorce, doubtless because of the hardness of their hearts.[60] But after Christ ordered the sword to be put away,[61] it is not proper for Christians to fight, except in the noblest of all battles against the most shameful enemies of the church, against love of money, against anger, against ambition, against the fear of death. These are our Philistines, our Nebuchadnezzars, our Moabites and our Ammonites,[62] with whom we must make no truce, with whom we must be unceasingly at war until the enemy is completely eliminated and peace is installed in their place. Unless we subdue these, there can be no real peace for anyone either with himself or with anyone else. This is the only war which can produce true peace. Anyone who has conquered in this war can have no wish to engage in war with any other mortal. I am not influenced in the least by the fact that some interpret the 'two swords'[63] as the two powers, ecclesiastical and civil – which are both claimed for the successors of Peter – for Christ allowed Peter to err [that is, to carry a sword] on this very point so that after he was ordered to put up his sword, no one should be left in any doubt that war, which seemed permissible before, was now forbidden.[64] 'But Peter fought,' we are told. He fought, but still as a Jew who had not yet received the truly Christian spirit. And he fought, not for his rights or his property as we do, nor for his own life, but for the life of his master. In a word, the man who fought was the one who a little later made the denial. If the example of his fighting attracts you then so should his denial. And though he erred out of honest affection, he was still reproved.

Moreover, if Christ approved this sort of defence – a quite absurd interpretation adopted by certain people – why is it that his whole life and teaching proclaim nothing but tolerance? Why does he send his disciples to meet tyrants armed only with their staff and their pouch? If the sword which Christ ordered them to buy after selling everything else,[65] stands for temperate defence against persecutors – as some interpret it not only ignorantly but wickedly – why did the martyrs never use it? This is where those rabbinical distinctions are brought forward: 'It is lawful for a paid soldier to fight, just as it is lawful for a butcher to exercise his skill in preparing meat. For the latter has learned to cut up animals, and the former men.' Even citizens may fight, but in a just war – 'just,' however, means any war declared in any way against any body by any prince – 'priests and monks are not allowed to brandish a sword, but they are allowed to be present and take command.' 'It is a sin to make war in a spirit of vengeance, but not out of concern for justice' but who does not think his own cause is just? 'Christ sent out his disciples without means of defence, but while he was still with them they had no need of defence. When the time came for Him to depart, He told them to take a pouch and a sword, the pouch against lack of food, the sword against their enemies. And then the words "Take no thought for the morrow," "Do good to them that hate you,"[66] and others of that sort were valid up to the time of his departure. Similar teachings of Paul or Peter are advice, not instructions.' It is with brilliant teachings of this kind that we feed the greed of princes and offer them the means of self-flattery. As if there were a danger that the world would have a rest from war one day, we defend war with the words of Christ; and as if we were afraid that men in their greed would get tired of piling up riches, we make Christ our authority for it, twisting his words to the point that it seems he commanded, not tolerated, the practices he had previously forbidden. Before the gospel came, the world had its laws; it punished, made war, gathered stores of wealth and food. Our Lord came not merely to tell us what was allowed – how far we might fall below perfection – but what goal we must strive for with all our might. Anyone who tries earnestly to dissuade men from war is suspected of heresy; and those who water down the strength of gospel teaching with falsehoods like these and offer princes opportunities to flatter their own desires, they are orthodox and doctors of divinity. A doctor who is truly Christian never approves of war; perhaps he admits it is permissible sometimes, but with reluctance and sorrow.

But this is dictated, we are told, by the law of nature, it has legal sanction, it is accepted by custom that we should meet force with force, that each of us should defend our own life, and our money too since it is our very life, as Hesiod[67] says. I admit that. But the grace of the gospel is more effective than all these, and prescribes that we should not curse those who curse us, that we should repay evil with good, that if someone takes away part of our possessions, we should give the whole, that we should pray even for those who try to kill us.[68] 'These sayings apply to the apostles,' we are told; but they apply still more to the whole people of Christ, and to the body, as we have said, which must be whole and complete, even if one member excels another in endowments. It may be that the teaching of Christ does not apply to those who do not hope for their reward in Christ; fighting for money, lands, and power is for those who mock at Christ's words, 'Blessed are the poor in spirit'[69] – that is, the rich are those who want nothing of wealth or honour in this world. Those for whom the greatest happiness is in riches fight to save their own lives, but they are people who do not understand that this is death rather than life, and that for the faithful immortality is prepared.

The objection is raised that some Roman pontiffs have both instigated and abetted wars, that there are pronouncements of the church fathers in which war is apparently mentioned with approval. There are indeed some like this, but they are from the later period, when the vigour of the Christian spirit was waning; and they are very few, whereas there are countless examples among writers of proven sanctity which argue against war. Why do those few come to mind rather than the rest? Why do we turn our eyes from Christ towards men and prefer to follow uncertain examples rather than the unquestioned authority? In the first place, the popes were men. Second, it is possible that they were badly advised, or not attentive, or lacking in prudence or piety. However, even in these cases, you will find there was no approval of the sort of war we are constantly waging. I could prove this with the clearest documentation if I did not want to avoid any longer delay in such a digression. Saint Bernard[70] praised warriors, but in terms that condemn all our forms of soldiering. But why am I influenced more by a work of Bernard, or an argument of Thomas,[71] rather than the teaching of Christ, which forbids us absolutely to resist evil, at least by the methods popularly used?

'But,' it is said, 'it is legitimate to sentence a criminal to punishment; therefore it is legitimate to take revenge on a state by war.' The answer that can be given to this is too long to be set out here. I shall say only that there is this difference: that in the courts a convicted criminal is punished in accordance with the laws, in war each side treats the other as guilty. In the first case, only the one who did wrong suffers and the example is visible for everyone. In the second case the greatest part of the suffering falls on those who least deserve to suffer, namely on farmers, old people, wives, orphans, and young girls. Moreover, if there is any advantage to be gained from this worst of all situations, it goes entirely to a small number of utterly criminal bandits, to the mercenary soldiery, to the brazen profiteers, perhaps to the few leaders who connived to stir up the war for this very purpose and who are never better off than when the state is on the rocks. In the courts, an individual is not spared in order to ensure the safety of all; in war, in order to take revenge on a few, or even on one person perhaps, we inflict cruel suffering on so many thousands of people who in no sense deserve it. It is better for the fault of a few to go unpunished than to demand some vague punishment of one individual or another and in the process draw ourselves and our loved ones, as well as our 'innocent enemies' – as we call them – into certain danger. Better leave the wound alone if you cannot treat it without serious harm to the whole body. If anyone cries that it is unjust not to punish a sinner, my answer is that it is much more unjust to call down absolute disaster on so many thousands of innocents who have not deserved it.

But these days almost every war is caused visibly by some 'titles' or other and by the ambitious alliances of princes who, in order to assert their dominion over some small bourg, seriously imperil their whole realm. Then this same thing that they have laid claim to with so much blood they sell or give away. Some one will say: 'Would you have princes fail to assert their rights?' I know it is not for some one like me to argue boldly about the business of princes, and even if it were safe to do so, it would take longer than I have time for here. I will say this only: if some claim or other seems to constitute a cause for war, then human affairs are in such a confused state, there have been so many changes, that there can be no one who does not have a claim. What nation has not at some time been driven out of its homeland or has not driven others out? How many migrations have there been from one place to another? How many times has there been a transfer of power this way and that, either by chance or by treaty? The Paduans should try to recover the site of Troy because Antenor[72] was once a Trojan. The Romans should try to recover Africa and Spain because these were once provinces of Rome. In addition, what we call 'rule' is administration; rights over men, free by nature, are not the same as rights over cattle. This same 'right' that you have was given by the consent of the people, and the same people who gave it, if I am not mistaken, have the power to take it away. Moreover, look what petty affairs are in question: it is not a matter of whether this or that state is to be subject to a good prince or slave to a tyrant, but whether it is reckoned to be Ferdinand's or Sigismund's, whether it pays tax to Philip or to Louis.[73] This is the all-important right for which the whole world is to be entangled in war and slaughter.

But let us admit that this 'right' is worth something, that there is no difference between a privately owned field and a state, no difference between the cattle bought with your money and men who are not only free but Christians. Still it is prudent to give some thought to whether this right is worth so much that you should pursue it at the cost of such huge detriment to your people. If you cannot show that you have the mind of a prince, at least act like a man of business. He takes no account of expense if he has seen clearly that it cannot be avoided except at the cost of heavier loss, and he considers it a gain if he has the good fortune to cut off a business with very small loss. At all events, in the case of a danger to the state you might follow the example from private life about which there is a popular, rather amusing story. There was a disagreement between two kinsmen about the division of property and since neither would yield to the other it looked as if the affair would go to court and the quarrel would be settled by the decision of the judges. Counsel had been consulted, the action was prepared, it was in the hands of the lawyers. The judges were addressed, the case opened, and the pleading began – that is, war was declared. At this moment one of them came to his senses just in time, invited his opponent to visit him privately, and spoke to him in these words: 'To start with, it is indecent for those whom nature has joined to be separated by money. In the second place the outcome of legal action is almost as uncertain as war. We have the power to start this but we cannot put an end to it. This whole case is about a hundred gold pieces. We shall spend twice that amount if we go to law on clerks, on investigators, on barristers, on solicitors, on judges, and on judges' friends. We shall have to be polite to them, flatter them and give them presents; and I say nothing of the worry of canvassing and the effort of running here and there. Even if I win on all possible points, it is still more trouble than gain. Why don't we think more of ourselves than of those robbers, and share between us the money which would be wasted on them? You give up half of yours, and I will give up the same of mine. In this way we shall be the richer for our friendship, which would otherwise be destroyed, and we shall avoid a great deal of trouble. And if you refuse to give up anything, I yield the whole case to you. I prefer to see this money go to a friend, not to those insatiable robbers. I shall have made an ample profit if I preserve my reputation, keep a friend and avoid such a host of troubles.' His opponent was moved both by the truth of this and by his kinsman's generosity. The matter was settled between themselves, to the rage of those gaping crows, the lawyers and the judges, whom they had tricked. In a matter of much greater danger, you should try to imitate the good sense of these men. Do not consider only what you may hope to gain, but the sacrifice of so many amenities, the dangers, the disasters you will also incur in order to gain it. If you weigh in the balance advantages and disadvantages and find that an unjust peace is preferable by far to a just war, why should you prefer a throw of the dice with Mars? Who but a madman would fish with a golden hook?[74] If you see that the cost is far greater than the profit, even if everything falls out well for you, is it not better to give way a little on your rights than to trade such countless ills for a small advantage? I would rather anyone had the title if my claim must be justified by the sacrifice of so much Christian blood. One man, whoever he may be, has held possession for many years, has become accustomed to the reins of government, is acknowledged by his subjects and carries out the office of ruler; then up will come another who has discovered some old claim from the chronicles or from some worn inscriptions, and turns a settled state of affairs upside down. Especially in these times when we see that nothing in human affairs keeps its place for long, but is the plaything of chance and ebbs and flows like the tide, what is the use of asserting one's claim with so much noise to something which will soon, by some quirk of chance, pass to someone else?

Finally, even if Christians cannot bring themselves to despise such trivialities as these, what need is there to fly immediately to arms? There are so many earnest and learned bishops in the world, so many venerable abbots, so many nobles of great age with the wisdom of long experience, so many councils, so many assemblies set up, not without reason, by our ancestors. Why are the childish disputes of such princes not settled by means of their arbitration? But the argument of those who make the pretext of defending the Church is more 'honourable' – as if, indeed, the Church were not really the people, or as if the whole dignity of the Church were in the wealth of the clergy, or as if the Church had originated, grown, and become established by means of wars and slaughter instead of by the blood of the martyrs, by their tolerance and by their scorn for life.

To me it does not even seem such a commendable matter that we repeatedly prepare war against the Turks. The Christian religion is indeed in a bad way if its safety depends on this sort of defence. Nor is it reasonable to expect good Christians to be made with such beginnings: what is obtained with the sword is also lost by the sword.[75] Would you bring Turks to Christ? Let us not display our wealth, our armies, our strength. Let them see in us not just the name 'Christians' but the sure marks of Christians: a blameless life, the desire to do good even to our enemies, an unshakeable tolerance of all injuries, a scorn for money, a disregard for glory, a life held cheap; and let them hear the heavenly teaching which accords with this sort of life. The best way to subdue the Turk is with these weapons. All too often nowadays we are wicked people fighting other wicked people. I will put it another way – and would that it were too daring rather than too true! – if you take away the name and sign of the cross, we are Turks fighting with Turks. If it is by armies that religion is established, if it is strengthened by the sword, and increased by wars, then let us defend it by the same means. But if everything has been achieved by different means to these, why do we adopt pagan ways as if we despaired of Christ's protection? 'Why should we not cut the throats of those who cut ours?' they say. Do you feel inferior if someone is more of a criminal than you are? Why do you not rob the robber? or revile the man who reviles you? or hate the man who hates you?[76] Do you think it is a Christian act to kill even the wicked – as we judge them to be, but who are still men whom Christ died to save – and so make a welcome sacrifice to the devil? You would give double pleasure to the enemy, because a man has been killed and because it was a Christian who did the killing. Most people, wishing to seem truly Christian, try to do as much harm as possible to the Turks; and what they cannot do they call down in the form of curses, although one might perceive this, by the same argument, as unchristian. In the same way some who wish to appear strictly orthodox heap fearful curses on those they call heretics when they themselves are perhaps more deserving of the name. If someone wants to appear orthodox, let him do his best to bring back the erring to a right mind by gentle reasoning. We spit on the Turks and think we are by this action fine Christians, when perhaps we are more detestable to God than the Turks themselves. If the first messengers of the gospel had had the same attitude towards us as we have towards the Turks, where should we be now who are Christian because of their forbearance? Confront the Turkish problem! Make the ungodly godly, if you can; if you cannot, then pray for it and I will recognize your Christian spirit.

There are so many orders of monks in the world who live by begging and who want to be thought of as pillars of the church; but out of all these thousands how many are there who hold life cheaply when it comes to spreading the religion of Christ? 'But there is no hope of that,' they say. Indeed there would be hope if the Dominicans and the Franciscans followed the ways of their founders; they were men who, I think, held the life of this world in supreme contempt. I hardly need mention the ways of the apostles. There would be no lack of miracles among us; indeed the glory of Christ would require it. At present those who pride themselves on being the vicars and successors of Peter, the prince of the church, and the other apostles, generally put their whole trust in human defences. They are indeed strict proponents of the true religion; they live in wealthy cities given over to luxury, where they are corrupted themselves more quickly than they can reform others and where there is an ample supply of pastors to teach the people and priests to sing God's praises. They dwell in princes' courts – and this is not the place to tell what they do there. If only it were nothing worse than a dog in a bath.[77] They sniff around for wills, they hunt for money, they are subject to the tyranny of princes; and in order not to appear idle they censure passages in books as erroneous, suspect, scandalous, irreverent, heretical, or schismatic.

The fact is they prefer to rule to the detriment of the Christian people than to extend the kingdom of Christ at any risk to themselves. But those whom we call Turks are in large part half-Christian and perhaps nearer to true Christianity than most of our own folk. How many are there among us who do not believe in the resurrection of the body and do not believe either that the soul survives the body? And meanwhile it is through them that an attack is directed against petty heretics who question whether the Roman pontiff has jurisdiction over souls tormented by the fires of purgatory.[78] Let us first cast out the beam from our own eye, then we can cast out the mote from our brother's eye.[79] The purpose of gospel faith is conduct worthy of Christ. Why do we insist on things which have no effect on morality and neglect others which are pillars of faith and will cause the whole structure to collapse at once if they are removed? Finally, who will believe us when we bear the cross as our device and the name of the gospel, if our whole life speaks at every moment of nothing but the world? Add to this that Christ, in whom there was no imperfection, nevertheless did not quench the smoking flax or break the bruised reed, as the prophecy said,[80] but cherished and tolerated the imperfect until it could become better. We are preparing to quench the whole of Asia and Africa with the sword, though most of the population there are either Christian or half-Christian. Why do we not rather acknowledge the first and cherish the second, reforming them mercifully?

But if we are seeking to expand the Empire, or if we crave their gold, why to such a worldly enterprise do we put the name of Christ? Why is it that, while we attack them with purely human means, we bring into obvious peril the whole of that very thing which remains to us in the world? What a small corner of the world is left to us! What a multitude of barbarians, and what a few we are to challenge them! But some one will say 'If God be for us, who can be against us?'[81] And he will have the right to say this if he relies on the protection of God alone. But what does Jesus Christ our commander say to those who strive with other weapons? 'He who strikes with the sword shall perish by the sword.'[82] If we wish to conquer for Christ, let us gird on the sword of the gospel word: let us take the helmet of salvation and the shield of faith,[83] and the rest of the truly apostolic armour. This is how it will come about that when we are conquered we shall make our greatest conquest.[84] But suppose that we are successful in war, who ever saw people being made true Christians by the sword, by slaughter, fire, and pillage? It is a lesser evil to say openly one is a Turk or Jew than to be a Christian hypocrite. 'But their assault on us must be driven off.' Why then do we invite them to assault us by our quarrels with each other? Certainly, if we are in agreement, they will not be able to attack us easily, and they are more likely be converted to the faith by our good offices if they are spared than if they are ruined. I would rather have a genuine Turk than a fake Christian. It is our business to sow the seed of the gospel; Christ will give the increase.[85] The harvest is plentiful, if the labourers are not lacking.[86] And yet for the sake of making a few Turks into bad and false Christians, how many good Christians do we make bad, and how many bad ones worse? For what else can be the result of such a turmoil of wars? I am reluctant to voice here the suspicion – which has all too often turned out to be true, alas! – that the rumour of war with the Turks has been put forward as an excuse for robbing the Christian population, so that it is broken with every sort of oppression and therefore is more servile to the tyranny of both sorts of princes.[87]

I say these things, not because I would entirely condemn an expedition against the Turks if they attack us of their own accord, but in order to ensure that we prosecute the war, which we claim to wage in the name of Christ, in a Christian spirit and with Christ's own weapons. Let them feel that they are being invited to be saved, not attacked for booty. Let us show them conduct worthy of the gospel, if we do not have the language to converse with them. Our manner of life itself will have considerable eloquence. Let us offer them a simple and truly apostolic profession of faith, not loaded with superfluous human points. Let us demand of them most of all those things which are plainly taught us by the sacred books and writings of the apostles. Agreement will be easier to reach on a few points and harmony will be more easily established if each is free to make his own sense of most questions, providing there is no contention.

But I shall have rather more to say about all these matters when I publish the book which I have entitled *Antipolemus*[88] and which I wrote some time ago during my stay in Rome for Pope Julius II when he was deliberating whether to make war against the Venetians – something to be deplored rather than refuted. If you examine the matter more closely you will find that almost all wars between Christians have arisen either from stupidity or from malice. A few youths, with no experience, have been inflamed by the bad examples of their forbears and of stories which fools have spread from foolish books. Then they have been encouraged by the calls of flatterers, goaded by lawyers and theologians, with the consent or connivance of bishops, perhaps even at their demand, and they have, rashly rather than wickedly, gone to war; and to the enormous suffering of the whole world they learn that war is something to be avoided at all costs. Others are driven to war by a secret hatred or ambition, others again by their ferocity of mind. For it is true that our *Iliad* contains 'nothing but the feverish doings of stupid kings and peoples.'[89]

There are some whose only reason for inciting war is to use it as a means to exercise their tyranny over their subjects more easily. For in times of peace the authority of the assembly, the dignity of the magistrates, the force of the laws stand in the way to some extent of the ruler doing what he likes. But once war is declared then the whole business of state is subject to the will of a few. Those whom the prince regards with favour are promoted; those with whom he is angry are cast down. They demand as much money as they like. Why say more? It is only then that they feel they are really kings. Meanwhile the generals act in collusion to pick the bones of the unhappy population. With people of this mentality, do you think they would be slow to seize any opportunity offered of making war?

Then we cloak our disease with respectable names. I crave the riches of the Turks and hide this with the defence of religion; I do what my hatred dictates and use the rights of the Church as an excuse. I am the slave of ambition, I am moved by anger, carried away by my wild, undisciplined character, and I give as an excuse some treaty broken, some friendship violated, some omission in regard to the laws of betrothal, or something else of the kind. It is astonishing how they can fail to achieve the very thing they are striving for, and while they are stupidly dodging this or that misfortune, they fall into another, or even much deeper into the original one. For really, if they are driven by desire for glory, it is much more splendid to preserve than to destroy, much finer to construct a city than to demolish it. Then, even supposing the war has the best possible outcome, it is a very small share of the glory that can be given to the prince, whereas a large part is due to the people whose money paid for the whole thing, a greater part usually to foreign soldiers and mercenaries, some to the generals, and the greatest part to fortune which is always the greatest factor, in war as in all other business. If it is high-mindedness that incites you to war, think, I beg you, how mistaken you are to act on that basis. You are not willing to yield to one person, a neighbouring ruler for instance, perhaps a kinsman, perhaps one who has deserved well of you in the past, yet how much more humiliating it is for you to be a suppliant, begging for help from barbarians – and what is even more unworthy, from men besmirched with every sort of crime, if indeed brutes of this sort can be called men – persuading, flattering, and wheedling villains, murderers, and robbers, for these are the people through whom war is most commonly waged. You try to look like a little tiger to your equal, and you have to force yourself to be servile to the lowest dregs of humanity. You get ready to drive some close neighbour out of his territory, and you have to let a rabble of the dirtiest scoundrels into your own. You don't trust your kinsman, yet you trust yourself to an armed mob? How much safer peace would have made you!

If you are lured by the idea of gain, make some calculations. War may seem attractive as long as you have not realized that you are incurring immeasurable expenditure for a return which is not only much smaller but uncertain too. But you were thinking of the interests of the state? There is no other way by which states go more quickly and completely to ruin than by war. Before you start, the harm you have already done to your country is greater than the good you would do if you were victorious. You exhaust the wealth of your citizens, you defile their homes with mourning and fill the whole country with robbers, thieves, and rapists. For these are the waste that war produces. And whereas before you could enjoy control of the whole of France, you are now excluded by your own act from many parts of it.[90] If you really love your people, why do you not think of questions like these? – 'Why should I expose this flower of youth to all these evils? Why am I going to deprive so many wives of their husbands, so many children of their parents? Why should some title or other, some uncertain right, be claimed at the price of my people's blood?' When war was undertaken on the pretext of defending the church, we have seen the clergy so crushed by frequent tithes that no enemy could have treated them with greater enmity. So because we use some silly means to avoid one pitfall, we throw ourselves of our own accord into another. Because we cannot suffer some slight insult, we subject ourselves to the greatest humiliations. Because we are ashamed to seem compliant to a prince, we become the suppliants of the basest of men. Because we rashly demand freedom, we entangle ourselves in the heaviest servitude. Because we chase after a little gain, we inflict immense losses on ourselves and on our people. A prudent man would weigh all this up in his mind; for a Christian, if he is truly Christian, a thing so hellish, so alien to both the life and teachings of Christ is something to be avoided, averted, and driven out by all possible means.

If, because of general perversity, there is no way of avoiding it, when you have left nothing untried and no stone unturned in your search for peace, then the best expedient will be to ensure that, being an evil thing, it is the exclusive responsibility of evil people, and is concluded with a minimum of bloodshed. For if we strive to be in fact what is said of us, that is, admiring or desiring nothing of this world, seeking only to take flight from it with as little burden as possible, striving with all our might towards heavenly things, placing our whole happiness in Christ alone, believing that whatever is truly good, truly glorious, truly joyful is founded only on him, holding firmly that the faithful cannot be harmed, pondering how empty and fleeting are the playthings of mortal existence, reflecting deeply what a difficult thing it is for man somehow to become like God and by a sort of untiring meditation be so purged here of the contagion of this world that, once this bodily cloak is laid aside, he can pass directly into the company of the angels. In short, if we show we have these three qualities without which no one deserves the name of Christian – innocence, so that we may be free of all vice; charity, so that we may do good as far as we can; and patience, so that we may bear with the wicked and, if possible, overcome evil with good – what war over trifles, I ask you, could possibly exist between us? If the story of Christ is an old wives' tale, why do we not frankly spurn it? Why do we glory in his name? If he is really 'the way, the truth, and the life'[91] why is there such a difference between this model and our whole way of thinking? If we acknowledge Christ as our authority, and if he is love, if he taught nothing, handed down nothing but love and peace, well, let us declare him, not by wearing his name and badge, but in our deeds and lives.

Let us embrace the cause of peace, so that Christ in return may acknowledge his own. It is to this end that popes, princes, and states must take counsel together. There has been enough shedding of Christian blood now. We have provided enough amusements for the enemies of the name of Christ. If the populace is in something of an uproar, as it usually is, it must be restrained by the rulers, who should be to the state what the eye is to the body, or reason to the mind. Or again, if the rulers make trouble, then it is up to popes to settle the disturbance with their wisdom and authority. Or rather may we become sick in the end of everlasting wars and be touched by the desire for peace. Calamity itself draws us to it; the world, exhausted by wrongs, begs for it; Christ beckons us to it; and to it we are exhorted by Pope Leo, tenth of this name, representative on earth of the true peacemaker, the Solomon, Jesus Christ, a lamb when it comes to doing harm, but a roaring lion against all that is opposed to piety, whose every wish, every counsel, and every effort are directed to uniting those joined by a common faith in a common bond of harmony. He is endeavouring to make the Church flourish, not by wealth or power, but by its own proper gifts. A magnificent task indeed, and one worthy of such a hero, descendant of the illustrious Medici whose civic wisdom brought the famous city of Florence its great flowering with a long period of peace, whose house was the home of all good learning. Leo himself was endowed with a serene and gentle character and was introduced, from earliest childhood,[92] as they say, to the humanities and the gentler Muses; he was educated among the most learned men, in the very lap of the Muses, and brought to the office of pontiff a life and reputation quite unsullied, unstained by the slightest suspicion of slander even in that freest of all cities, Rome. Leo did not thrust himself forward for this office but, when he least expected it, his name was called as by a divine voice to bring help to a world grown weary with a prolonged turmoil of war. Let Julius[93] have the glory of making war; let him keep his victories; let him keep his splendid triumphs. Whether such things are fitting for a Christian pontiff is not for such as myself to declare. I shall say only this: that man's glory, such as it was, was accompanied by the ruin and misery of a very great number of people. The return of peace to the world will produce far more true glory for our Leo, than all those wars valiantly undertaken or successfully waged all over the world could produce for Julius. But this digression will seem to be an undue delay for those who prefer to hear about proverbs rather than about peace and war.

1 *Art of War* 3.12
2 A fragment (87 Bergk) cited by Stobaeus *Eclogae* 49.9.3, according to Henri Estienne, slightly mistranslated by Erasmus (he says it should read 'is horrified in his heart')
3 Horace *Epistles* 1.18.86–7
4 Erasmus makes a play on the words *amor*, love, and *amarum*, bitter.
5 A slightly confused memory of *Rhetoric* 2.12.6–9 (1389a) and 2.13.7 (1389b)
6 *Adages* I x 51
7 Cf Virgil's description of the Fury Allecto in *Aeneid* 7.324–492.
8 The multi-headed hydra which grew two or three heads to replace one cut off (Hesiod *Theogony* 313–5, Servius on Virgil *Aeneid* 6.287); also *Adages* I iii 27 'A Lerna of troubles'
9 Allecto, in Virgil *Aeneid* 7.337–8 which follows
10 Roman goddess of war; but it is Allecto who cracks her whip in *Aeneid* 7.451.
11 Cf *Aeneid* 1.294–6.
12 Servius on Virgil *Aeneid* 1.22 and Donatus *Ars grammatica* 3.6 ed Keil 4.402. For *bellua* see Festus Pompeius p 30 Lindsay.
13 Varro *On the Latin Language* 7.31 (alluded to in II i 86)
14 Pliny *Natural History* 7.1.5
15 The Emperor Maximilian's plan to marry Anne of Brittany was forestalled by Charles VIII of France.
16 See above, III vii 1* n 40.
17 Juvenal 2.83
18 Diogenes Laertius 8.13, Plutarch *De esu carnium* in *Moralia* 993A, and Ovid *Metamorphoses* 15.60–142. Pythagoras condemns the

practice of eating flesh but does not speak of the custom mentioned in the following sentence.
19 Cf *Adages* III v 1.
20 *Metamorphoses* 15.88
21 *Metamorphoses* 15.120
22 Cacus was a brigand (Virgil *Aeneid* 8.194, Livy 1.7.5, Ovid *Fasti* 1.550) and Busiris an Egyptian king (Cicero *Republic* 3.11.15, Virgil *Georgics* 3.5), both killed by Hercules.
23 Varro *On the Latin Language* 5.86, Livy 1.32.5–6, Cicero *On Duties* 1.11.36, Sallust *Historiarum fragmenta* 3.61.17
24 Not among the Symbols of Pythagoras (*Adages* I i 2). Diogenes Laertius reports a number of precepts of Pythagoras and various opinions about them, but not this.
25 *Adages* I ii 9
26 Psalm 91:5–7 and 13
27 Ie, mercenaries; cf *Adages* I vi 14 'Risk it on a Carian.'
28 Sallust *Jugurtha* 10.6; cf Otto 418.
29 Horace *Odes* 4.5.23
30 Cf Terence *Phormio* 575, Seneca *Letters* 108.28, and *Adages* II vi 37, Old age is sickness itself.
31 *Iliad* 17.446–7
32 *Adages* II viii 34
33 *Adages* I x 95
34 John 13:34 and 15:12
35 John 14:27
36 John 17:21
37 1 Chronicles 22:9
38 2 Samuel 7:12–17, 1 Kings 8:16–19, 1 Chronicles 22:8
39 Matthew 5:17 and 44, Luke 6:27
40 Luke 2:14
41 Psalm 76:2; an interpretation rather than a quotation from the psalm, which actually says 'in Salem ... in Zion.' One of the Songs of Asaph, one of the three musicians whom David put in charge of music in the temple (1 Chronicles 6:31) and a seer (2 Chronicles 29:30); twelve psalms (50 and 73–83), all of a prophetical character, are assigned to him.
42 Matthew 11:29
43 Matthew 5:3
44 Matthew 5:11
45 Matthew 5:39
46 John 15:5
47 Romans 12:5, Ephesians 4:16 and 5:23
48 Matthew 6:10
49 For Democritus see Diogenes Laertius 9.44; for the link between him and Empedocles on the subject of multiple worlds, see Cicero *On the Nature of the Gods* 1.26.73.
50 *Adages* IV iii 94
51 *Adages* II iii 27
52 Ie, charity begins at home; cf *Adages* I iii 91.
53 Herodotus 7.20 and 35
54 Quintus Curtius *Life of Alexander the Great* 9.6.20
55 *De ira* 2.23.4, 3.16.4
56 The *paterpatratus* was the chief of the *fetiales*.
57 Plutarch *Quaestiones Romanae* in *Moralia* 273E–F

58 Xenophon *Cyropaedia* 4.1.3–4
59 2 Corinthians 3:6
60 Matthew 19:8
61 Matthew 26:52 and John 18:11
62 Philistines, Moabites, and Ammonites were traditional biblical enemies.
63 Luke 22:38
64 Matthew 26:51–2
65 Luke 22:36
66 Matthew 6:25, Luke 12:22, Matthew 5:44
67 *Works and Days* 686
68 Matthew 5:42 and 44, Luke 6:27–35
69 Matthew 5:3
70 *Sermo* II *Ad milites* 3 (*PL* 182.924–5)
71 *Summa theologica* IIa IIae 40
72 Virgil *Aeneid* 1.242–9
73 All names of rulers in recent history
74 *Adages* II ii 60
75 Matthew 26:52
76 Allusions to Luke 6:27–8
77 *Adages* I iv 39* 'What has a dog to do with a bath?'
78 Allusion to the traffic in indulgences
79 Matthew 7:3
80 Matthew 12:20, Isaiah 42:3
81 Romans 8:31
82 Matthew 26:52
83 Ephesians 6:17 and 16
84 Cf Romans 8:36–7.
85 Cf 1 Corinthians 3:6–7.
86 Matthew 9:37, Luke 10:2
87 Ie, secular and ecclesiastical
88 The *Antipolemus* (or 'Against War') was never published; it was written for Cardinal Riario during Erasmus' stay in Rome in 1509 (see CWE 27 161).
89 Horace *Epistles* 1.2.8
90 A general comment, but an implied reader may be Francis I of France.
91 John 14:6
92 *Adages* I vii 52
93 A contrast between two Medici popes, Leo X and Julius II, the latter a notorious warmonger mocked in the famous dialogue *Julius exclusus*

IV i 52
Reddidit Harpocratem / He turned him into Harpocrates

Erasmus first wrote this for Collectanea *no 172. The proverb came into English as Tilley* H 177 *'To be a Harpocrates.' It was well known in antiquity (Otto 791) and was related to another phrase, 'Lay your finger on your lips' (in the satirist Juvenal 1.160), which also found its way into English (Tilley* F 239*). The gesture was the subject of an emblem poem by Alciato (no 11), who rewrote the epigram in the* Greek Anthology *10.98. Harpocrates was from Pharos (or Alexandria) in Egypt and was a form*

Cùm tacet haud quicquam differt sapientibus amẽs,
Stultitiæ est index linguaq; uoxq; suæ:
Ergo premat labias, digitoq; silentia signet,
Et sese Pharium uertat in Harpocratem.
Aiiij

He turned him into Harpocrates This is the emblem entitled 'Silence' in Andrea Alciato's *Book of Emblems* (here illustrated in the edition of Paris 1540, p 7). The text of this emblem (no 11), reads: 'When he is silent, a foolish man differs not a bit from the wise. Both tongue and voice are the index of his foolishness – therefore let him press his lips, and with his finger mark his silences, and let him turn himself into a Pharian Harpocrates.' It is related to Erasmus' adage IV i 52*. (Thomas Fisher Rare Book Library, University of Toronto) *of Horus, the sun-god, traditionally represented as a boy with his finger held to his lips (Augustine,* City of God *18.5; Ovid,* Metamorphoses *9.692; Varro* On the Latin Language *5.57). In Catullus 102, the speaker claims that he can be trusted to keep his friend Cornelius' secrets, as a 'very Harpocrates.'*

In his *Epigrams* Catullus[1] said by way of a proverb: 'He turned him into Harpocrates,' meaning: He imposed silence. The poem goes like this:

Gellius had heard that his uncle was in the habit of reproving loudly
Anyone who enjoyed love's pleasures or talked about them.
Determined that this should not happen to himself, he gave his uncle's own wife a 'massage,'
And turned his uncle into a figure of Harpocrates.
He did whatever he liked, for now even if he made his uncle himself
Perform fellatio,[2] Uncle would not utter a word.

Harpocrates[3] was pictured in ancient times as a god who, by a finger raised to his lips, enjoined silence, rather like the Roman goddess Angerona.[4]

1 74.4, the context for the passage then provided
2 Cf *Adages* III vii 70.
3 Plutarch 'Isis and Osiris' in *Moralia* 378C; Politian *Miscellanea* 83
4 See Pliny *Natural History* 3.65, Macrobius *Saturnalia* 1.10.7.

IV i 97
Mulierem ornat silientium / Silence becomes a woman

Proverbs about women and garrulity are common in many languages and this proverb is a typical patriarchal injunction (Tosi 1386, 1388), found in English as Tilley S 447, *'Silence is the best ornament of a woman' (and compare* M 45 *'Maidens should be seen and not heard'). Presumably woman is to be silent to allow man to speak more. Though the injunction might strike us as foolish now, the proverb is, as Erasmus shows, very old. Here he does not question the way social codes and prohibitions are built into the basic cliché stock of language.*

Sophocles[1] in his *Ajax the Whipbearer*: 'Silence is always a seemly ornament for women.' This is a proverbial statement which Servius[2] quotes from Sophocles in his commentary on book 1 of the *Aeneid*. Woman is by nature a talkative animal and is respected for nothing as much as for her silence, especially in the company of men when the talk is of serious matters. The source is Homer[3] who says several times: 'Speech shall be for men.' And Saint Paul[4] does not give women the right to speak, at least in church, but says they should question their husbands at home.

1 *Ajax* 293
2 Servius on *Aeneid* 1.561 (the reference is found in the first edition of Servius [Rome, c 1470], but omitted in the modern editions; ASD II-7, 95)
3 Homer *Odyssey* 1.358
4 1 Corinthians 14:34–5

IV V 1
Ne bos quidem pereat / Not even an ox would be lost

A proverb that begins on the subject of good neighbours, on having them and on being one. The idea is that a good neighbour will not steal one's ox, a bad neighbour may. Friendship is a central theme in the Adages; *the work begins with 'Between friends all is common' (I i 1*) and the topical index in the 1536 edition lists over sixty other proverbs on this same subject. Here neighbours and friends are interpreted broadly, as was common at the time, to include patrons and benefactors and much of the essay is a revealing study of the art of receiving patronage. Archbishop William Warham (*Contemporaries *3:427–31) was a great benefactor to Erasmus, and his interest in good learning allows Erasmus to write at length also on proper schooling in the arts.*

In some earlier proverbs we have already shown the great value of having a good neighbour and the troublesomeness of having a bad one. But it is profitable to stress again and again those features that make for a happy life so as to fix them more deeply in our minds. For having a good neighbour is important in almost all aspects of our life, not just when buying property or a farm. Accordingly, Porcius Cato's words[1] about having a good neighbour pertain not only to farmers, but also to each one of us. Indeed, if anyone of advanced age reviews the whole course of his life, he will come to realize that most of his good fortune and bad sprang from having good or bad neighbours. Columella[2] quotes a verse of Hesiod as if it were proverbial: 'Nor would an ox be lost unless you have a wicked neighbour.' But the loss of an ox is slight when compared with those misfortunes that one suffers at the hands of unscrupulous associates, false friends, or unfaithful wives and servants. Some have thought that Cato's view is to be rejected since the kind of neighbour we have is not in our control: 'sometimes death or other circumstances bring us new neighbours.' This is undeniable, but it was wise advice of Cato's that a farmer should take care, as far as he can, to have a good neighbour, and not only a good neighbour, but also an obliging one. (For a man who is not obliging can still be good.) Two things in particular will help to achieve this: being very careful when buying land, and being accommodating and helpful to one's neighbour. For we often have a bad neighbour because we ourselves behave like one. As Columella[3] so stylishly says:

> As a wise man bears with fortitude the misfortunes of chance, so a madman creates his own bad fortune. This happens to the man who spends his money only to acquire a good-for-nothing neighbour, when, if born from free parents, he might have heard even in earliest childhood, 'Nor would an ox be lost unless you have a wicked neighbour.' This applies not only to an ox, but to all parts of our estate. Indeed many have chosen to deprive themselves of their household gods and have fled from their homes because of their neighbours' wrongdoing – unless we think that whole nations abandoned their ancestral lands and made for distant regions for any reason other than that they could not tolerate wicked neighbours. I mean the Achaeans and the Iberians, the Albanians too, as well as the Sicilians, and, to touch on our own beginnings, the Pelasgians, the Aborigines and the Arcadians. And, to speak not only of calamities that afflicted whole peoples, tradition has handed down the memory of individuals who were hateful neighbours both in the regions

> of Greece and here in Hesperia itself. Could anyone have tolerated living next to the infamous Autolycus? Did Cacus, who lived on the Aventine hill, bring any joy to his neighbours on the Palatine? I prefer to mention persons of the past than those of the present so as not to name my own neighbour, who does not allow a tree of any great size on our land to stand, or any seedbed or any vine stake to remain undisturbed, or even our herds to graze without their being carefully watched. For what my opinion is worth, then, Marcus Porcius was right in thinking that such nuisances were to be avoided and in especially forewarning the farmer-to-be not to put himself into such a situation of his own accord.

So much for Columella, who, with an eloquence that has something of the flavour of a declamation, has both supported Cato and informed us what a pest a bad neighbour is. And yet Cato[4] has views not only on a neighbour's character but also on how well cared for is his property. 'Observe,' he says, 'how prosperous your neighbours look. In a fertile region they should be thriving.' For sometimes healthy crops show that the land is good, but in soil that is not very fertile they reveal the industriousness of the farmer. Moreover, just as a hardworking man stimulates his neighbour's household with the desire to farm well, so neighbours who are lazy and extravagant corrupt it. Similarly, having an over-powerful neighbour weighs hard upon those of little means, while extremely poor neighbours are always paring your resources, either by begging or by stealing. With sour-tempered and dishonest neighbours there are incessant disputes: about boundaries, damages incurred, rainwater from the roof, rights of way, the view from the house, or the blocking of light. But if circumstances have given us such a neighbour and if we cannot move our residence, all that we can do is to change him from a bad neighbour into a good one by being very obliging ourselves and certainly to avoid making him more troublesome by provoking him. The most shameful thing will be to turn a helpful neighbour into a disagreeable one by our own behaviour. Clearly this is the point of Cato's advice,[5] 'Be good to your neighbours.' And in case you might think it sufficient if you yourself refrain from injuring your neighbour, he adds, 'Do not allow your household to err in this way.' Next he points out the advantages of having good neighbours. He says, 'If you are popular with your neighbours, it will be easier for you to sell your products, contract out jobs, hire workmen. If you are building, they will help you with labour, animals, materials. If, heaven forbid, the need ever arises, they will be glad to defend you.'

Now, at one time, those who put up their farm for sale would inform the auctioneer of the features that made the property attractive: healthy climate, convenient location, fertile soil, well-constructed buildings. But when Themistocles,[6] a man of the keenest intellect, was selling his farm, he gave instructions that to attractive features such as these there should be added 'good neighbours.' This action was at first received with widespread laughter and mockery; later it was realized that to commend land in this way was of especial importance. To have an agreeable way of life in all its aspects the kind of neighbour each person chooses for himself is of the highest importance, as is also how he treats a neighbour he happens to acquire.

A prince who seeks new territory that he cannot protect without great difficulty and without spending all the resources of his ancestral realm creates bad neighbours for himself. On the contrary, a prince who appoints to his service loyal, intelligent counsellors and magistrates of irreproachable character who are devoted to their country wins good neighbours. It is also of the greatest importance which nations he joins together through marriage. If consideration of dowry or rank prompts him to take a wife who has a disagreeable character and insolent relatives, he is creating bad neighbours for himself. The prince who makes a treaty of friendship with those who are unscrupulous is seeking out bad neighbours. The man whose desire for prestige makes him rush to join a college or a monastery whose members are irreligious or even superstitious is acquiring hostile neighbours. The first precaution, then, should be in choosing associates, the next in correcting them, the final one in fleeing from those that are incorrigible. But even when one flees there is need of caution. Otherwise, if it is not done properly, fleeing from a fault leads one into a vice. And it often happens that in our loathing for one evil we rush headlong into a different, more serious one. Those who have chosen a friend judiciously rarely have regrets about the friendship. And it is often our fault that a friendship breaks up, because we do not treat our good friends well and also because we do not know how to put up with or correct friends who are unhelpful. No less in the wrong are those who do not know how to extract themselves from harmful friends whom they have encountered, but either cling to those whom they secretly detest or break off the friendship suddenly instead of allowing it to dissolve gradually.

The same thing happens to people in my situation in choosing and keeping patrons and supporters of our studies. We pass over those who present themselves, or we warmly accept those that do not suit us, or, if we have someone suitable, we do not exert ourselves to foster his good will towards us by performing services in return. I made most grievous errors of the first kind when I was young. Indeed if I had responded to the favours of the important men who had begun to embrace me I would have made something of myself in literature. But an excessive love of independence caused me to wrestle for a long time with treacherous friends and persistent poverty. And this would not have come to an end had it not been for the great William Warham,[7] Archbishop of Canterbury, a man to be revered more for his outstanding virtues, worthy of the highest prelate, than for the dignity of his title and office. I was like a fugitive that he trapped with a net and enticed into his friendship. After only a brief taste of his kindness I went off to Italy. When I was lingering there with no thought at all of going back to Britain, of his own accord he invited me back with the offer of a benefice. This too was treated with disdain. But when another wind returned me to England, he put me under such obligation to him that I surrendered to him, unwilling though I was. He achieved this, not so much by his kindness, which was, and still is, unequalled, as by an amiable and pleasant disposition and a wonderful constancy of affection – extremely rare in men of the highest rank. These qualities were the bait with which he enticed me into his service. In this way I was captured, much to my advantage, fortunate simply in his being the Maecenas[8] that befell me, but I would have been by far the most fortunate of men if it had happened sooner. I do not know whether he has regrets about me as his protégé, but I have certainly not repaid to my own satisfaction his kindnesses with my services to him, and I do not think that I will ever be able to do so. Accordingly, I must ask all who are devoted to good letters and to religion and who have derived from my works anything that pleased them to give thanks to this most holy prelate instead of to me, and indeed repay him if they can. They will repay him if they will not allow his memory to fade away among the generations to come. It is to his generosity they owe whatever they have drawn from my books – if they have actually drawn anything of value from them.

On all sides there is the clamour of complaints from those bewailing that they do not have a Maecenas to foster their studies. And yet Maecenas did not immediately embrace Virgil or Horace, and neither Maevius[9] nor Bavius had a Maecenas. The first thing a young man should do is to provide an outstanding specimen of his work as a pledge that what is given him will not be wasted. Let him not think it sufficient to have carried off gifts (or, more accurately, plunder) by any means at all. Generosity is not to be sought by shameless begging, but by continuously improving one's writings and character. Land that never fails to repay with considerable interest whatever a farmer entrusts to it invites him to sow seed more copiously.

Nor should one continually change patrons, abandoning one whom you have exhausted and then seeking another who is fresh and undepleted. Do not shake one oak[10] and then gather acorns under another. You should serve only one or two, and do so as if you are always going to rely on them. How many do we see at present who by their behaviour bring odium to literary studies and shame and unpopularity to their patrons! One way to show gratitude is to celebrate a patron's name in what you write and say, but how you praise someone is of great importance. Hollow-sounding praise prompts disbelief even if what is said is true. The result is that instead of thinking more highly of the person praised a reader thinks worse of the person doing the praising. Extravagant praise brings ill-will rather than glory. Those who extol those things that are condemned by good and wise men are actually censuring those whom they are praising.

First of all, the content of your encomium should be true; this should then be handled so as also to seem believable. Away with the hyperbole of certain poets by which they transform at will a mortal into a god. Depict in particular those virtues that win favour and goodwill, such as piety, honesty, purity in thought and deed, humility, generosity, openness, and affability. Nothing is more prone to envy human nature, or more captious in judging others. If, therefore, you have to touch on any of these qualities that the general public admires so much that it envies those who possess them, you must handle this skilfully, so that he who is praised will not have to fear the evil eye of envy. No one envies the rich man who acts not as the owner, but as the steward of possessions that he has received by the kindness of fortune or has acquired honestly. And no one envies a powerful man who uses his power for the good of his country, and who is as self-effacing in humility as he is exalted in rank, winning over even the low-born by his affability. No one envies a handsome man when in addition to his physical appearance he has also propriety and good morals. No one envies those who are healthy or have lived long lives if they use their health or years to benefit many others.

Whoever lacks the talent or skill for treating these things in the appropriate way should abstain from encomia rather than be like a bad painter who turns a beautiful form into an inferior one through his clumsiness. Perhaps Alexander the Great was too fastidious when he would not allow himself to be painted by anyone but Apelles.[11] Yet no handsome person would wish to be painted by a Fulvus or a Rutuba.[12] Let what you bring into public view be such that it promises to be remembered by posterity. Finally, praise must be so tempered that the duty you are performing may not appear to have been prompted by the person you are praising (for no one seeks or even tolerates praise less than those who especially deserve it), but rather by virtue itself, which even against its will has glory in its train,[13] and by the desire to inspire others to similar achievements. In this way not only will it be profitable to praise a man who has deserved it, but the risk of envy and the suspicion of flattery will also be avoided. When praising the dead, however, one should be much less inhibited in unleashing the power of which eloquence is capable, since in these circumstance envy is felt much less keenly and the suspicion of flattery is diminished.

So far I have shown how scholars can commend themselves to their patrons. Now I shall touch briefly on the ways in which they have the power to win universal support for their own scholarly activities as well. For in many places the study of languages and of what is called 'good letters' meets burning hostility. This is partly the fault of the older generation, who think that the acquisition of any of the new learning by the young detracts from their authority. Content with what they learned as children, they do not allow anything different to be taught, not do they bear to learn it themselves, either because the thought of doing so annoys them or because they are ashamed of their ignorance. In part too this is the fault of those who attack these ancient disciplines as new. For in this group there are some who are intolerably insolent; as soon as they have learned twelve words of Latin and five of Greek they think that they are a Demosthenes or a Cicero; they babble on in their writings, which are quite silly and sometimes even venomous; with incredible arrogance they spurn all liberal studies, and rant and rave in a scurrilous fashion at those who study them as a profession. And there are also some who use good letters for the worst of ends, to promote discord through blasphemy, and to disturb, damage, and destroy the harmony and tranquillity of Christendom. But in the past those who were learned in such studies would settle strife among princes with their eloquence, wage war with the leaders of heretical sects, celebrate the memory of the saints, sing the praises of Christ in verse and prose, and urge men to despise this earthly world and to love heavenly things. Such were Basil, Nazianzenus, Ambrose, Prudentius, and Lactantius, but they are not objects of hostile criticism, because they used their knowledge of languages and classical literature in the service of their pious works.

Fields of study, however, are customarily judged by the character of those engaged in them. For example, nowadays, many loathe the Gospel because of the immorality of some who use it for self-promotion. By guarding 'against every appearance of evil,' Paul[14] glorifies his Gospel, 'having become all things to all men' so as to profit all. If those who profess letters were like him and commended their profession by living pure lives and by using courteous and temperate language, they would reap a much richer harvest and incur much less hostility. On the other hand, if the older generation accepted, with civility and calmness, such studies as old friends being repatriated instead of as new immigrants, they would realize that their addition brings them considerable enlightenment and profit. As it is, they are waging a never-ending war with old friends as if they are fighting with enemies. Those things that are very ancient they call 'new,' and they term as 'ancient' what is new. The early doctors of the Church had a knowledge of Scripture that was combined with mastery of languages and of secular literature. We see the same thing in ancient philosophy, medicine and law. Where do Aristotle and Hippocrates utter solecisms? Are not Plato and Galen eloquent? How skilled in both languages were the ancient jurists! The purity and majesty of the Latin language is revealed by the very fragments that the boastful Justinian[15] thrust upon us instead of complete works, though even they are full of the most unbelievable textual errors.

What *is* new is drumming the modes of signification[16] into the heads of children to teach them grammar, and reading out lists of senseless words that teach them nothing but how to speak improperly. What *is* new is accepting young men into the study of philosophy, law, medicine, and theology when they understand nothing in the ancient authors because of their ignorance of the way they speak. What *is* new is to be excluded from the holy shrine of theology unless you have sweated long over Averroes and Aristotle. What *is* new is stuffing young candidates for a degree in philosophy with sophistic rubbish and imaginary problems. All these do is torture the brain! What *is* new is that in our schools different answers are given according to whether one follows the path of the Thomists, Scotists, Nominalists, or Realists. What *is* new is the exclusion there of arguments taken from the founts of divine Scripture, and the acceptance only of those that are drawn from Aristotle, papal decretals, schoolmen's tenets, definitions of professors of canon law, and precedents from Roman law, which are usually pointless and distorted. If new things offend us, these are the things that are really new. If we approve of what is old, it is the oldest disciplines that are now being laid to rest – unless perhaps what goes back to the time of Origen is new, and what came into being three hundred years ago and has continuously deteriorated since then is old.

But some persons who are even more hostile to such studies do not shrink from babbling, both privately and publicly, and indeed even in sermons, about how these are the source of all heresies, not noticing that this slander applies to Jerome, Ambrose, and Augustine, and many others – the doctors of the church in which it takes such pride. When hearing confession they din the ears of young men with such stupid nonsense as 'Beware of the Greeks, lest you become a heretic; avoid

Hebraic literature lest you become like the Jews; throw away Cicero lest you be damned along with him.' What grave admonitions! They do not realize that the boys will spout out such words to all and sundry, for all sensible people to laugh at. They drop similar words into the ears of parents, their aim being to have the children's education entrusted to them. Women and simple ordinary folk are easily taken in by sanctimonious deceit. But you might just as well entrust a sheep to a wolf as entrust children to such 'maws'![17] What do I hear? 'Were the Waldensians,[18] the Poor of Lyons, or Wyclif versed in languages and good letters?' Surely it does not follow that Jerome was a heretic because he was pre-eminent in his knowledge of languages and all kinds of literature. If anyone who knew only French wrote heretical views in his own language, would we immediately issue a general admonition that no one should learn French? Recently they have even persuaded the courts of princes that all this turmoil, of Lutheranism and the peasants' revolt,[19] had its source in the study of languages and classical literature. Courts have their Midases and Thrasos,[20] and the more naive the highest princes are and the more they indulge their inclinations the more exposed they are to the tricks of such men. If a person who knows Greek and Hebrew runs the risk of heresy because Luther is not unskilled in these languages, why is such a person not said to be safe because of John, bishop of Rochester,[21] and Girolamo Aleandro,[22] archbishop of Brindisi, who are stout defenders of the tottering church? The latter excels in all languages, the former is embracing the study of three languages with extraordinary zeal even though he is in his declining years.

They add another slander as well. When a young man admits his sins in confession, they hear of some licentious behaviour, a defect that belongs particularly to those of such an age. They ask what authors he is reading. When they hear that it is Virgil or Lucian, they blame his studies for what is a vice of their time of life (or of general human weakness), immediately making literature the cause instead of youthfulness, as if they do not hear much worse things from those who have never read even a word of literature. To be sure, while the study of literature does not free us from all vices, it is undeniable that it protects those at a dangerous age from many of them. Yet nothing is so sacred that it can not be used as a pretext for wrongdoing by someone who is naturally prone to wicked behaviour. But if we should remove whatever provides the slightest opportunity for immorality, why does the requirement of celibacy receive such praise? Do they think no one knows what 'a Lerna of troubles'[23] springs from that?

But, I ask you, what profit will there be if all honourable disciplines collapse in ruin because those who devote themselves to learning are tearing each other to pieces? We see that this has already happened to a great extent in some places. Without such disciplines, however, humans no longer live like humans but like beasts. The only course left for us, then, is that the study of languages and the study of good letters should return from exile and, like plants springing up again from the roots, make their way, with courtesy and civility, into the society of those disciplines that have ruled now for many centuries in the universities, without attacking anyone's particular subject of study but rather helping all disciplines. Let them make some concession to a profession's prestige, to long-established practices that have become second-nature, and to the advanced age of many practitioners, not readily adaptable to change. Let them leave those who are incurable to follow their own inclination so as not to stir up greater catastrophes. Let them win over those who are more treatable with timely and flattering advice. Let them advise, help, and correct, as a conscientious attendant advises, helps, and corrects her mistress. Theology is by rights the queen of all disciplines, but she will be more distinguished and more enlightened if she receives into her service such useful attendants with the appropriate friendliness. Philosophy is a very splendid subject, but it would win much more esteem by acknowledging old friends. Jurisprudence is a noble mistress, but such elegant servants will bring no little adornment to her. Medicine is a pre-eminent discipline, but is almost blind without knowledge of the ancient languages and literature. If the disciplines share with each other what each possesses, all will become richer and more splendid.

I would like to advise monarchs not to listen to the kinds of whispering that I have been talking about. Rather, let them think how much profit and prestige will accrue to their lands from such disciplines, as it did in the past. Finally, all will be more prosperous, both publicly and privately, if each is a good neighbour to his neighbour. To return to the proverb, it agrees with what has been mentioned elsewhere, Something bad from a bad neighbour, used by Demosthenes in his speech against Callicteas:[24] 'Nothing is more harmful, men of Athens, than to acquire a neighbour who is wicked and not content with what he has.'

1 Cato, cited by Columella *Res rustica* 1.3.5
2 Columella *Res rustica* 1.3.5–7 (see long passage below), here citing Hesiod *Works and Days* 348
3 See preceding note.
4 Cato *De agricultura* 1.2
5 Cato *De agricultura* 4
6 Plutarch *Themistocles* 18; cf *Adages* I i 32; I x 73.
7 William Warham (1450–1532), archbishop of Canterbury in 1503, and lord chancellor of England 1504–15, was a generous benefactor of Erasmus, giving him in 1509 the living of Aldington, later commuted to a pension.
8 Maecenas, adviser of the emperor Augustus, was patron of Virgil and Horace.
9 Maevius and Bavius were two minor poets attacked by Virgil *Eclogues* 3.90.
10 *Adages* I v 34 'Go and shake another oak-tree'
11 Apelles was the renowned painter of the fourth century BC; Horace refers to an edict of Alexander forbidding anyone other than Apelles to paint him (*Epistles* 2.1.239–40); cf also Pliny *Natural History* 7.125.
12 Gladiators referred to by Horace at *Satires* 2.7.96
13 Cf Seneca *Letters* 79.13, 'Glory is virtue's shadow and will accompany it even against its will'; Cicero *Tusculan Disputations* 1.91, 109; also *Adages* IV viii 71 'Virtue produces glory.'
14 The sentence combines three quotes from Paul: 1 Thessalonians 5:22, 2 Thessalonians 3:1, 1 Corinthians 9:22.
15 Justinian, the eastern Roman emperor AD 527–65, organized the consolidation of earlier Roman law into three volumes, the *Codex*, the *Institutions*, and the *Digest* or *Pandects*. In this achievement he took great pride; see the prefaces to the *Institutions* and *Digest*.
16 Erasmus is here attacking speculative grammar, a philosophical approach to the teaching of language that was popular from the thirteenth century; he himself endured it in his childhood (see CWE 26 345).
17 Cf *Adages* II viii 78 'Idle bellies' (*ventres*), applied, according to Erasmus, to 'gross eaters, slaves

of their stomachs and digestions.'

18 The Waldensians were an evangelical group, also called 'the Poor of Lyons,' started by a rich merchant of that city, named Valdes, who renounced his possessions to live in poverty. John Wyclif (c 1330–84) is associated with the first complete English translation of the Vulgate, and wrote voluminously in Latin. It is doubtful whether he knew Greek. Both the Waldensians and Wyclif incurred charges of heresy. The point of Erasmus' facetious contrast of them with Jerome may be simply that knowledge of or expertise in classical languages and literature has nothing to do with holding heretical views.

19 The peasants' revolt of 1524–5, which occurred throughout much of what Erasmus describes as Germany, was a protest against serfdom and other constraints. Its outbreak at this time was connected with the aims of the Protestant reformers and, at least initially, Luther was sympathetic to it.

20 King Midas was given ass's ears by Apollo; see *Adages* I iii 67 'Midas has ass's ears' – 'properly applied to stupid people.' Thraso is the name of a braggart soldier in Terence's *Eunuchus* who is stupid as well as vain.

21 John Fisher (1469–1535), a friend and correspondent of Erasmus, was appointed bishop of Rochester in 1504. He did not undertake serious study of Greek and Hebrew until his mid- to late-forties. He wrote against Luther and other reformers.

22 Girolamo Aleandro (1480–1542) was renowned for his learning and intellectual powers and he rose to cardinal in the church. When Erasmus was preparing the 1508 edition of the *Adages*, Aleandro lent him a manuscript of the collection of proverbs by Apostolius. For more on their complex relationship, see *Contemporaries* 1:28–32.

23 *Adages* I iii 27

24 *Adages* I i 32, used in Demosthenes *Against Callicles* 55.1 (not 'Callicteas').

IV vi 35
Auris Batava / A Batavian ear

This proverb also appeared back at III ii 48*. The essay stands out in the collection because of Erasmus' short but highly spirited digression in praise of his homeland, written despite his general distaste for his countrymen. In the 1508 edition, this was the concluding essay.*

Just as the Greeks say Βοιώτιον οὖς, that is 'A Boeotian ear,' referring to someone who is dull and stupid, so in book 6 of his *Epigrams* Martial[1] said *Batava auris*, 'The ear of a Batavian,' of someone who is unrefined, graceless, and mean-spirited:

Are you, says he, the poet Martial,
Whose risqué jests are plainly caught
By all but those with a Batavian ear.

'Batavian' (*Batavam*) is the reading of Domizio Calderini,[2] although some had read 'austere' (*severam*).

The Batavians were a German tribe, 'part of the Catti, who were expelled as a result of civil war. They then occupied the northernmost part of the coastal region of Gaul, at that time uninhabited, and also an island situated between two stretches of water, being washed by the ocean at the front, and bounded by the Rhine at the sides and back.'[3] This tribe was not only formidable in war, as a result of much experience in the Germanic wars, but it was also very wealthy, since its resources were not drained by the demands of the Roman army. It had an alliance with the empire to supply only men and arms. This is what Tacitus tells us at greater length in book 20. Many scholars agree (and there are no opinions to the contrary) that the island mentioned by Tacitus is what is now called Holland, a land that I will always honour and revere since I owe my life's beginning to it. And I only hope that the honour I can bring to it will match the pride it gives me. Although Martial accuses this people of a lack of any sophistication and Lucan[4] calls them 'ferocious,' I think that both charges can be turned into praise, if they actually apply to us. Which people has not been rather primitive at some time? And when was the Roman race more deserving of praise than when the only arts it knew were warfare and agriculture? But if anyone will argue that what was once said against the Batavians applies to what we are now, what higher praise can be given my dear Holland than for people to say that it abhors Martial's humour, which even the author himself describes as indecent. I even wish that all Christians had 'Dutch ears' so that they would not grant audience to that poet's corrupting witticisms or certainly not find them appealing. If anyone wishes to regard this as 'a lack of sophistication,' we shall gladly admit the charge, one we share with the high-principled Spartans, the ancient Sabines, the noble Catos. I think, however, that Lucan calls the Batavians 'ferocious,' in the sense that Virgil[5] calls the Romans 'spirited.'

If one looks at how they conduct themselves in everyday life, no other race is more humane or generous and less wild or fierce. By nature they are straightforward, free of treachery and deceit, prone to no serious vices, although they are somewhat too fond of pleasure, particularly of feasting. The reason for this, I think, is the marvellous abundance of everything that customarily stimulates the pursuit of pleasure. This abundance comes partly from the ease with which they can import goods (since the country is located at the mouths of two rivers, the Rhine and the Meuse, and part of it is washed by the ocean), and partly from the natural fertility of the region itself, since it is everywhere intersected by navigable rivers that are well stocked with fish and abounds in rich pastures. Moreover, the marshes and glades provide an inexhaustible supply of birds. Accordingly, it is said that no other region can be found containing so many towns in such a small area. Admittedly, they are of modest size but they have an incredibly attractive appearance.[6] For the splendour of its domestic furnishings, merchants who have travelled over most of the world regard Holland as unequalled. No country in the world has a larger number of moderately well-educated citizens, though not as many as one would expect are outstandingly erudite, particularly in ancient studies. The reason is either the luxury in which they live or their greater reverence for moral excellence than for distinction in scholarship. For it is undisputable, as many points show, that they are not lacking in intellectual power. I, however, have it only to a modest, even tiny, degree, as is true of everything else of me.

1 Martial 6.82.4–6 (Boeotians were depicted as stupid peasants by many ancient writers)

2 Domizio Calderini (1446–78), the Veronese humanist, wrote commentaries on Juvenal and the *Silvae* of Statius as well as on Martial (see *Contemporaries* 1:243–4).

3 Tacitus *Histories* 4.12. The next two sentences paraphrase part of this same section. Erasmus gives the reference as book 20 since the *Annals* and *Histories* of Tacitus

were numbered consecutively in the early printed editions. Hence the first book of the *Histories* was book 17, following what we now know as book 16 of the *Annals*. ASD II-8, 37 n 436 says that the source is probably not not only Tacitus but also Raimondo Marliano's *Index locorum* or 'Index of Places,' a commentary on Caesar.

4 Lucan 1.431
5 Virgil *Georgics* 3.346
6 The translation adopts the interpretation of *politia* in ASD II-8, 42 n 470.

IV ix 25
Usus est altera natura / Custom is a second nature

Shakespeare's Hamlet, advising his mother to make a habit of not going to Claudius' bed, argues that 'use almost can change the stamp of nature' (3.4.170). This is a commonplace observation in the Renaissance, well known from the classical sources (cf Otto 426 and Tosi 159) and basic to ideas of education in the Renaissance, including in Erasmus' De pueris instituendis *(CWE 26 311). Pascal took it further: 'Custom is our nature' and 'What are our natural principles, but principles of custom?'* (Pensées, *nos 89, 92 ed Brunschvicg) There are many variations in English: 'Once a use, ever a custom' (Tilley U 22), 'Use is another nature' (C 932), or, Shakespeare again, 'How use doth breed a habit in a man'* (Two Gentlemen of Verona *5.4.1).*

Nothing is more celebrated than this saying, Ἔθος ἄλλη φύσις, Custom is a second nature. Nothing is stronger or more powerful than nature. And so the Satirist[1] writes, 'Nature, more powerful than any watchfulness or diligence.' Doing something habitually, however, is equal in power to nature or at least is very close to it.

Aristotle[2] discusses what is pleasurable in book 1 of the *Rhetorica*. He defines as pleasurable those things that are in accordance with nature or those things that we have been accustomed to do. For he thinks that the difference between nature and custom is the same as that between 'always' and 'often'. For what nature has planted in us is always with us, while what habituation has fixed in us is frequently so. Accordingly, that man[3] who told us to choose, right from a tender age, to perform the noblest actions, so that these would also become pleasurable through habituation, gave very sound advice.

1 Juvenal 10.303
2 Aristotle *Rhetoric* 1.11 (1369b34ff)
3 Cf Aristotle *Nicomachean Ethics* 2.1.7 (1103b23–4) and *Rhetoric* 1.11.4 (1370a12–14); perhaps Quintilian *Institutes* 2.4.20.

V i 42
Nihil dulcius quam omnia scire / Nothing is sweeter than to know everything

In book 4 of the *Letters to Atticus*, in the one that begins 'I was delighted,' Marcus Tullius[1] quotes the following verse as if it was extremely well known: Οὐδὲν γλυκύτερον ἢ πᾶν εἰδέναι, 'Nothing is sweeter than to know absolutely everything.' (The verse[2] is corrupt and will scan if one reads Οὐδὲν γλυκύτερον ἔστιν ἢ παντ' εἰδέναι.) And then Cicero adds, 'Since I am so curious, tell me in detail[3] what happened on the first day, what happened on the second, what have the censors – and Appius and the people's darling, that emasculated Appuleius – been up to?' One also sometimes comes across the following expression in Cicero's *Letters*:[4] Πάντα περὶ πάντων, 'Everything about everything.'

1 Cicero *Letters to Atticus* 4.11.2
2 Menander *Epitrepontes* frag 2 Koerte
3 Cicero is asking about a gladiatorial show and for some gossip about Appius Claudius Pulcher and his brother Publius Clodius Pulcher, whom he calls an 'emasculated Appuleius' (Appuleius Saturninus was a politician of an earlier generation who opposed personal power in the republic).
4 *Letters to Friends* 15.17.1, 12.20

List of Adages

Index

Note: Part A lists the titles of the 119 selected adages in a standard Latin form. Part B is a general index in English and includes subjects and names. The main and many additional proverbs are listed, often under several headings, with the indication '(prov).' If there is an italicized word in the entry, the main listing for the proverb is found under that word. If the proverb is the subject of one of the selected essays by Erasmus, the adage number is given; additional references elsewhere in the book follow. Not all the proverbs in Erasmus' introduction are included here as his essay is itself in places virtually an index. Citation analyses are provided in ASD and a cumulative index is promised for CWE 30.

A / Latin titles

B / General